# UKRAINE WAR

*Military Perspectives and Strategic Reflections*

# UKRAINE WAR

## *Military Perspectives and Strategic Reflections*

*Editors*

Sujan Chinoy
Abhay Kumar Singh
Vivek Chadha

MANOHAR PARRIKAR INSTITUTE FOR DEFENCE STUDIES AND ANALYSES

PENTAGON PRESS LLP

First published in 2024 by
PENTAGON PRESS LLP
206, Peacock Lane, Shahpur Jat
New Delhi-110049, India
Contact: 011-26490600

Typeset in AGaramond, 11 Point
Printed by Aegean Offset Printers, Greater Noida, U.P.

ISBN 978-81-968722-8-1 (HB)



**www.pentagonpress.in**

# Contents

# List of Contributors

**Cmde Abhay Kumar Singh (Retd)** is a Research Fellow at the Manohar Parrikar IDSA. His research interests include maritime geopolitics and strategic developments in the Indo-Pacific region. A frequent contributor to journals and periodicals on geopolitical issues, he has authored a book on the dynamics of India-China relations titled "India-China Rivalry: Asymmetric No Longer: An Assessment of China's Evolving Perceptions of India.

**Brig Akhelesh Bhargava (Retd)**, was commissioned in June 1983 in Army Air Defence. He has done B Tech (Electronics), MBA Finance and a graduate of Defence Services Staff College. He has written articles related to Army Air Defence, Satellites, Drones, Electronic Warfare, etc. He is a SSB Trainer, a financial advisor and represents Delhi State in Masters Swimming Nationals.

**Lt Col Akshat Upadhyay** is a Research Fellow at the Manohar Parrikar IDSA. His research interests include emerging technologies, changing character of warfare, AI, unmanned systems and military history. He is the author of a book on coercive diplomacy against Pakistan and his recent paper is "DIY Warfare: A New Warfighting Paradigm", published in Strategic Analysis, a peer-reviewed journal of MP-IDSA.

**Maj Gen Amarjit Singh (Retd)** is the Director of Gyan Chakra Think Tank located at Chandigarh. He has edited two books; one on India's Military Strategy and one on Indian Strategic Thought. He has been associated with the Defence Department of Panjab University as a Strategic and Military expert. He has been conducting regular discussions on strategic subjects as part of the Gyan Chakra Think Tank enabling research scholars and serving officer to develop strategic thinking.

**AVM Anil Golani (Retd)** was a Jaguar Pilot, Qualified Flying Instructor, Examiner; Commanded AD Direction Centre, Operational base, Maritime Air Operations.

Completed the International Security & Strategy course at the Royal College of Defence Studies, London. Served in A&N Command as the AF Component Commander, Strategic Forces Command as the Chief Staff Officer (Air Vector), and Chief Instructor, Air Force, at DSSC, Wellington. Co-edited 'Air Power and Emerging Technologies'; 2022 and 'Indian Air Force in its Centennial Decade'; 2023. He took over as ADG, CAPS on 07 May 2021.

**Lt Gen (Dr) Anil Kapoor AVSM, VSM (Retd)** superannuated as the Director General Electronics and Mechanical Engineers. He is a Board Member Technology Innovation Hub Governing Body and a Professor of Practice at IIT Tirupati. The General Officer is a strategic advisor to a number of global think tanks and an international speaker on technology strategy, transformational leadership, design thinking and supply chain management.

**Col Deepak Kumar** is a former Research Fellow at the Manohar Parrikar Institute for Defence Studies and Analyses (MP-IDSA). He holds a PhD in Defence and Strategic Studies and his research interests include Eurasia, military and strategic studies, and ancient Indian history. He has written on the Armenia-Azerbaijan conflict, the Central Asian Region, and the Russia-Ukraine war. His monograph titled "Central Asia: Key to Engaging China and Russia" is a significant contribution to his field of study.

**Prof (Dr) Dinesh Kumar Pandey** is a Master Fighter Controller, was a Director of Air Staff Inspections and Director of the Joint Control and Analysis Center. He has been a Professor at the School of Business (Aviation Management) at Galgotias University. Co-edited 'Road to Atmanirbhar Aerospace'. He is currently a Senior Fellow at CAPS, a member of the Advisory Council of Greater Noida Institute of Technology (GNOIT) and a member of the Advisory Board (Academic Affairs) at Foreign Policy School, New Delhi.

**Dr Jason Wahlang** is a Research Analyst at the Europe and Eurasia Centre at the Manohar Parrikar IDSA. His research interests include peace and conflict, genocide studies, foreign policy and identity politics in Eurasia. His Ph.D. thesis was on the Politics of Memory and the 'Armenian Genocide.'

**Krutika Patil** is a science and technology writer based in Canada, possessing a keen interest in emerging military technology, cybersecurity, internet governance, and telecommunications. Previously, she worked as a researcher on the Cybersecurity Project at the Manohar Parrikar Institute for Defence Studies and Analyses (MP-IDSA) in New Delhi. There, she was involved in multiple projects and contributed significantly to various think tanks and academic journals, including authoring peer-reviewed papers.

**Dr R Vignesh** is a Research Analyst at the Manohar Parrikar IDSA. His research area includes Maritime Security Issues in the Indian Ocean Region, Geopolitics of the Indo-Pacific, Naval Warfare and Military Diplomacy. He is the recipient of the prestigious Research Fellowship awarded by the History Division Ministry of Defence in 2016.

**Col Rajneesh Singh (Retd)** is a Research Fellow at MP-IDSA. His areas of research include higher defence management, military studies and self-reliance in defence production. He is the author of the Monograph titled Sanctions on Russia: A Study of Economic in the Contemporary World.

**Dr. Rajorshi Roy** is Associate Fellow at the Manohar Parrikar Institute for Defence Studies and Analyses (MP-IDSA). His research interests include Eurasian security architecture as well as the foreign, defence, security and domestic policies of Russia and the Central Asian countries.

**Dr S Samuel C Rajiv** is Associate Fellow at the Defence Economics and Industry Centre at MP-IDSA and Editor of the MP-IDSA Website. He earned his PhD from School of International Studies, JNU. His latest book is The India-Israel Strategic Partnership: Contours, Opportunities and Challenges (Pentagon Press LLP, 2023).

**Amb Sujan Chinoy** is the Director General of the Manohar Parrikar Institute for Defence Studies and Analyses (MP-IDSA), New Delhi since 2019. A career diplomat from 1981-2018, he was Ambassador to Japan and Mexico and the Consul General of India in Shanghai and Sydney, besides serving at India's Missions at the UN and Saudi Arabia. A specialist on China, East Asia and politico-security issues, he anchored confidence-building measures (CBMs) with China on the boundary dispute from 1996-2000. At the National Security Council Secretariat (NSCS) from 2008-2012, he handled external and internal security policy, including in the extended neighbourhood of the Indo-Pacific. He was the Chair of the Think20 engagement group for India's G20 Presidency.

He is the author of "World Upside Down: India Recalibrates Its Geopolitics" published in July 2023 by HarperCollins. He writes regularly for newspapers and journals and has a well-known presence on the international think-tank circuit.

**Dr. Swasti Rao** is Associate Fellow at the Europe and Eurasia Centre, Manohar Parrikar Institute for Defence Studies and Analyses (MP-IDSA). Her ongoing book project at the MP-IDSA revolves around the theme of "*Conflicts in Europe amidst shifting Power Structures and Europe's Indo-Pacific outreach*". An alumnus of JNU, India; Tsukuba University, Japan and IHEDN, France; she is a recipient of Japanese Education Ministry Fellowship (MEXT) in 2011 and the 'Okita Memorial Scholarship' in 2010 from ICCR. Before joining IDSA she was an academic.

**Col Vivek Chadha (Retd)** is a Senior Fellow at the Manohar Parrikar IDSA. His research interests include military studies, counter terrorism and indic heritage texts. His recent single author book is titled CDS and Beyond: Integration of the Indian Armed Forces.

# 1

# Introduction

*Sujan Chinoy*

The Ukraine conflict has lingered on, quite unexpectedly. Russia's so-called special military operation has met with great resistance and a pushback. The question of morality apart, reverses on the battlefield have not prevented Russia from legislating a new geography for itself through the referendum and consequent redrawing of its own map. The West has flooded Ukraine with intelligence and weapons, but how long will this endure?

Neither Ukraine nor Russia is making military gains along a frontline that has solidified after prolonged fighting, with victories and reverses for both sides. By all accounts, Russia has not given up as its fresh mobilisation suggests. Neither has Ukraine, but it is finding it difficult to keep up the barrage in the face of acute shortages of munition. Both sides have experienced tumult in their military hierarchies, and both have made use of asymmetrical means to erode the confidence of the adversary, including targeted assassinations. The cost of any reconstruction, post-settlement, can only be imagined. Who will pay for all that?

Meanwhile, the world faces disruptions in supply chains of food, fuel and fertilisers. More relevantly, the Ukraine War has created a false narrative that India must face a binary choice between 'good' and 'evil' forces, that is, between a liberal and democratic cohort led by the West and its antithesis in Russia. Such a dilemma is being extended to a stark choice between Russian arms and American ones. Even the energy needs of a large country such as India, with 1.4 billion people, now also the world's fastest growing economy, are frequently under the scanner; if India buys crude oil and LNG from Russia, it is tantamount to sacrilege in the eyes of critics. The yardstick is different if European Union countries or

Japan are constrained to continue their purchases of Russian energy supplies. Japan, in fact, has increased its offtake of LNG from Russia. It is instructive to remember and to remind others that energy is a fungible commodity and that someone, somewhere, is bound to use it.

The Ukraine crisis has demonstrated the many shortcomings of the United Nations Security Council (UNSC). The UNSC failed to reach a consensus on condemning Russia for its 'special military operation', which the West deems as an invasion. Russia, on its part, portrays it as an act of self-defence against the growing eastward expansion of North Atlantic Treaty Organization (NATO). Divergent interests of its Permanent Members, especially the United States (US), the United Kingdom and France on one side and Russia and China on the other, have created a stasis in the UNSC. This only underscores the fact that we are today in a world that is neither bipolar nor multipolar—it is a fractured world.

The crisis has strengthened the trans-Atlantic partnership. It has undone the weakening of ties during the Trump presidency. Europe, initially divided over policy towards Russia, has come together in an unprecedented manner. The NATO stands rejuvenated. Russia's actions have also caused consternation in other parts of Europe, as a result of which NATO is expanding its membership and defence budgets have witnessed spikes in Germany and the Netherlands, to name just a few.

The war in Ukraine is bound to impact the Indo–Pacific region. A stronger trans-Atlantic strategic partnership and a stronger, more focused NATO will be capable of dealing more effectively with other challenges as well. Japan is now closely examining three challenges, that is, China, North Korea and Russia. Japan's diplomatic Bluebook has cited Russia as being in illegal occupation of its northern territories for decades. Interestingly, there are several references to Taiwan, which suggest that the cross-strait situation is a matter of concern for other regional powers as well. Japan has revised its national security strategy and decided to double its defence budget. China has been cited as an unprecedented strategic challenge for the country.

The strengthening of alliance partnerships is not restricted to the European theatre. Both the trans-Atlantic and trans-Pacific alliances have been strengthened in recent times. There are attempts underway to fuse the two theatres not only because China and Russia are deepening their strategic partnership and conducting joint exercises in the East and South Seas as well as the Pacific Ocean, but also because of the apprehension that China might be emboldened to mount an invasion of Taiwan in the wake of Russia's 'special military operation' in Ukraine.

The Ukraine conflict, inevitably, has broader strategic implications for India's national security, whether in regard to traditional supplies of arms and equipment from Russia and Ukraine or choosing energy options at optimal prices for the continued growth of its economy.

Right from the beginning of the war in Ukraine, India has taken a principled position. India called for an immediate cessation of hostilities and advocated a peaceful resolution of differences through diplomacy and dialogue. Respect for sovereignty and territorial integrity and a rules-based international order are inherent in the Indian position. India has also provided considerable humanitarian assistance to Ukraine.

India's position on the war in Ukraine and its relations with Russia are sui generis. On Ukraine, there is considerable understanding of India's position among Western countries, as observed during Prime Minister Modi's interactions with European leaders during his three-nation tour to Germany, Denmark and France in 2022. India's relations with Russia are a legacy issue. There is perhaps a better understanding in the West of India's relations with Russia as compared to China's relations with Russia, which are viewed through the prism of geostrategic contestation.

We at Manohar Parrikar Institute for Defence Studies and Analyses undertook a project for the government during the initial stages of the conflict. We, however, realised that any attempt at drawing lessons prematurely could lead to misleading conclusions. Instead of absolutist conjectures, we were more interested in identifying broader trends. The absence of fulsome information, more particularly the widespread disinformation on all sides, made this task more difficult.

Much water has flown under the bridge since then. Along the way, the world has been introduced to a dazzling array of new weapons, missiles and drones that question the very relevance of established battlefield platforms such as tanks, for instance.

Some broad conclusions, however tentative and open to challenge, are evident:

First, treaty alliance partnerships are not a pre-requisite for allies to come to one's aid. Ukraine is still not part of NATO; nor does it have a treaty arrangement with any Western country and yet it has received a great deal of assistance. What does this mean for India, given its strategic autonomy, in a potential conflict with its larger neighbour? Will India's Quad partners and others be equally forthcoming in terms of intelligence sharing and provisioning of military equipment?

Second, a military conflict can easily erupt when red lines are crossed. In this case, Russia clearly believes its red lines with regard to NATO expansion and activity were crossed; conversely, it appears that Russia has also crossed the red lines laid down by Ukraine and the West. It is a moot question whether Russia has a right in perpetuity to claim Ukraine as part of its 'sphere of influence' based on a distant historical past that may bear no relevance to the aspirations of the Ukrainian people in the 21st century.

Third, what is the potential for escalation in Ukraine to the nuclear realm? At the start of the conflict, Russia put its nuclear forces on alert, and it is good that the US did not react in the same manner. Ironically, at the start of the year, just before the Russian 'special military operation' in Ukraine was launched on 24 February 2022, the Permanent Members of the UNSC (the five nuclear weapons states) had passed a unanimous resolution on 3 January 2022, calling for reinforcing the Nuclear Non-Proliferation Treaty's key tenets of disarmament, non-proliferation and peaceful uses of nuclear energy. What is more, they had affirmed that a nuclear war cannot be won and must never be fought. That homily stood out in sharp contrast to the sharpening of rhetoric about a possible escalation to nuclear weapons just a few weeks later.

The potential for escalation between two adversaries of which only one is a nuclear weapons state is different from a situation wherein both sides possess nuclear weapons. Ukraine is a non-nuclear weapons state and is not under any nuclear umbrella. Russia has not ruled out the use of nuclear weapons in the face of an 'existential threat'. Given that it has already absorbed Crimea, and more recently, four more regions taken in the war with Ukraine, one could speculate about the possible resort to a nuclear option by Russia in the event that a nuclear weapons state tries to pry away these territories.

Fourth, the historical irredentist claims of Russia over Ukraine and that of China over Taiwan appear to be similar, but Taiwan has a special relationship with the US under the Taiwan Relations Act of 1979. Logically, therefore, Taiwan would expect the US to directly enter the fray in the event of Chinese aggression. Does this, and the inability of Russia's war machine to prevail in Ukraine, harbour any sobering lessons for the People's Liberation Army (PLA)?

Fifth, have we entered the era of protracted conflicts in which no country can prevail over another quite so easily despite asymmetries in comprehensive national power, especially military power? Over time, the strategic community had perhaps concluded that future wars would be swift and short. The Ukraine conflict challenges this notion. For that matter, so does the Israel–Hamas conflict in Gaza. Prolonged wars have a debilitating effect on all belligerents, faced with mounting military expenditure amidst distressed economic activity. The economic implications of long-drawn conflicts, the capacity of the defence industrial base to support it, the morale of the armed forces and public opinion, all have an impact on the outcomes.

Lastly, India is in the process of modernising its armed forces. In India, there is great emphasis on *Atmanirbhar Bharat* and Make in India in the defence sector. What lessons do we draw from the Ukraine conflict for our own security needs, particularly with reference to potential disruptions in critical supply chains of military spares, equipment and munitions?

This book, *Ukraine War: Military Perspectives and Strategic Reflections*, presents a comprehensive assessment of the ongoing conflict. Divided into five sections, the 15 chapters delve into the geopolitical backdrop of the conflict, highlight its operational narrative, dissect the components of military power, explore the impact of disruptive technologies and examine the strategic ramifications of this ongoing war.

We are confident that this compendium of writings will prove to be invaluable for scholars, students, academicians and policymakers alike.

# SECTION I

# Overview of the Ukrainian Conflict

# 2

# The Geopolitical Background of the War in Ukraine

*Swasti Rao*

## INTRODUCTION

The Russia–Ukraine war that started with Russia's special military operation in Ukraine on February 24, 2022, has been the largest military conflict in Europe since the end of World War II. The larger context of this long, convoluted war between neighbours can be understood better after first analysing its geopolitical and historical background.

The war in 2022 was not a standalone war but an escalation of an ongoing conflict with roots in historical, geopolitical and civilisation tensions that manifested in 2014 over Crimea.

While relations between the two countries have been strained since the collapse of the Soviet Union in 1991, the history of rivalry goes a long way back. The 2022 war, in the words of historian Serhii Plokhi, 'produced a nineteenth-century war fought with twentieth-century tactics and twenty-first-century weaponry'.

There is much lying in the folds of this statement that needs to be unravelled. On the one hand, it reflects the commonality and diversity in the ideological underpinnings in identities of Russian and Ukrainian statehood and their people. On the other hand, when coupled with geopolitical, strategic and economic instruments of statecraft, it has resulted in the much deteriorated security situation that East Europe is reeling under today. All of this has confounding implications for the rest of the world.

## RESEARCH QUESTIONS

The Russia–Ukraine war is a unique case study not only because it has shredded the post-Cold War European security order but has also raised important questions on states' quest of national identities and their perception of security dilemmas.

This chapter will analyse some of the most fundamental questions that arise while studying the Ukraine War. Namely, why have Russia and Ukraine remained mired in a long-standing conflict over decades? Why are the roots of the conflict so deep despite the two countries' strong civilisational and historical links as one sovereign country in the community of states up until 1991? What has been the role of other European states and the North Atlantic Treaty Organization (NATO) in this regard? Finally, what is the role of the complex geo-economics of the post-Cold War European theatre in exacerbating tensions between the two sides?

## METHODOLOGICAL TOOLS AND FRAMEWORK

### Methodology

This section delves into the broad methodological frameworks used in writing this chapter. Since it deals with analysing the events of the past embedded in histories with multiple narratives, the chapter takes the view that its historiography[1] is done carefully to avoid lending one's own meaning to the unfolding of events. The historiography used in the current piece rests on two broad methodological frameworks: contextualism and the securitisation theory.

For a fair historical analysis of several entwined factors, the analytical framework of 'Contextualism', first proposed by Quentin Skinner, is deployed. While the method itself has undergone stages of evolution and revision, the basic tenet remains as valid as it was when it was first proposed. The key assertion here is centrality ***of the context*** in which certain interpretation of ideas and events emerged and in which they were interpreted, understood and internalised by successive generations of analysts, researchers and the common people.

Therefore, as per the tool provided by Quentin Skinner, this chapter will analyse the geopolitical background of the Russia–Ukraine war by first 'contextualising' the unfolding of events and then by 'contextualising' the agency of the states that are directly affected by the war. That brings in picture the interests of the East European states and their experience.

The chapter wishes to avoid **two major** analytical fallacies stemming from reductionist explanations of the Ukraine War as offered by offensive realism.[2]

This approach regards the war in Ukraine as a product of NATO's eastward expansion.[3] While it does provide a part of the causality, but such reductionism robs the East European states of valid agency and overlooks the historical-geopolitical churnings within the Union of Soviet Socialist Republics (USSR), the subsequent Russian state and its relations with its neighbours.

By implication, it also renders the neighbours' perspectives inconsequential in the larger scheme of East European security situation in the last 40 years.

In this regard, a significant limitation of the theory of offensive realism championed by John Mearshimer must be highlighted.[4] First, offensive realism's sole focus on big state behaviour assumes that the small states of the international system don't seem to matter. It simply looks at them as insignificant counterweights, weighting to be sucked into great power competition.

Second, offensive realism's focus on great power politics results in an inability to explain the phenomenon of middle order multipolarity, a distinguishing feature of the global order today. Careful observation shows that this fallacy is also related to undermining the agency of states that are not 'great powers'. One of the strongest rebuttals to Mearshimer's offensive realism applied to Russia–Ukraine has come from the Finnish scholar and politician Dr Alexander Stubb, who has successfully established the agency of East European states such as Sweden, Finland and Poland as crucial in determining the outcomes of the war.[5] In fact, Kleinschimt argued in 2018 that the offensive realist explanations of Russia's actions in Ukraine are inconsistent with the available empirical knowledge of the conflict in Ukraine and with the structural logic postulated by the offensive realist theory itself. He argued instead that the war in Ukraine could be better understood as a conflict about the incompatibility of the Russian state structure to cope with the imperatives of functional differentiation theory.

One of the lasting legacies of the post-modern, post-realist turn in international relations would perhaps be the acceptance of the complexity of the world order that defies a one-dimensional pathway of evolution and explanation. No grand theory has been successful at explaining the events of the world, especially that of geopolitics. The question of agency remains critical, and the value of rightfully contextualising events will always remain valid.

The second methodological framework used in the chapter is securitisation theory, with developments added by the differentiation theories. This variety of theorising is found to be most suitable for analysing the actions of three main actors—Russia, Ukraine and European states—across the different strands of their ethnic, national, demographic and economic experiences. Generations of analysts of the securitisation school have successfully suggested that security should be seen as a construct or an act where the central issue is not whether the threats are real or not, but the *ways* in which a certain issue can be socially constructed as a threat.

This leads the Copenhagen school to define securitisation as an 'act' that has to fulfil three rhetorical criteria.[6]

> It is a discursive process by means of which an actor (1) claims that a referent object is existentially threatened, (2) demands the right to take extraordinary countermeasures to deal with that the threat, and (3) convinces an audience that rule-breaking behavior to counter the threat is justified.

This approach successfully explains the actions of the Russian state that have been condemned by the West as 'unprovoked'.[7] When analysed from this lens, the Russian actions in Ukraine are not as unprovoked as assumed even when legally problematic according to the UN Charter, post-Cold War security guarantees and international law—a part that will be discussed in the subsequent sections.

As mentioned earlier, differentiation theories have significantly added to the explanatory framework of the securitisation discourse.[8] To put it most simply, adherents of the analytical framework of differentiation derived from sociology and anthropology have argued that it can and should be applied to International Relations (IR) theory when studying discourses on securitisation. Barry Buzan and Mathias Albert have argued that by adapting the differentiation theory to its more complex, layered subject matter, the discipline of international relations can develop it into a holistic theory and explanatory framework. Differentiation, as defined by Buzan et al, is about how to distinguish and analyse the components that make up any social whole, here relevant for understanding the Russia–Ukraine war.

Therefore, this war is a complex entity where developments and actions are better understood when viewed through the lens of the securitisation discourse with its rich additions from differentiation theories while keeping the analysis contextualised correctly at all times.

## Context Setting

There are four distinct strands of differentiation that highlight four distinct components that together make the larger context of analysis within which the Russia–Ukraine conflicts have evolved in the historical context.

These four components need to be understood separately and in relation with each other for understanding their role in the Russia-Ukraine war of 2022.

They can be summarised as:

> (i) civilisational legacy and conflicting identitarian narrative; (ii) ideology of the Russian state and its continuation under 'Putinism'; (iii) legal aspect of the post-World War II security guarantees and the role of NATO; and (iv) complex geo-economics of the European theatre.

It is important to re-iterate at the outset that these four differentiated strands that are required to contextualise the Ukraine War need separate analysis but are interrelated and make the larger background in which the events of 2022 unfolded.

### *Civilisational Legacy and the Making of Conflicting Identities*

Who are the Ukrainian people? There is definitely a civilisational and ideological underpinning to why Ukraine remains such a contested geopolitical space for Russia. A quick flashback of how these respective national identities have formed in the last millennium is a fascinating study.

**Kyiv as the Cradle of Russian Civilisation:** Kyiv, the capital city of Ukraine today, was the heart of the 'Kyivan Rus' state a thousand years ago. Between the 8th and the 10th century, predominantly Swedish traders sailed from the Baltic to the Black Sea and started to settle around the region of what is now Kyiv. They were referred to as Rus (literally, men who rowed since they were closely associated with rivers/water bodies).[9] Subsequently, the ethnic merging of the Rus people with Slavic, Baltic and Finnish tribes led to what came to be known as Kyivan Rus. That is how Kyiv has come to be regarded as the mother of Rus cities, its status being denoted as the capital of the Kyivan Rus state.

**How was Russia born from Kyivan Rus?:** Around the 13th century, expansion of the Mongols reached the Kyivan Rus state with key Mongol victories. By 1237, the Mongols had completely taken over Kyivan Rus. These victories led to the breakup of the Kyivan states, which remained under the dominion of the Golden Horde for a few centuries.[10]

It was during this period that the Grand Duchy of Moscow began to rise, eventually becoming the heart of what is now Russia and providing a new focal point for the Rus people.[11]

As for Ukraine, as the control of the Golden Horde started to diminish, Ukraine got absorbed in the Grand Duchy of Lithuania and then the Polish-

Lithuanian Commonwealth. Then came the era of the Cossacks that strengthened the Ukrainian identity[12] as distinct from others in the region but connected to Russia. When there was an emergence of Ukraine during the 19th century and a Ukrainian identity began to form more fully, it remained closely linked with that of the Cossacks and the role they played in consolidating the Kyivan people against the Polish–Lithuanian Commonwealth.

Back in the 16th century, the Cossacks began to resist the control of the Polish–Lithuanian Commonwealth and rebelled in favour of joining Russia. This is known as the 1648 Khmelnytsky Uprising.[13]

In 1654, the Cossacks signed the Treaty of Pereyaslav with the Tsar, breaking the supremacy of the Polish–Lithuanian Commonwealth, their allegiance shifting to the Russian Tsar and remaining with the Russian state until early 19th century.

So far the question of Crimea has not arisen, which was a part of the Ottoman Empire. Following a war between the Ottoman and Russian empires, Crimea was briefly independent before being annexed by Russia under Catherine the Great in 1783.[14] War returned to Crimea from 1853 to 1856 when the Russian Empire again fought a coalition of the Ottoman Empire, France and the United Kingdom (UK) and lost to them.[15] Under the Treaty of Paris, signed on March 30, 1856, Russia was forbidden from placing bases in the Black Sea. The embarrassment of losing Crimea was crucial in the modernisation of the Russian Empire and overall military capabilities.

This also explains the roots of Russia's insistence of taking back the peninsula in 2014 despite legally signing a document that first gave Crimea back to Ukraine in 1954 and then acknowledged Crimea being a part of Ukraine in 1991 as well. Russia considers Crimea as having a major role in Russia's power projection across centuries. This part shall be covered in more detail in the section on legal aspect of security guarantees.

To conclude, the importance of Kyivan Rus, and Kyiv, today is obvious from the fact that the Rus tribes still bear its name. There is 'Rus' in Russian and Belarusian and Kyiv is the capital of Ukraine. This explains why the city has a hold over the collective imagination of the people in the region, going beyond the legal borders of today. It was important to the birth of Russia. Until the advent of the 20th century, owing to that common civilisational ethos, Russia considered Ukrainians and Belarusians as ethnically Russians but referred to both groups as Little Russians.[16]

This thousand-year old connection is the beginning of the explanation of the present-day wars. It explains why populations are willing to fight for places that exert a 'pull' on how they perceive their identities.

However, there still remains a gap in understanding how and why did the Ukrainian identity become separate and hostile to this common civilisational ethos.

As East Europe remained mired in wars, by the early 1800s, there was a discernible and growing separatist movement in Ukraine. This led Imperial Russia to impose a ban on the teaching of Ukrainian language in schools in an effort to eradicate the threat to the Russian Empire.[17] In the wake of the Bolshevik Revolution in Russia in 1917, Ukraine briefly became an independent nation before becoming a part of the USSR. Russia and Ukraine were two of the signatories of the founding documents of the USSR in 1922.[18] With its sweeping, fertile plains, Ukraine became the breadbasket of the Soviet Union, making it an invaluable part of the USSR. Subsequently, USSR became one of the dominant forces in world politics for the rest of the 20th century.

However, according to the Ukrainian people, joining the USSR did not settle the question of their identity but worsened it. To understand the forging of a separate Ukrainian identity, an analysis of the Soviet era experiences is required.

Perhaps the most devastating blow to the Ukrainian people came from the Holodomor (literally meaning 'death by hunger'), a state-sponsored famine between 1930–33, created by Stalin's government. This resulted in the death of approximately 4 million Ukrainians. In the experiences of the Ukrainian people then, the suffering of the Holodomor is a pivotal point of reference. During the World War II, about 1.5 million Ukrainian Jews were killed along with 5–7 million overall Ukrainian casualties and a post-war famine yet again claimed a million more lives.

**Re-emergence of the Crimean Question in Soviet Russia:** From the perspective of the current analysis undertaken here, it is important to mention that in 1954 the Soviet Union transferred the control of Crimea to Soviet Ukraine (then part of USSR).[19] The basis of this transfer was 'the integral character of the economy, the territorial proximity and the close economic and cultural ties between the Crimea Province and the Ukrainian SSR'. It was also to commemorate the 300th anniversary of Ukraine's union with Russia.[20] This union had happened through the 'Treaty of Pereyaslav' that the Ukrainian Cossacks had signed with Tsarist Russia in 1654 (discussed in an earlier section of this chapter). As discussed later, this became the legal basis on which Ukraine got Crimea in 1991 as well.

The Ukrainian misgiving with its status in USSR was also exacerbated with the Chernobyl nuclear disaster of 1986. Chernobyl is situated in Ukraine. On the fateful day on April 26, 1986, during a test procedure in reactor-4, power decreased and made the reactor unstable. The subsequent explosion remains one of the only two nuclear disasters in human history alongside the 2011 Fukushima disaster in Japan.

Five years later, the USSR collapsed and an independent Ukraine with an evolved and pronounced Ukrainian identity found itself as an independent nation finally. In the same year a referendum and an election were held. To the question: do you support the act of declaration of independence of Ukraine, 92.3 per cent voted (out of 84 per cent of the population that took part) in favour of an independent Ukraine.

In the ensuing presidential elections, six candidates ran, each forwarding their own narrative of consolidating the Ukrainian identity. Leonid Kravchuk was elected the first President.

This heightened sense of Ukrainian identity played a key role in the subsequent political revolutions in the young Ukrainian state, namely, the Orange Revolution of 2004 and the Maidan Revolution of 2014—both having conflicting narratives from the Russian perspective that regarded them as engineered by the Central Intelligence Agency (CIA). Both will be discussed shortly.

### *'Putinism'[21] in the Evolution of the Russian state post-1991*

The resurgence of the Russian state in the post-Cold War era is ascribed to the personality of one man alone—its long-standing President, Vladimir Putin. The binding ideological glue that President Putin has successfully deployed to invoke a strong state has been encapsulated as 'Putinism'. It is an ideology devoted to connecting Russia's past to visions of cultural achievement and the image of a strong Russian state.[22] It has been a long, arduous and skilful task and is reflected in distinct events and expressions by President Putin.

**Power Cacuum in Russia during 1990s:** The Russian state in the 1990s was a weakened agency, mired in internal power struggles and uprisings. Russian political leaders were still struggling to find their footing after their destinies were changed by a stroke of a pen by President Boris Yeltsin. Bigger geopolitical questions and narratives of 'sphere of influence' had to be put on the backburner as pressing requirements such as food distribution had become an insurmountable problem in the aftermath of the Soviet disintegration. The decade of the 90s saw separatism thrive in Chechnya as the economic and geostrategic profile of Russia declined. The general mood was that of gloom and frustration as millions of citizens lost their savings to hyperinflation. Uncertainty descended on its people in all walks of life.

Vladimir Putin, freshly resigned from the KGB and then deputy mayor of St. Petersburg, was merely 39 years old when Russia became a new country. He had returned after serving for five years as a liaison officer between the KGB and the Stasi (the East German secret police)[23] in Germany. Son of an officer in the NKVD, the Soviet Secret Police, he was not new to the world of foreign intelligence.

Even after the KGB was reconstituted into four different domestic services by a decree passed by Boris Yeltsin in 1991, and despite an alleged official resignation from the agency, Vladimir Putin continued to remain influential in the higher echelons of Russian political sphere by undertaking newer roles successfully.

**Putin's Rise to Power:** His big opportunity arrived with Yeltsin's inability to deal with the separatist movements in Chechnya. Putin's ascent to power began with the promise of crushing separatism with an iron hand. In August 1999, he was named Prime Minister when Yeltsin refused to condone a re-invasion of Chechnya. Soon, the hugely unpopular Yeltsin stepped down and Putin was appointed President and has remained in power ever since, serving either as the President or the Prime Minister.

It is noteworthy that Putin developed his own approach to 'war' as an essential tool of statecraft. He vowed to crush the Chechen uprising and avenge the humiliating defeat of the Yelstin years. With his ascent to power rose the expectations to consolidate the Russian state agency, which lay subverted by the Chechen uprisings and the weakness exhibited by Yeltsin. When he became President in 2000, Putin presented himself as a saviour, moderniser and an ideologue that people could trust and look up to.[24] Commentators have noted that back then his ideology was more or less neutral to both Europe and the United States (US) and was focussed solely on building the strength of the Russian state.

The defeatist decisions of the Yeltsin years during the 1990s came to be perceived as a mark of a weak Russian state, which was put on the path of redemption in the 2000s as Putin came to power.

In the years between 2000 and 2023, Putin's ideas have evolved into more crystallised forms, justifying the unity between the Russian races transcending sovereign borders.[25]

The early years of his presidency focussed on national consolidation around the idea of stability. The first expression of his ideas came in late 1999 when he published an article 'Russia at the Turn of Millennium'.[26] In that article Putin laid out his vision for the country. He rejected Communism as well as Western-style democracy and suggested a third way for Russia to derive strength from its traditions.

A more sustained effort at developing a patriotic and 'greater' Russia narrative emerged after a surge in protests in 2011 and 2012; this suddenly increased before the war in Ukraine started.

The content analysis of his assorted writings across different platforms suggests that he borrows heavily from czarist and Soviet themes as well as from other intellectual sources such as the 20th century radical right.[27]

**Putinism and the First European War in the post-Cold War Era:** The first decade of Putin's presidency was a co-optive foreign policy towards the West and friendly pictures of Putin with his Western counterparts were a common sight. When Russia hosted its first G8 meeting in 2006 it became a testimony to a synergistic alliance with the Western economic grouping.

However, all of that changed in 2008 when Georgia was attacked by Russia on August 8 that year. Although the relationship between the two countries had been worsening since the pro-democracy Colour Revolution in Georgia in 2003,[28] Russia's full-fledged military response to Georgia's shelling of its breakaway province was considered farfetched. The West, invested in the path to engage Russia owing to good relations between them and Putin, called merely for a ceasefire and seemed to be in a hurry to return to business as usual of the Merkel years.[29] The ceasefire agreement was initiated by French President Nicolas Sarkozy and explains the Franco–German approach of favouring diplomatic solutions such as the Normandy Talks in the years that followed.[30]

While the Georgian War lasted merely a few days, its repercussions shaped the geopolitics of what followed in 2014 and then in 2022.[31]

The pattern in Putin's ambitions for Russia reclaiming its lost sphere of influence became more visible after the Russo–Georgian war in 2008.

By 2009, the Russian state had embarked upon its version of 'securitisation'—a process of aligning Russian culture and history with matters of national security.

Testimony to such securitisation is the 2009 National Security Strategy that explicitly warned against attempts to revise Russia's history as having security repercussions for its neighbours.[32]

By the mid 2010s, public engagement with his ideas on the glory of the Russian Empire further increased.

**Russia's Red Lines to NATO:** It is interesting to note that the Georgian War of 2008 came within six months of NATO's Bucharest Summit where it was declared that Ukraine and Georgia will be NATO members someday. Russia's response was included the first unapologetic rebuttal by Putin against NATO expansion, which also affirmed his red lines to NATO expansion that had begun into Central and East Europe after 1991.

While Russia's stand towards NATO's red lines cannot be defended on legal grounds as all states are entitled to their sovereign decisions, but to argue so without referring to its heavily loaded context would be incorrect and a folly.

Therefore, under Putin, from the mid 2000s, there has been an internal push in Russia to reclaim its lost influence through exerting control on the destinies of the ex-Soviet states, forcing them to either remain as buffer zones between Russia and NATO borders or face wars with perpetuating frozen conflicts. This internal push is not only fuelled by Putin's personality cult alone, but also by the powerful group, the inner circle, that the President has established to rule the vast lands of Russia for the last 23 years.[33] The inner circle also has a role to play in how the fates of Russia and its neighbours, especially Ukraine, have been entwined in conflict and bloodshed for the larger period of their modern histories.

The collective binding thought portrayed by President Putin ever since he came to power in 2000 through his policies, decisions and writings has been termed 'Putinism'. The success of Putinism lies in its discursive appeal that garners support in the Russian people and therefore it thrives. That is what has made the fight for Ukraine an ideological and existential fight for the values of Russia.

### *Legal Aspects of Security Guarantees after 1991 and the Role of NATO*

After the collapse of the Soviet Union, Ukraine became an independent state along with 14 others—Estonia, Latvia, Lithuania (Baltic States), Belarus, Moldova, the three Caucasian states of Georgia, Armenia and Azerbaijan and the five Central Asian states of Kazakhstan, Uzbekistan, Tajikistan, Turkmenistan and Kyrgyzstan.

Post-1991, Ukraine became the third-largest holder of Soviet-era nuclear weapons. Not just the weapons, it also possessed warheads and the capacity to make more. Although the software that controlled them was in Russian hands, it led to a precarious situation on the status of nuclear weapons stationed in Ukraine.

**1994 Budapest Memorandum on Security Assurances:**[34] The origins of the Budapest Memorandum lie in the lengthy bargaining between Russia and the US with the newly independent Ukraine to persuade Kyiv to transfer all Soviet-made nuclear weapons that it had inherited from the USSR to Russia.

Meeting at the sidelines of the Budapest Summit of the Conference on Security and Cooperation in Europe (CSCE) in December 1994, the big powers decided to sign a legal instrument to decide the matter.

This legal statement signed by Russia, the UK and the United States of America (USA) that extended security assurances to Belarus, Kazakhstan and Ukraine in return for transferring all the Soviet-made nuclear warheads on their territory to Russia came to be known as the Budapest Memorandum on Security Assurances. The Russian actions in 2014 were a clear violation of the Budapest Memorandum. It sparked an intense debate on the reliability of the legally signed documents as Russia's disregard for the Budapest Memorandum has raised fundamental questions about the future of the international order. In hindsight this seems to be a correct misgiving as the war of 2022 proved yet again

**1997 Treaty on Friendship, Cooperation and Partnership between Ukraine and the Russian Federation:**[35] After the successful negotiation of the Budapest security assurances, Russia and Ukraine signed a friendship treaty designed to strengthen the weak bonds between the two neighbouring states. The treaty was signed in Kiev, the Ukrainian capital, on Boris N. Yeltsin's first trip there as the President of Russia. The main points of the 1997 Treaty stressed on political and commercial cooperation between the countries. It also included a joint statement on the Black Sea Fleet that would permit Russia to operate on Ukrainian territory. In lieu, Russia agreed to write off most of Ukraine's enormous debt to Moscow, which was mostly outstanding payments for Russian oil.

Once again, the corner stone of this treaty was Russia's written promise to respect the territorial sovereignty and integrity of Ukraine as per the 1991 borders.

After Russia's unilateral actions in Crimea in 2014, the National Security and Defense Council (NSDC) of Ukraine decided not to extend the 1997 Treaty, which expired on March 31, 2019.

The flouting of 1994 and 1997 legal instruments[36] by Russia shows that there is indeed an incompatibility of the Russian state's pursuit of its strategic objectives with the legal and historical components of functional differentiation in the East European order.

**East European Security Situation and NATO's Expansion:** East Europe saw a rapid decline in Russia's influence after 1991 as the country remained mired in internal challenges discussed earlier. The newly found Central and East European states found themselves between a defeated Russia and an ascending liberal order from the West that promised prosperity and freedom. From the perspective of the East European states, joining the affluent Western bloc seemed a more winsome strategy as the tide was turning. This became the dynamic for NATO's eastward expansion, which, contrary to popular belief, is a demand driven geopolitical expansion in Europe.

There is little doubt that from the perspective of Russia's securitisation objectives, NATO's entry into the buffer states around Russia—Ukraine, Georgia, Belarus and Moldova—was and is considered a direct threat to Russia's security.[37] And it would be wrong to assume that the West had no idea of how far they were encroaching into the idea of Russia's securitisation imperatives when NATO membership was expanding in Russia's backyard.

A clearer understanding of this dynamic emerges when the perspective of the ex-Soviet states is taken into account.

The ex-Soviet states' push towards the West came from how they perceived their state security as being under threat from their bigger neighbour, which could not accept their sovereignty and territorial integrity being at par with its own. One of the unresolved dilemmas that the ex-Soviet states grapple with till today is the agency of their sovereignty and statehood being undermined by Russia in the quest of maintaining its sphere of influence.[38] From the perspective of the ex-Soviet states, then the quest to chase stability of their statehood became their securitisation imperative, which they thought could be best achieved by getting the guarantee of NATO's Article 5.

**Why did NATO Expand Eastward After 1991?:** NATO was a military alliance put together in 1949 during the Cold War to expand the US' sphere of influence. It had its rival in the Soviet-engineered Warsaw Pact of 1955, which fell apart when the USSR collapsed. Several analysts have questioned the rationale of the existence of NATO after the Cold War ended.[39] But their claims have been refuted by those who point out that NATO predates the Warsaw Pact. They further argue that as a military alliance functioning in Europe for 40 years it has every rationale to re-invent its role in the European theatre.

The first challenge before NATO in the post-Cold War era came immediately after the Berlin Wall came down in November 1989[40] and East Germany collapsed into disorganisation.

The bitter criticism that NATO received in the 90s and later in 2001 came from its indefensible misadventures in Iraq and Afghanistan rather than from its role in European security. Critics should be able to maintain a distinction between the two contexts. The tendency to assume that NATO pushed expansion in Eastern Europe is fallacious because it does not stand any test of analysis.

**A Demand Driven Expansion:** NATO expanded periodically after 1991 but its expansion was sought by, not pushed upon, the East European states. Records suggest that UK and US military officials prioritised re-inventing the alliance instead of expanding it per se because they saw little merit in expanding membership.[41] The smaller, unstable and poor countries of East Europe were considered to be a de-stabilising addition to the alliance while bringing little in terms of financial commitments.

Nonetheless, analysis of the final agreements pertaining to German Unification clearly shows that all sides had agreed to the inherent rights of states to join any organisation they deem fit, a principal first expressed in the Helsinki Act of 1975.

Therefore, the much touted 'verbal assurance' given to Gorbachev by Bush at the time of fall of the Berlin Wall has not found valid reference because all agreements had widely accepted the Helsinki Act.

NATO's dynamic in East Europe developed gradually and Russia seems to have been on board.

The following points bring out the gradual and steady progress of NATO in the East European states and its relationship with Russia:

**NATO's Partnership for Peace Programme (PfP) in 1994:** This programme was open to all the former Warsaw Pact countries and the rest of Europe and was designed to open larger collaborations toward overall peace and stability in Europe. Different groups in East Europe actively participated in the PfP programme. Russia was given a special status within the PfP but since the nature was informal, it did not mean the formal expansion of NATO.

President Bill Clinton took several measures to co-opt Russia in the security theatre of Western Europe. He pushed a new partnership embodied in the NATO–Russia Founding Act signed in May 1997, which created the NATO–Russia Permanent Joint Council (PJC) to provide Russia a voice within the alliance itself. However, to argue that it meant significantly for Russia would also be an error. It remained a formality and just like how Russia found itself on the margins of decisions taken inside NATO, Russia too ignored the Joint Council and pursued its national interests regardless.

**First Round of NATO Expansion in 1999:** The popularity of NATO in the East European theatre grew by leaps and bounds when ex-Warsaw state members—Poland, the Czech Republic and Hungary started to lobby vigorously to join NATO.[42] They saw NATO as a means to provide them with additional security from possible Russian aggression and joined NATO in 1999. Russia did object to this citing the 'verbal assurance' Gorbachev was given, which became a frequent point of reference in Russian objections to NATO expansion thereafter.

**Groups such as the GUAM Group:** GUAM emerged out of the 1996 talks in Vienna on amending the Conventional Forces in Europe (CFE) Treaty.[43] The governments of Georgia, Ukraine, Azerbaijan and Moldova decided to pool their diplomatic resources to resist Russia's efforts to station its weapons in or near the territory of the organisation's member states. GUAM was later expanded to GUAM following Uzbekistan's accession to the organisation in April 1999. One of the primary objectives of the group was to foster closer ties with NATO's PfP programme to safeguard their sovereignty.

**NATO–Russia Council of 2022:** In 2002, the NATO–Russia cooperation was further strengthened with the establishment of the NATO–Russia Council (NRC). However, it proved to be of little significance in the larger scheme of East European geopolitics. NRC proved incapable of improving NATO's relations with Russia and in the words of Condoleezza Rice, 'made little progress, because the Kremlin never fully embraced it'.

**Second Round of NATO Expansion:** 2002 onwards, a new set of Central and Eastern European states sought inclusion in NATO. In addition to the states, such as Slovakia, Bulgaria and Romania, that NATO had not accepted in the first round, Latvia, Lithuania and Estonia too sought membership.

This brought a different kind of tension between NATO and Russia as these states would be the first former Soviet Union states to be admitted into NATO and would directly border Russia. Putin had come to power in Russia by then and objected to this enlargement citing the familiar 'verbal assurance' clause. But he was also eager to not let normalisation with the West and subsequent improvement in Russian energy sales to Europe be off tracked. The reader must be reminded that this was also the phase of the early years of 'Putinism' when the focus was on consolidating Russia's national stature.

By 2004, Bulgaria, Romania, Slovakia, Slovenia and the three Baltic states joined NATO. In 2009, Albania and Croatia joined as well.

**NATO's Membership Action Plan (MAP) of 1999:** Meant as an enabler for other East European and Balkan states to join the alliance, NATO came up with an accession plan.

Therefore, an overview of NATO's expansion and subsequent improvement in Russia–NATO ties between 1991–2008 shows that while the balance was tilted in favour of NATO and Russia objected to the West not honouring the 'verbal assurance' it was not hostile in the least. Putin's discomfort with ex-Warsaw Pact states and then ex-Soviet states joining NATO seems to have been offset by his desire to have stable relations with the West and specially the US/NATO.

Russia's red lines to NATO's expansion emerged in 2008 when Putin launched the first European war against Georgia six months after the NATO summit at Bucharest just because the summit concluded with a declaration of future inclusion of the two states of Ukraine and Georgia.

Bucharest Summit of 2008 was, in principle, no different from the Helsinki Act of 1975 which was adhered to every time NATO expanded after 1991. Similarly, Georgia's and Ukraine's accession to NATO was also fundamentally no different from the Baltic States' accession because all these were ex-Soviet states. What then explains Putin's strong military response to Bucharest Summit when erstwhile NATO accessions by ex-Warsaw pact as well as the ex-Soviet states did not elicit it.

Perhaps it was the aligning of more factors that led to Putin declaring war on Georgia. First, the resurgence of Russian state agency, and second, the coming to power of pro-Western governments in both Georgia in 2003 and Ukraine in 2004 through the colour revolutions.

In the case of Ukraine, there was an the added factor of Crimea's status that had legally remained with Ukraine but in whose capital, Sevastopol, Russia had stationed the headquarters of its Black Sea Fleet. Ukraine's entry into NATO would have meant an increased complexity on the status of Russia's Black Sea Fleet.

Therefore, to argue that the West was oblivious of the red lines in the case of Ukraine is an unconvincing argument, especially after the turn of events in 2008.

Perhaps, there was also a realisation in Russia of the utility of the grey zone of frozen conflicts in these countries. Disturbed borders, as long as they remained unresolved, would block their entry into NATO. These frozen conflicts could be perpetuated with relatively little effort and through extra state agencies that would neither trigger coordinated response from the West nor let these countries join NATO.

Ukraine had watched the Russo–Georgian war with bated breath as the pro-democracy Orange Revolution swept through the country.

Now is a good time to re-visit the Ukraine question.

What about the Russia–Ukraine relations?

**The Orange Revolution 2004:** Despite all the security assurances given to Ukraine in the form of Budapest security assurances and the Russia–Ukraine friendship treaty of 1997, Russia was aware of the pro-West tilt in Ukraine. The Ukrainian people wanted to have the candidate they voted for as the President and rose up against the Kremlin-backed candidate. Eventually the election results were overturned and Kremlin-backed Victor Yanukovych was replaced with the democratically elected Victor Yuschneko.

After the 2008 Georgian War, the struggle in Ukraine to fight its internal corruption also accelerated. The Kyiv appellate court ruled on June 13, 2010, and posthumously convicted Stalin, Molotov and Ukrainian leaders of genocide against the Ukrainian people during the Holodomor famine.

This reinforced the sense of Ukrainian identity, which had re-crystallised after the Orange Revolution and further distanced the country from Russia.

Russian analysts, on the other hand, termed the Orange Revolution and its aftermath a CIA-funded uprising, which Ukraine and other East European countries have rejected.

**The Maidan Revolution 2014:** The Revolution of Dignity also called the Maidan Revolution, erupted from Yanokovych's refusal to sign the European Union (EU) accession agreement. During the protests 130 people were killed, including police officers, and this led to early presidential elections.

In the same year, a pro-Russian uprising in eastern Ukraine began fighting in the Donbas region. This was said to be supported by Russia in the same way as in the Georgian War in 2008.

The European states, now further dependent on Russia for cheap energy, tried the same diplomatic route they had tried with Georgia. In the midst of Franco–German negotiations under the Normandy Format talks, something more dramatic happened.

An army of 'Little Green Men' took Crimea back for Russia. The West was shocked but put half-hearted sanctions on Russia, which did little to Russia's stable energy revenues. On the contrary, it helped Russia build a formidable chest of $640 bn foreign reserves[44] and $150 bn in sovereign wealth fund[45] for launching the war of February 2022.

A year later, President Putin praised the 'Little Green Men' and other special forces who fought for getting Crimea back to Russia. 2014 was also the first time that Wagner troops, among other private armies, masqueraded as Little Green Men. Back then, however, Prigozhin's connection with the Wagner Group was not formally established.

**Frozen Conflicts:** The similarity between the 2008 Georgian and 2014 Ukrainian experience shows the utility of frozen conflicts in the pro-Russia regions of ex-Soviet states where large swaths of ethnic Russians have been living since the Soviet times. As argued earlier, a frozen conflict in the Donbas region of Ukraine and the taking back of Crimea, flouting the internationally recognised borders of 1991 and the security assurances of 1994 and 1997 were enough to stop Ukraine from joining NATO.

What then explains the Russian War of 2022?

**Militarisation of Ukraine by the West:** For Russia then, it was ***not*** only the red line of Ukraine's NATO accession that seems to be the tipping point because that was not going to be crossed in the foreseeable future. It was ***also*** the steady militarisation[46] of the country by the CIA[47] after 2014 and the training of Ukrainian Armed Forces by the West that created a security threat to Russia, regardless of whether Ukraine joined NATO or not.

There is little doubt that the parallel strands of thoughts such as NATO's eastward expansion, Russia's ideological struggle with the West to save Russia's traditional values, militarisation of its neighbour pumped up with Western training and weapons and, last but not the least, Putin's public image as the saviour of the Russian state—all joined the complex web of narratives that finally led to the special military operation of February 24, 2022.

The recent American retreat from Afghanistan in 2020, its sharpening focus on the Indo–Pacific and the astounding degree of dependence that Europe had on Russia for oil and gas, exacerbated by France's fallout with NATO, seems to have also played a role in perpetuating the decision on the special military operation.

Now comes the role of the last component of the complex geo-economics of the European theatre, which is at the heart of Europe–Russia relations after 1991.

### *The Complex Geo-economics of the European Theatre*

Post-1991, Europe thrived on the peace dividend of the European security order. It was a three-pronged existence that allowed Europe to focus solely on economic performance by, first, outsourcing Europe's security to NATO; second, relying on a reliable supply of cheap natural gas and oil from Russia and third, intensifying trade relations with China.

At the time of Russia's special military operation of February 2022, the EU was importing 40–50 per cent of its imported natural gas and 30 per cent of its crude oil imports from Russia alone. Germany, the economic engine of Europe, was the largest destination of these energy imports.

Over reliance of European heavy industry on energy imports, which seems to be a foreign policy blunder in hindsight, was not the foregone conclusion during the post-Cold War years.[48] Getting cheap energy from Russia was thought to be the best formula of the now fallen neo-liberal logic. It was a meticulously crafted design by leaders of Germany and France to co-opt Russia into the European theatre. In hindsight, however, the three-pronged existence of creating security, energy and trade dependencies has rendered the bloc incapable of converting its geo-economic heft into geopolitical traction or fending for its own security.

**Weaponization of Energy in the European Theatre:** Gabriel Collins has identified more than a dozen discrete instances before 2022 where Russian entities used price and physical volume manipulation of crude oil or natural gas supplies—often amid political tensions—to pressurise consumers located in Central and Eastern Europe and the former Soviet countries.[49]

In the context of Ukraine alone, Russia has weaponized Europe's energy reliance on itself not once but at least twice before 2022. Analysts point out that the kind of weaponization of energy that has been seen in the context of the Russia–Ukraine war has not been observed in international politics after the 1970s oil crisis. Energy geopolitics and its weaponization has been a critical driver in the battle for Ukraine and has a complex history of its own. For brevity, this chapter divides post 1991 Russia's energy weaponization towards European countries in two phases.

**First Phase of Energy Weaponization by Russia:** Russia had been targeting East European countries with selective gas cuts as a pressure tool against Ukraine since the winter of 2005–06.[50] All of 2004, Russia gave extraordinarily cheap gas to Ukraine to support the image of Kremlin-backed candidate Victor Yanukovych. But the voters voted overwhelmingly in support of the pro-democracy candidate Victor Yushchenko. This is the background to the Orange Revolution already discussed in the previous sections.

Dispute emerged between the Ukrainian state-controlled oil and gas company Naftogaz Ukraine and the Russian national gas supplier Gazprom in 2005 March. The disagreements concerned natural gas supplies, prices and debts. In addition of outstanding payments Russia accused Kyiv of re-selling the gas to the EU via a complex network of pipelines going into Europe. The crisis peaked in January 2006 when Russia cut of supply. It affected not only Ukraine but also European countries that relied on Russia for their gas.

Until 2005, Ukraine was the major transit for about 80 per cent of Russian gas going into Europe.

Beginning of 2006, a deal was signed between Russia and Ukraine to end the gas dispute and gas started flowing again to Ukraine and Europe. However, it soon became a political issue as the parliament of Ukraine, Rada, voted to dismiss the Prime Minister for dubious dealings in the gas deal.

According to the EU, this was the first time that Brussles recognised Putin's willingness to use energy as a geopolitical tool.

While successive US administrations[51] had been warning the bloc of an excessive reliance on Russia, but driven by Germany the bloc had created a synergy with Russia in a win-win cost-efficient quid pro quo.

In the US warnings was also an implicit fact that the US wanted to sell more of its own gas to Europe. For the Europeans, however, getting cheap natural gas via Soviet-era pipelines was seen as a preferred option due to its cost effectiveness and as it ensured that Russian endeavours remain entwined with the larger European economic machine.[52]

**Second Phase of Energy Weaponization by Russia:** The issue of outstanding payments and reselling Russian gas to other actors in re-emerged in 2009. The Russian natural gas company Gazprom refused to send gas to Ukraine until the

Ukrainian gas company Naftogaz paid its accumulating debts for previous gas supplies. The dispute began towards the end of 2008 with a series of failed negotiations, and on January 1, 2009, Russia cut off gas supplies to Ukraine.[53] Matters got out of hand when on January 7, 2009, Russia halted gas supplies to Ukraine for almost two weeks in the peak of winter. As a result, the entire south-eastern Europe that received gas via the Ukraine transit entered a period of unprecedented energy crisis.

This was the rationale behind the Nord Streams, a set of offshore pipelines meant to bring natural gas directly from Russia into Europe under the Baltic Sea, bypassing the Ukraine transit. Nord Stream-1 was thought to solve this crisis of the south-eastern and central-eastern European states that found themselves vulnerable each time tensions between Russia and Ukraine stirred. However, its viability remains disputed because it would have also increased Europe's overall dependence on Russia even if it bypassed Ukraine.

**Era of the Nord Streams:** Hailed by supporters as a purely commercial project and by detractors as a political tool to enhance Europe's economic dependence on Russia, a set of pipelines called the Nord Steam-1 and later Nord Stream-2 project of promised to change the existing landscape of natural gas flowing from Russia into Europe. Expectedly, it was vehemently opposed by the US but was backed by Russia and Germany.

Nord Stream-1 went into operation in 2012. Nord Stream-2 was completed in September 2021, but it could never transport any gas. Nord Stream 1 and 2 were both twin pipelines, and together they could carry up to 110 bcm of gas (out of the 140 bcm total imported volumes from Russia) directly from Russia into Germany.

From the very beginning Nord Stream-2 was mired in controversy and faced adamant opposition in particular from the US and Poland, who believed that Germany was making itself and the rest of Europe further dependant on Russian energy. Ukraine opposed the Nord Streams as they made Ukraine lose out on the annual transit fee from Russia, which was a major source of its income.

The US made it clear that bilateral relations would be badly affected if Nord Stream-2 went into operation.

As luck would have it, Nord Stream-2 never went into operation. On September 26, 2022, twin blasts, later confirmed by Swedish authorities as manmade explosions, were reported in the Nord Streams.[54]

The case is still undecided and the latest report by the Washington Post points a finger at Ukraine having done it.[55] That said, the case is far from solved.

It maybe concluded that the gas pipeline project sits at an intersection of several geopolitical and geo-economic crosscurrents[56] that have come to shape economic security as well as the geostrategic balance of Europe in the way that Europe responds to successive years of energy weaponization.

## CONCLUSION

The larger context of the Russia–Ukraine war in 2022 is complex and entwined and merits analysis in a rigorous methodological framework. The methodological framework within which the four interrelated components of the Russia–Ukraine war have been analysed are taken from Quentin Skinner's contextualism and securitisation theory adapted to differentiation. The former argues for keeping the analysis of past events rooted in relevant contexts at all times, while the latter provides a more robust mechanism to explain the role of social, anthropological and other factors in determining the security discourse in Russia, Ukraine and East Europe. Such a contextualised analysis is finetuned to analysing the security concerns of each actor and its subsequent actions, which reductionist approaches such as offensive realism tend to miss.

The four components analysed separately and in relation to each other in this chapter are: (i) civilisational legacy and the conflicting identitarian narrative, (ii) ideology of the Russian state and its continuation under 'Putinism', (iii) legal aspect of the post-World War II security guarantees and the role of NATO and (iv) the complex geo-economics of the European theatre.

With careful analysis of the humongous background of the Russia–Ukraine war of 2022, the further chapters dealing with specifics of the war may be understood better.

## NOTES

1 Writing of critical historical narration

2 Patrick James, "Offensive Realism", in *Realism and International Relations: A Graphic Turn Toward Scientific Progress, Oxford* Academic, November 2022, pp. 494–516.

3 John Mearshimer, (740) The Causes and Consequences of the Ukraine War, YouTube, June 16, 2022, at https://www.youtube.com/watch?v=qciVozNtCDM. Accessed on October 25, 2023.

4 Gavin Jacobson, "The Tragedy of John Mearsheimer", *New Statesman,* September 27, 2023.

5 Alexander Stubb, (740) Why Mearsheimer Is Wrong About Russia and the War in Ukraine.

Five Arguments from Alexander Stubb, YouTube, July 8, 2022, at https://www.youtube.com/watch?v=vlB-pRqdyBg. Accessed on August 29, 2023.

6 Rens van Munster, 'Securitization,' *Oxford Bibliographies*, June 26, 2012, at https://www.oxfordbibliographies.com/display/document/obo-9780199743292/obo-9780199743292-0091.xml (Accessed October 20, 2023)

7 Jeremy Herb, Donald Judd and Phil Mattingly, "Biden condemns 'Russia's unprovoked and unjustified attack on Ukraine' | CNN Politics", February 24, 2002.

8 Barry Buzan and Mathias Albert, "Differentiation: A sociological approach to international relations theory - Barry Buzan, Mathias Albert, 2010 (sagepub.com), March 16, 2010. (Accessed on 16 October 2023).

9 Omeljan Prtsak, 'The Origin of Rus', 36 (3), 1977, pp. 249–73 (Accessed October 16, 2023).

10 Golden Horde - World History Encyclopedia (Accessed October 22, 2022).

11 Janet Martin, "The emergence of Moscow (1359–1462) (Chapter 7) - The Cambridge History of Russia", March 28, 2008.

12 'Why Are Cossacks Key to Understanding the Ukrainian Nation?,' *UkraineWorld*, March 2019 (Accessed October 25, 2023).

13 Cossack-Polish War (encyclopediaofukraine.com) (Accessed September 20, 2023).

14 Marc Kramer, "Why Did Russia Give Away Crimea Sixty Years Ago? | Wilson Center" (Accessed on October 19, 2023).

15 Florence Nightingale's experiences that led to the professionalising of nursing are traced back to this era.

16 Jeffrey Mankoff, "The belief that Russians and Ukrainians share a common identity has deep roots - The Washington Post", The Washington Post, February 10, 2022.

17 A short guide to the linguicide of the Ukrainian language | Infographics - Euromaidan Press (Accessed on October 21, 2023).

18 Jonathan Davis, The Birth of the Soviet Union and the Death of the Russian Revolution - JSTOR Daily, December 21, 2022.

19 Meeting of the Presidium of the Supreme Soviet of the Union of Soviet Socialist Republics | Wilson Center Digital Archive (Accessed October 26, 2023).

20 Krishnadev Calamur, "Crimea: A Gift To Ukraine Becomes A Political Flash Point : Parallels : NPR," February 27, 2014.

21 Maria Snegovaya, Michael Kimmage, and Jade McGlynn, "The Ideology of Putinism", Center for Strategic & International Studies, September 2023. (Accessed on 23 October 2023).

22 Ibid.

23 Catherine Belton, *Putin's People*, London, Williams Collins, 2020, pp. 22–23.

24 Maria Snegovaya, Michael Kimmage, and Jade McGlynn, "The Ideology of Putinism", Center for Strategic & International Studies, September 2023. (Accessed on October 23, 2023).

25 Vladimir Putin, "Article by Vladimir Putin "On the Historical Unity of Russians and Ukrainians", President of Russia (kremlin.ru)," July 12, 2021.

26 Vladimir Putin, "Putin on RUSSIA & MILLENNIUM (uoregon.edu)", 1999 (Accessed November 1, 2023).

27 Maria Snegovaya, Michael Kimmage and Jade McGlynn, The Ideology of Putinism: Is It Sustainable? (csis.org), Center for Strategic & International Studies, September 27, 2023.

28 Federica Prandin, "RIAC: Color revolutions and regime change in Georgia and Ukraine (russiancouncil.ru)," August 5, 2019.

29 This part is covered in the geo-economics of the European theatre.

30 Swasti Rao, "Relevance of Normandy Format Talks in the Ukrainian Crisis | Manohar Parrikar Institute for Defence Studies and Analyses (idsa.in)", February 15, 2022.

31 Peter Dickinson, "The 2008 Russo-Georgian War: Putin's green light - Atlantic Council," August 7, 2021.

32 Carolina Vendil Pallin, "(21) Security Policy and Strategic Consequences | Carolina Vendil Pallin - Academia.edu", 2014 (Accessed November 1, 2023).

33 Catherine Belton, *Putin's People*, London, Williams Collins, 2020, pp 23.

34 The Budapest Memorandum (Accessed July 5, 2023).

35 Treaty on Friendship, Cooperation, and Partnership between Ukraine and the Russian Federation on JSTOR (Accessed July 6, 2023).

36 John B. Bellinger, "How Russia's Invasion of Ukraine Violates International Law | Council on Foreign Relations (cfr.org)", February 28, 2022.

37 Roy Allison, "Russian 'deniable' intervention in Ukraine: how and why Russia broke the rules on JSTOR", International Affairs, November 2014.

38 James Kilner, "Vladimir Putin's veiled threat to ex-Soviet states: 'You're part of historic Russia' (telegraph.co.uk)", June 18, 2022.

39 Marc J.Rice, "NATO's New Order: The Alliance After the Cold War | Origins (osu.edu)", March 2016.

40 John Johnson, "Remember, Remember the 9th of November": The Fall of the Berlin Wall | Origins (osu.edu)" October 2014.

41 Robert H Wealy, "Critique of NATO's Expansion | Origins (osu.edu)", October 1997 (Accessed October 31, 2023).

42 NATO's New Order: The Alliance After the Cold War | Origins (osu.edu) (Accessed on October 28, 2023).

43 Daryl Kimbal, "The Conventional Armed Forces in Europe (CFE) Treaty and the Adapted CFE Treaty at a Glance | Arms Control Association," (Accessed October 31, 2023).

44 Nicholas Gordon, "Sanctions on Russia's central bank reveal fatal flaw in sanction-proofing strategy | Fortune," March 3, 2022.

45 John Hyatt, "How Putin Used Russia's Sovereign Wealth Fund To Create A 'State-Sponsored Oligarchy' (forbes.com)," March 8, 2022.

46 Amy Mackinon and Jack Detsch, "Ukraine's Military Has Come a Long Way Since 2014—and So Has Russia's (foreignpolicy.com)", December 23, 2021.

47 Evan Simko-Bednarski, "Ukrainians got secret CIA training after Russia's Crimea invasion (nypost.com)," March 16, 2022.

48 Patrik Wintour, "'We were all wrong': how Germany got hooked on Russian energy | Germany | The Guardian," June 2, 2022.

49 Gabriel Collins, "Russia's Use of the "Energy Weapon" in Europe | Baker Institute," July 18, 2017.

50 Alexander Motyl, "Ukraine vs. Russia: The Politics of an Energy Crisis on JSTOR", Vol.7, No.4, October-December 2005. (Accessed on October 26, 2023).

51 How Europe Got Hooked on Russian Gas Despite Reagan's Warnings - *The New York Times* (nytimes.com), March 23, 2022.

52 Richard J Anderson, "Europe's Dependence on Russian Natural Gas: Perspectives and Recommendations for a Long-term Strategy | George C. Marshall European Center For Security

Studies (marshallcenter.org)," September 2008.

53 BBC NEWS | Europe | Russia to cut Ukraine gas supply", January 5, 2009.

54 Miranda Bryant, "Key details behind Nord Stream pipeline blasts revealed by scientists | Nord Stream 1 pipeline | The Guardian", September 26, 2022.

55 Ukrainian military officer coordinated Nord Stream pipeline attack that shocked and mystified the West, *The Washington Post*, November 11, 2023.

56 Swasti Rao, "Intersecting Geo-economics and Geopolitics: Nord Stream 2 and Europe | Manohar Parrikar Institute for Defence Studies and Analyses (idsa.in)", December 10, 2021.

# 3

# Tracking Russia–Ukraine War: A Conflict that Defied Expectations

*Abhay K Singh*

Russia's special military operation in Ukraine, which began on February 24, 2022, was expected to be short and swift. Given the disparity in the military power and rather demonstrative superiority of the Russian military, most analysts had concluded that the Ukrainian military stood little chance of resisting it in a conventional war. Russia expected that it would win in a matter of days by quickly overwhelming the Ukrainian Army. As per the United States (US) Intelligence assessment, the best-case scenario was that the remnants of Ukraine's defeated forces would mount an insurgency, a guerrilla war against the Russian occupiers.[1]

Unarguably, these early assessments proved to be wildly off the mark.[2] Ukraine fought back with determination and halted Moscow's advances. Having gravely miscalculated, and faced with determined resistance and operational problems, Russia has refocused its war effort in Ukraine's eastern region. Ukraine's swift territorial gains during the spirited counteroffensive in September 2022 had raised tentative hopes of war termination on Ukraine's terms, which did not materialise. Since then, the war has seen a multitude of ebbs and flows, which include a renewed Russian winter/spring offensive followed by a much-vaunted Ukrainian counteroffensive in the summer of 2023. None of which has resulted in any significant territorial change or major strategic advantages to any side.

The war in Ukraine has repeatedly confounded expectations.[3] While Russia has not been able to achieve its military objectives, Ukrainian forces despite their heroic endeavours and modern equipment from the West have not been able to recapture enough territory to put their leaders in a strong position at any subsequent negotiations. As of early December 2023, the Russia–Ukraine war remains stalemated in a protracted war of attrition.

The chapter provides an overview of key developments in the various phases of the war, intending to provide contextual references to specific analyses in subsequent chapters of the book. After a brief overview of Russia's envisaged war plans, the chapter describes key events in the five phases of the war:

- Phase 1: Russian Invasion of Ukraine (February 24–March 30, 2022)
- Phase 2: Russia's Revised War Objectives and the Battle for Donbas (April–August 2022)
- Phase 3: Ukrainian Counteroffensive (September–November 2022)
- Phase 4: Russian Winter–Spring Campaign (November 2022– May 2023)
- Phase 5: Ukraine's Counteroffensive (June–November 2023)

## RUSSIA'S PLAN OF INVASION

As highlighted in the previous chapter, Russia–Ukrainian war that began on February 24 was not a standalone war but an escalation of the 2014 conflict over Crimea with roots in historical, geopolitical and civilisation tensions. While the Minsk agreements has allowed the Russian occupation of Crimea and Russian-supported militia occupation of the Donbas region in a sort of 'frozen conflict', President Zelensky's outreach to NATO and efforts towards reintegration of occupied territory has caused significant consternation in the Kremlin. In March and April 2021, Russia built up its forces near the Russia–Ukraine border and again in both Russia and Belarus between October 2021 and February 2022 while denying any plan to invade Ukraine.[4] The objectives of this military build-up were threefold. First, it aimed to compel Western governments to re-initiate the Minsk II negotiations and coerce Kyiv to make concessions to avert a conflict. Second, it catered for a rapid build-up of forces through the pre-positioned military equipment around Ukraine. Third, it allowed Moscow to gauge international reaction.[5]

Russia's plan for Ukraine's invasion was made by Russia's Federal Security Service (FSB) and a core group within the presidential administration, supported by senior officials in the Ministry of Defence. Even though the Kremlin maintained a very high level of operational security during the planning phase, US intelligence agencies claimed to have received an indication of invasion in October 2021.[6]

While the actual details of Russia's plan for invasion would have to await archival disclosure, the general framework of the Russian invasion was created around a number of crucial presumptions:[7]

- Making quick progress in operation was essential to preventing an international diplomatic backlash.
- Removing Ukraine's leaders would make it easier for pro-Russian Ukrainians to publicly endorse the occupation.
- Managing economics, energy, and heating would be a good method to keep the majority of the impassive Ukrainian population under control.
- Russian military could defeat the Ukrainian military in combat.

Accordingly, Russia's operational plan envisaged the following major military-strategic tasks for the Russian military:[8]

- By dismantling its air, sea, and air defence units, weaken Ukraine's military power.
- Fixing the Ukrainian Ground Forces in Donbas will help defeat them.
- Removal of Ukraine's military and political leadership and seizing important centres of political and economic power, will weaken Ukraine's resolve and ability to resist.
- Mislead the Ukrainian government through false information regarding Russia's invasion, including date, time, location, and extent.

Although operational security was guaranteed by a very small number of planners, this posed significant implementation issues. The strategy for completing the aforementioned military-strategic tasks became difficult because of the divergent methods needed to achieve the goals of effective deception and spreading national will. The latter required speed, whereas the former would have required a prolonged moulding process before to the invasion. According to assessments, Russian strategists did not carry out persistent shaping operations before to the invasion because they were overly optimistic about the disruptive effect that speed alone may have on weakening Ukraine's resolve to resist. [9]

In the broad term, the invasion would start with a huge missile and bombing campaign directed against Ukraine's air defences, airfields, ammunition storage depots, and Command and Control (C2) infrastructure. Critical infrastructure, such railroads and power plants, would not be targeted since they were essential to Russia's post war plan to control and administer Ukraine. Russia's special services were tasked to eliminate Ukraine's political leadership. Russia's Special Forces and air-assault soldiers were assigned the task of seizing Ukraine's power plants, airfields, water supplies, central bank, and parliament.

As per the plan, Ukraine's administrative centre on the left (eatern) bank of Dnipro river along with Kyiv, Kherson, Mykolaiv, Odesa, a were to be cleared and occupied by Russia's Ground Forces as they concurrently advanced under multiple groups of forces along diverse lines of operation. [10]

The primary attempt to encircle and take control of Kiev was made along the northern axis. One force, using the tactical sign "V," was formed in the Belarusian Gomel region and given the directive to attack Kiev via the right (western) bank of the Dnipro River. The second group was ordered to encircle Kyiv from the left (eastern) side. They were established in the Bryansk region of Russia and utilised the tactical symbol "O."

The tactical symbol "Z" in a square denoted units under the command of the Southern Military District Command Post. They were told to launch an assault from the seized Crimea in order to encircle Mariupol, seize control of the Dnipro bridges, and march along the North Crimean Water Canal, Enerhodar, and the Zaporizhzhia Nuclear Power Plant.

The Western Military District Command Post forces supplemented by conscripts from occupied Luhansk and Donetsk were assigned the tactical symbol "Z". This force was projected from Kursk, Belgorod, and Voronezh to encircle the Ukrainian troops in Donbas along the Lozova-Gulyapole line or the Barvinkovo–Velika Novosilka line. This encirclement aimed to cut off almost half of the Ukrainian forces positioned in the area.

All the way up to the battalion tactical group, the Ground Forces were allocated areas and tasks. The goal for the mechanised forces was frequently to quickly seize, then isolate and screen important targets. With due emphasis on speed of advance, units were instructed to advance in administrative columns by road and to bypass initial resistance during the transit. It was envisaged that Russian units would switch over to stabilisation operations by D+10.

The Black Sea Fleet's components and its amphibious units made formed the last group of Russian forces. On the Kherson–Mykolaiv–Odesa corridor, two amphibious task groups were established with an instruction to land ahead of the advancing Russian Ground Forces. The planned deployment of amphibious forces aimed to capture strategic locations and chokepoints along the coast beyond Mykolaiv in order to facilitate the swift advance of ground forces. The Black Sea Fleet was also tasked with providing support for a large strike campaign by launching Kalibre cruise missiles deep inside Ukraine and for blockading the Ukrainian coast.

The stabilisation phase of operations was to commence after D+10. Russia's conventional forces were to transition into a supporting role to Russia's special services, which were tasked to set up necessary administrative organisations on the occupied territories.

The subsequent section will show that while Russian forces had some successes—including attacks on airfields and civilian infrastructure—but the plan soon began to unravel due to poor planning, faulty intelligence and significant underestimation of the Ukraine's tenacious resistance and overwhelming Western support.

## PHASE 1: RUSSIAN INVASION OF UKRAINE (FEBRUARY 24–MARCH 30, 2022)

President Putin declared an all-out assault on Ukraine on February 24, just as UN representatives were openly pleading with Russia to pull back from the verge of war. The declaration of war was followed by massive rocket and missile attacks on several Ukrainian cities, including the capital Kyiv, the country's second-largest city Kharkiv, and the southern city of Odessa.[11] The stated objective of the 'special military operation' was to demilitarise and 'denazify' Ukraine and warn the West of grave consequences if they decided to interfere.[12] Russian forces began a synchronised multidimensional offensive using land, air and naval forces simultaneously from the northern, western and southern directions of Ukraine.[13] Even though US intelligence had forewarned of Kremlin plans for a full-scale invasion of Ukraine, most observers were taken aback by the attack's magnitude.[14]

A vast, all-encompassing aerial strike campaign across Ukraine marked the start of the invasion. Prior to the strikes, Ukraine's air defence and defensive radar installations were heavily targeted with electronic attacks, and flying decoys were used in large quantities to overwhelm the air defence network. Ballistic and cruise missiles that were fired from air, sea, and ground-based launch systems followed next. [15] Furthermore, Russian planes entered Ukrainian airspace in order to attack tactical targets. In accordance with Russian doctrine, the high-value target list for the initial aerial strike comprised industrial facilities, fuel and energy storage facilities, air defence installations, command and control (C2) infrastructure, ammunition storage stations, and troop assembly zones.[16] Strangely, outside from situations where it was necessary for a tactical outcome, Ukrainian transport infrastructure was not targeted. A three-pronged invasion that attacked the capital city of Kyiv, as well as the cities of Kharkiv and Kherson, respectively, came right after the aerial strikes.

**Figure 1: Russian Invasion of Ukraine, February 24, 2024**

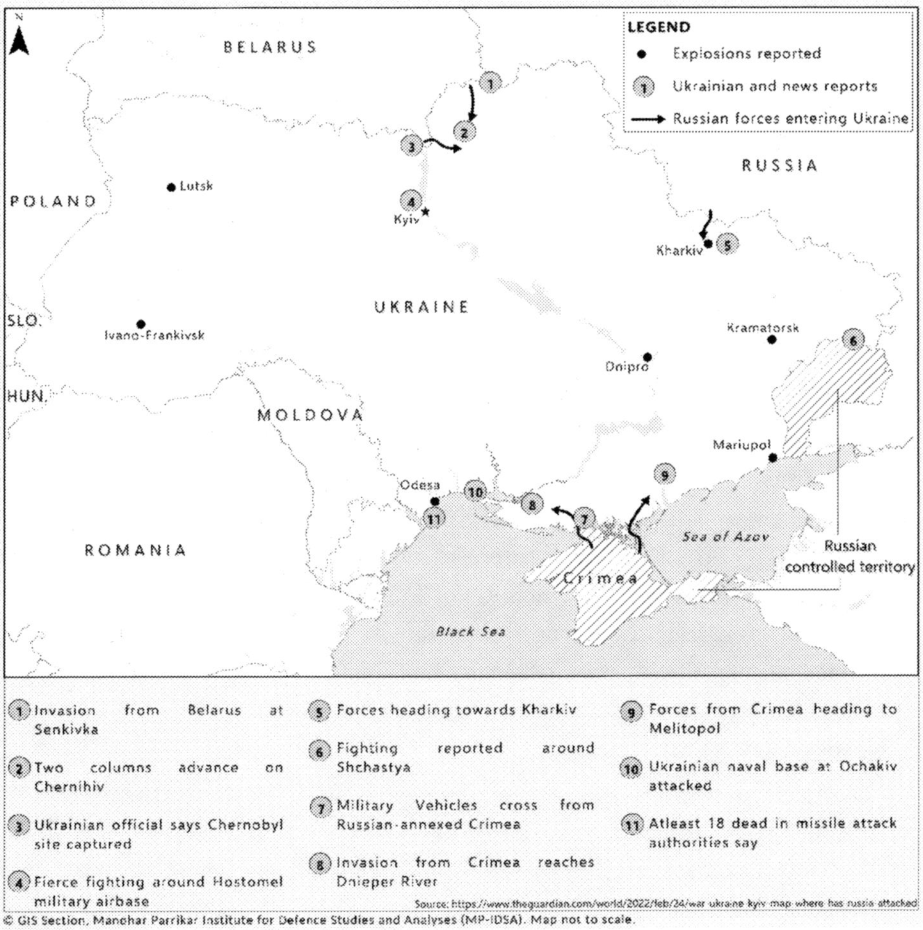


*Source: Guardian.*[17]

## Failed Dash to Kyiv

Later during the day on February 24, 2023, Russian helicopters and airborne troops attempted to capture Hostomel Airfield, a strategic airbase close to Kyiv which soon turned into a ferocious battle.

According to the Russian plan, Hostomel Airport (also called Antonov Airport) would be quickly taken over and utilised as a staging ground for Kyiv's eventual encirclement and annexation. Russian VDV forces launched a heliborne operation to establish a bridgehead for follow-on echelons. Defending Ukrainian troops were completely surprised by Russia's heliborne assault, despite a warning from

Central Intelligence Agency Director William J. Burns in January 2022 about Hostomel being a key target during the Russian offensive.[18]

The airport's defences were weakened during the raid by Mi-35 and Ka-52 attack helicopters operating out of Belarus which facilitated the landing of Mi-8 transport helicopters transporting VDV airborne troops without incident. At Hostomel, two waves of air-assault forces, each with ten helicopters, touched down. These helicopters reached the objective successfully and avoided detection by flying Nap-of-the-earth (NOE) along the Dnipro River from Belarus. Two helicopters were shot down at Hostomel by MANPADS during the first wave. As Ukrainian defences were largely left intact during the initial softening phase and Russian forces lacked necessary air support during the air assault, the VDV troops faced fierce counterattack from defending forces from the touchdown itself. Heavy artillery fire met these Russian VDV forces as they landed, and a mechanised counterattack cleared them from the airfield.[19]

The Ukrainian Air Force (UAF) faced significant danger due to the speed and strategy of the Russian advance. The Russian ground forces quickly moved towards Kyiv from Gomel, where there were very few Ukrainian troops. Major difficulties arose from the axis past Chernihiv, as Ukrainian forces found themselves trapped between their positions. Many Ukrainian battalions were left cut off and behind Russian lines because invading forces were instructed to bypass resistance whenever possible.

Russian ground forces that were stationed in Belarus were able to break through Ukraine's defences near Ivankiv and quickly advanced towards Hostomel. During their advance, they faced multiple ambushes by Ukrainian forces who were fighting to maintain control of the airport against the VDV troops. Despite the resistance, on February 25th, the Russian forces were able to successfully occupy Hostomel Airport.[20]

Following the Russian invasion of Ukraine, the Russian Army and VDV began utilizing Hostomel as a forward operating base. Their goal was to launch an advance on Kyiv. However, their efforts were met with resistance, and the invasion began to stall. Fuel shortages forced entire troops to withdraw, including the famed 40-mile convoy.

Despite these setbacks, the freshly arrived Russian Army and VDV troops attempted to fan out from Hostomel airport to extend their offensive into Bucha and Irpin. These largely uncoordinated pushes encountered fierce resistance in the form of ambushes at Bucha and Hostomel with significant casualties and equipment losses.

Russia had planned to overthrow the government in Kyiv through a less costly approach of encircling the capital, creating chaos through acts of sabotage, and establishing stronger connections with pro-Kremlin politicians who could potentially take control of the country. They intended to avoid a direct assault on the city. They also attempted to sow discord within the Ukrainian government, but these efforts were unsuccessful.[21]

On the western side, Russia's convoy of combat and supply trucks tried to encircle the capital while on the eastern side, its group of forces on the Chernihiv-Sumy line aimed to surround Kyiv. These Ground Forces clusters were supported by missile attacks on Boryspil International Airport and aerial assaults that aimed to take control of Antonov Airport and Vasylkiv Airbase. On the first day of the conflict, Russia also gained control of the Chornobyl nuclear power plant, which provided a direct route to Kyiv via the regional road P02. On February 25, the Russian Ministry of Defence declared that Chernihiv was under siege which would aid the eastward encirclement of Kyiv.[22]

The Russian strategy aimed to capture Kyiv quickly by using speed and deception to keep Ukrainian soldiers away from the capital. The strategy was successful in deceiving the Ukrainian forces, and north of Kyiv, the Russians gained a 12:1 force ratio advantage. However, the same operational security that made the deception possible also left Russian soldiers tactically unprepared to implement the plan effectively. The absence of alternative courses of action was the biggest flaw in the Russian plan. Consequently, as Ukraine mobilised, Russian forces saw their positions steadily deteriorate as speed failed to yield the intended effects.[23]

Despite careful planning by the Russian military to quickly take over Ukraine, they were caught off guard by the fierce resistance put up by the Ukrainian forces. The Russian troops had no idea where their opponents would strike or how to effectively fight back. [24] The ambushes in Hostomel and Bucha not only caused significant losses to the Russian side but also made them realize the challenges they would face as they advanced closer to Kyiv.

The events that followed were of great importance. The Russian Army and VDV, who had surrounded Kyiv, became stationary and waited for additional supplies and for the 40-mile convoy to complete the encirclement of Kyiv. However, the complete encirclement never happened due to the Russian forces' inability to adjust to the changed situation. They had to bunker down on the roadsides and defend themselves against Ukrainian artillery and drone strikes.

The Russian forces faced poor or absent leadership, a shortage of supplies, regular shelling, and significant fatalities, which affected their morale.[25] The situation worsened as they began to experience increasing harassment from drones, commonly used to scan targets for artillery, as well as from Special Operations Forces (SOF). These forces were inflicting significant casualties at night, and Russia was unprepared to face them, due to its inadequate investment in night gear for its soldiers.

## Annexation of Southern and Eastern Ukraine

Russia's aim to regain control of the Black Sea was closely linked to its conflict in southern Ukraine. On February 24, Russia took control of Snake Island, which could have been used as a base for coastal missile operations or as a supply station in the event of an amphibious attack on Odesa.

**Figure 2: Russia's Southern and Eastern Offensive[26]**

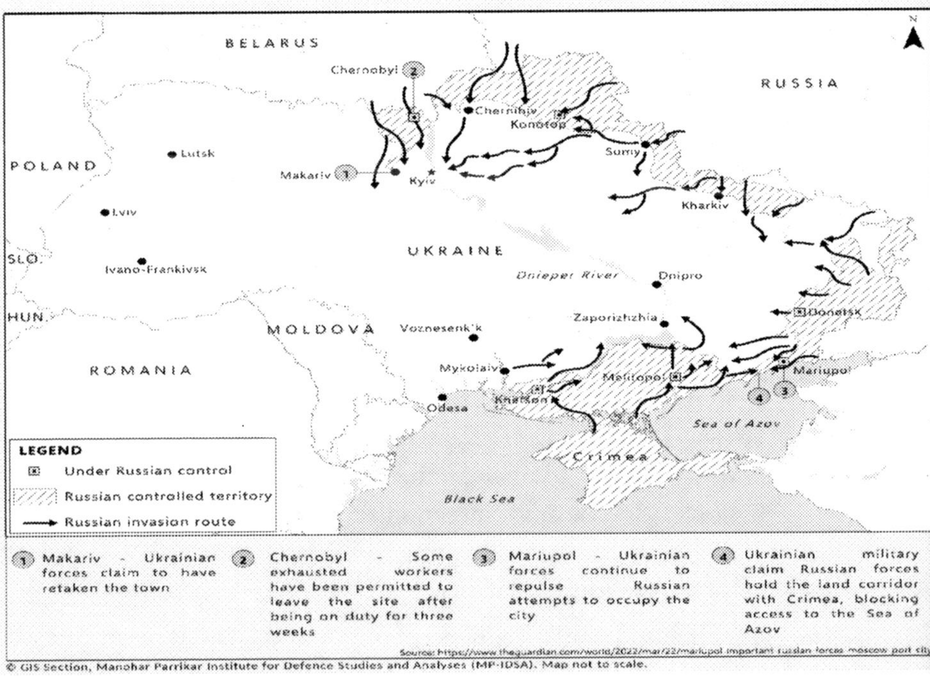


Russia swiftly transferred its invading troops from Crimea to Kherson and Melitopol in Zaporizhzhia Oblast, after successfully conquering Snake Island. Within the first 48 hours of the conflict, Russia gained control of Nova Kakhovka and the Antonovskiy Bridge in Kherson, which crosses the Dnieper River and leads to Mykolaiv. Despite Ukrainian retaliation, Russia besieged Kherson on February 27 and subsequently moved from Kherson International Airport to the Kherson-Mykolaiv highway on March 1. On March 2, Russia declared victory in Kherson.[27]

Russian forces followed the invasion plan and broke out from Crimea to the south. They faced little opposition while crossing into northern Ukraine. With minimal resistance, they captured Melitopol and Kherson and proceeded to encircle Mariupol, putting the city under siege.

According to experts, Ukraine did not put up strong resistance to Russia's numerical advantage in the Kherson region because it feared that sending a large force would have given Russia the chance to annex other areas like Mykolaiv or Odesa.[28] However, Russia's attacks on Odesa and Mykolaiv were not very successful. In March, Russian forces were forced to withdraw to the southern parts of Mykolaiv Oblast after losing the battle of Snihurivka, which was later incorporated into Kherson.

The main objective of Russia's Donbas Offensive was to capture the city of Mariupol and create a land bridge to Crimea. With a population of over 430,000 and two significant metallurgical companies along with the largest port on the Sea of Azov, Mariupol was a crucial target for the Russian invasion. If they managed to gain control of Mariupol, Russia could establish a land bridge to Crimea and take over the entire northern shore of the Sea of Azov.[29]

Russia combined an amphibious landing by the Black Sea Fleet on the Sea of Azov with artillery bombardment as it advanced on Mariupol through the territory of Donetskaya Narodnaya Respublika (DNR). The Assault on the city began on February 24 with an aim to capture Mariupol and cut it off from the nearby Ukrainian Forces. The initial ground attack was resisted by the defenders, but the Russian forces managed to land and carry on with their mission.

Mariupol's fall was virtually assured after the Ukrainian Army lost its crucial defensive position at Volnovakha, north of Mariupol, on February 27, and Berdyansk fell to Russian forces who had broken out of the Crimea on the same day. The Russian forces stepped up their bombardment of Mariupol after failing to drive the city's defenders from their positions.

As of March 2, the Russians had surrounded Mariupol by blocking all of its exits. They were encircling the city from the west, advancing from the areas of Donbas that they controlled, and from the recently taken city of Berdyansk. The

Russian forces intensified their bombardment of Mariupol after failing to push the city's defenders from their concealed positions. However, the city's defences severely damaged the Russian troops that were advancing. By the beginning of April, Russia had taken control of much of the city. After seizing the SBU (Sluzhba bezpeky Ukrainy i.e. Security Service of Ukraine) building and the military headquarters of the Azov Regiment in central Mariupol, the Russian forces focused on demolishing the last stronghold of Ukrainian resistance, which was located in the Azovstal steel complex. A tenacious pocket of resistance in the sprawling steel plant continued till May 17, 2022. [30]

Russian efforts to repair the majority of the Ukrainian Armed Forces in Donbas turned out to be nearly perfect. The Russian forces were unable to reallocate Ukrainian soldiers from this theatre, despite their limited success against the defensive positions along the line of contact. In Luhansk, Russia also conducted military operations, securing control over 93 percent of the oblast, with the exception of Severodonetsk and Lysychansk.

**Figure 3: Russian Invasion, Day 35**

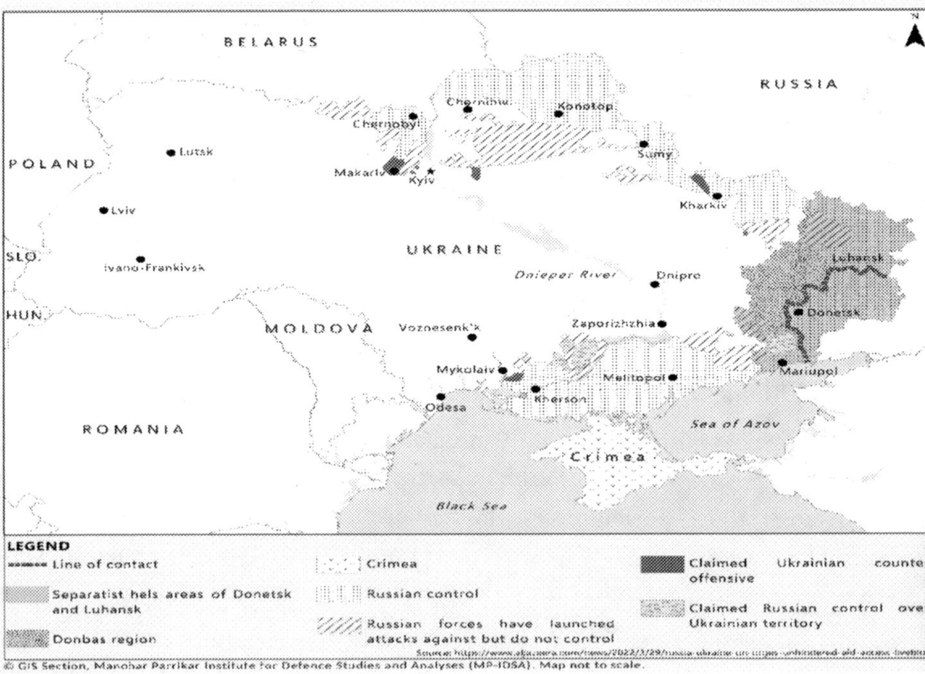


*Source: Al Jazeera.*[31]

The Russian advance towards Kharkiv didn't go according to plan, resulting in heavy casualties for their troops. Russian Special Forces arrived in the city on light vehicles and became separated from their conventional supporting units. When asked to surrender, the troops claimed that the Ukrainian defenders would be outnumbered once the follow-on units arrived. Due to differing levels of preparedness, coordination between the Russian Special Forces and Conventional troops was challenging and the advanced parties were subsequently destroyed. Despite the setback, Russian forces continued holding the area around the city and proceeded with their planned advance, assisted by extensive artillery bombardment.

## PHASE 2: RUSSIA'S REVISED WAR OBJECTIVES AND THE BATTLE FOR DONBAS (APRIL–AUGUST 2022)

By the end of March, the front lines had become more stable. While Russia had made some progress in the east, it was facing resistance on all other fronts. Ukrainian forces had successfully repelled Russian attacks near Kyiv and Kharkiv and also in the southern Ukraine. However, the separatist-controlled Donbas region remained the only area from where the Russian military was advancing eastward.[32]

Russian military forces were forced to temporarily halt their operations due to logistical challenges they faced in various locations throughout the country. The forces were stretched thin because the invasion was spread out along four different axes. These axes included driving from Belarus to Kyiv in the south, driving from farther east into Donbas and Sumy in northeastern Ukraine, and driving northward out of Crimea.[33] Broader signs of stalled operation across multiple axes compelled the Kremlin to pivot Russia's military strategy in Ukraine from a regime change mission to a Donbas-centric campaign.

On March 29, 2022, the Russian Deputy Minister of Defence announced that operations in the areas around Kyiv and Chernihiv would be significantly reduced. This move is aimed at building mutual trust and creating the necessary conditions for further negotiations. According to an earlier statement by Russia's defence ministry, the main objectives of the operation's first stage have been achieved. The attack on Kyiv was intended to deceive Ukrainian forces and divert their attention from the real fight in Donbas. The Russian Ministry of Defence confirmed that the "main tasks of the first stage of the operation" have been completed. Accordingly, Russian forces have begun evacuating from northern Ukraine and are moving towards Belarus.[34] Numerous accounts of mass killings and atrocities against civilians surfaced after Russian forces withdrew.[35]

**Figure 4: Russian Offensive as of March 30, 2022**

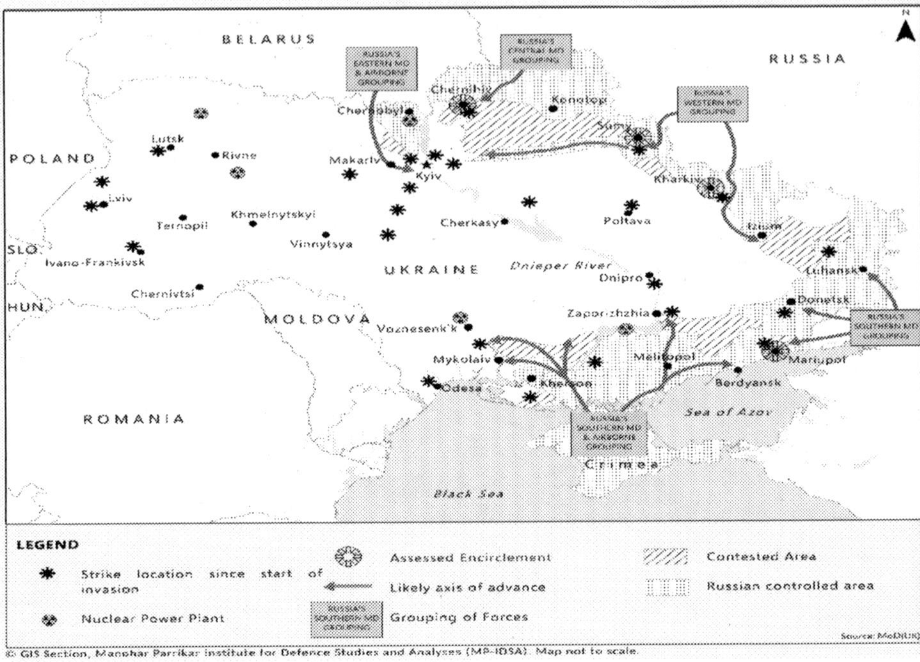


*Source:* MoD (UK).

Russia has continued its offensive operations in eastern Ukraine on a limited scale as it restructured its forces that were withdrawn from northern Ukraine. Russian soldiers carried out small-scale attacks south of Izyum while regrouping for future offensive operations in Kharkiv Oblast. At the same time, Russian forces moved north along a front stretching from the outskirts of Zaporizhzhia on the Dnieper to Mariupol on the coast, while attempting to move south from the north bank of the Donets River near Izyum, a town located 125 km southeast of Kharkiv. The aim of the attack was to trap the Ukrainian forces fighting against Russian proxies in Donbas. It is believed that nearly 40% of the Ukrainian army was stationed in that area. If Russia had succeeded in encircling them, it would have been a devastating setback for Ukraine.

**Figure 5: Battle for Donbas, April 2022**

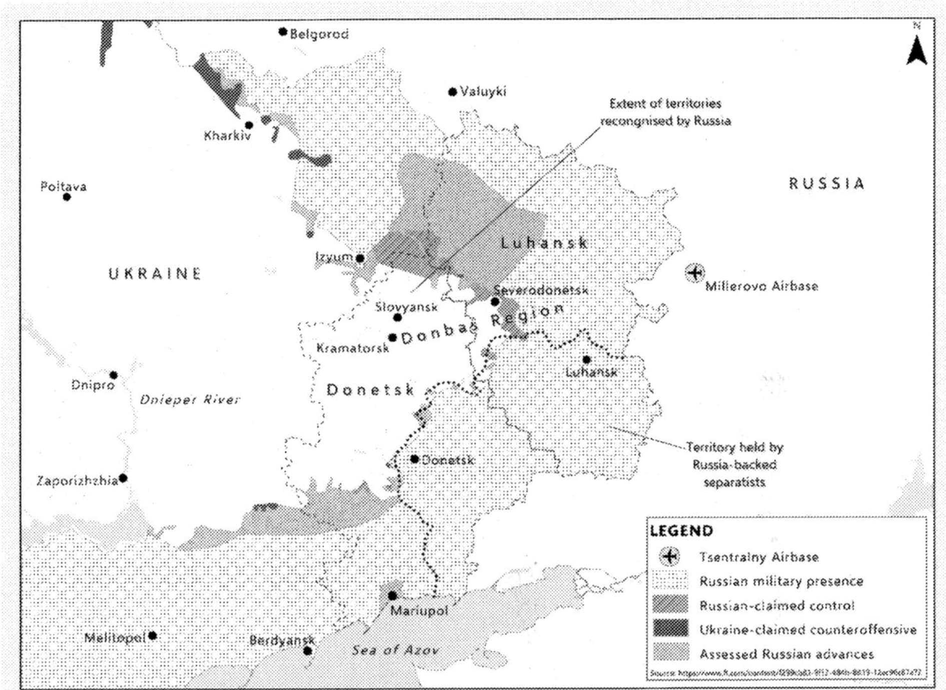


© GIS Section, Manohar Parrikar Institute for Defence Studies and Analyses (MP-IDSA). Map not to scale.

*Source: Financial Times.*[36]

Russian forces launched a large-scale operation in east Ukraine on April 18, 2022, intending to take full control of Luhansk and Donetsk oblasts. The commander of the Central Military District, Rustam Minnekayev, stated that this operation marked the "second phase" of Russia's invasion of Ukraine. The goal of this phase is to completely annex Donbas and southern Ukraine, and to establish a land corridor with Transnistria, an internationally unrecognized breakaway republic that is occupied by Russia, but is considered part of Moldova.[37]

The planned offensive operation in eastern Ukraine was not very successful. There was only minimal progress made near Popasna, Marinka, and Severodonetsk, and limited territorial gains were achieved around Izyum. Russia's main objectives were the cities of Kramatorsk and Slovyansk, which were both located deep inside Ukrainian borders and vital to regaining control of Donbas. Moscow intended to attack them from three different directions: from the west via Severodonetsk (the path that led troops into Kreminna), from the south via Izyum, and from the north via Donetsk.

Despite the use of concentrated artillery, Russian soldiers faced difficulty in penetrating the well-prepared fortifications of Ukrainian forces in eastern Ukraine. The frontline in the heavily contested Donbas region remained intact due to strong opposition from the Ukrainians.

Russian forces had initially planned to fully encircle Ukrainian forces from Donetsk City to Izyum. However, by mid-May on April 18, they had abandoned this plan in favour of completing the takeover of Luhansk Oblast. The Russian forces coordinated their efforts in the eastern Donetsk Oblast to capture Severodonetsk from the north, while in the south, they attempted a shallower encirclement than what was initially planned.[38]

While Russia did not succeed in isolating Ukrainian forces in JFO, it made steady progress in the conduct of its eastern offensive in the Donbas through incremental advances in and around the Severodonetsk–Lysychansk area. On May 6, Russian and Luhansk People's Republic (LPR) forces made gains in the outskirts of Sievierodonetsk, capturing several surrounding villages.[39] After significantly weakening defences through artillery attacks, Russia launched a ground assault on May 27, 2022. Notwithstanding tenacious resistance by Ukrainian forces, Russia finally captured the city on June 15, 2022.[40]

On June 30, 2022, Russian soldiers withdrew from "Snake Island," a small but strategically important Ukrainian islet located in the Black Sea, due to the constant missile strikes and attacks carried out by the Ukrainian army.[41] The persistent artillery and missile assaults by the Ukrainian forces had made it difficult for Russia to maintain control over the island. As a result, Russia's hold over the crucial Black Sea grain transport corridors was weakened, leading to their abrupt retreat. However, the Russian Ministry of Defence presented this as "a gesture of goodwill" to avoid obstructing UN efforts to enable grain exports from Ukraine.[42]

In the first week of July, Russian forces took control of Lysychansk after indiscriminate shelling had already destroyed the city. The fall of Lysychansk, along with nearby Syeverodonetsk, marked the end of the last significant population centres in the Luhansk region returning under Russian control. [43] This offensive marked the furthest point of Russia's push eastward.

On July 04, 2022, Russian President Vladimir Putin announced that his country's soldiers had won a major victory in Ukraine's eastern Luhansk region. Ukrainian troops had retreated from their last stronghold in the city of Lysychansk. Following this, Russian forces quickly shifted their focus to the adjacent province of Donetsk. Though the Kremlin ordered an "operational pause" for the Russian military from July 4 to July 16, offensive operations on Siversk in Donetsk began as soon as Lysychansk fell.[44]

Russia's military operations in Donetsk were less successful when compared to those in Luhansk. The collapse of the attack on Siversk onslaught hindered Russian offensives in other areas of Donetsk. In the latter part of July 2022, Russian forces managed to gain some territory south of Bakhmut, but their attempts to launch a larger offensive against Bakhmut failed. For the following six months, Russian attackers made fruitless attempts at bloody assaults on the Bakhmut stronghold in the Donetsk Oblast of Ukraine. By the end of August 2022, the Russian summer offensive appeared to lose momentum, and the frontline transformed into a slow-moving attritional battle of inches.

## PHASE 3: UKRAINIAN COUNTEROFFENSIVES (SEPTEMBER–NOVEMBER 2022)

Even though Ukrainian forces had thwarted the attempt by Russian forces to occupy their capital Kyiv, Russian forces retreated, concentrated their power in the south and east and continued to pummel Ukrainian forces. Ukraine had survived but one-quarter of its territory was still occupied, and Russian forces continued to pummel Ukrainian forces along with progressive nibbling of Ukrainian territory in the south and east.

By the sixth month of the war, both sides appeared to be stuck in a stalemate. Russia gained complete control of Severodonetsk in early July, but their subsequent advances in the east failed to materialize.[45] The front line remained mostly static, and both sides were engaged in long-range artillery battles. Ukrainian forces were able to use US-supplied HIMAR to target Russian munitions and logistics facilities that were located far from the front line.

The conflict in Ukraine entered its third phase in mid-August. With advanced weaponry, innovative strategies, and sufficient funding from NATO, Ukraine spent months preparing for a counteroffensive in the south.

Long-range weapons supplied by the US and Europe helped stabilise the front line, preventing further advances by Russian forces and allowing Ukraine to plan an offensive to retake significant territory. Ukrainian authorities hinted at an imminent offensive in June to reclaim their southern region, particularly Kherson.[46] On August 29, 2023, Natalia Humeniuk, a spokesperson for Ukraine's Southern Military Command, announced that Ukraine had commenced "offensive actions on multiple fronts".[47]

Ukraine's counteroffensive achieved immediate successes in the Kherson direction, as the villages of Novodmytrivka, Arkhangelsk, Tomyna Balka and Pravdyne were swiftly recaptured. Oleksii Arestovych, an advisor to Ukraine's presidential office, confirmed that the Ukrainian Armed Forces had 'broken through the frontlines in several sectors' and were shelling ferry crossing points that Russia used for resupply purposes in Kherson. Russian troops reportedly retreated closer to the Dnipro River and were crossing its left bank.[48] Russian troops reportedly retreated closer to the Dnipro River and were crossing its left bank. Notwithstanding these early successes, the Ukrainian military remained rather circumspect and prepared for 'positional warfare' or an 'imitation' counteroffensive as Russia had an overwhelming advantage in missile capabilities and the efficacy of HIMARS in a full-scale counteroffensive was unclear.[49]

On September 7, Valery Zaluzhny, Ukraine's Military Commander publicly revealed the scope and objectives of the counteroffensive.[50] He argued that the most significant Russian military threat to Ukraine emanated from the south, as Russia could use advances along this axis to threaten Odesa, Mykolaiv, Kryvyi Rih and eventually central and western Ukraine. Zaluzhny highlighted Russia's control over Crimea, which allowed for nationwide strikes and strength along the Zaporizhzhia axis via the Gulyai Pole as significant threats. To counter these Russian threats, Zaluzhny proposed assembling 10–20 combined military brigades and neutralising Russia's 2,000 km missile strike range by securing equipment such as MGM-140B ATACMS Block 1A surface-to-surface missiles. These NATO-style arms deliveries would be paired with indigenous Ukrainian weapons development, including the domestic production of long-range missiles. By collapsing the gravitational centre of Russia's military operations and carrying out Saky airbase-style strikes that inflicted pain on Russia, Zaluzhny hoped to achieve decisive breakthroughs in 2023 and prevent Russian long-range missile strikes from creating a years-long war.

Immediately after the announcement of the counteroffensive by Kyiv, the Russian Ministry of Defence claimed that Ukraine had launched unsuccessful offensives in Mykolaiv and Kherson, which had cost it 560 personnel, 26 tanks and two Su-25 jets.[51] In Russia's assessment, Ukraine lacked the material capacity for an effective counterattack. Russian defence analysts believed that Ukraine's counteroffensive was a symbolic display of Kyiv's ability to strike Russian territory, which built on its attacks on Crimea, shelling of Donetsk and Darya Dugina's murder on the outskirts of Moscow was unlikely to result in major territorial change.[52]

Ukraine's battlefield progress in Kherson was slow but steady. Ukrainian forces broadened the frontlines in Kherson to over 100 miles in width as they tried to prevent Russian troops from concentrating, and escalated sabotage attacks on pro-Russian collaborators. The ultimate aim of Ukraine's southern offensive was to seize control over territories in the north and west of the Dnipro River and liberate the city of Kherson. Ukraine also wanted to secure control of the Nova Kakhovka hydroelectric plant and the North Crimean Canal, which Russia had occupied on the first day of the war, as Russia had destroyed a dam on the canal to divert Dnipro River water to Crimea. Beyond its sporadic capture of villages, Ukraine made noteworthy progress towards enhancing its battlefield position in Kherson. Ukraine managed to establish three lines of attack on Kherson by September 3. The Kherson attack was intended to capture Russian-occupied territory to the west of the Dnieper River. It aimed to bring Kherson city and three strategically important river crossings within its artillery range.

**Figure 6: Objectives of the Kherson Offensive**

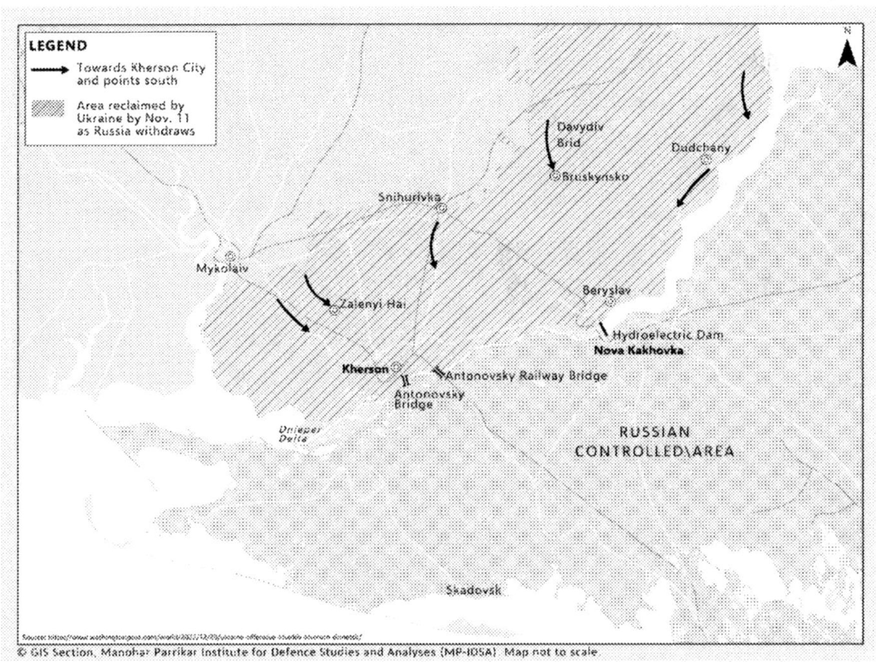


*Source: Washington Post.*[53]

Despite its apparent commitment to a southern-centric counteroffensive, Ukraine stealthily prepared for a blitzkrieg liberation of Kharkiv.[54] Subsequent information has revealed that collaboration with the US and wargaming played an instrumental role in shaping Ukraine's counteroffensive strategy. The Pentagon advised Kyiv to restrict the operation's objectives and geographical scope, in order to avoid over-committing and getting bogged down on multiple fronts.[55] Ukrainians chose to disregard this advice and choose to mount a blithering offensive in the Kharkiv region.

Russia had decided to move some of its well-equipped forces to the south due to Kharkiv's preparations for a southern attack. As a result, the front in Kharkiv was not heavily manned. However, Ukraine was able to deceive Russia into thinking that the operation in Kherson was the only thing that it was focused on, even though it involved more troops than the one in Kharkiv.[56]

At the tactical level, the Ukrainian military employed a clever deception strategy to aid their northeastern thrust.[57] They initiated a ruse at Balakliya, which involved only about 15 tanks, to mislead the Russian forces into believing that it was merely a feint to pin them down and prevent their redeployment to defend against the supposed main counter-offensive in the Kherson region. To conceal their preparations, the Ukrainians deliberately reduced the amount of heavy weaponry in the attack force. For instance, they thinned out some weapons, such as HIMARS rocket launchers, from the attack force in Kharkiv, and relied on a relatively small number of tanks to break through in the first wave. This cunning tactic allowed them to achieve their objectives without alerting the enemy to their true intentions.[58] The Russian front collapsed quickly, which allowed the onslaught to expand in a "domino" manner.

Starting on September 5th, the Ukrainian military launched a counteroffensive in the northeastern Kharkiv region, during which they managed to liberate almost the entire province in just a few days.[59] By September 8th, which was only three days after the start of the offensive, Ukrainian troops had already arrived on the outskirts of Izyum, following a lightning-fast attack that overran Russia's northeastern flank. In less than a day, the Ukrainian army had managed to surround the town of Balakliya, which was on the frontline of the battle. Two days later, Ukrainian forces took control of Kupyansk, a vital rail hub that was previously connected to Moscow. On September 10th, at first light, Ukrainian forces broke into the heart of Izyum itself. By September 13th, the Ukrainian army had retaken 3,800 square kilometres of the Kharkiv region through their rapid counteroffensive.[60]

The Russian military, being understaffed and under-equipped, couldn't hold onto a vast territory as indicated by the Kharkiv assault. This unexpected attack caught the Kremlin by surprise and proved to Ukraine's supporters that the billions of dollars invested in military hardware and financial aid were worth their value.[61]

**Figure 7: The Kharkiv Offensive**

*Source: Washington Post.*[62]

Russia's defeat in Kharkiv coincided with military setbacks elsewhere on the frontlines. Russian shelling of Kupiansk, which persisted in the days following the Kharkiv defeat, did not stem the momentum of Ukraine's northeastern counteroffensive. Russia attempted to slow Ukraine's advance by blowing up a dam on the Inhulets River, which flooded parts of the Kherson frontline. On September 19, Ukraine captured Bilohorivka, a suburb of Lysychansk, which ensured that Russia no longer had complete control of Luhansk.[63]

On September 24, it was reported that military commanders from Russia had requested to move to more secure positions due to the worsening situation at the Kherson frontline. However, President Putin intervened and prohibited any retreat that could result in the surrender of Kherson city.[64]

In October 2022, the Ukrainian forces continued their offensive along the eastern and southern fronts. The Ukrainian forces made incremental progress as they advanced into Luhansk Oblast after taking over Lyman.[65] However, the Ukrainian breakthrough in the southern sector around Kherson was more difficult compared to the quick advances in the northeast near Kharkiv. As Ukraine advanced in both the east and the south, Russia's two fronts were under pressure. To improve coordination among the forces stationed in the war zone, Russia appointed General Sergei Surovikin as their first overall commander for the conflict in Ukraine in order to improve coordination fighting on two fronts simultaneously.[66]

In October 2022, Ukrainian forces successfully removed Russian soldiers from the Charivne and Chkalov settlements in the southern Kherson sector. However, the challenging terrain and wet weather made the counteroffensive against Russian soldiers in this region more difficult than in the northeast. Despite these challenges, Russia's control over the city of Kherson appeared to be increasingly threatened. In a television broadcast, General Sergei Surovikin acknowledged that the situation in Kherson was "not easy."

On the 9th of November 2022, General Surovikin informed Russia's Defense Minister Sergei Shoigu through a televised briefing that it would be most sensible to establish a new defensive line on the eastern bank of the Dnieper River due to current circumstances. The General also stated that Russia's position in Kherson had become untenable. On the 11th of November, the Russian evacuation from the east bank of Dnipro was completed before dawn. The withdrawal from Kherson was well planned, in contrast to the disorganized retreat from Kharkiv. The Russian forces were able to successfully remove their weapons and supplies during this well-executed withdrawal.[67]

Ukrainian forces arrived in Kherson on November 11th after Russian forces withdrew from their eight-month-long occupation of the southeast city. President Zelensky of Ukraine visited the city of Kherson on November 14th to celebrate its liberation.[68]

## PHASE 4: RUSSIAN WINTER–SPRING CAMPAIGN (NOVEMBER 2022–MAY 2023)

By early November 2022 indications had begun to emerge that Russia may intensify its offensive operation in Donetsk province with the availability of additional mobilised servicemen along with forces withdrawn from western Kherson.[69]

Between November 11 and December 10, Russian forces launched an attack on southern and northern Donetsk Oblast in Ukraine. Their goal was to breach Ukraine's defences in Bakhmut, Soledar, Pavlivka, and Vuhledar. During this time, there were intense battles along the Bakhmut-Soledar axis, which included trench fighting, drone warfare, artillery duels, and small-scale ground assaults. These battles were fought in extremely cold weather. Both the Russian and Ukrainian forces brought reinforcements to the Bakhmut-Soledar axis from other fronts.[70]

The Bakhmut front was a site of intense fighting during the freezing winter weather. The combat was marked by trench warfare, artillery duels, and small-scale Russian probing attacks. The Wagner Group Private Military Company (PMC) forces, along with Russian regular troops, aimed to breach the defence lines on the city's eastern and southern flanks. The ground assaults into the city and its suburbs, which Ukraine had transformed into strongholds, were led by PMC Wagner fighters.[71] In December 2022, the Russian military attempted to encircle Bakhmut from multiple directions in a pincer movement in order to gain control over most of the supply routes leading to the city.

Due to the lack of significant advancements in the front lines and the high number of casualties suffered by both Russian and Ukrainian forces every day, the conflict in Bakhmut was commonly referred to as a "meat grinder." [72] In an attempt to encircle Bakhmut, Russian forces intensified their efforts during the winter. On December 27, Wagner took control of Ukrainian defence lines in the salt-mining town of Soledar, and by January 16, 2023, Soledar had fallen to the Russian forces, causing a weakening of Bakhmut's defensive flanks to the northeast.[73]

The news about a major restructuring of the military command in Russia came while the ongoing battle in the eastern town of Soledar continued to rage on. Moscow has appointed General Valery Gerasimov, the current Chief of Staff, as the supreme commander of the conflict in Ukraine. General Gerasimov, who has been in his role for almost a decade, played a key role in the initial planning of the conflict in Ukraine. His appointment is widely interpreted as a signal of an impending Russian offensive aimed at seizing territory quickly in the upcoming spring offensive.[74]

**Figure 8: The Russian Spring Offensive**

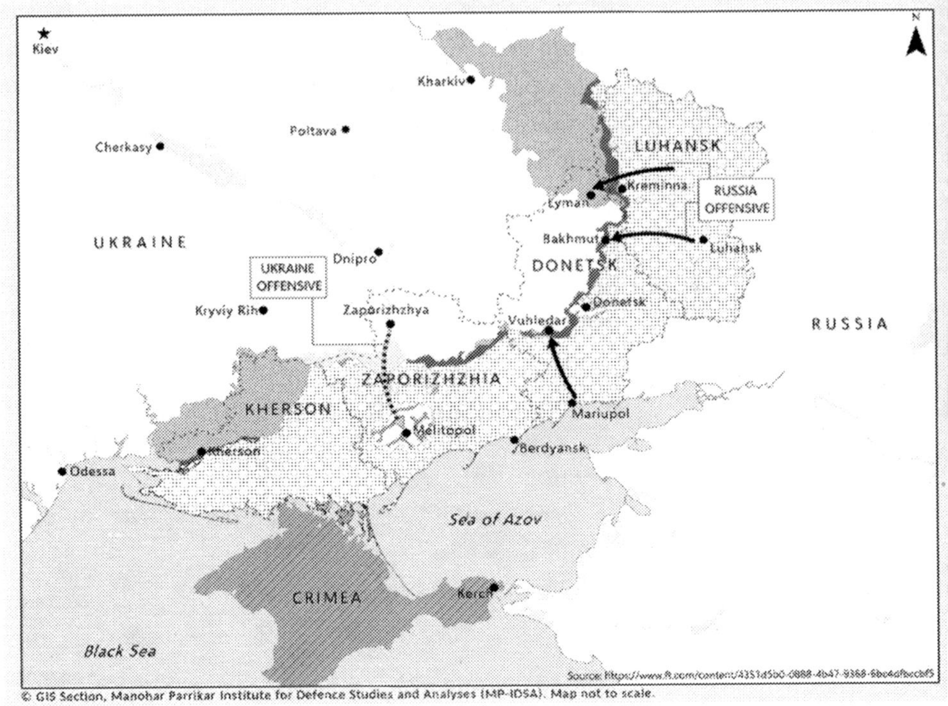


*Source: Financial Time.*[75]

On January 24, 2023, a huge attack on the city of Vuhledar marked the start of the Russian spring offensive. The 40th and 155th Naval Infantry units, two of Russia's most accomplished units, were part of this unsuccessful onslaught. At least 130 armoured vehicles, including 36 tanks, were lost, greatly damaging both brigades. The Russian army underestimated the strength of the Ukrainian army and the challenging terrain, which was filled with landmines.[76]

Although the Ukrainian forces were able to temporarily halt the Russian offensive, they suffered significant losses. Following the capture of Soledar, the Russian forces, led by Wagner fighters, were able to surround Bakhmut from the northeast and gain control of a section of the roadway that leads to Siversk.

In early February, Russia started deploying a large number of troops to the Bakhmut combat zone in anticipation of a critical point in the conflict. On February 11th, 2023, the defences along the northern flank of Bakhmut were breached, resulting in the withdrawal of Ukrainian forces. In addition, Russian troops carried out reconnaissance operations in the north near Kreminna and in the south near Vuhledar.[77]

Russian forces crossed the M-03 and launched attacks on Berkhivka and Yahidne, which are located northwest of Bakhmut, by February 22. The Ukrainian military reported that they were able to repel the attacks following intense combat. However, on February 26, Wagner announced that both settlements had been seized, while the Ukrainian military staff stated that the Russian attacks were still "unsuccessful".[78]

On March 7, Ukraine retreated west of the Bakhmutka River, which resulted in eastern Bakhmut being ceded to Russian forces. By March 16, Wagner claimed to have made progress along the M-03 highway, and extended the buffer zone north and west of Bakhmut while taking control of the villages of Zaliznianske and Dubovo-Vasylivka. However, Ukrainian defences stopped the advance along this axis by March 19, and successfully fended off attacks on the settlements of Orikhovo-Vasylivka, Bohdanivka, and Khromove.[79]

Conflicts in the Avdiivka area escalated in February and March of 2023 during the Bakhmut battle, as Russian forces attempted to encircle the city.[80] With ground troops moving into the outskirts of Avdiivka from the north and northeast, Russian forces increased their airstrikes in the region. By March 21, they had captured Vesele, located 7 km north of Avdiivka, and Krasnohorivka, located around 9 km north of Avdiivka. The fierce battle for Marinka continued further to the south, but despite intense urban warfare with Ukrainian troops, Russian ground forces made very little progress on the ground.[81]

As of March 2023, the Russian assault had considerably slowed down while intense fighting continued. The fierce battle inside Bakhmut continued until April and May of the same year. By May 18, the Russian forces had seized control of 95% of the city, after pushing the Ukrainian defenders into a neighborhood in the southwest that was known as the "nest." It was reported that Ukraine had concentrated a significant number of defending units in that area.[82] From May 10 onwards, Ukraine launched counterattacks on Bakhmut's southern and northwest flanks, while Wagner fighters gradually advanced inside the city.[83]

On May 20, Wagner fighters entered Bakhmut and announced that they had taken control of the city, despite facing counterattacks from Ukrainian forces. They also stated their intention to withdraw from the front line once the clearing operations were completed and be replaced by regular Russian soldiers. However, Ukraine disputed the claim that Bakhmut had fallen, stating that their forces were in the process of encircling the city. On May 21, 2023, Wagner forces were successful in pushing the Ukrainian soldiers outside of Bakhmut.[84]

For both sides, Bakhmut seemed like an odd place to make a stand as the location had limited strategic importance. Nevertheless, the town became highly symbolic as a representation of Ukrainian tenacious resistance and Russian commanders' doggedly determination to achieve a rather costly victory in a relatively unknown area of eastern Ukraine.[85]

Beginning November 2022, Russia began fortifying strong and defendable positions along the entire frontline by using natural obstacles such as rivers. They were simultaneously waging a beleaguered offensive in the east. These defensive fortifications consisted of deep trenches called tank traps and miles-long rows of concrete pyramids known as dragon's teeth. The purpose of these fortifications was to slow down the Ukrainian advance and push them into predetermined areas where Russian forces could target them. Additionally, Russia constructed kilometres of pillboxes and trenches to fend off invading columns. Large-scale minefields were also set up in the gaps between the defensive lines.[86]

**Figure 9: Russian Fortification in Ukraine**

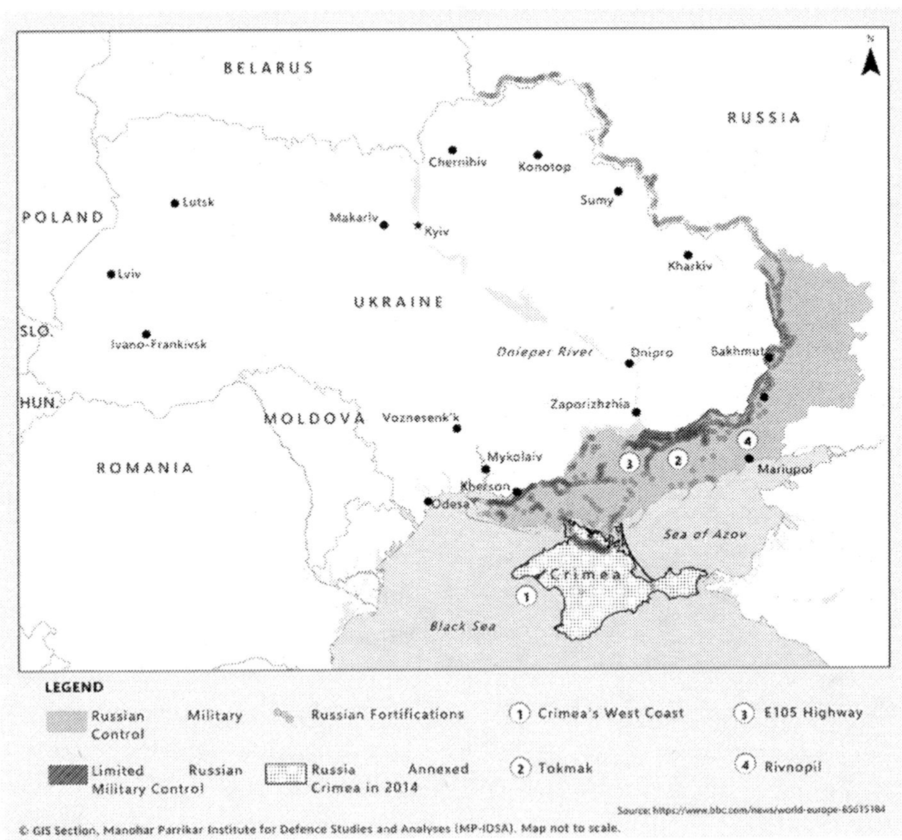


*Source: BBC.*[87]

Over time, fortifications started to emerge across the entire frontline as well as within the occupied territories. These fortifications included approaches to Melitopol in the Zaporizhzhia region, close to the airbase near Berdyansk on the coast of the Sea of Azov which is a significant shipping hub, and also in Crimea both on the western coast of the peninsula and on the Perekop isthmus.

The northern region of Zaporizhzhia witnessed the construction of some of the largest fortifications in preparation for a possible attack by the Ukrainian Armed Forces to disrupt the "land bridge" from Crimea. Additionally, the towns of Tokmak, Pologi, Ocheretovatoye, and Bilmak, situated northeast of Melitopol, were surrounded by protective fortifications on all sides.[88]

Large fortifications also appeared all along the boundary of the formerly Russian-controlled Luhansk region, especially in front of earlier captured cities of Sievierodonetsk, Lysychansk, and Popasna. These defensive preparations played significant role in the next phase of the war.

## PHASE 5: UKRAINE'S COUNTEROFFENSIVE (JUNE–NOVEMBER 2023)

On June 4, 2023, the Ukrainian forces carried out a "large-scale" attack on five fronts in the southeast of the Donetsk region in eastern Ukraine. This attack was backed by hundreds of armored vehicles, howitzers, and tanks provided by the West and was planned and prepared for many months. In a swift move, The Ukrainian forces successfully captured Novodonetske on June 4 and 5, a town located southwest of Russia-held Donetsk city, and continued their advance towards Velyka Novosilka. This marked the beginning of a new phase of the combat.[89] Ukraine also significantly increased its missile and rocket attacks on Russian locations behind the battle lines in the southern areas. The attacks have been focused on the central province of Zaporizhia, specifically the towns of Mykhailivka, Melitopol, and Tokmak. These towns provide a second possible route to the Sea of Azov.

On June 7, it was reported that four columns of Ukrainian forces, comprising up to 120 armored vehicles and 12 tanks, were moving from Orikhiv to Tokmak. Tokmak is a town situated on the "land bridge" that connects Crimea with theseized territory. This offensive thrust in Zaporizhia marked the start of Ukraine's long-awaited counteroffensive along the 1,000 km frontline.[90]

Ukraine aimed to launch an offensive attack in the spring of 2023 and began planning for it in February of the same year. However, due to weather-related delays, troop training, and weapon delivery delays, the offensive had to be postponed until the summer.[91] Furthermore, the Pentagon document leaks, which revealed some secret US intelligence information regarding the planned Ukrainian counteroffensive, also contributed to the delay. As a result, Ukraine had to modify some of its operational plans and timelines.[92]

In contrast to Ukraine, Russia began preparing its defenses in November 2022. They built a massive defensive system that included landmines, ditches, artillery positions, and trenches to slow down any counteroffensive. These fortifications are considered the most extensive defensive works in Europe since World War II. By April 2023, Russia had constructed an 800-kilometer defensive line in anticipation of a potential Ukrainian attack. The last lines of defense built by Russia covered a distance of approximately 2,000 kilometers, stretching from the Belarusian border to the Dnieper Delta. Enormous minefields were established by Russia using anti-tank mines along the whole frontline, covering an estimated area of 170,000 square kilometers in Ukraine, including mines placed by Ukraine in the Donbas region the year before.[93]

There were high expectations for Ukraine's summer offensive due to their successful earlier counteroffensive, expected lack of resistance from Russian forces, and the delivery of new advanced Western weapons. Additionally, a new crop of Western-trained Ukrainian recruits added to the anticipation. However, some analysts expressed skepticism, pointing out that the Russian fortifications along the vast frontline were heavily mined and formidable, making the upcoming counteroffensive a potential slog.[94]

In May 2023, the Ukrainian military started targeting Russian forces with rocket and missile attacks on command posts, barracks, depots, and transport nodes located far behind the front lines. Throughout May, the Ukrainian forces carried out "localized" counterattacks on the flanks of Bakhmut, as part of the larger battle in the city. By early June 2023, the Ukrainian forces claimed to have made considerable advances of several hundred meters in various regions around Bakhmut's flanks. Additionally, Ukraine utilized diversionary tactics, such as cross-border attacks into Belgorod led by pro-Ukrainian militias.[95] Starting from June 03, the Ukrainian 37th Marine Brigade engaged in a slow but consistent offensive action on the Zaporizhzhia front around the frontline settlement of Novodonetske in Donetsk Oblast. On June 03, 2023, President Zelenskyy announced Ukraine's readiness to launch a counteroffensive.[96]

On June 4th and 5th, Ukrainian forces made progress in their offensive campaign. They advanced towards Velyka Novosilka and Novodonetske, which were previously under Russian control. Additionally, they started to probe the entire front spanning over 1,000 km from Kherson in the south to Luhansk in the northeast.[97]

On June 6th, a significant event occurred on the southern side of the Russian left flank when the Kakhovka Dam collapsed, causing extensive flooding in the province of Kherson. It remains unclear who destroyed the dam and the power plant on the Dnipro River, which was under Russian control at the time. The dam's collapse severely impeded the planned counteroffensive by Ukrainian forces in the Dnieper region.

The Ukrainian counteroffensive broadly progressed along three axes:[98]

- In northern Donetsk, it attempted to outflank the Russian troops and Wagner mercenaries hunkered down around Bakhmut. An easterly arc progressed in the area around the bloodily contested town of Bakhmut and in Luhansk province. Another aimed south and southeast from Velyka Novosilka and Vuhledar in Donetsk province.
- On the southern front, where the Donetsk region meets Zaporizhzhia, the Ukrainians gradually advanced south from the town of Velyka Novosilka.
- The third phase of the counteroffensive in the western Zaporizhzhia region, situated on the left bank of the Dnipro river, aimed to break through the southern part of the Orikhiv settlement. The objective was to advance towards the strategically important Russian-occupied city of Melitopol and eventually reach the Sea of Azov.

Despite high expectations, the counteroffensive launched by Ukraine proved to be a difficult and grueling battle. The Russian fortifications along the vast frontline were heavily mined, resulting in significant damage and destruction of Ukrainian weaponry – up to 20 per cent in the first two weeks of the counteroffensive. Though this rate of loss reduced to 10 per cent in the following weeks, the counteroffensive itself slowed down and even halted in some places due to the strong defensive resistance of the Russian troops.

Despite suffering significant equipment losses and high casualties, the Ukrainian forces were only able to recapture a mere five miles out of the planned 60 miles advance to reach the sea in the south and split the Russian forces into two. Although some tactical gains were made, especially in the Western Zaporizhzhia region, the overall Russian defensive line remained mostly intact.

**Figure 10: Main Axes of Ukraine's Counteroffensive**

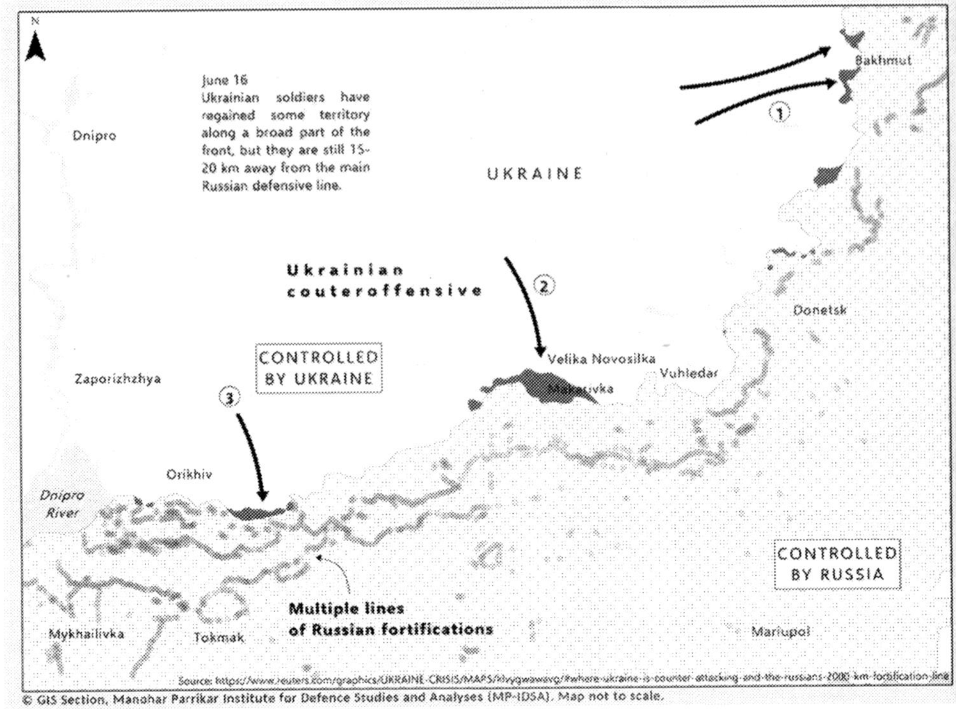


*Source: Reuters.*[99]

Due to the mounting loss of tanks in dense and overlapping minefields, the Ukrainians adapted their tactics by switching to platoon-sized infantry units, often conducting operations at night. This changed approach made further progress grueling and slow.[100]

Russian defensive line showed remarkable resilience in the face of relentless Ukrainian attacks on multiple axes across the embattled frontier. Entrenched Russian troops on the frontline held back the Ukrainian counteroffensive even when an unsuccessful putsch by the Wagner Group created serious internal turmoil in Russia in June 2023.[101]

By the end of August, it was becoming apparent that the pace of counteroffensive had virtually stalled even though Ukraine claimed 'partial success' in its counteroffensive through some 'tactically significant' advances in its southern axis of counteroffensive. While the capture of Robotyne, a small village along the main axis of attack, was not a grand prize itself, it indicated that Ukrainian troops might have at last reached the so-called Surovikin line, the first layer of minefields, tank traps, trenches and bunkers installed by the Russians. With Robotyne firmly in Ukraine's hands, Kyiv's forces began to shift east to their next objective and Russia's main line of defence around the village of Verbove. However, Russian troops soon readjusted their defences and halted further Ukrainian progress.[102]

Russian soldiers successfully employed an innovative concept known as the "elastic defence tactics" to counter the Ukrainian attack. This tactic involves a shallow retreat followed by a decisive counterattack. When Ukrainian forces advanced, the Russian soldiers would retreat to a second line of defense, luring the enemy into a vulnerable position, and then launch a counterattack. By doing so, they prevented the Ukrainian forces from taking control of a strategic position and using it to launch further attacks.[103]

On September 13, Ukraine carried out a drone and missile attack on the Sevmorzavod dry dock in Sevastopol, Crimea. The attack targeted one of the six kilo-class submarines that had the capability to launch cruise missiles close to the Ukrainian coast, as well as an amphibious landing ship. The Russian S-400 air defense system was also destroyed by Ukrainian drones and cruise missiles on the following day. Another group of cruise missiles hit a pier in Sevastopol on September 23, one day after the headquarters was attacked. Russia retaliated by launching several waves of drone strikes throughout Ukrainian territory during the night.[104]

During October 2023, Russian forces began to exhibit limited offensive posture. In one of its biggest pushes since spring. Russia launched a sustained offensive centred on Avdiivka, a heavily fortified Ukrainian-held area close to the Russian-held capital of Donetsk province.[105] The goal of the Russian assault was to encircle the Ukrainian defenders creating a "cauldron" and turn the war's narrative around Russia regaining the initiative.

Russia had committed elements of up to eight brigades with close air support to the Avdiivaka sector in the offensive.[106] However, just as the Ukrainians throughout the summer had found breaking down well-prepared defences extremely tough, Russians also suffered significant losses in their assault. During an estimated gain of less than two square miles of territory, Russia is estimated to have lost about 50 tanks and 100-odd armoured vehicles. Sitting in an indent—surrounded on almost three sides by Russian forces—Avdiivka remains a symbol of a grinding war in which neither side has made a decisive breakthrough in more than a year.[107]

In early November, a handful of Ukrainian troops reached the occupied side of the Dnipro River and established a foothold in Russian-controlled territory in the Kherson region.[108] The number of Ukrainian troops engaging in the operation was estimated to be in the dozens to several hundred, and they were reportedly fighting Russian forces fiercely on the other side of the river. While the Russians have acknowledged the presence of a small number of Ukrainian soldiers, these troops did not make much headway beyond a small beachhead.[109]

Ukrainian counteroffensive has thus far remained far short of declared objectives and has made only modest progress on the flanks of Bakhmut and in the south in the Zaporizhia province. After five months into their counteroffensive, Ukrainian forces has only been able to make progress of just 17 kilometres.[110] A combination of weary units, limited ammunition and wet weather is likely to considerably slow offensives during the winter while some small-unit infantry attacks may continue.

In an essay and interview with The Economist, Ukraine's top general Valery Zaluzhny acknowledges that Ukraine is at a stalemate with Russia and that a deep and beautiful breakthrough is unlikely to happen.[111] General Valery Zaluzhny's first comprehensive assessment of the campaign highlighted that the battlefront in Ukraine reminded him of the great conflict of a century ago. In his view, 'Just like in the First World War, we have reached the level of technology that puts us into a stalemate', The general assesses that unless there is a significant technological advancement to end the impasse, 'there will most likely be no deep and beautiful breakthrough'.

On the contrary, the President of Ukraine, Volodymyr Zelenskiy, has reiterated his position that now is not the right time to negotiate with Russia. He also denied that any Western leaders were pressuring him to change his stance. Additionally, Zelenskiy rejected the assessment of his commander-in-chief regarding the state of stalemate in the ongoing war. [112] The divergence of views on the state of war at the strategic level in Kyiv is being interpreted as a serious divergence of views between the civilian and military wings of Ukraine's leadership.

## FUTURE TRAJECTORY: WAR WITHOUT AN END?

Unarguably, the Ukraine war has defied every expectation. War in Ukraine as it unfolded was very different was envisaged by belligerents as well as the strategic community. Prior to February 2022, there was a widespread belief that Russia would be able to easily defeat Ukraine's air defenses and carry out a swift ground campaign that would result in the capture of Kyiv. Some experts even suggested that it may not be worth arming Kyiv for a conventional interstate war, given Ukraine's perceived inability to resist such an attack. [113] However, Ukraine not only halted the Russian onslaught but showing tenacious determination and perseverance recovered more than half the territory captured by Russian forces during the last 18 months or so.

On the other hand, while Russia has certainly not been able to achieve its early objectives, it continues to marshal resources for a protracted war. The Russian economy has, thus far, shown remarkable resilience in withstanding the impact of sanctions imposed by the West. Russians' support for the ongoing conflict in Ukraine has not collapsed notwithstanding limited protest against mobilisation and the short-lived Wagner rebellion.

Ebbs and the flow of nearly two years of war in Ukraine epitomises classic Clausewitzian truism about war being a 'complex of interactions, multi-layered and often unpredictable'.[114] It is increasingly evident that both sides are now dug in for a protracted conflict, which could potentially be a multi-year war.

The two countries seem to have drawn divergent inferences from the extant evidence of stalemate. Ukraine remains optimistic about Western support and expects that such support will continue to increase Russia holds the belief that the United States and its allies will eventually withdraw their support for Ukraine, especially as the costs of the war increase. Both sides are confident about their relative power and ability to win, which makes it difficult to end the war. This mutual optimism has historically prolonged wars and made it challenging to reach peace agreements.[115]

## NOTES

1 James Risen Klippenstein Ken, 'The CIA Thought Putin Would Quickly Conquer Ukraine. Why Did They Get It So Wrong?,' *The Intercept*, October 5, 2022, at https://theintercept.com/2022/10/05/russia-ukraine-putin-cia/,(Accessed November 12, 2023).

2 Phillips O'Brien, 'The War That Defied Expectations,' *Foreign Affairs*, July 27, 2023, at https://www.foreignaffairs.com/ukraine/war-defied-expectations. (Accessed August 4, 2023).

3 'Ukraine Faces a Long War. A Change of Course Is Needed,' *The Economist*, September 21, 2023, at https://www.economist.com/leaders/2023/09/21/ukraine-faces-a-long-war-a-change-of-course-is-needed (Accessed November 23, 2023).

4 Adam Taylor, *'Russia's Attack on Ukraine Came after Months of Denials It Would Attack,' The Washington Post*, February 24, 2022, at https://www.washingtonpost.com/world/2022/02/24/ukraine-russia-denials/ (Accessed November 23, 2023).

5 Julian E. Barnes, Michael Crowley and Eric Schmitt, 'Russia Positioning Helicopters, in Possible Sign of Ukraine Plans,' *The New York Times* sec. U.S., January 10, 2022, at https://www.nytimes.com/2022/01/10/us/politics/russia-ukraine-helicopters.html. (Accessed January 12, 2022).

6 Shane Harris, Karen DeYoung, Isabelle Khurshudyan, Ashley Parker and Liz Sly, 'Road to War: U.S. Struggled to Convince Allies, and Zelensky, of Risk of Invasion,' *The Washington Post*, August 16, 2023, at https://www.washingtonpost.com/national-security/interactive/2022/ukraine-road-to-war/ (Accessed November 23, 2023).

7 Mykhaylo Zabrodskyi, Jack Watling, Oleksandr V Danylyuk and Nick Reynolds, 'Preliminary Lessons in Conventional Warfighting from Russia's Invasion of Ukraine: February–July 2022,' Royal United Services Institute for Defence and Security Studies, at https://static.rusi.org/359-SR-Ukraine-Preliminary-Lessons-Feb-July-2022-web-final.pdf. (Accessed July 6, 2023)

8 Ibid.

9 Greg Miller and Catherine Belton, "Russia's Spies Misread Ukraine and Misled Kremlin as War Loomed," Washington Post, Aug 19, 2022, https://www.washingtonpost.com/world/interactive/2022/russia-fsb-intelligence-ukraine-war/ (Accessed January 11, 2023)

10 Zabrodskyi, no. 7.

11 Eleanor Sly, 'How Did Russia's Invasion of Ukraine Unfold?,' *The Independent*, February 24, 2022, at https://www.independent.co.uk/news/world/europe/timeline-russia-invasion-ukraine-b2022544.html (Accessed April 10, 2022).

12 'Briefing by Foreign Ministry Spokeswoman Maria Zakharova, Moscow, July 20, 2023,' The Ministry of Foreign Affairs of the Russian Federation, July 20, 2023, at https://mid.ru/en/foreign_policy/news/1897910/ (Accessed November 17, 2023).

13 Tim Lister, Tara John, and Paul P. Murphy, "Here's What We Know about How Russia's Invasion of Ukraine Unfolded," News, CNN, February 24, 2022, https://edition.cnn.com/2022/02/24/europe/ukraine-russia-attack-timeline-intl/index.html. (Accessed November 17, 2023).

14 Michael D. Shear, 'Russia-Ukraine Tensions: Citing U.S. Intelligence, Biden Says Putin Has Decided to Invade Ukraine,' *The New York Times* sec. World, February 18, 2022, at https://www.nytimes.com/live/2022/02/18/world/russia-ukraine-biden-putin (Accessed March 8, 2022)

15 'How Did Russia's Invasion of Ukraine Unfold?,' no. 11.

16 Zabrodskyi, no. 7.

17 Dan Sabbagh and Peter Beaumont, 'War in Ukraine: Where Has Russia Attacked?,' *The Guardian* sec. World News, February 24, 2022, at https://www.theguardian.com/world/2022/feb/24/war-ukraine-kyiv-map-where-has-russia-attacked.

18 Michael R. Gordon, Bojan Panceyski, Neomie Bisserbe and Marcus Walker, 'Vladimir Putin's 20-Year March to War in Ukraine—and How the West Mishandled It,' *The Wall Street Journal* sec. Life, April 1, 2022, at https://www.wsj.com/articles/vladimir-putins-20-year-march-to-war-in-ukraineand-how-the-west-mishandled-it-11648826461 (Accessed June 22, 2022)

19 Oryx, 'Destination Disaster: Russia's Failure At Hostomel Airport,' *Oryx* (blog), at https://www.oryxspioenkop.com/2022/04/destination-disaster-russias-failure-at.html. (Accessed November 17, 2023).

20 'The Battle of Hostomel Airport: A Key Moment in Russia's Defeat in Kyiv,' War on the Rocks, August 10, 2023, at https://warontherocks.com/2023/08/the-battle-of-hostomel-airport-a-key-moment-in-russias-defeat-in-kyiv/ (Accessed August 22, 2023)

21 Paul Sonne, Isabelle Khurshudyan, Serhiy Morgunov and Kostiantyn Khudov., 'Battle for Kyiv: Ukrainian Valor, Russian Blunders Combined to Save the Capital,' *The Washington Post*, at https://www.washingtonpost.com/national-security/interactive/2022/kyiv-battle-ukraine-survival/ (Accessed November 17, 2023).

22 'Russian Forces Cut off Ukraine's Chernihiv City, Mayor Says,' *Reuters* sec. World, March 25,

2022, at https://www.reuters.com/world/ukrainian-city-chernihiv-cut-off-by-russian-forces-regional-governor-2022-03-25/ (Accessed March 30, 2022).

23 Zabrodskyi, no. 7.

24 Visual Storytelling Team in London, 'How Russia's Mistakes and Ukrainian Resistance Altered Putin's War,' March 18, 2022, at https://ig.ft.com/russias-war-in-ukraine-mapped (Accessed April 3, 2022).

25 Oryx, no. 19.

26 Bermet Talant, 'Why Is Mariupol so Important to Russian Forces?,' *The Guardian* sec. World News, March 22, 2022, at https://www.theguardian.com/world/2022/mar/22/mariupol-important-russian-forces-moscow-port-city (Accessed March 26, 2022).

27 Michael Schwirtz and Richard Pérez-Peña, 'First Ukraine City Falls as Russia Strikes More Civilian Targets,' *The New York Times* sec. World, March 2, 2022, at https://www.nytimes.com/2022/03/02/world/europe/kherson-ukraine-russia.html (Accessed March 26, 2022).

28 Samuel Ramani, *Putin's War on Ukraine: Russia's Campaign for Global Counter-Revolution,* Hurst & Company, London, 2023.

29 Talant, no. 26.

30 'Mariupol: Key Moments in the Siege of the City,' *BBC News* sec. Europe, May 17, 2022, at https://www.bbc.com/news/world-europe-61179093 (Accessed May 21, 2022).

31 David Child, Umut Uras, Zaheena Rasheed, Ali Harb and Federica Marsi, 'Russia-Ukraine Latest Updates: No Let up in Attacks on Chernihiv,' *Al Jazeera*, March 30, 2022, at https://www.aljazeera.com/news/2022/3/29/russia-ukraine-un-urges-unhindered-aid-access-liveblog (Accessed April 10, 2022).

32 'Maps: Tracking the Russian Invasion of Ukraine,' *The New York Times* sec. World, February 14, 2022, at https://www.nytimes.com/interactive/2022/world/europe/ukraine-maps.html (Accessed March 1, 2022).

33 'What Next for Russia?,' *The Economist*, April 2, 2022, at https://www.economist.com/briefing/2022/04/02/what-next-for-russia (Accessed April 10, 2022).

34 'Russia Says It Will Sharply Cut Military Activity near Kyiv, Chernihiv,' *Reuters* sec. Europe, March 29, 2022, at https://www.reuters.com/world/europe/russia-says-it-will-drastically-cut-military-activity-near-kyiv-chernihiv-2022-03-29/ (Accessed April 10, 2022).

35 Matthew Mpoke Bigg, "An Abyss of Fear': A Report Accuses Russia of Further Abuses against Civilians.,' *The New York Times* sec. World, July 24, 2022, at https://www.nytimes.com/2022/07/24/world/europe/russia-torture-ukraine-human-rights-watch.html (Accessed August 12, 2022).

36 Henry Foy, John Paul Rathbone and Felicia Schwartz, 'The Battle for Donbas: 'The Real Test of This War',' *Financial Times* sec. The Big Read, April 25, 2022, at https://www.ft.com/content/f299cb83-9f12-484b-8839-12ec96c87a72 (Accessed May 2, 2022).

37 Andrew Roth, 'Russian Commander Suggests Plan Is for Permanent Occupation of South Ukraine,' *The Guardian* sec. World News, April 22, 2022, at https://www.theguardian.com/world/2022/apr/22/ukraine-south-occupation-russian-military-chief-rustam-minnekayev (Accessed May 5, 2022).

38 ISW Press, 'Russian Offensive Campaign Assessment, May 15,' Institute for the Study of War, May 15, 2022, at https://www.understandingwar.org/backgrounder/russian-offensive-campaign-assessment-may-15 (Accessed May 22, 2022).

39 ISW Press, 'Russian Offensive Campaign Assessment, May 6,' Institute for the Study of War, May 6, 2022, at https://www.understandingwar.org/backgrounder/russian-offensive-campaign-assessment-may-6 (Accessed May 22, 2022).

40 Yuras Karmanau, 'Russians Control 80% of Key Ukraine City, Cut Escape Routes,' *AP News*,June 15, 2022, at https://apnews.com/article/russia-ukraine-business-government-and-politics-01f6d1c027ce68791667ffaafb61e30c (Accessed November 22, 2022).

41 Marc Santora and Ivan Nechepurenko, 'Ukraine Drives Russian Forces from Snake Island, a Setback for Moscow,' *The New York Times* sec. World, June 30, 2022, at https://www.nytimes.com/2022/06/30/world/europe/ukraine-russia-snake-island.html (Accessed July 4, 2022).

42 'Russian Army Draws down from Snake Island in Goodwill Grain Gesture,' *TASS*, June 30, 2022, at https://tass.com/defense/1473763?utm_source=google.com&utm_medium=organic &utm_ campaign=google.com&utm_referrer=google.com (Accessed July 4, 2022).

43 Thomas Gibbons-Neff, Kamila Hrabchuk and Vivian Yee, 'As City Falls, Ukraine's Last Hope in Luhansk Falls With It,' *The New York Times* sec. World, July 3, 2022, at https://www.nytimes.com/2022/07/03/world/europe/ukraine-war-lysychansk.html (Accessed July 4, 2022).

44 Andrew E. Kramer and Steven Erlanger, 'Moscow Signals a Shift to a More Aggressive Phase of Ukraine War,' *The New York Times* sec. World, July 16, 2022, at https://www.nytimes.com/2022/07/16/world/europe/russia-ukraine-donbas-shoigu-pause.html (Accessed July 21, 2022).

45 'Six Months of War in Ukraine,' *The Economist*, August 24, 2022, at https://www.economist.com/interactive/europe/2022/08/24/six-months-of-war-in-ukraine (Accessed August 27, 2022).

46 'Ukraine Should See Impact of Kherson Counterattack from August, Spy Chief Says,' *Reuters* sec. Europe, June 25, 2022, at https://www.reuters.com/world/europe/ukraine-should-see-impact-kherson-counterattack-august-spy-chief-2022-06-25/ (Accessed July 15, 2022).

47 'Ukraine Says Long-Anticipated Southern Offensive Has Begun,' *Reuters* sec. World, August 29, 2022, at https://www.reuters.com/world/ukraine-says-long-anticipated-southern-offensive-has-begun-2022-08-29/ (Accessed August 30, 2022).

48 Olga Voitovych, Jo Shelley, Tara John, Olha Konovalova and Rebecca Wright, "Ukraine Claims Early Success in Counteroffensive as Zelensky Vows to 'Chase' Russians to the Border," CNN, August 30, 2022, at https://www.cnn.com/2022/08/30/europe/ukraine-kherson-counteroffensive-intl/index.html (Accessed September 6, 2022).

49 Yaroslav Trofimov, 'Ukraine Braces for Brutal Fight for Occupied Southern Regions as Referendum Looms,' *The Wall Street Journal* sec. World, August 3, 2022, at https://www.wsj.com/articles/ukraine-braces-for-brutal-fight-for-occupied-southern-regions-as-referendum-looms-11659519001 (Accessed September 6, 2022).

50 'Perspektyvy zabezpechennya viys'kovoyi kampaniyi 2023 roku: ukrayins'kyy pohlyad (Prospects for Securing the Military Campaign of 2023: The Ukrainian View),' Ukrinform, September 7, 2022, at https://www.ukrinform.ua/rubric-ato/3566162-ak-zabezpeciti-voennu-kampaniu-u-2023-roci-ukrainskij-poglad.html (Accessed September 10, 2022).

51 'Minoborony Rossii zayavilo o neudavsheysya popytke napadeniya na VSU (The Russian Ministry Of Defence Announced a Failed Attack Attempt by the Armed Forces of Ukraine),' RIA Novosti, August 29, 2022, at https://ria.ru/20220829/nastuplenie-1813011342.html (Accessed September 6, 2022).

52 Samuel Ramani, no. 28, p. 181.

53 'Inside the Ukrainian Counteroffensive That Shocked Putin and Reshaped the War,' *The Washington Post*, December 29, 2022, at https://www.washingtonpost.com/world/2022/12/29/ukraine-offensive-kharkiv-kherson-donetsk/ (Accessed January 4, 2023).

54 Huw Dylan, David V. Gioe and Joe Littell, 'The Kherson Ruse: Ukraine and the Art of

Military Deception,' Modern War Institute, October 12, 2022, at https://mwi.westpoint.edu/the-kherson-ruse-ukraine-and-the-art-of-military-deception/ (Accessed December 12, 2022).

55 Katie Bo Lillis and Natasha Bertrand, 'US War-Gamed with Ukraine Ahead of Counteroffensive and Encouraged More Limited Mission,' *CNN*, August 31, 2022, at https://www.cnn.com/2022/08/31/politics/ukraine-us-wargames-counteroffensive/index.html (Accessed September 13, 2022).

56 Isobel Koshiw, Lorenzo Tondo and Artem Mazhulin, 'Ukraine's Southern Offensive 'Was Designed to Trick Russia',' *The Guardian* sec. World News, September 10, 2022, at https://www.theguardian.com/world/2022/sep/10/ukraines-publicised-southern-offensive-was-disinformation-campaign (Accessed September 13, 2022).

57 Tom Balmforth, 'Ukraine Blindsides Russia with Northeastern Thrust at Supply Hub,' *Reuters* sec. Europe, September 9, 2022, at https://www.reuters.com/world/europe/ukraine-blindsides-russia-with-northeastern-thrust-supply-hub-2022-09-09/ (Accessed September 13, 2022).

58 'Is Russia on the Run?,' *The Economist*, September 11, 2022, at https://www.economist.com/europe/2022/09/11/is-russia-on-the-run. (Accessed September 13, 2022).

59 Mark Townsend, Lorenzo Tondo and Isobel Koshiw, 'Ukrainian Counter-Offensive in North-East Inflicts a Defeat on Moscow,' *The Observer* sec. World News, September 10, 2022, at https://www.theguardian.com/world/2022/sep/10/ukrainian-forces-kupiansk-advances-north-east-russia-izyum (Accessed September 13, 2022).

60 'Ukraine Says Northeastern Offensive Has Retaken 3,800 Sq. Km in a Week,' *Reuters* sec. Europe, September 13, 2022, at https://www.reuters.com/world/europe/ukraine-says-northeastern-offensive-has-retaken-3800-sq-km-week-2022-09-13/ (Accessed September 13, 2022).

61 Isabelle Khurshudyan, Paul Sonne, Serhiy Morgunov and Kamila Hrabchuk., 'Inside the Ukrainian Counteroffensive That Shocked Putin and Reshaped the War,' *The Washington Post*, December 29, 2022, at https://www.washingtonpost.com/world/2022/12/29/ukraine-offensive-kharkiv-kherson-donetsk/ (Accessed January 6, 2023).

62 Ibid

63 Ramani, no. 28, p. 183.

64 Julian E. Barnes, Helene Cooper, Eric Schmitt and Michael Schwirtz,' As Russian Losses Mount in Ukraine, Putin Gets More Involved in War Strategy,' *The New York Times* sec. U.S., September 23, 2022, at https://www.nytimes.com/2022/09/23/us/politics/putin-ukraine.html (Accessed September 25, 2022).

65 Yaroslav Trofimov, 'Ukraine Pushes South Into Strategic Kherson Region,' *The Wall Street Journal,* October 3, 2022, at https://www.wsj.com/articles/ukraine-pushes-south-into-strategic-kherson-region-11664795231 (Accessed November 10, 2023).

66 Neil MacFarquhar and Cassandra Vinograd, 'Russia Names New General, Surovikin, to Lead Forces in Ukraine,' *The New York Times*, October 22, 2022 at https://www.nytimes.com/2022/10/08/world/europe/russia-ukraine-general-sergei-surovikin.html (Accessed November 19, 2023).

67 'Russia Says It Is Abandoning the Ukrainian City of Kherson,' *The Economist*, November 9, 2022, at https://www.economist.com/europe/2022/11/09/russia-says-it-is-abandoning-the-ukrainian-city-of-kherson. (Accessed November 10, 2023).

68 Michael E. Miller, 'Visiting Liberated Kherson, Zelensky Sees 'Beginning of the End of the War',' *Washington Post*, November 14, 2022, at https://www.washingtonpost.com/world/2022/11/14/kherson-zelensky-atrocities-ukraine-war/ (Accessed November 16, 2022).

69 Max Seddon, John Paul Rathbone and Roman Olearchyk, 'Military Briefing: Russia Prepares

Ukraine Spring Offensive,' *Financial Times* sec. Ukraine military briefing, February 15, 2023, at https://www.ft.com/content/164360c3-1b37-46c9-b26a-4444d2045eef (Accessed March 13, 2023).

70 'Russian Offensive Campaign Assessment, November 29, 2023,' Institute for the Study of War, November 29, 2023, at http://dev-isw.bivings.com/ (Accessed October 31, 2023).

71 Gerrard Kaonga, 'Wagner Group Repels Fresh Ukrainian Advances in Battle for Bakhmut—Report,' *Newsweek*, December 08, 2022, at, https://www.newsweek.com/russia-ukraine-wagner-group-attack-battle-bakhmut-study-war-latest-1765549 (Accessed October 31, 2023).

72 Andew Osborn and Felix Light,'Analysis: Russia's Grim Battle for Bakhmut May Yield Pyrrhic Victory at Best,' *Reuters*, December 20, 2022, at, https://www.reuters.com/world/europe/grim-battle-bakhmut-may-yield-only-pyrrhic-victory-russia-2022-12-20/ (Accessed December 18, 2022).

73 Matthew Mpoke Bigg and Michael Schwirtz, 'Ukraine Says That Its Forces Have Retreated from Soledar after an Intense Battle,' *The New York Times* sec. World, January 25, 2023, at https://www.nytimes.com/2023/01/25/world/europe/ukraine-soledar-retreat.html (Accessed January 29, 2023).

74 Helene Cooper, Julian E. Barnes and Eric Schmitt, 'To Fix Its Problems in Ukraine, Russia Turns to the Architect of the War,' *The New York Times* sec. U.S., January 28, 2023, at https://www.nytimes.com/2023/01/28/us/politics/russia-generals-ukraine.html (Accessed January 29, 2023).

75 Seddon, Rathbone, and Olearchyk, no. 69.

76 Tim Lister, "Like Turkeys at a Shooting Range': Mauling of Russian Forces in Donetsk Hotspot May Signal Problems to Come,' *CNN*, February 13, 2023, at https://www.cnn.com/2023/02/13/europe/russia-ukraine-vuhledar-donetsk-fiasco-intl/index.html (Accessed February 16, 2023).

77 Christopher Miller, 'Battle of Bakhmut Nears Tipping Point as Russia Intensifies Offensive,' *Financial Times* sec. War in Ukraine, February 2, 2023, at https://www.ft.com/content/0bfe39c1-6d68-4e72-9fe2-9f54b7efa2bd (Accessed February 16, 2023).

78 'Russia's Prigozhin, Ukraine Give Varying Accounts on Fighting near Bakhmut,' *Reuters*, February 26, 2023, at https://www.reuters.com/world/europe/russias-prigozhin-says-wagner-fighters-capture-ukrainian-village-near-bakhmut-2023-02-25/ (Accessed February 28, 2023).

79 Hanna Arhirova, 'Russian Forces Claim Progress in Bakhmut but No End in Sight,' *AP News*, March 9, 2023, at https://apnews.com/article/russia-ukraine-war-bakhmut-a9f4d5c3d3b1c6f6fcc7e9abc69cc7b6 (Accessed March 15, 2023).

80 'Ukraine Says Eastern Town of Avdiivka Could Become 'Second Bakhmut',' *Reuters*, March 20, 2023, at https://www.reuters.com/world/europe/ukraine-says-eastern-town-avdiivka-could-become-second-bakhmut-2023-03-20/ (Accessed March 24, 2023).

81 Sophia Ankel,'Before-and-after Photos Show How Russia's Invasion Reduced a Ukrainian City to a Post-Apocalyptic Wasteland,' *Business Insider India*, March 7, 2023, at https://www.businessinsider.in/international/news/before-and-after-photos-show-how-russias-invasion-reduced-a-ukrainian-city-to-a-post-apocalyptic-wasteland/articleshow/98480212.cms (Accessed March 14, 2023).

82 Erin Banco, 'Wagner Still Holds Significant Territory in Bakhmut, U.S. Officials Say,' POLITICO, May 10, 2023, at https://www.politico.com/news/2023/05/10/wagner-russia-bakhmut-ukraine-00096255 (Accessed May 21, 2023).

83 Tim Lister and Yulia Kesaieva, 'Wagner Units Have Pulled Back to Bakhmut Due to Alleged Lack of Coordination with Russian Army, Ukraine Says,' *CNN*, May 10, 2023,at https://

www.cnn.com/europe/live-news/russia-ukraine-war-news-05-10-23/index.html (Accessed May 21, 2023).

84 'Russia Says Ukrainian City of Bakhmut Captured,' *Reuters*, May 21, 2023, at https://www.reuters.com/world/europe/russias-wagner-claims-bakhmut-kyiv-says-situation-critical-2023-05-20/ (Accessed May 24, 2023).

85 Marc Santora, 'The Battle for Bakhmut, in Photos,' *The New York Times* sec. World, May 23, 2023, at https://www.nytimes.com/2023/05/23/world/europe/bakhmut-photos-ukraine.html (Accessed May 24, 2023).

86 Marco Hernandez and Josh Holder, 'Defenses Carved Into the Earth,' *The New York Times* sec. World, December 14, 2022, at https://www.nytimes.com/interactive/2022/12/14/world/europe/russian-trench-fortifications-in-ukraine.html (Accessed December 17, 2022).

87 'Ukraine War: Satellite Images Reveal Russian Defences before Major Assault,' *BBC News* sec. Europe, May 21, 2023, at https://www.bbc.com/news/world-europe-65615184 (Accessed May 24, 2023).

88 "Dragon's Teeth,' Hedgehogs and Minefields: How Russia Is Preparing to Defend Occupied Ukrainian Areas,' *The Moscow Times*, May 23, 2023, at https://www.themoscowtimes.com/2023/05/23/dragons-teeth-hedgehogs-and-minefields-how-russia-is-preparing-to-defend-occupied-ukrainian-areas-a81234 (Accessed May 24, 2023).

89 Andrew E. Kramer et al., 'U.S. Officials See Signs of a Counteroffensive in Ukraine,' *The New York Times* sec. World, June 5, 2023, at https://www.nytimes.com/live/2023/06/05/world/russia-ukraine-news (Accessed June 11, 2023).

90 'Ukraine's Counter-Offensive Is Gathering Pace,' *The Economist*, June 7, 2023, at https://www.economist.com/briefing/2023/06/07/ukraines-counter-offensive-is-gathering-pace (Accessed June 11, 2023).

91 'Why Ukraine's Counteroffensive against Russia Still Hasn't Begun,' *PBS NewsHour*, May 19, 2023, at https://www.pbs.org/newshour/world/why-ukraines-counteroffensive-against-russia-still-hasnt-begun (Accessed May 24, 2023).

92 'Ukraine Alters Counter-Offensive Plans after Document Leak,' *Reuters* sec. Europe, April 10, 2023, at https://www.reuters.com/world/europe/ukraine-alters-counter-offensive-plans-after-document-leak-cnn-2023-04-10/ (Accessed April 12, 2023).

93 Marco Hernandez and Josh Holder, 'Defenses Carved Into the Earth,' *The New York Times* sec. World, December 14, 2022, at https://www.nytimes.com/interactive/2022/12/14/world/europe/russian-trench-fortifications-in-ukraine.html (Accessed December 17, 2022).

94 Jen Kirby, 'What Went Wrong in Ukraine's Counteroffensive,' Vox, August 8, 2023, at https://www.vox.com/23819064/ukraine-war-counteroffensive-russia-mines-tanks (Accessed August 12, 2023).

95 Andrew E. Kramer, 'Pro-Ukraine Fighters Behind Cross-Border Attack Pledge More to Come,' *The New York Times* sec. World, May 24, 2023, at https://www.nytimes.com/live/2023/05/24/world/russia-ukraine-news (Accessed May 25, 2022).

96 'Zelenskiy Says Ukraine Ready to Launch Counteroffensive,' *Reuters*, at https://www.reuters.com/world/europe/zelenskiy-says-ukraine-ready-launch-counteroffensive-2023-06-03/ (Accessed October 30, 2023).

97 'Ukraine's Counter-Offensive Is Gathering Pace,' no. 90.

98 Jen Kirby, 'A Guide to Understanding the Ukrainian Counteroffensive,' Vox, June 10, 2023, at https://www.vox.com/2023/6/10/23750041/russia-ukraine-war-counteroffensive-begins-explained.

99 Mariano Zafra and Jon McClure, 'Where Ukraine Is Counter-Attacking and the Russian's

2,000 Km Fortification Line,' *Reuters*, June 26, 2023, at https://www.reuters.com/graphics/UKRAINE-CRISIS/MAPS/klvygwawavg/#where-ukraine-is-counter-attacking-and-the-russians-2000-km-fortification-line (Accessed June 29, 2023).

100 Lara Jakes, Andrew E. Kramer and Eric Schmitt, 'After Suffering Heavy Losses, Ukrainians Paused to Rethink Strategy,' *The New York Times* sec. U.S., July 15, 2023, at https://www.nytimes.com/2023/07/15/us/politics/ukraine-leopards-bradleys-counteroffensive.htm (Accessed July 18, 2023).

101 'Mutiny and Mayhem in Russia a Probable Boon for Ukraine,' *NBC News*, June 27, 2023, at https://www.nbcnews.com/news/world/russian-mutiny-prigozhin-ukraine-forces-counteroffensive-rcna91214 (Accessed July 18, 2023).

102 Thomas Gibbons-Neff and Lauren Leatherby, 'Ukraine Has Gained Ground. But It Has Much Farther to Go,' *The New York Times* sec. World, September 20, 2023, at https://www.nytimes.com/interactive/2023/09/20/world/europe/ukraine-war-counteroffensive-robotyne.html (Accessed September 22, 2023).

103 Matthew Mpoke Bigg, 'Russian Troops Cede Ground and Strike Back, Frustrating Ukraine's Counteroffensive,' *The New York Times* sec. World, October 3, 2023, at https://www.ny times.com/2023/10/03/world/europe/russia-ukraine-elastic-defense-counteroffensive. html (Accessed October 30, 2023).

104 'Ukraine Attacks Russian Black Sea Navy HQ in Crimea,' *Reuters*, September 22, 2023, at https://www.reuters.com/world/europe/russian-official-says-ukraine-struck-black-sea-navy-hq-with-missile-2023-09-22/ (Accessed October 30, 2023).

105 'Now Russia Is Fighting to Gain Territory in the East of Ukraine,' *The Economist*, October 14, 2023, at https://www.economist.com/europe/2023/10/14/now-russia-is-fighting-to-gain-territory-in-the-east-of-ukraine (Accessed November 29, 2023).

106 AP, 'Russia Says It Shot down 36 Ukrainian Drones as Fighting Grinds on in Ukraine's East,' *The Hindu* sec. World, October 29, 2023, at https://www.thehindu.com/news/international/russia-says-it-shot-down-36-ukrainian-drones-as-fighting-grinds-on-in-ukraines-east/article67473053.ece (Accessed October 30, 2023).

107 'Ukraine's Avdiivka Empties in Face of Russian Assaults,' *France 24*, November 27, 2023, at https://www.france24.com/en/live-news/20231127-ukraine-s-avdiivka-empties-in-face-of-russian-assaults (Accessed November 30, 2023).

108 Tom Burgis, 'Ukraine Troops Defend Vital Foothold on Russian-Controlled Dnipro River,' *The Guardian* sec. World News, November 3, 2023, at https://www.theguardian.com/world/2023/nov/03/ukraine-troops-defend-vital-foothold-on-russian-controlled-dnipro-river (Accessed November 29, 2023).

109 Tom Balmforth and Yuliia Dysa, 'Ukrainian Troops Operate in Occupied Kherson Region after Crossing River,' *Reuters*, November 16, 2023, sec. Europe, at https://www.reuters.com/world/europe/ukraine-presses-russian-forces-along-dnipro-river-near-kherson-kyiv-2023-11-15/ (Accessed November 29, 2023).

110 'Ukraine's Top General: War with Russia Has Reached Stalemate,' POLITICO, November 2, 2023, at https://www.politico.eu/article/valery-zaluzhny-ukraine-top-general-war-russia-reach-stalemate/ (Accessed November 29, 2023).

111 'Ukraine's Commander-in-Chief on the Breakthrough He Needs to Beat Russia,' *The Economist*, November 1, 2023, at https://www.economist.com/europe/2023/11/01/ukraines-commander-in-chief-on-the-breakthrough-he-needs-to-beat-russia (Accessed November 29, 2023).

112 Sam Jones and Luke Harding, 'Zelenskiy Denies Ukrainian General's Claim War Is at Stalemate,' *The Guardian* sec. World News, November 5, 2023, at https://www.theguardian.com/world/

2023/nov/05/zelenskiy-denies-ukrainian-generals-claim-war-is-at-stalemate (Accessed November 29, 2023).

113 Barry Gander, 'What Conventional Military Analysis Missed About Russia,' Medium, August 29, 2023, at https://barry-gander.medium.com/what-conventional-military-analysis-missed-about-russia-6a9ebb35424 (Accessed November 29, 2023).

114 Hugh Smith, 'Clausewitz's Definition of War and Its Limits,' *Military Strategy Magazine*, at https://www.militarystrategymagazine.com/article/clausewitzs-definition-of-war-and-its-limits/ (Accessed November 29, 2023).

115 Samuel Charap and Miranda Priebe, 'Avoiding a Long War: U.S. Policy and the Trajectory of the Russia-Ukraine Conflict,' RAND Corporation, January 25, 2023, at https://www.rand.org/pubs/perspectives/PEA2510-1.html (Accessed November 29, 2023).

# SECTION II

# Role and Impact of the Various Components of Military Power

# 4

# Efficacy of Armoured Warfare in the Modern Battlefield

*Amarjit Singh*

## INTRODUCTION

The tank and manoeuvre are the essence of armoured warfare. The tank is the prime instrument of armoured warfare and manoeuvre is the key technique to employ this instrument. The tank represents a protected, highly mobile and precision direct firing weapon system and manoeuvre is the art of creating surprise and disrupting the enemy's mind and operational plans by using the element of movement of forces with skill and care. Manoeuvre is more of an attitude of mind than an arrow on the map.[1] The efficacy of armoured warfare in the modern battlefield will be determined by examining whether success in future wars have in their character a need for the tank and has the space and time for employment of manoeuvre. The tank was a technology that transformed the second-generation warfare of firepower and trenches into the third generation[2] of warfare that involved thinking up new ideas in tactics of which manoeuvre using tanks was the prime inspiration. This generation was characterised by non-linearity of battle lines, surprise and swift movement of potent firepower to occupy strategic spaces behind enemy defences. Conventional wars of the last century have time and again proved the tank to be a battle winning factor. Striking victories of the tank in battle have, but naturally, led to research and development of a potent anti-tank weapon. The race between the tank and the anti-tank has been a sine curve between the technological advancement of the tank and anti-tank weapon systems. When the curve is against the tank, questions arise about the efficacy of the tank as a battle winning factor. If this is coupled with manoeuvre that is done without skill and care (as in the UkraineWar 2022), the need to re-examine the efficacy of armoured warfare will necessarily become mandatory. Armoured warfare is a combination of tanks and mechanised infantry. The term 'tank' used in this article is a combination of the tank and the infantry's armoured fighting vehicle that are complimentary to each other.

Many military strategists have already predicted the unsuitability of the tank in the future battle. Their arguments are based on the fact that the last classical armoured battle, where two large, armoured forces manoeuvred against each other in a decisive battle, occurred in 1973, the Arab–Israeli War.[3] This may be correct only to justify the end of large tank versus tank battle in open desert terrain. We have to consider the spectacular use of armoured forces in the Gulf War (Operation Desert Storm and Operation Iraqi Freedom) where engagements were decisive and the tank provided the cutting edge. It has been stated that since Iraq, Lebanon, Georgia and Syria, armoured formations either followed or supported the application of air power and artillery, and their units were committed piecemeal in urban terrain.[4] This argument is based on an inter se domination between arms. No one arm has won the battle on its own; it is the integration of the strengths of each arm that creates success. If the future battle requires a re-orientation of battle groups, the generalship should rebalance rather than predict the demise of the tank as a failed weapon platform.

## EMPLOYMENT OF TANKS IN THE UKRAINE WAR

The first two months of the Ukraine War was a depiction of a graveyard of Russian tanks that were destroyed by superior Western-based intelligence and hi-technology anti-tank weapons that North Atlantic Treaty Organisation (NATO) had supplied to the Ukrainian Army. Tanks were seen employing unprofessional battle tactics, moving in straight lines along roads and even trapped in *cul-de-sacs*. Moreover, Russia's operational plan involved advancing along multiple axis of advance, many of which were not in mutual support, and Russian Ground Forces units were tasked with advancing at an extremely rapid rate. This rapid pace outstripped the support of the infantry and the artillery. Then there was the factor of 'mud'[5] (a major factor in World War II) that prevented tanks from manoeuvring to tactical advantageous positions. This armour was confronted with the most technologically advanced anti-tank systems supplied by Western countries. The casualties were large and at times dramatic enough to hit headlines of TV channels. When you add up these battle indicators the conclusion is fairly obvious to military analysts and some professional soldiers, who have since come out with numerous articles degrading the tank. Much of this can be filtered down as part of Western propaganda and the fog of war but there is some reality in this. The 'concept of employment' of armoured warfare, which has come into question because of the battle outcomes in Ukraine, includes:

(a) **Tanks and decisive battles.** Tanks are designed to fight decisive contact battles. In the Ukraine War the information that permeates is that the tanks failed to get a decision in battle. This is seen in the concept of the failure to capture of Kiev in a blitzkrieg move by tanks and by heliborne operations. The journalistic view of this battle has centred more on the destroyed tank rather than where the tank was destroyed and where it had manoeuvred. The War is still an ongoing process and to conclude that the tank has lost its capability to fight a decisive battle would be premature. One of the important lessons of the Ukraine War is the understanding of winning and losing. The Russians withdrew from their initial failed operations in a remarkable short strategic time frame, bearing huge loss of face both domestically and on the world platform but have managed to salvage their armoured columns to live and fight another day. But what has been lost is the confidence in tanks in decisive battles.

(b) **Anti-tank weapons.** The one factor that tilted the scales in favour of anti-tank weapons was their extended range that out-gunned the tank in effective range of engagement. This allowed anti-tank weapons to be fired from relatively safe positions. The second factor was the lethality, which breached the tank's armour with ease. The low levels of battlefield awareness of tank crews and longer ranges of the multitudes of hi-tech anti-tank weapons have proved very effective in stopping and destroying a tank column. These anti-tank weapons are light, man-portable, attack the vulnerable top of the tank and are self-guided in a 'fire and forget' mode. The number of these weapons deployed is over the ratio of 10:1 and are very cost effective. The advent of drones and loitering ammunitions has been the cause of many destroyed tanks. The first effective drone strikes were witnessed in the Second Nagorno–Karabakh War in 2021. The anti-tank weapons have questioned the 'protection' or the armour of the tank. In order to increase the levels of protection the weight of the tank goes up and so does the cost. The tank design, which is a balance of firepower, protection and mobility, may require a relook in the technological advancement of this weapon system.

(c) **Manoeuvre.** Movement and manoeuvre are an important war fighting function. It involves employing forces to achieve a position of relative advantage over the enemy. Direct fire and close combat are an inherent part of manoeuvre. Their effects are surprise, shock and momentum, leading to the dislocation of enemy's plans and positions. The main strength of tanks is the ability to manoeuvre to the flanks and towards more advantageous ground. If this capability is removed, then the tank is just a fortified static pill box. The adage 'if it can be seen, it will be hit' becomes true for the tank that is incapable of manoeuvre. The Russian ground plan did not demonstrate any form of manoeuvre, except a link up operation with heli-borne forces at the Hostomel Airfield, which also failed. In armoured warfare, manoeuvre is a factor of time, speed, space and opportunity, which can be executed only by an agile, educated and situationally aware commander. Tanks under a dull commander will be destroyed. Russian armoured columns in the initial phase of operations did not exhibit any form of manoeuvre and this led to the destruction of the large, in line and static columns of tanks.

(d) **Tank tactics.** Tanks are employed in troops, which basically have three or four tanks. Fire and move are the basic tactics, that is, one half is in firing positions to pin the enemy while the other half moves to positions closer to the objective. The basic operation requires space and time. If this is mastered, then armoured warfare will always be successful. The problem arises when there is little space and less time. It is at this moment that the whole point of ingenuity, training and flexibility of tank commanders comes into play. Here the tank commander's situational awareness is a battle winning factor. Reports from the initial battle in Ukraine did not indicate any such tank tactics and therefore it suffered casualties. However, now, after a year of fighting the tank tactics that we are seeing are very effective and tanks are proving instrumental in winning small battles, which has been the pattern of operations in the Ukraine War. It is exhilarating to see brave tank commanders making successful deep manoeuvres into enemy territory at high speed using high rates of precise fire and returning to their firm bases.

(e) **Combined arms concept.** The initial Russian invasion was probably based on the false premise that the Ukrainian Army will not put up any resistance. Russian commanders made minimal attempts in planning and executing a coherent combined-arms operation, which inherently requires detailed coordination and planning between air and ground forces at the higher level and armour, infantry and artillery at the tactical level. Russian spearheads simply drove toward cities, unprepared to a fight an all-arms battle. Russian tank units were tasked with advancing at an extremely rapid rate, and at a point were beyond infantry, artillery, electronic support and air defence coverage, further exacerbating the thin logistics support. The rapid advance exposed the supply lines to ambushes from territorial defence forces. As a result, the initial phase of this war cannot be a good indication of how effective tanks and other systems would prove to be in a better-organised military operation where the tank is well supported in a combined arms team. Many of the supposed weaknesses of tanks were a result of these mistakes and not a reflection of their technical relevance in modern warfare.

(f) **Command and control.** The initial evidence of photographs of long lines of tanks on roads, crossing built up areas, which provide ideal anti-tank firing positions, indicate an unprofessional use of tanks. This is an indicator of incompetent leadership, both at tactical and operational levels. The plan completely disregarded the enemy's capability to fight battles. It was well known that after the coup in Ukraine in 2014, NATO was training at least four Ukrainian battalions to NATO standards per year with NATO weapons.[6] What is apparent is that the commanders had failed to re-orientate themselves from years of peace to an intense battle. Sun Tzu says, 'The art of war is of vital importance to the State. It is a matter of life and death, a road either to safety or to ruin. Hence it is a subject of inquiry which can on no account be neglected.' The neglect of Russian field commanders was apparent in the initial phases of the war.

(g) **Tank casualties.** As per the Oryx Blog, Russians have lost 1,831 tanks[7] of which 1,087 were destroyed, 91 were damaged, 103 abandoned and 550 captured. These figures indicate that nearly 40 per cent of the casualties were not due to enemy action and could be attributed to poor training, obsolete vintage and unprofessional handling of tanks. From the photographic evidence it can be easily concluded that many of the tanks listed as destroyed were first abandoned by their crews and destroyed by Ukrainian soldiers who either could not or chose not to capture them. This figure is nearly the same for Ukrainian tanks. In Chechnya (1999–2000) Russians lost 122 out of 146 tanks and infantry fighting vehicles. The stated under-performance of the tank can be attributed to 'competence' rather than the character of the tank in the modern battlefield. In simple words, the tanks themselves were not the problem—they were simply poorly employed. Three key issues explain Russia's tank losses: lack of warning and preparation, poor strategy, which exacerbated logistics issues, and insufficient infantry to protect them.[8] Tanks form the vanguard for all close quarter combat. This naturally implies that they will sustain casualties. For a commander each casualty must enforce and contribute to success in battle and each casualty must be studied for its technical performance and its tactical employment to learn lessons.

(h) **Logistics.** Tanks are extremely logistics-intensive weapon systems. They require routine maintenance, spare parts and substantial fuel and lubricants to keep them operational. Logistics planning is more important for tank regiments than for any other type of military unit. Many of the damaged, abandoned and captured tanks in the initial phase of war were due to running out of fuel. (In the intense cold of February, the Russian tank crews burnt fuel to warm themselves during the wait in their assembly areas before the start of operations and thereby ran out of fuel.) The logistics just could not keep up with the speed of the leading columns. For every crew member of the tank there is a requirement of one maintenance staff, which turns out to be heavy on manpower.

## The Ukrainian Counteroffensive June 2023

The Ukrainian counteroffensive of September–October 2022 was considered a success, but it was actually a redeployment of Russian forces to better defended positions and a better logistical support. The success of this counteroffensive gave confidence to Ukrainians and the NATO that the Russians could be defeated if the Ukraine forces were given more sophisticated arms, especially tanks. This conclusive thinking came to the decision to provide Ukraine with Leopard tanks from Germany, Challengers from the United Kingdom (UK) and Abrams from the United States of America (USA), which would form the centre of the counteroffensive to defeat the Russians. The analysis of the June 2023 counteroffensive with reference to armoured warfare has highlighted the following:

(a) **Numbers (of tanks).** The number of tanks provided to Ukraine was incredibly low, which would not be enough even for a local counterattack let alone a national one over a thousand kilometres. In Indian terms it would be one squadron of Leopards and one squadron of Challengers, which could be organised at best into two combat teams. One combat team covers a frontage of roughly five kilometres. Such numbers cannot generate combat power for a successful counteroffensive.

(b) **Technological capability of tanks.** The technological capability of Leopards and Challengers is approximately only one generation ahead of the T-72. They cannot defeat the modern anti-tank missiles. The technology of these tanks did not come into play in the counteroffensive as they were used and employed in the way one would use the T-80 or T-72 and therefore met with the same fate. Each technology capability of a weapon system requires innovative tactics to bring out the advantage of superior technology. The employment and the performance of the Leopard tank have proved to be a failure. If used similarly the Abrams of USA would meet the same fate.

(c) **Remotely delivered mines.** Remotely delivered mines have proved to restrict the mobility of advancing armoured columns. A very large number of tanks and infantry fighting vehicles were destroyed by mines. The Ukrainians failed to negotiate the minefield laid by the Russians. Remotely delivered mines have been very effective in stopping armoured columns. Tanks without individual mine clearing have no chance of advancing through a minefield, especially those that are covered by artillery and anti-tank weapons.

(d) **The attack helicopter.** The attack helicopter has been re-invented as a battle winning factor. The Ka-52 of Russia has bounced back as a tank killer. Its employment and tactics have been well researched by Russia. It has developed a defence against anti-aircraft missiles, vastly improved its optics for target acquisition and above all supports an anti-tank missile of a 10 kilometre range, giving it the capability to fire at the enemy from secure positions. The Ukrainian tank forces did not take the weapon system seriously after it saw its failure in the initial Russian invasion in February 2022.

(e) **The man behind the gun.** In a serious analysis of the counteroffensive, the factor that, in my opinion, was the main reason for the failure was the 'man behind the gun'. In today's battlefield technology takes centre stage but the man behind the gun is of paramount importance. The deduction is that no nation can build an army, which is well trained, in one or two years. It requires years of thinking, war gaming, training, equipping and psychologically orienting the soldier and the leader to produce an army.

## ARMOURED WARFARE

The main emphasis of the analysis of the Ukraine War is concentrated on the tank and its destruction. The armoured tactics used by Ukraine and the Russians have been largely similar, differing only in the numbers employed. The information coming out from the war has a distinct undertone of discrediting the Russian tank design and underplaying the role of armoured formations. Armoured warfare as such has not been discussed. If we look at the war with the tank in perspective, we can conclude that thousands of tanks have been destroyed and the tank seems to an obsolete technology for modern war. But if we look at the war with armoured warfare in perspective, we see that Russia had captured 119,000[9] square kilometres of Ukrainian territory over a frontage of 2,200 kilometres. This will be the biggest territorial gain after World War (WW) II. Such territory was not even captured in Kuwait or in Iraq where the modern-day tank was very effectively employed. Armoured warfare in this capture of territory can only be considered as a success. If we relate combat power and manpower, we find that tank crews, who comprise 4 per cent of the overall Russian Army's manpower, contributed to 40 per cent of the combat power generated. (The dynamics of combat power are leadership, firepower, information, mobility and survivability).[10]Even today after a year of war and the hype of tank destruction, it is the tank that is leading all operations in Ukraine on both sides. Tanks form the vanguard of offensive forces and therefore will suffer the maximum casualties. To achieve success commanders must have the heart to bear casualties. The nature of war is violent, and this violence results in casualties. The essence is evaluation of the success achieved versus casualties suffered. Conventional wisdom of the current journalist and strategists on the efficacy of armoured warfare in the Ukraine War is clearly a hasty conclusion. It's becoming quite apparent that armoured dominance on a battlefield in Ukraine could still turn the tide, dramatically. This fact gets corroborated by the fact that the President of Ukraine has pressed very hard to get modern battle tanks from NATO and Western countries to give him the potential to defend and create a capability of a counteroffensive. This reflects his confidence in armoured warfare to fight decisive battles.

Several media reports are inconspicuous to general public, but for an analyst they have immense value about efficacy of systems, such as a New York Times report on fighting near Izyum states the following: 'Tanks in particular have become a serious menace, fighters said, often coming within a mile of the battalion's positions and wreaking absolute havoc. Already this month, 13 soldiers with the battalion have been killed and more than 60 wounded.' In *Panzer Ace*, the published memoirs of Richard von Rosen, a German tank commander in WW II, Rosen retells occasions where Soviet anti-tank guns were quickly silenced, leaving their infantry at the mercy of the armoured formations and leading to heavy enemy losses.

The next analysis in verifying the efficacy of armoured warfare is to study the characteristics of the next generation of war and examine the role of the tank in this environment. The next generation of war will be a clash of ideologically opposing cultures and civilisations. The territorial and economic equations will not be the foremost objects of war. For the underdog the cost of war has no meaning, it is his survival. In this fight for survival all conventions will be set aside. The war will be fought in the grey zone;[11] war will be multi-modal, multi-domain[12] and multi-spatial (land, sea, air, space, cyber, psychological and cognitive). Weapons will be high precision, lethal, long range and mobile. The complexity of war will be non-linear and fast in tempo. The only linearity in war will be 'time', which highlights the speed of decisions and actions. No one service, space, domain or mode can win the war on its own but there will be a muddled integration. However, the ultimate victory will be perceived on land. The Iraq War, the Afghanistan experience, Vietnam, Korea and now Ukraine all indicate that ultimately the battles fought on land will prevail and contact battles will hold the key to achieve war objectives that satisfy the political aims. The review of armoured warfare comes under the ambit of the strategic discussion that the era of conventional war is over and therefore weapon platforms such as the tank, warship and the fighter jet will lose their predominance to the cyber platforms, economic sanctions, soft power and cognitive attacks. The myth that conventional war is passé, as professed by politicians and some defence analysts, stands on infirm ground. Ultimately it is 'hard power' that counts to impose one's will on the adversary. The tanks represent hard power and will continue to enjoy a unique and indomitable position on the battlefield in the foreseeable future. As long as nations have belligerent adversaries, unsettled borders and ideological differences, physical presence of fighting men and machines on ground will be essential. They are the symbol of hard power and the signature of strength.

The main factor troubling analysts is the potency of anti-tank weapons against the tank. Anti-tank platforms will continue to evolve and hunt the tank. The US Army Field Manual FM 17-10 published in 1942 states: 'The conditions which should exist or be created for their (Tanks) successful action are air superiority in the decisive area of employment, surprise, favourable terrain, and absence of or neutralization of massed defensive means'. The massed defensive means against tanks have been acknowledged in 1942. Tanks have continued to prevail with counter technologies and adaptive tactics. Balanced survivability is a concept that entails technologies and tactics blending together. This entails that the tank must not to be seen, if seen must not be hit and if hit must not be destroyed.[13] Tanks are evolving. In the Ukraine War the bulk of the tanks that were destroyed by anti-tank systems were of the 1970's vintage, namely the T-62 and the T-72. The Armata, Leopard and the Abrams are still to arrive at this battlefield. Armour has to be employed with modern technology, innovative tactics, superior training and bold leadership with the concept of an all-arms integrated operations. The tank and the tank crew have the basic character to prevail over such challenges and perform way beyond expectations; they are both built and trained in this character and tend to live up to it. Adaptation to changing challenges is one of the hallmarks of armour (see the cope cages built by Russians on turrets of tanks to attenuate top attack anti-tank warheads). Generals of all armies will continue to choose tanks as one part of their élite offensive forces and politicians and diplomats will continue to negotiate from the power that flows out of its guns. It will remain the first choice of a physical and psychological manoeuvre. The tank will provide credence to the other modes and domains of war. Deterrence and the battle in the grey zone will be fought with the pretext that one has a tank fleet to precipitate the fear of violence.

Armoured warfare is re-inventing itself. Schools of armoured warfare of leading armies are huddled in discussions to invent new technologies and tactics to increase the effectiveness of armour. The tank is no longer a weapon system of open plains, its employment in built up towns and cities as well as in jungles and forest lands (employment of the Terminator in the Serebryanka forest in Luhansk Oblast) has been verified in the current Ukraine War. The employment of tanks at an altitude above 12,000 ft in Ladakh[14] in the boundary clash between India and China in 2021 has not only proved to be a military success but a political and diplomatic victory where bargaining could be done from strength as well. One factor of our diplomatic strength in Ladakh could be attributed to us fielding our main battle tank (T-90) against China's light tank. The tank has adapted to the new centres of gravity of operational battles into towns, forests and high-altitude areas with the operational concepts of the adaptive manoeuvre and the meat grinder. The key to success of tanks is its integration with artillery, infantry and informational systems in the battlefield. Network centric warfare is the future of armoured warfare. The idea is not to make the tank invincible but to accept a finite degree of casualties in order to achieve the military aim.

Sun Tzu, in his *The Art of War*, says, 'Strategy without tactics is the slowest route to victory. Tactics without strategy is the noise before defeat.' It was the Russian tactics that can be faulted in failure of mechanised warfare. Tanks have to be employed in numbers that are above a critical mass, which has to be substantially higher than the adversary's to win a decisive battle. Russians have adopted the Battalion Tactical Group (BTG) formation, which inherently divides the concentration of armour. The concept of operating in small teams is gaining ground in the present generalship of most armies, including our own. This is about 'thinking big and fighting small'. We have downsized our armoured formations to brigade size groups; such a concept may produce tactical results but would fall short at a strategic level at the battle of the centre of gravity where concentration and centralised control is the battle winning factor. Generals who have the heart and acumen to command large forces and the stomach for casualties will achieve strategic victories. In the Ukraine War the strategy of 'meat grinder' is gaining ground in towns, whereas small strategic manoeuvres are also seen to isolate large towns and tactically trap enemy forces. In both strategies, armoured formations play an important role.

The next area of study in armoured warfare is operational art. Understanding and creating a new geometry of the modern battlefield is the challenge for armoured warfare. A war is no longer two dimensional. Systems such as long-range artillery, drones and electronic warfare can defeat anti-tank weapons before the tank appears on the battlefield at the right time and the right place. The sequencing of tactical plans into the strategic plan is operational art. All systems of support, time and space have to be integrated in an art form to derive the magnificence of the tank. In a fiercely contested battle, the side with better operational art will win the day. The requirement is intense training and education of commanders to enable them to devise new tactics and battle procedures to defeat the dominance of anti-tank weapons. The experience in Ukraine will surely invigorate the Rommels and Guderians of today to revolutionise the employment of armour. The tank in the hands of an accomplished commander can be a formidable weapon. Commanders determine the success or failure through the decisions they make, the actions they inspire and their will to win, the tank is but a tool in their hands.

## Philosophies of Employment

There is a marked difference in the employment of armoured forces in battle between the West and the Russians. Russians believe in massed employment of tanks and rely on numbers and lethality rather than accuracy. Their tanks are smaller, lighter (45 tons) with lower levels of protection but make it up by fielding large numbers in battle, which evolved the concept of 10 guns to one target. Using large numbers increase the number of casualties, and this is what has happened in the initial phase in the Ukraine War. The Russians cater for high casualties in their operational concept. The Western countries, on the other hand, believe in accuracy and survivability. Their tanks are larger, heavier (60 tons) with very high accuracy and lethality, working on the concept of one gun one target. The number of tanks the Western countries can field is relatively far lower than the Russians and thus every casualty hurts their capability. The Indian Armoured Corps has the unique distinction of fielding Russian tanks but using the Western philosophy of employment. This is very apparent when we designed our own tank (Arjun). This has turned out to be 60 tons with a more accurate gun than the best tank in the world, but we find it difficult to integrate it with our offensive formations due to strategic mobility and hence the Arjun tank has been relegated to obscure defensive formations.

## Nuclear Warfare Environment

The strongest argument of the importance of the tank and armoured operations is its survivability in a nuclear war environment. The modern tank is the only offensive weapon system that is capable of fighting during a tactical nuclear exchange; it can even fight through the aftermath, isolated from nuclear fallout. The tank can survive a nuclear blast if it is on the periphery of ground zero. This capability is vital for any armed forces of the future. An attack by tactical nuclear weapons is a distinct possibility in the present and in the future. The threat is alive in the current Ukraine War. It is prevalent in our sub-continent. The only weapon system that can survive a nuclear blast and still carry out its operational mission is the tank. The tank's capability of surviving a chemical, biological and nuclear environment will make it the number one choice of weapon system of all strategists. This capability has potential of employment in extrication of forces from contaminated areas as also in nuclear disasters in the civilian domain. If there is a potent threat of nuclear war, then it becomes imperative that the country should have a potent armoured force. The tank provides a deterrence force for nuclear blackmail and nuclear terrorism as it can survive a nuclear attack and launch a counter.

## THE INDIAN WAY OF WAR FIGHTING

The Indian military is still evolving its war fighting philosophy. The lack of integration and dispersion in command between its Air Force, Navy and the Army precludes a common war fighting philosophy in India. Western military experts conclude this factor to be paramount in India's inability to fight a large war campaign in an integrated theatre. The Army fights its own battle on the ground. Within the Army there is a fair amount of integration of arms, but not enough. The terrain of our battlefields range from high-altitude, mountains to plains to deserts, which determines which arm becomes the lead arm in an operation. The plains sector is still considered to be the area where the decisive battle will be fought and where conventional deterrence has been developed. This makes the tank an important weapon system of the Indian Army. Many Indian generals have spoken of the demise of the tank in their commentary but do not give an alternate. It becomes important to carefully examine the propaganda and the truth of the information of tank battles in Ukraine because India fields 90 per cent tanks of Russian origin. There is danger of crews losing confidence purely due to propaganda. This is why comments of analysts in India can have extreme consequences.

India has the experience of fighting with tanks in the 1965 and 1971 wars. The Ukraine War gives more insight for the future tank battle. The Indian Army is already engaged in re-inventing its armour force. Some suggested lines of study are:

(a) Develop strong tactics to degrade and overwhelm the anti-tank systems. The superiority of tanks in the next war will only be in the context of the absence of anti-tank weapons. How to achieve this condition is the challenge.

(b) Work on innovative methods to increase protection of tanks. There is no end to innovative ideas at the unit level to increase protection. As a simple way of innovation we used sandbags during Op Parakram to improve protection from the top. The Defence Research and Development Organisation (DRDO) should be tasked with this study on a long-term basis.

(c) Improve on the tank technology of the T-90 and Arjun tank. Producing a light tank is not a very good idea given the lethality of infantry hand held anti tank weapons despite it having power logistic requirement. There is no limit to technology. There must be a clear distinction between technologies, which are either purely motivated by financial gain or which are needed by crews in battle conditions. The crews must demand technologies that suit them.

(d) The awareness of crews on the battlefield is one of the most important factors in survivability and effectiveness. The two systems that provide awareness to the crews are reconnaissance and battlefield management systems. Awareness of both commanders and the crews will enable the precise employment of the tank with superior tactics. In this context it is important that tanks are well supported by integrated reconnaissance elements that forewarn and inform while battlefield management systems assist commanders to make quick and precise decisions.

(e) Work towards integration with air assets such as attack helicopters and ground attack aircraft. The Army must demand of the Air Force to acquire ground attack aircraft (type of A 10 or the like) to have an intimate integration to produce quick and decisive results on the ground. Air superiority fighters should be employed to facilitate the use of such ground attack aircraft.

(f) Focus on the training of crews and commanders, which is always an ongoing process. It is important to develop the feeling of elite superiority with a balanced aggressive attitude amongst the commanders of armoured formations. Crews and commanders must constantly improve upon their tactics, techniques and procedures.

(a) Institute regular study groups involving academia, veterans and service personnel to evolve and modernise tank tactics and strategy.

## CONCLUSION

War is a necessary evil and its very nature is violence and destruction. There is a thought that war can be fought from a distance, guided and controlled from safe bunkers by technicians using computers but in the end someone will come visiting this bunker with a weapon in hand. The last stage of war, no matter how it is configured, will be a violent decisive contact battle with a chilling number of casualties. The commander will have to choose his weapons for this battle based on the circumstances and the terrain as his survival and the survival of his clan depends on it.

*"Zelensky demands 500 tanks from NATO"*[15]

## NOTES

1 Professor Alex Danchev,'Liddell Hart and Manoeuvre,'*The RUSI Journal*, 143(6), 1998, pp. 33–5, DOI: 10.1080/03071849808446325

2 William SLind, KeithNightengale, John F.Schmitt, Joseph W.Sutton and Gary I. Wilson,'The Changing Face of War: Into the Fourth Generation,' Marine Corps Gazette, October 1989, pp. 22–6.

3 Raj Shukla, "Future of Warfare in the Changing Technological Context: An Indian Military Perspective", in RP Rajagopalan (ed.),*Global Policy, Future Warfare and Technology: Issues and Strategies*, ORF, New Delhi, 2022, p 61.

4 Ibid, p. 61.

5 Holly Ellyatt, 'How Ukraine's Mud Became a Secret Weapon in Its Defense Against Russia,'*Europe News*, April 21, 2022.

6 Daniel Michaels, 'The Secret of Ukraine's Military Success: Years of NATO Training,'*Wall Street Journal*, April 13, 2022.

7 Oryx Blog, "Attack on Europe: Documenting Russian Equipment Losses During the 2022 Russian Invasion of Ukraine" at https://www.oryxspioenkop.com/2022/02/attack-on-europe-documenting-equipment.html. Accessed on 18 Dec 2023

8 Rob Lee, "The Tank Is Not Obsolete, and Other Observations About the Future Of Combat", War on The Rocks, September 6, 2022, at https://warontherocks.com/2022/09/the-tank-is-not-obsolete-and-other-observations-about-the-future-of-combat/ Accessed on 18 Dec 2023

9 Natalie Croker, Byron Manley and Tim Lister,"The turning points in Russia's invasion of Ukraine", *CNN*September 30, 2022.

10 FM 3-0 Operations, Department of the Army, United States of America, October 2022, p. 2.3.

11 "Aboli Dhawade asked: What is Grey Zone Warfare?"at https://idsa.in/askanexpert/what-is-grey-zone-warfare. Accessed on 19 Dec 2023

12 FM 3-0 Operations, Department of the Army, United States of America, October 2022.

13 Lt Gen AB Shivane PVSM AVSM VSM (Retd), 'Eleven Big Lessons for the Employment of Tanks in Future Battle space: The Russia–Ukraine Conflict,'*Centre for Land Warfare Studies*, April 29, 2022.

14 B S Dhanoa, 'Why Ladakh needs Tanks,' Observer Research Foundation, 22July 2020, at https://www.orfonline.org/expert-speak/why-ladakh-needs-tanks/. Accessed on 17 Dec 2023

15 'Zelensky: Ukraine needs 300–500 tanks,'*The Kyiv Independent*, March 18, 2023.

# 5

# Impact of Artillery, Precision-Guided Munitions (PGMs) and Missiles

*Deepak Kumar*

## INTRODUCTION

An overwhelming employment of artillery, rockets and missiles has been the most decisive feature of the ongoing Russia–Ukraine conflict. Their foreboding threat has influenced strategic calculations and prompted caution in the military decision-making process. In the Tactical Battle Area (TBA), mechanised forces are hesitant in making bold advances. The devastation caused by artillery guns, rocket and land missile forces in the contact and depth battles have impacted their roles. Washington Post has reported that 'the war has seen relatively few infantry engagements or tank-on-tank battles; Russia, rather, is concentrating overwhelming artillery power on relatively small areas to blast its way forward in a path of grave destruction'.[1] Tanks and aircraft are forced to incorporate countermeasures and mitigation tactics in order to adapt to the threat landscape of artillery and missiles. In the operational depth, rockets and missiles have carried out 'shaping' operations by engaging logistics and command & control (C2) centres, troop concentrations, airfields and supply routes. Artillery and missile fires have resulted in widespread damage to cities and towns. Such 'non-contact' strikes have targeted the adversary's ability to project force and hinder offensive capabilities. This article delves into the impact of artillery, Precision-Guided Munitions (PGMs) and ground launched ballistic missiles in the Russia–Ukraine conflict, highlighting the strategic advantage they provide, their role in offensive and defensive operations and the implications for the overall trajectory of the war.

## CONCEPTUAL ISSUES

The Russian Army doctrine emphasises generating 'mass' through overwhelming use of firepower.[2] The design of military operations of Russia is centred around employing massed artillery to saturate the adversary, disrupt enemy formations, inflict casualties, cover defensive voids and restrict attempts for reinforcements and counterattacks. Suffice to mention, artillery and missile forces, the main proponents of firepower, are regarded as a combat arm in the Russian Army. The Russian warfighting doctrine is that of surrounding the enemy by mechanised forces and calling in massed artillery fire to destroy the surrounded forces.[3] The United Kingdom (UK) think-tank Royal United Services Institute (RUSI), calls the Russian Army as 'an artillery army with a lot of tanks'.[4] Dave Johnson, a RAND researcher had this to say, 'This is what the Russians do: they just hunker down, they conquer with Artillery, and they occupy with infantry'.[5]

## EMPLOYMENT OF ARTILLERY BY RUSSIA

### Sub-optimal Application of Fire

The Russia–Ukraine conflict appears to have begun in a copybook style with deliberate preparatory fires. Russia attempted to carry out the stated aim of 'demilitarisation' of Ukraine through systematic destruction. Massed guns, missiles and rocket strikes were ranged on Ukraine's military bases and North Atlantic Treaty Organisation (NATO) training areas. The destruction of the Ukrainian defence industry was done by engaging ammunition, fuel and logistics dumps in depth. On the 'Kiev' front, Russia's failed 'blitzkrieg' type attempt to capture 'Kiev', some reports suggest, was due to the inability of artillery to provide effective massed fire in time and close fires in space. Unarguably, Russians employed their artillery less than optimally?[6]

### Relapse to Attritional Fire Doctrine

After the attempt to capture Kyiv failed in February–March 2022, Russians reverted to their 'doctrinal template' of an artillery-oriented attrition warfare commencing April 2022. This entailed pummelling with the longest range, heaviest artillery available in Eastern Ukraine. Due to dominating Russian artillery fires and the resulting destruction, Ukraine had lost control over strategically important cities of Severodonetsk and Lyschansk by June 2022. While Russia, aided by massive attritional artillery fire, could expand control over territories in Crimea and Donbass regions, Ukraine due to resulting losses in men and resources found itself hampered to concentrate or launch counterattacks.

In the current phase of conflict, artillery barrages and missile strikes are being employed by Russia as part of 'encirclement' operations.[7] This was seen in the Battle of Severo–Donetsk and recently in the Battle of Bakhmut. This type of operation involves denying ingress/egress to an enemy trapped or fixed by mechanised forces through the use of artillery. The infantry is used as screens to protect artillery gun areas, act as observers or spotters and mop up the surviving enemy after an artillery barrage.

## EMPLOYMENT OF ARTILLERY BY UKRAINE

Ukraine in contrast, fought with available artillery, majority of them 122 mm and 152 mm calibres of ex-Soviet vintage in the initial phases. The response was barely effective, and the Ukraine artillery found itself outranged and outnumbered, resulting in ceding major territorial gains in Eastern Ukraine and the Donbass region in particular. An important reason for Ukraine's dismal performance of artillery was its low numbers. To stave off the artillery asymmetry, the United States (US) and NATO sent modern artillery weapons but in limited numbers. These included France's CAESAR, 155 mm self-propelled howitzer (Range 46 km), M777 155 mm howitzers (40 km), British M119A3 towed light gun (17 km), German Panzerhaubite 2000 SP howitzers and High Mobility Artillery Rocket Systems (HIMARS).[8] Ukraine's artillery doctrine began to shift on the lines of Western armies, which centres on generating 'mass' through 'manoeuvre' and 'precision fires'. The introduction of Western artillery equipment and ammunition have provided Ukraine with a much-needed technological edge and has been successful in stalling further Russian gains. The unrelenting shelling of key Ukrainian cities witnessed in the early stages of the conflict through long range rockets and missiles has ebbed considerably due to Ukraine's capability to counter and target Russian depth areas.

## EMPLOYMENT OF MULTIPLE LAUNCH ROCKET SYSTEMS (MLRS)

Grad BM-21 'Hail' is the most widely used rocket artillery system by both sides. An upgraded version of BM-21 was introduced as the 9K51M Tornado-G system by Russia in 2014. The 'Tornado' is equipped with automated fire control and GLONASS navigation system. Ukraine also has a derivative version of the BM-21, introduced in 2014 and known as the RM-70, originally developed to meet the requirements of the then Czechoslovak Army. BM-27 'Uragan' is another system in service with both Russia and Ukraine. It has a larger 220 mm calibre rocket with a greater payload and range. A third similar system in service with both armies is the BM-30 'Smerch', having 300 mm rockets.

Ukraine has employed the British M270, American HIMARS and German MARS II rocket launchers, which it received in 2022.[9] These precision long range rocket systems with accuracies of around 10 m have been widely regarded as being instrumental in slowing down Russian operations. During the counteroffensives in Kharkiv and Kherson oblasts, Ukraine successfully engaged Russian air defence and electronic warfare systems with HIMARS rockets. Precision rocket fires forced Russia to relocate vital military equipment beyond the HIMARS range of 50 km. Ukraine has since asked the United States (US) for the 300 km range Army Tactical Missile Systems (ATACMS), which too can be fired from HIMARS. The reason Ukraine wants to procure this missile is because of its range. The US did not acquiesce to Ukraine's request for ATACMS for a long time. It had instead provided Ukraine with Guided Multiple Launch Rocket System (GMLRS) rockets in June 2022,[10] which are compatible with M270 and HIMARS and could hit targets up to 70 km. In September 2023, the United States eventually yielded and provided Ukraine with the 150 kms range version of ATACMS.[11] This newly acquired capability is likely to alter the dynamics of the battlefield to an extent. Russian commanders may have to reconsider their force posturing and relocate high-value targets out of ATACMS range. The precision of the ATACMS is likely to pose a challenge for Russian air defence systems to intercept Ukrainian strikes as ATACMS was originally designed to destroy enemy surface-to-air missile defence weapons by blanketing them with hundreds of individual bomblets.[12] With this newly acquired capability, Ukraine can target Russian air defence systems deployed to protect the Russian army in southern and eastern Ukraine. Ukrainian forces may also aim to target army maintenance sites and weapons storage facilities, forcing Russian army to relocate these high-value targets further away from the front lines. The Russian military relies heavily on helicopters to counter Ukraine's offensive operations and prevent breakthroughs. The freedom of action of Russian attack helicopters could be affected with the arrival of ATACMS. To illustrate the effectiveness of its new found capabilities, Ukraine launched strikes with ATACMS on two Russian airfields located in Berdyansk and Luhansk as part of 'Operation Dragonfly'.[13] According to Ukrainian Special Operations Forces, the attacks caused substantial damage to Russian military assets and infrastructure including helicopters, an ammunition depot, and an air defence launcher.[14] It must however be mentioned that the cluster munition version of ATACMS provided by the United States in limited numbers to Ukraine are not capable of decisively changing the dynamics of the war. To effectively target major logistics links and fortified command posts, Ukraine would require the single warhead longer range version of the ATACMS and in much greater numbers.

## EMPLOYMENT OF BALLISTIC MISSILES

Russia reportedly launched some 100 missiles from land and sea on the first day of the conflict.[15] This includes rockets, surface-to-air missiles, cruise missiles and short- and medium-range ballistic missiles. According to Reuters, on October 10, 2022, several missiles struck junctions, parks and popular tourist destinations in Kyiv, the country's capital. 'The barrage of dozens of cruise missiles fired from air, land and sea was the biggest wave of air strikes to hit away from the front line, at least since the initial volleys on the war's first day, February 24'.[16]

Russia has mostly used the less sophisticated Tochka (NATO name SS-21 Scrab) Tochka-U (upgraded Tochka) and Kh-22, an anti-ship missile against ground targets. This seems to indicate a low availability of precision missiles. Tochka is a Short-Range Ballistic Missile (SRBM) that has a range of 70 km and is capable of carrying chemical, nuclear or conventional warheads. Tochka-U has a range of 75 km and can carry a 100-kiloton nuclear warhead or a 1,000-pound high-explosive bomb. It is fired from a mobile launcher and has an accuracy of 100 m.

Iskander-M (NATO name, SS-26 Stone) is another missile used by Russia. The 500 km short-range missile is the main in-service SRBM of Russia. It was first used in combat in 2008 during the Georgia conflict. It is designed to bypass missile defences by flying at a low trajectory and manoeuvring in flight. With an accuracy of 2–5 meters, Iskander-M is capable of carrying high explosive warheads of 1,000–1,500 pounds. It can also carry thermobaric, fragmentation, nuclear and penetration warheads. According to some analysts, the much-publicised Kh-47M2 'Kinzhal' hypersonic missile is the air-launched version of Iskander-M missile. Russian SRBM attacks have targeted Western armament supplies, making it difficult for the Ukrainian Air Force to use airfields for operations.[17] These missile strikes have been accurate, as is evident from the damage observed at airports and other targeted locations. It points to the use of precision-guided missiles; Russia was not known in the past to use precision-guided missiles, unlike the US. There have been missile strikes on Ukrainian air bases and depth areas using Kailbr missiles, which is indicative of engagement of strategic military assets and to convey a message that conventional missiles can be successfully used below the nuclear threshold. The subsonic 3M14 Kalibr (NATO name, SS-N-30A), has a 450-kg payload and 1,500–2,500 km range.

## EMPLOYMENT OF PRECISION-GUIDED MUNITIONS (PGMS)

Precision-guided munitions utilise advance guidance systems, including Global Positioning System (GPS), laser or radar guidance, to achieve high precision and minimise collateral damage. On the tactical battlefield, guided artillery ammunitions have been used to target vulnerable points on tanks, such as turret rings and engine compartments. Russians have tended to use more of standard artillery ammunition compared to PGMs. The rationale is that massed artillery can saturate the area, suppress the enemy and is more effective when enemy location is not known. It is also more economical compared to PGMs.

Ukraine on the other hand has used PGMs in larger measure. A crucial component of Ukraine's precision-guided artillery munition arsenal is the M982 Excalibur rounds. These rounds, supplied by the US, are equipped with GPS guidance systems, allowing for precise targeting of enemy positions by guns such as M-777 155 mm howitzers and other 155 mm artillery weapons supplied by Western allies. With a range of 40 km, the Excalibur rounds have been highly effective in accurately hitting Russian targets such as tanks, armoured vehicles and artillery positions. This capability has significantly levelled the playing field for Ukraine. Additionally, Ukraine has acquired BONUS and SMArt 155 rounds. These have infrared-seeking submunitions that are attached to small chutes. On being fired, they look for infrared signatures of armoured vehicles. When a vehicle is spotted, the submunition fires a shaped charge on the target.

So far as rocket artillery is concerned, the ability to execute precision fires by rocket artillery has been a redeeming feature of the conflict considering MLRS are traditionally designed as area weapons with high dispersion at the target area. One of the most revered rocket systems, as discussed earlier, has been the HIMARS. By employing laser designators, Ukrainian forces could paint targets for the rockets, enabling accurate strikes on otherwise inaccessible enemy assets.

## DIFFERENCES IN APPROACH FROM PREVIOUS WARS

### Spinoffs of Modern Artillery

The arrival of advanced artillery systems from Western allies provided Ukraine with the means to level the playing field. The Western systems are modern, quicker to fire and are more lethal. They use advanced tactical computers, are better at counter-battery fire, easier to repair due to modular parts that can be replaced in field rather than wait for repairs and are straightforward to use. The precision and effectiveness of these systems provided Ukraine with means to inflict heavy casualties on Russian forces and disrupt their logistical capabilities and supply lines in the deep battle. At the tactical level, Ukraine was able to innovatively apply the firepower of sophisticated and agile Western systems in what is now being referred to as 'firepower ambush' and 'track and kill' operations.[18]

## Asymmetricity of Resources

Russia in pure numerical terms does not have any significant superiority in combat manpower, considering it has not officially called out any mobilisation. However, it does have a numerically superior artillery compared to Ukraine and a significantly many times larger rocket artillery and ballistic missiles force. This has been advantageous in generating a larger volume of artillery and missile fires in order to capture important objectives. The delivery of massive volumes of artillery has been made possible because of its large ammunition holdings at the divisional and brigade level. Ukraine, on the other hand, despite a small artillery is struggling to provide ammunition for its ex-Soviet 152 mm artillery shells.

## Grouping and Control of Artillery

The performance of Russian Battalion Tactical Groups (BTGs) has come under the microscope. It was believed before the conflict commenced that Russia had organised and integrated up to three artillery batteries into each of the BTGs for a more intimate and responsive fire. On the ground, however, several BTGs only had older short-range mortars and howitzers. Most of the brigade and divisional artillery resources were retained centrally. This often led to delays and inaccurate appreciation of firepower requirements and delivery. The Russian artillery under many BTGs was saddled with poor communications, resulting in getting out of contact with manoeuvre forces at critical times. On several occasions, BTG artillery units had to resort to using commercial mobile phones, giving away their locations and inviting counter artillery fire. According to many military analysts, the Russian artillery operated independently and not in close support of manoeuvre forces, leading to delays in supporting fire missions.[19]

## Role of UAVs and Drones in Extending Artillery Effects

Unmanned aerial vehicles (UAVs) and drones have played a prominent role in the current conflict compared to earlier wars. In several battles in Kherson and

Kharkhiv, long-range artillery rockets were integrated with UAVs to observe and direct fires and provide real-time damage assessment. Small hand-held drones made available to artillery units have changed the operational tempo of artillery, shortening time-critical targeting and firing cycles from about half an hour to 3–5 minutes.[20]

The Western armies follow a 'Reconnaissance Fire Complex' concept. In this, drones are cued with dedicated firepower resources, fire direction and a battlefield management centre to execute swift and time critical missions. As the conflict continues, both countries have employed commercial drones as 'artillery spotters.' They operate together with artillery batteries, sometimes with even 1–2 guns to deliver fires. Ukrainian commanders are reported to have said that 'the "Sea Eagle" Orlan 10 UAV has directed many of the up to 20,000 artillery shells that Russia has fired daily on Ukrainian positions in 2022, killing up to 100 soldiers per day."[21] Russians have used laser designators fitted in the larger Orlan-30 drones to guide Krasnopol precision rounds.[22]

## Force Multiplier Role of PGM's

In earlier wars, artillery barrages were employed, which were less accurate and caused collateral damage. HIMARS has proven to be a game changer in this regard. The rockets' precision is due to an inertial navigation system, comprising gyroscopes and accelerometers, that provides precise location information to the rockets, enabling striking accuracy within just a few meters. Their effectiveness is enhanced due to advanced Intelligence, Surveillance and Reconnaissance (ISR) capabilities of Ukraine to acquire targeting data and in the software to process and transmit the data quickly. Due to precision targeting, the number of rockets needed for successful engagements reduced. This was critical, considering the challenges faced by the West in meeting Ukraine's requirements for ammunition.

## Exploiting Shoot and Scoot Capabilities of Mounted Systems

Alongside improved accuracy, the rockets' artillery systems on both sides are mounted on a wheeled or tracked chassis, thus can relocate quickly after firing and thereby avoid counter-battery fires or attempts to locate them. This has significantly improved their survivability. The 'shoot and scoot' capabilities of mounted guns and MRLS integrated with drones, radars and targeting technology have enabled a tactical shift by both sides to carry out effective Counter-artillery Battery (CB) operations.

## INNOVATIVE PRACTICES

### Development of Advanced Software Tools

Ukraine has developed an application software named Geographic Information System of Artillery (GIS Arta), which functions like the cab ride sharing application 'Uber'. The application collects battlefield intelligence and creates targeting information in a bottom-up manner much similar to a cab ride sharing application. UAVs, drones, reconnaissance parties, forward observers can share enemy locations in real time through a number of devices available to a Ukrainian soldier in an encrypted multi-band network using satellite, internet and radio as the media. The data is corroborated at the operations centre and fire orders are given to an appropriate resource in range. The uniqueness of the application is that it can be interfaced even to an individual smartphone, which means that the fire orders can be given to any resource in range and even multiple resources. According to reports, many Ukrainian citizens were given this application to report the locations of Russian troops in real time. Targeting information was transmitted over mobile networks and shared with artillery systems through applications such as Google Meet. In this manner, citizens could share the location of targets. The different artillery batteries or any other fire delivery means in range in turn would each receive their individual extrapolated targeting data in real time from the operations centre. Ukrainian operators have also collaborated with US analysts stationed in Europe to obtain targeting data from satellites and other assets.[23]

### Modifications to Enhance Accuracy

Both sides have carried out modifications to enhance the accuracies of conventional artillery shells through the use of digital maps and drones.[24] Ukraine has used small commercial drones, such as Leleka-100 and Spectator-M, for artillery observation and an inexpensive tablet computer running the 'Nettle' system,[25] to adjust fire. In March 2022, Oleksiy Arestovych, adviser to the office of President Volodymyr Zelensky, in a media briefing mentioned that, 'a standard platoon defensive position took normally took 60–90 artillery rounds to destroy, but with drone-guided fire this was reduced to just 9 rounds, and that drones had been supplied to all artillery units'.[26] Another innovation made by Ukrainian gunners has been that of fitting laser designators on commercial quadcopters to illuminate targets. Kvitnyk PGMs were fired by 155 mm self-propelled howitzers with a common fuse setting as the laser beam to ride the 'designated' beam and destroy the target.[27]

### Use of Asymmetric Tactics

Ukraine has employed 'asymmetric' tactics to counter Russian artillery. Specially trained artillery and special forces observers have been reported to sneak in close to Russian units and guide armed drones and fires of long-range Western systems such as HIMARS rockets. Likewise, Russia has been known to employ the Wagner Group and Private Military Companies (PMCs) in conjunction with their armed forces to direct artillery fires.[28]

### Exploiting Artificial Intelligence

The conflict has been a testing ground for emerging technologies such as Artificial Intelligence (AI). For instance, an automated guidance and fire control system has been installed in the Russian Msta-SM 2S19M2 howitzers so that each combat vehicle can communicate with the battalion and battery command posts. In order to effectively employ firepower and coordinate attacks of all the active vehicles on the battlefield, AI is being used to transmit information about each shot fired by individual combat vehicles.[29] Likewise, an AI-enabled acoustic monitor is being used by Ukraine to detect missiles by evaluating acoustic signals. Developed by a startup named Zvook, it operates as a network of multiple devices. Zvook's sensors can pinpoint the object's speed and direction, enabling defenders to intercept accurately and effectively.[30]

## TAKEAWAYS FOR INDIA

(a) Static frontiers and improved ISR till the lowest levels have exposed the vulnerabilities of infantry and armour to lead assaults. Attack by artillery followed by mopping up by armour and infantry will become the new normal. Artillery, missiles and rockets will become the instruments of orchestrating strategic and operational fires as fighter aircraft will find difficulty in operations due to modern air defence capabilities, UAVs and drones. The Russia–Ukraine conflict has reignited the debate on the offensive capabilities of artillery. India needs to take a *de novo* look at having a commensurate doctrine for artillery and shift the status of its artillery to that of a combat arm.

(b) The Ukraine conflict makes a case for artillery's modernisation priorities, especially the focus on long-range fires after it has become obvious that Ukraine's artillery had been outranged by Russians. The arrival of artillery weapons such as HIMARS from Western allies turned the tide in many ways for Ukraine. It is imperative for India to consider the aspect of Long-

Range Precision Fires (LRPF), extended-range gun systems and Precision Strike Missile (PrSM) capabilities. India meanwhile must continue strengthening and modernising its artillery capabilities through procurement of modern artillery systems such as M-777 and K9 self-propelled howitzers and the development of indigenous systems such as Advanced Towed Artillery Guns (ATAGs) and Dhanush. Mobility is another issue for artillery fire systems. The proliferation of ISR capabilities: drones, manned aerial platforms and low-cost space systems have created vulnerabilities for sluggish moving towed systems. The survivability of towed artillery systems in modern warfare amidst integrated counter batter fire systems is difficult. Ukraine has received a number of truck-mounted howitzers from Western countries, which it has employed successfully. France, UK and Israel have invested in truck-mounted 155 mm howitzers. These systems have the ability to rapidly deploy, execute a fire mission and then redeploy. There exists a case for having a greater share of mounted guns in our inventory vis-a-vis towed guns.

(c) The effectiveness of artillery is enhanced when PGMs are utilised. Both Russia and Ukraine have employed large numbers of precision and unguided projectiles in the conflict. Russian massed artillery barrages expended enormous quantities of ammunition to degrade Ukrainian targets, while NATO's HIMARS were able to destroy Russian ammunition dumps and command posts with minimal ammunition expenditures. The cost of a PGM is a few hundred times that of a conventional artillery shell. This leads to the question of identifying the appropriate balance between holding of precision and conventional ammunition. With modern-day ISR and Battlefield Transparency (BFT) available to commanders, even dumb bombs can be 'smartened' to a certain degree. A case exists for development of guidance kits on conventional ammunition to obviate costs. Indian artillery needs to consider this aspect seriously.

(d) Both Ukraine and Russia have faced 'ISR voids' during crucial stages in the absence of a layered and overlapping ISR grid. For example, Russia paid the price for not having a successful observation in the initial stages of conflict during the Kiev offensive and the failed attack on Hostomel airport. This would have allowed them to control fires in the depth areas, protect vital grounds and prevent reinforcements. Likewise, in the Kherson offensive in late 2022, Russia could successfully cross the Dnieper River and re-enforce its defensive lines using Nova Khakovka and Antonovskiy bridges and five ferry crossing points. Unobserved artillery rocket strikes on the crossing points by Ukraine was not successful. Had artillery observers been available to Ukraine to direct long-range rocket artillery to strike armour assembly areas before the Dnieper River crossings, Russia would have found it difficult to employ its armour. This reinforces the need for real-time targeting data for artillery and missile systems.

(e) Future conflicts between equal adversaries are unlikely to be short and decisive as was being imagined. These conflicts can end up in a frozen stalemate and become a battle of attrition involving artillery duels. The country that exhausts its resources first may ultimately lose. In the early phases of the conflict, Russian artillery gunners made mistakes in their artillery logistics plans and as a result the artillery ammunition expenditure surpassed the availability and replenishment capabilities. India must be prepared for long-term engagement conflicts and ensure the availability of sufficient artillery resources, including ammunition reserves.

(f) With regard to artillery ammunition, a key aspect to come out of the conflict is of the use of archaic methods of stocking and movement of artillery ammunition. Russia has revealed its vulnerabilities in the World War era dependence on fixed railways to move artillery ammunition. This is in stark comparison to the Western armies, which use trucks, modern highways and palletised ammunition. Another Russian vulnerability with respect to artillery ammunition has been its centralised ammunition dumps at the divisional and brigade level. With the modern BFT resources available, it is difficult to conceal and defend such lucrative targets from precision attacks. Ukraine seems to have copied this playbook by undertaking attack by HIMARS using precision munition on Russian ammunition dumps.

(g) Gun areas present a lucrative target for drones. The conflict has shown how low tech and commercially available drones can be used as a weapon. The security of Russian gun areas was severely undermined by cheap shoulder-fired Ukrainian missiles and drones. Counter drone systems must become an inventory item in gun areas.

(h) The weaponization of the smartphone is a reality now. The conflict has highlighted the importance of open-source intelligence, including social media posts, in gathering information and targeting enemy artillery assets and gun areas. Civilians throughout Ukraine and a hostile population have fed target intelligence data that can be cross-checked with other users or intelligence inputs. Indian artillery must prepare itself for such threats in the future.

(j) An aspect which has not been deliberated enough is the use of AI and data analytics in artillery target acquisition and engagement process. It is possible to analyse and compare large volume of target data obtained from multiple sources including 'legacy' signatures and produce quick actionable target input for use by artillery assets. AI would be able to identify the targets, suggest priority, time, reason and justification for engagement.

(k) A key shortcoming of Western artillery systems has been their inability to sustain long periods of engagements due to serviceability issues. The conflict has shown that in artillery battles, serviceability is an important factor. This aspect should be factored especially for ex-import artillery resources.

(l) Cutting edge commercial technology and startups are force multipliers. The conflict has shown how Ukraine could leverage commercially available technology to develop battlefield systems that the West has taken years and considerable expenses to develop. Ukraine's GIS Arta was able to demonstrate many capabilities of far more expensive systems such as the US's Net Warrior and Joint Battle Command Platform and Germany's ADLER.

(m) The use of low-cost commercial satellites to obtain targeting and battlefield data has been a revelation. Commercial satellite operators such as Capella Space and Black Sky have been reported to provide Ukraine with useful and timely targeting data.[31] When Ukraine encountered jamming and Electronic Warfare (EW) issues, they shifted their artillery computers from encrypted radio to commercial STARLINK GPS of Elon Musk. The Russian COMINT systems could not interfere and jam the new system. A fusion of civil and military minds and resources is an imperative to draw out the best outcomes.

## CONCLUSION

Artillery, missiles and rockets have had a profound impact on tactics and strategy in the ongoing Russia–Ukraine war. The strategic deployment of advanced artillery systems, such as the HIMARS rocket artillery vehicle, has proven to be a game changer for Ukraine. By disrupting Russian operations and weakening their logistical capabilities, Ukraine managed to hold its ground and counter Russian aggression. The ability to deliver precision strikes from a distance provides a significant advantage to those who possess advanced artillery capabilities. From artillery barrages raining destruction upon cities and towns to precision-guided missiles targeting key military infrastructure, their impact can be seen not only on the battle spaces but also on the civilian infrastructure, causing humanitarian situation and geopolitical ramifications. When the armed forces of both countries were slogging for small swaths of territory from static frontlines and their mechanised forces not able to generate operational manoeuvres, artillery on both sides with long-range guns, rockets and missiles orchestrated operational fires to open the battlefield. The US Defense Secretary, Lloyd Austin, has said that 'long-range fires will prove "decisive" in the war'.[32] As the conflict escalated, both sides quickly realised the importance of deploying advanced artillery systems to gain an upper hand on the battlefield. As the conflict continues, the impact of artillery will undoubtedly shape the future of the Russia–Ukraine conflict and influence the strategies and tactics employed by both sides. Their employment will continue to play a pivotal role in shaping the battle space, altering war fighting strategies and influencing military operations.

## NOTES

1 Siobhan O' Grady and others, 'They're in Hell, Hail of Russian Artillery Tests Ukrainian Morale,' at https://www.washingtonpost.com/world/2022/06/04/ukraine-east-artillery-war/ (accessed on June 22, 2023)

2 Lucian Staiano-Daniels, 'Why Russia Keeps Turning to Mass Firepower,' at https://foreignpolicy.com/2022/06/19/why-russia-keeps-turning-to-mass-firepower/(accessed on June 10, 2023)

3 A Primer, 'The Russian Way of Warfare, RAND Corporation, 2017' at https://www.rand.org/pubs/perspectives/PE231.html (accessed on June 25, 2023)

4 Sam Cranny-Evans, 'The Role of Artillery in a War Between Russia and Ukraine,'February 14, 2022 at https://rusi.org/explore-our-research/publications/commentary/role-artillery-war-between-russia-and-ukraine#:~:text=The%20Russian%20army%20has%20been,bear%20against%20an%20opponent%27s%20forces (accessed on May 20, 2023)

5 Lara Seligman and others, 'Outgunned. Outmanned. Outnumbered. Out planned?,' *Politico*, June 16, 2022, at https://www.politico.com/newsletters/national-security-daily/2022/06/16/outgunned-outmanned-outnumbered-outplanned-00040024 (accessed on June 22, 2023)

6 David Axe, 'Russia Has More Artillery Than Ukraine. But Russian Gunners Have A Bad Habit Of Shelling ... Nothing.'Forbes, December 18, 2022, at https://www.forbes.com/sites/davidaxe/2022/12/18/russia-has-more-artillery-than-ukraine-but-russian-gunners-have-a-bad-habit-of-shelling—nothing/?sh=139e6cc2aed7 (accessed on June 22, 2023)

7 Maj Gen (Dr) Mandip Singh, SM, VSM (Retd), 'Russia–Ukrainian War–Artillery ad maximum,'Salute, September 22, 2022 at https://salute.co.in/russia-ukrainian-war-artillery-ad-maximum/ (accessed on June 22, 2023)

8 Reuters, 'Ukraine Gets More U.S., German Rocket Launcher Systems - Minister,'Reuters, August 1, 2022 at https://www.reuters.com/world/ukraine-gets-more-us-german-rocket-launcher-systems-minister-2022-08-01/ (accessed on June 15, 2023)

9 Ibid.

10 https://www.defense.gov/News/Releases/Release/Article/3064556/joint-statement-by-the-united-states-department-of-defense-the-ministry-of-defe/ (accessed on November 11, 2023)

11 Emma Graham-Harrison, "US agrees to send long-range missiles to Ukraine in military boost for Kyiv", The Guardian, September 23, 2023, https://www.theguardian.com/world/2023/sep/23/us-agrees-to-send-long-range-missiles-atacms-to-ukraine-in-military-boost-for-kyiv (accessed on November 11, 2023)

12 Ismay John, "The Missile Ukraine Wants Is One the U.S. Says It Doesn't Need", The New York Times, October 6, 2022, https://www.nytimes.com/2022/10/06/us/ukraine-war-missile.html (accessed on November 11, 2023)

13 Novikov Illia, "Ukraine claims a major strike on Russian airfields and thanks US for providing long-range missiles", AP, October 18, 2023, https://apnews.com/article/russia-ukraine-war-avdiivka-attacks-8b5fd038c7e496dcb8f015b759b74666 (accessed on November 11, 2023)

14 Dysa Yulia, "Ukraine uses US long-range missiles to strike Moscow-occupied territories", Reuters, October 18, 2023, https://www.reuters.com/world/europe/ukraine-says-it-strikes-russias-military-equipment-near-luhansk-2023-10-17/ (accessed on November 11, 2023)

15 Eleanor Watson, 'Russian Assault on Ukraine Included 100 Missiles and 75 Bombers, U.S. Official Says,'CBS News, February 24, 2022 at https://www.cbsnews.com/news/russia-ukraine-100-missiles-75-bombers-us-official/ (accessed on June 25, 2023)

16 Max Hunder and Jonathan Landay, 'Russia Launches Biggest Air Strikes Since Start of Ukraine War,'Reuters, October 11, 2022 at https://www.reuters.com/world/europe/russias-ria-state-agency-reports-fuel-tank-fire-kerch-bridge-crimea-2022-10-08/ (accessed on July 2, 2023)

17 Vijainder K Thakur, 'Russia Bombs Ukraine's MiG-29 Air Base After Striking Its Su-24MR Facility To Cripple Its Counter Offensive,' The EurAsian Times, June 11, 2023 at https://eurasiantimes.com/russia-bombs-ukraines-mig-29-air-base-after-striking-its/ (accessed on July 2, 2023)

18 Lt Gen P R Shankar (R), 'Artillery and Firepower : Lessons from the Ukrainian War-Part 8,' at https://gunnersshot.com/2022/06/11/artillery-and-firepower-part-8-lessons-from-the-ukrainian-war-by-lt-gen-p-r-shankar-r/ (accessed on July 3, 2023)

19 Sebastian Roblin, 'The Secrets of Russia's Artillery War in Ukraine,'Business Insider, July 12, 2022 at https://www.businessinsider.com/how-russia-is-waging-its-war-with-artillery-in-ukraine-2022-7?IR=T (accessed on June 25, 2023)

20 Dominika Kunertova, 'The War in Ukraine Shows the Game-changing Effect of Drones Depends on the Game,' at https://www.tandfonline.com/doi/full/10.1080/00963402.2023.2178180?scroll=top&needAccess=true&role=tab (accessed on July 3, 2023)

21 Stephen Grey and others, 'The Global Supply Trail That Leads to Russia's Killer Drones,'Reuters, December 15, 2022 at https://www.reuters.com/world/europe/global-supply-trail-that-leads-russias-killer-drones-2022-12-15/ (accessed on July 3, 2023)

22 David Axe, 'Russia's High-Tech Artillery System Was Supposed to Win the War In Ukraine. But Troops Didn't Know How to Use It,' Forbes, November 25, 2022 at https://www.forbes.com/sites/davidaxe/2022/11/25/russias-high-tech-artillery-system-was-supposed-to-win-the-war-in-ukraine-but-troops-dont-know-how-to-use-it/?sh=4e99870d56ac (accessed on June 22, 2023)

23 TASS, 'Ukrainian Officials Admit They Rely on US Data for Precision Targeting,' at https://tass.com/world/1574397 (accessed on June 24, 2023)

24 Maj Gen (Dr) Mandip Singh, SM, VSM (Retd), 'Russia–Ukrainian War–Artillery ad maximum,'Salute, September 22, 2022 at https://salute.co.in/russia-ukrainian-war-artillery-ad-maximum/ (accessed on July 3, 2023)

25 Nettle is supplied as a tactical system compatible with NATO-standard secure communications and is used from divisional command down to individual vehicles. It maps battle lines and targets and calculates artillery fire missions. It is specifically designed to work with drones, receiving data and using it to calculate the adjustment needed. The gunner changes angle and azimuth accordingly, and shells land on target.

26 David Hambling, 'How Ukraine's Artillery is Doing More Damage Than Russia's, Even with Fewer Rounds,' Business Insider, April 26, 2023 at https://www.businessinsider.com/ukraine-artillery-does-more-damage-with-fewer-rounds-than-russia-2023-4?IR=T#:~:text=Ukraine%20is%20killing%20more%20by%20fighting%20smarter &text=The%20solution %20to %20this%20paradox,to%20pick%20off%20individual%20targets (accessed on July 3, 2023)

27 Ibid.

28 "Moscow's Mercenary Wars: The Expansion of Russian Private Military Companies, CSIS September 2020 at https://russianpmcs.csis.org (accessed on July 3, 2023)

29 Sharath Kumar Nair, 'A Closer Look at Russia's AI-powered Artillery,'January 26, 2022 at https://analyticsindiamag.com/a-closer-look-at-russias-ai-powered-artillery/ (accessed on July 5, 2023)

30 Ben Wodecki, 'Ukraine War One Year On: How AI Has Shaped the Battlefield,' at https://aibusiness.com/verticals/ukraine-war-one-year-on-how-ai-has-shaped-the-battlefield (accessed on July 5, 2023)

31 'How Commercial Satellites Are Shaping the Ukraine Conflict,' *The Economic Times*, March 5, 2022 at https://economictimes.indiatimes.com/news/international/world-news/how-commercial-satellites-are-shaping-the-ukraine-conflict/articleshow/90001565.cms?from=mdr (accessed on June 29, 2023)

32 Dan Lamothe, 'Western Artillery Surging into Ukraine Will Reshape War with Russia,'The Washington Post, April 30, 2022 at https://www.washingtonpost.com/national-security/2022/04/30/ukraine-russia-artillery/ (accessed on June 22, 2023)

# 6

# Role of Airpower in the Russia–Ukraine Conflict

*Anil Golani and Dinesh Kumar Pandey*

## INTRODUCTION

The conflict between Russia and Ukraine has observed the implementation of diverse military strategies and tactics. The utilisation of airpower has been significant in contemporary warfare, exerting a profound influence on the results of military engagements, including notable instances such as World War II, the Gulf War and diverse counterinsurgency operations. Airpower, an inalienable instrument of national military power, facilitates expeditious mobility, reconnaissance capabilities and the capacity to exert force across extensive distances.

Political and geographical disagreements, notably those involving Crimea and the Donbas area, caused the Russia–Ukraine war. Crimea's annexation by Russia in 2014, followed by the emergence of pro-Russian separatist movements in eastern Ukraine resulted in a military confrontation between the two countries.[1] The Russian Federation and Ukraine have implemented a range of military strategies during the ongoing conflict, encompassing conventional ground operations, asymmetric warfare and the deployment of airpower. The utilisation of airspace, including heliborne and drone operations, is exerting a significant impact on the trajectory and duration of the conflict.

Russia's invasion of Ukraine in the early hours of February 24, 2022, was intended to last just a few days and conclude with the swift seizure of Kyiv. This objective, however, could not be fulfilled as Ukraine successfully repelled Russian forces with an unwavering resolve and abundant physical and moral support, including weapons provided by Western nations. Russia, nevertheless, could occupy the 'Donbas' region of eastern Ukraine with the help of the Wagner Group.

Notwithstanding various warfare shifts, it is imperative to acknowledge that the conflict remains a persistent and unresolved issue. Contrarily, it seems to be evolving into a prolonged, attritional battle that will likely assess the resilience and determination of Ukraine and Western powers.

The utilisation of airpower has emerged as a prominent element within the broader military strategies employed by Russia and Ukraine in the context of the ongoing conflict between the two nations. The proliferation of technological advancements and the widespread accessibility of contemporary aircraft have significantly amplified the potential influence of airpower on resolving disputes.

The Russian Air Force, significantly larger than the Ukrainian Air Force, was underutilised. Moscow may have done this to reduce battle damage and control particular areas. The forces deployed drones, attack helicopters and fixed-wing aircraft. Russia's advanced air force aids its ground soldiers while Ukraine fights Russia. Ukraine shows how airpower and heliborne operations dominate modern conflict.

## THE CONCEPT OF AIRPOWER

Airpower refers to the capacity to employ various aerospace assets, including aircraft and related help such as UAVs, missiles, satellites and other relevant technologies, to achieve strategic, operational and tactical objectives in war. The utilisation of airpower in contemporary warfare is of considerable importance due to its ability to enhance various aspects such as velocity, scope, accuracy, adaptability and promptness across diverse operational contexts.[2] Airpower can serve as a deterrent against acts of aggression, project military strength, aid allied nations, acquire valuable intelligence and facilitate the delivery of humanitarian assistance.[3]

The field of airpower has undergone significant transformation throughout the past century, transitioning from a peripheral and experimental stature to a preeminent and essential one. This technology has significantly transformed the dynamics of warfare through its facilitation of manoeuvrability, tempo, lethality, and network-centric capabilities.[4] Nevertheless, utilising airpower initiates novel obstacles and risks in the contemporary era, including asymmetric warfare, hybrid threats, anti-access/area denial strategies, cyber-attacks and space warfare. Hence, it is imperative for airpower to consistently evolve and foster innovation to uphold its significance and efficacy in forthcoming times.[5]

The mere presence of an inventory of airpower resources is insufficient; effectively utilising these assets is of utmost significance. Exploiting the advantages of strategic deployment and tactical employment may be instrumental in achieving a certain level of air dominance, thereby facilitating the efficient execution of operational missions. The control of airspace additionally enables the establishment of air supremacy, a strategic advantage wherein a particular force possesses absolute dominance over air warfare and airpower vis-à-vis opposing troops, rendering them unable to impede operations effectively.

## Air Superiority

The concept of air superiority entails the establishment of dominion over specific airspace by a particular party, thereby restricting the adversary's capacity to conduct unrestricted operations within the aerial realm. This strategy enables the prevailing force to execute operations with a diminished level of risk, simultaneously impeding the adversary's activities.

Russia possesses a competent air force with state-of-the-art fighter aircraft and advanced Air Defence (AD) systems. The Russian Aerospace Forces, known in Russian as 'Voyenno-Kosmicheskiye Sily (VKS)', effectively employed its air superiority capabilities for a limited period during March 2023 to assert dominance over critical regions and execute strategic bombing operations targeting Ukrainian objectives. The operational presence of the Airborne Warning and Control System (AWACS) and Airborne Early Warning and Control (AEW&C) platforms has been conspicuously scarce. Perhaps the apprehension stemmed from the potentiality of being subjected to firearm-inflicted harm and therefore the scope of fighter strikes was duly curtailed.[6] Two issues have hindered AWACS's (A-50M) effectiveness throughout the battle. The Ukrainian military has found the A-50 easy to weaken electronically and has succeeded. Second, because the Russian air operation is subservient to the Ground Forces, A-50M surveillance information is not usually conveyed directly to Combat Air Patrol (CAP) fighters or long-range Ground-Based Air Defence (GBAD) units such as S-400 batteries.[7] One of the primary reasons for Russia's failure to achieve its objectives is how the war has been fought from the beginning. No combined arms or joint strategy was used to prosecute operations to achieve the desired goal.

Russians believe that the commencement of a significant battle with NATO would include a considerable missile aviation strike, and they must be ready to respond to it.[8] Thus, the VKS employed limited air resources. However, according to a report by the London-based think tank, Royal United Services Institute (RUSI), the involvement of Russia's aviation units in the war has been limited, primarily attributed to their inability to breach Ukrainian ADs effectively. According to military analysts, Russia has thus far been unable to achieve a critical objective that holds significant importance for commanders in war: establishing air superiority.[9]

That said, Ukraine has also encountered difficulties in attaining air superiority due to the presence of a more formidable opponent. Most of the Ukrainian Air Force, or the 'Povitryani Syly Ukrayiny (PSU)' aircraft involved in the conflict, initially operated with onboard systems at least one generation behind the Russian platforms they were tasked with defending against. Nevertheless, the PSU has implemented various strategies to mitigate Russia's prevailing airpower superiority, such as deploying AD systems in collaboration with Western allies and the rapid shoot-and-scoot tactics for shoulder-fired surface-to-air missiles.

The contest for air superiority has exerted a substantial influence on the overall trajectory of the conflict, including having a significant impact on ground operations. The effort to achieve a certain degree of control of air has resulted in the curtailment of Ukraine's military operations and exerted a notable influence on the morale of both Ukrainian and Russian forces.

## AIR FORCE HOLDINGS

Russia possesses a formidable fleet of 4,182 aircraft, starkly contrasting Ukraine's more modest inventory of 312 aircraft. Figure 1 (shown on next page) is a visual representation that elucidates the comparative analysis of the aerial military capabilities possessed by the nations of Russia and Ukraine, specifically for the year 2023. The Ukrainian government currently has a relatively modest fleet of 69 fighter aircraft, which pales compared to the considerably more substantial inventory of 773 fighter aircraft held by the Russian Federation.[10]

### Ukraine's Air Force (PSU)

Ukraine currently maintains the 27th largest air force globally and Europe's 7th largest air force. This is primarily attributed to the effective maintenance of its older aircraft by its domestic defence industry, Ukroboronprom, and its subsidiary, Antonov. The primary fleet of the Air Force continues to predominantly comprise aircraft of Soviet origin. The Ukrainian Air Force and AD forces include 36,300

**Figure 1: Comparison of the Air Forces of Russia and Ukraine**

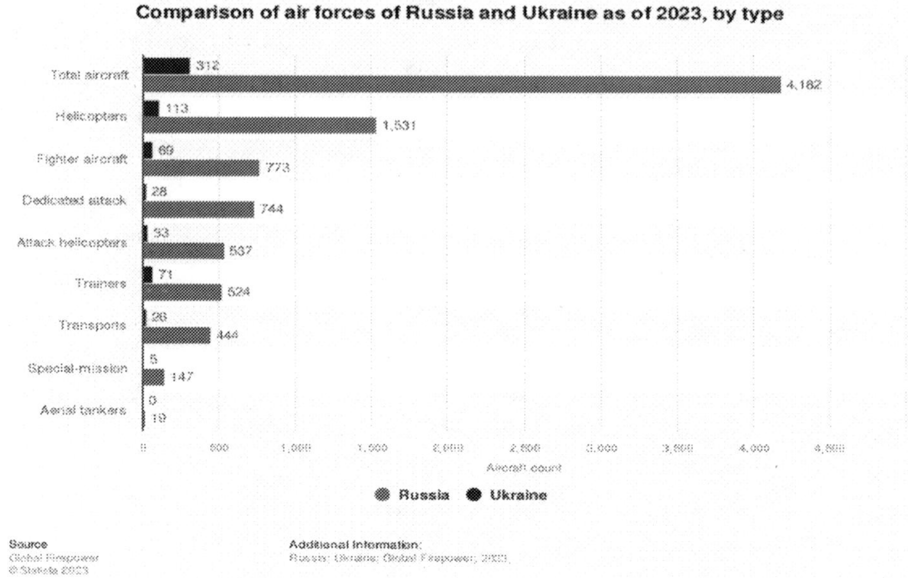


*Source:* Global Firepower, 'Comparison of Air Forces of Russia and Ukraine As Of 2023, By Type,' Statista, February 7, 2023, at https://www.statista.com/statistics/1293414/airpower-of-russia-and-ukraine-in-comparison/ (Accessed July 9, 2023).

personnel.[11] The PSU has the following types of military aircraft: anti-aircraft missile complexes and AD radars.[12]

(a) Multi-purpose fighter MiG-29
(b) Assault Fighters: Su-27, Su-25, Su-24
(c) Front all-weather bomber Su-24MR
(d) Transport aircraft: IL-76MD, An-26, An-24, An-30, Tu-134
(e) Helicopter: Mi-8MT
(f) Training and combat aircraft: L-39
(g) Anti-aircraft missile complexes: C-300PS, C-300PT, Buk-M1, 73H6
(h) Radars: Long-range: Radar-5H84AMA; Medium-Range: P-18M & 35D6M

## Russian Aerospace Forces (VKS)

The Russian Air Force is recognised as the 2nd largest air force globally, boasting a fleet of various aircraft. There are eight bomber squadrons, consisting of four squadrons operating Tu-22M3/MR aircraft, three squadrons operating Tu-95MS aircraft and one squadron operating Tu-160 aircraft. There are a total of 37 fighter squadrons in operation, consisting of eight squadrons equipped with MiG-29 aircraft, three squadrons operating MiG-29SMT, 11 squadrons operating MiG-31 or MiG-31BM, 10 squadrons operating Su-27, four squadrons operating Su-27SM1 or Su-30M2 and one squadron operating Su-27SM3 or Su-30M2.[13]

According to Military Balance-2023, released by the International Institute for Strategic Studies (IISS), the Aerospace Forces aircraft holdings are appended below:[14]

**VKS AIRCRAFT: 1,153 combat-capable**

(a) **BBR 137**:
[60 Tu-22M3 Backfire C; 1 Tu-22MR Backfire† (1 in overhaul); 33 Tu-95MS Bear; 27 Tu-95MS mod Bear; 7 Tu-160 Blackjack; 7 Tu-160 mod Blackjack; 2 Tu-160M Blackjack (in test)]

(b) **FTR 185**: 70 MiG-29/MiG-29UB Fulcrum; 85 MiG-31 BM Foxhound C; 12 Su-27 Flanker B; 18 Su-27UB Flanker C

(c) **FGA 410+:** 15 MiG-29SMT Fulcrum; 2 MiG-29UBT Fulcrum; 6 MiG-35S/UB Fulcrum (in test); 47 Su-27SM Flanker J; 24 Su-27SM3 Flanker; 19 Su-30M2 Flanker G; ε80 Su-30SM Flanker H; ε105 Su-34 Fullback; 7+ Su-34 mod Fullback; 99 Su-35S Flanker M; 6 Su-57 Felon

(d) **ATK 262**: 12 MiG-31K; 70 Su-24M/M2 Fencer; 40 Su-25 Frogfoot; ε125 Su-25SM/SM3 Frogfoot; 15 Su-25UB Frogfoot

(e) **ISR 58**: 4 An-30 Clank; up to 50 Su-24MR Fencer*; 2 Tu214ON; 2 Tu-214R

(f) **EW:** 3 Il-22PP Mute

(g) **ELINT 31**: 14 Il-20M Coot A; 5 Il-22 Coot B; 12 Il-22M Coot B

(h) **AEW&C 10**: 3 A-50 Mainstay; 7 A-50U Mainstay

(i) **C2 8**: 2 Il-80 Maxdome; 1 Il-82; 4 Tu-214SR; 1 Tu-214PU-SBUS

(j) **TKR 15**: 5 Il-78 Midas; 10 Il-78M Midas

(k) **TPT 446**: [Heavy: 125+Med: 65+ Light: 224+Pax: 32]

(l) **Heavy 125**:
[11 An-124 Condor; 4 An-22 Cock; 98 Il-76MD Candid; 3 Il-76MD-M Candid; 9 Il-76MD-90A Candid;]

(m) **Medium 65** An-12BK Cub

(n) **Light 224**:
[ε113 An26 Curl; 25 An-72 Coaler; 5 An-140; 27 L-410; 54 Tu-134 Crusty; PAX 32: 15 An-148-100E; 17 Tu-154 Careless]; PAX:32.

(o) **TRG 262**: [35 DA42T; 118 L-39 Albatros; 109 Yak-130 Mitten*]

**HELICOPTERS**

(p) **ATK 361+**:
[ε105 Ka-52A Hokum B; 100 Mi-24D/V/P Hind; 80+ Mi-28N Havoc B; 13 Mi-28UB Havoc; ε60 Mi-35 Hind]

(q) **EW:** ε20 Mi-8MTPR-1 Hip

(r) **TPT 313**:
[**Heavy 33** Mi-26/Mi-26T Halo;
**Medium 280** Mi-8/AMTSh/AMTSh-VA/MT/MTV-5/MTV-5-1 Hip]

(s) **TRG 69**:
[19 Ka-226U; 50 Ansat-U]

**UNINHABITED AERIAL VEHICLES**

(t) **CISR**: [**Heavy**: some Inokhodets; **Medium:** Forpost R; Mohajer 6]

(u) **ISR**: [Medium: Forpost (Searcher II)]

## LOSSES DENTING THE AIRPOWER

The enigmatic fog of war often veils many elements, including elusive and misleading loss figures. According to the top U.S. Air Force commander for Europe, Ukraine has lost approximately 60 aircraft since the renewed invasion by Russia in February 2022. Conversely, the Russian forces have suffered a more significant loss, with over 70 jets reported as casualties. Following the initial failure of Russia's expansive air force to achieve air superiority during the early stages of the conflict, the current state of the aerial situation has evolved into a scenario characterised by mutual denial.[15]

### Losses

The quantification of aircraft losses incurred during the Russia–Ukraine conflict can be found across multiple sources, with biases that are inherent to the source. According to the Ministry of Ukraine, the Russian losses till the 552nd day (July 11, 2023) are as appended below:[16]

(a) Russian Aircraft: 315
(b) Russian Helicopters: 310
(c) Russian UAVs: 3693
(d) Air Defence Systems: 414

## HELICOPTER OPERATIONS

Russia has utilised heliborne operations to conduct troop insertions, resupply missions and provide fire support to its forces in the Ukraine conflict. Helicopters have been used to deploy special forces, reinforce critical positions and conduct surveillance. Ukraine has also employed heliborne forces to enhance its military capabilities in the conflict. Helicopters have been utilised for troop transportation, medical evacuation and reconnaissance missions. These operations have provided flexibility and agility to Ukrainian forces in their engagements with Russian-backed separatists.

Heliborne operations have played a significant role in the Russia–Ukraine conflict by enabling rapid deployments, enhancing situational awareness and supporting ground forces. However, limitations such as vulnerability to anti-aircraft systems, adverse weather conditions and logistical constraints should also be considered when assessing their overall impact.

During the Global Air and Space Chiefs conference on July 13, 2023, RAF Air Chief Marshal Rich Knighton said, 'During the past 16 months of military engagement in Ukraine, Russia has incurred a loss of 86 fixed-wing aircraft and 90 helicopters'.[17] These figures are in variance to Ukrainian official data.

The initial operation of the Russian attack helicopter fleet involved the execution of assertive hunter-killer missions situated outside the Ukrainian front-lines, with relatively frequent occurrences of penetrating depths of up to 50 km. These helicopters used a combination of unguided rockets and cannon fire against troop concentrations and soft-skinned vehicles and Anti-Tank Guided Missiles (ATGMs) against armoured vehicles and other hardened targets. Nevertheless, the Russian military experienced significant casualties from Man-Portable Air Defence Systems (MANPADS), prompting a change in tactics. The frequency of penetrating missions decreased, giving way to rocket 'lofting' attacks from a secure distance. Later, there has been a notable trend of cautious employment of Russian attack helicopters, primarily relying on standoff rocket strikes, which has effectively reduced their role to that of airborne rocket artillery assets. Despite taking such precautions, they have been frequently shot down by Ukrainian frontline units utilising MANPADS, Javelin and occasionally ATGMs.[18]

Currently, Ka-52 and Mi-8 helicopters and other rotary-wing aircraft are engaged in short-range operations near the front-lines, adversely affecting specific Ukrainian endeavours. Russia has augmented its attack helicopter capabilities in southern Ukraine, granting the Russians a strategic edge in a region characterised by intensified hostilities.[19]

The emergence of Russian attack helicopters, such as the Ka-52 Alligators, poses a significant threat to the ground forces of Ukraine. These helicopters possess the capability to inflict damage through the utilisation of a 30 mm cannon or anti-tank missiles. Ukraine has to promptly engage these helicopters with AD missiles to prevent the elimination of their heavy armour, including tanks and infantry fighting vehicles.[20]

## DRONE OPERATIONS

Russia and Ukraine failed to attain air superiority in the ongoing conflict, prompting both parties to use drones as a comparatively less risky approach to engage in aerial attacks against ground targets. The employment of drones has substantially influenced the conflict between Russia and Ukraine. Both factions have used drones to gather intelligence. According to official statements, Russia asserts its possession of over 1,000 compact and adaptable Orlan-10 Unmanned Aerial Vehicles (UAVs), which are purportedly employed for reconnaissance and targeting, jamming and intercepting surveillance communications.[21]

The usage of drones has enabled Ukraine to conduct surveillance and engage in activities that would otherwise be unattainable, thereby facilitating the monitoring and provocation of Russian military personnel. The Ukrainian Air Force has established a contingent of UAVs, commonly called a 'Drone Army', to engage in conflict with Russia. Although drones lack the comparable firepower of fighter jets, they have demonstrated efficacy in their distinct manner of utilisation and Russia's utilisation of Iranian-manufactured Kamikaze drone infrastructure has proven to be a noteworthy and economically efficient approach in neutralising Ukrainian aerial defence systems while simultaneously achieving successful air-to-ground strikes.

Ukraine resorted to drones to counter Russian airpower. In the ongoing conflict in the eastern region of Ukraine, Ukrainian forces have utilised UAVs, such as the Bayraktar TB2 manufactured in Turkey, as well as quadcopters for artillery observation. Ukraine has employed commercially available UAVs to deploy explosive devices, a tactic ISIS has used against U.S.-backed forces in Iraq and Syria.[22] The Turkish-made Bayraktar and Akinci drones have played a prominent role in Ukraine's war effort. Ukraine has praised the TB2 and Akinci as effective weapons that have changed the nature of warfare. They have been credited in various videos and reports with destroying Russian tanks, armoured defences, patrol boats and AD systems. This has had a significant impact on the conduct of military operations as they have enabled combatants to effectively monitor the positioning and mobility of troops, enhanced the precision of conventional weaponry, exerted pressure on and disrupted enemy forces and captured visual evidence of successful operations for subsequent dissemination to garner support and undermine the morale of opposing Russian forces.[23]

As Russia persistently deployed loitering munitions and missiles towards Ukrainian cities, Ukraine was compelled to allocate its already limited AD resources between two primary objectives: supporting front-line operations and safeguarding civilians as well as critical infrastructure.

## AD OPERATIONS

The suboptimal utilisation of Destruction of Enemy Air Defences/Suppression of Enemy Air Defences (DEAD/SEAD) tactics by the VKS has inadvertently facilitated a robust response from the PSU in the AD arena. The utilisation of Air-Launched Cruise Missiles (ALCMs) by the VKS appears inadequate, as there is a notable dependency on Surface-to-Surface Missiles (SSMs).

The transition of the VKS Concept of Operations (CONOPS) towards utilising Anti-Radiation Missiles (ARMs) in October 2022 holds considerable significance. Enhanced outcomes in DEAD have been observed. The utilisation of ARM systems such as Kh-31 and Kh-58 has been significant in the concerted efforts to subdue the Ukrainian GBADS.[24] In November 2022, RUSI noted that Su-30SM and Su-35S jets frequently fired the Kh-31P and Kh-58 ARMs to disable Ukrainian Surface-to-Air Missile (SAM) radars.[25] The frequency of S-300 system losses to the PSU is observed to be approximately two to three per week. Furthermore, it has come to notice that PSU's Mig-29 aircraft have undergone modifications to enable the carriage of AGM-88 HARM missiles aimed at high-frequency radar, resulting in efficient employment.[26]

The absence of VKS' dominance over the airspace is ascribed to the ingenious and adaptable utilisation of AD systems by the PSU. Its implementation of shoot-and-scoot tactics and deployment of MANPADS has proven instrumental. The utilisation of the philosophy of asset dispersal has proven to be effective in PSU's efforts to alleviate the detrimental effects incurred by the presence of Air-Launched Cruise Missiles (ALCMs) and Surface-to-Surface Missiles (SSMs).

The significant losses incurred by the VKS Helicopters and Transport aircraft can be attributed to the suboptimal utilisation of passive Electronic Countermeasures (ECM). The VKS successfully implemented an offensive strategy by deploying S-400 systems in Belarus and Crimea, as a robust deterrent against potential incursions by attackers seeking to infiltrate the PSU air command within their territories.

## Encountering Aerial Threats

The performance of SAM systems, particularly the S-400, against aerial threats, specifically aircraft, is highly effective. The PSU has attributed multiple aircraft losses to the S-400 missile defence system engagements. The Ukrainian SA-11 and S-300 SAM systems demonstrated the stipulated effectiveness. The Russian strike aircraft were compelled to operate at lower altitudes while penetrating Ukraine-defended zones to evade the lethal range of SAMs.[27]

The attribution of notable aircraft kills to MANPADS is of considerable importance. The Su-25 and Su-34 fleets have experienced significant losses, most likely due to using Stinger and IGLA SAM systems. The Ukrainian Pechora system demonstrated effectiveness in its anti-aircraft capabilities. The considerable number of aircraft lost by both factions is evidence of the efficacy of a well-distributed AD system.

The integrated air and missile defence systems have proven highly effective in countering airborne threats. Consequently, they have refrained from conducting flights over each other's respective territories.[28]

## Anti-missile and Stand-off Weapon (SOW) Operations

The interception of Russian Tochka-U and Iskander missiles is challenging due to the absence of well-suited interceptor missiles. The interception of the Iskander missile poses a significant challenge due to its quasi-ballistic manoeuvring capabilities. Approximately 80–90 per cent of the Russian Air Launched Cruise Missiles [specifically, the Kh-101 (RS-AS-23A Kodiak) and Kh-55 (RS-AS-15B Kent) variants] launched by Tu-95M bombers were intercepted. However, the Russian S-400 systems demonstrated notable effectiveness in intercepting missiles, successfully blocking approximately 80–90 per cent of Ukraine's launches. This accomplishment was primarily attributed to utilising the S-400 systems with the Storm Shadow systems.

## Anti-Drone Operations

A significant proportion of UAVs of both factions were rendered inoperable.

UAVs are not operating without facing any consequences, as evidenced by the notable losses incurred by the TB2, Akinci and the escalating number of Shahed 136 casualties. UAVs were observed to have been incapacitated due to ground-based attacks and Electronic Countermeasures (ECM) implementation.[29]

Russia's Electronic Warfare (EW) capabilities remain formidable, as evidenced by at least one significant system deployed every 10 km along the front. These systems have a strong bias towards neutralising UAVs and typically do not prioritise efforts to mitigate their impact on other operations. The monthly losses of Ukrainian UAVs are estimated to be around 10,000.[30]

## Countering Hypersonic Threats

The anti-missile air defence systems were utilised for intercepting hypersonic missiles, which are characterised by extremely high speeds. The Patriot missile system reportedly successfully intercepted the Russian Kinzhal hypersonic missile. The Russians, however, did not confirm the same. The interception of Kinzhal missiles is not game-changing due to their pseudo-hypersonic characteristics. Contemporary hypersonic cruise missiles, such as the Russian Zircon, as well as quasi-ballistic Hypersonic Glide Vehicles (HGVs), such as the Avanguard and DF-ZF, have proven to be considerably challenging to intercept.

## Efficacy of the AD Networks

The performance of AD networks, specifically the VKS Integrated Air Defence System (IADS), has been limited. This can be attributed to reliance on outdated concepts, inadequate technological capabilities, insufficient real-time data transfer and a lack of comprehensive training.

Real-time transmission of intelligence data from the A-50, the Russian AWACS, and radar information from ground-based sensors was not directly communicated to the weapon system. The tactical data was transmitted through a ground relay post and an IL-20M 'Coot' airborne command post to the GBADS and CAP fighters. This communication pathway led to a notable increase in the response time between the sensor and the shooter.

The development of Russian concepts and technology has enhanced the AD network. During the conflict, the integration of Strelets-M, the Integrated Command and Communication System (ICCS), and Andromeda-D, the battlefield management systems, took place. The specific details regarding the capabilities are currently not available.

Ukraine employs an essential Air Defence Control and Reporting System (ADCRS). Despite the absence of a networked environment, a series of noteworthy and influential AD operations were carried out, primarily attributed to the guiding principles of mobility, agility and the innovative utilisation of AD systems.[31]

### Cutting-edge Tactics, Techniques, and Procedures (TTP)

UAVs have been strategically utilised by the VKS to achieve AD saturation. Furthermore, during the Neptune missile strike, lethal armaments were effectively utilised to distract the detection systems of the appreciated Russian naval vessel Moskva.[32] Additionally, it is worth noting that these anti-tank weapon systems, commonly called MANPADS, were instrumental in achieving this tactical objective.

The efficacy of SAM systems, particularly the S-400, exhibits a commendable level of proficiency when countering aerial targets, particularly aircraft. The PSU has ascribed several aircraft losses to engagements involving the S-400 system. The efficacy of the Ukrainian SA-11 and S-300 SAM systems is notable as they compelled Russian strike aircraft to adopt lower altitudes during their incursions into Ukrainian airspace.

The notable aerial victories can be attributed to the utilisation of MANPADS, resulting in considerable attrition inflicted upon the fleets of SU-25 and SU-34 aircraft (presumably employing Stinger and IGLA missiles). The efficacy of shoulder-fired anti-defence weapons remains admirable.[33]

## RUSSIANS' SUBOPTIMAL PERFORMANCE

The potential of airpower has remained untapped despite Russia's evident superiority in quantity and quality in this domain. Russia was unable to neutralise Ukrainian AD assets effectively. None of the airfields, particularly those in the western regions, were subjected to any assault. There exists a certain degree of uncertainty regarding the operational efficacy of the Russian Air Force, primarily attributable to their relatively constrained involvement within the Syrian theatre of conflict. While Russia has been diligently preserving its resources in anticipation of potential escalation, the losses incurred by Russia have surpassed initial projections.[34]

The lack of success of Russian airpower in Ukraine can be ascribed to the incompetence of the Russian military in terms of air campaign planning, as well as their inability to effectively counter Ukraine's formidable GBAD capabilities. The Russian military's efforts for SEAD were notably unsuccessful, while Ukraine, on the other hand, achieved success through its effective countermeasures. The outcome of the aerial defeat can be attributed to the Russian Air Force's indecisiveness in applying the appropriate doctrine precepts during the conflict. There was a notable dependence on what the Russian Chief of Staff Valeriy Gerasimov and other military strategists referred to as 'non-contact' warfare, a concept extensively expounded upon in Russian military sources and official documents. However, this approach proved impracticable during the Ukrainian conflict.[35]

## RUSSIA'S REVISED AIRPOWER STRATEGY

According to RUSI, the Russian military acknowledged its deficiencies and implemented measures to enhance coordination and responsiveness. In Watling and Reynolds' opinion, Russia encountered ongoing challenges in effectively addressing emerging threats; however, it has demonstrated a capacity for adaptation over time. Enhancements in multiple sectors of Russia's military have been observed, encompassing its engineering divisions and the tank and artillery brigades. The report also emphasised the robustness of the nation's AD capabilities and its highly effective EW systems.[36]

As per the report, Putin's forces have undergone adaptations to enhance their effectiveness following a period of underwhelming performance during the war. However, these units continue to encounter a significant challenge from the substantial number of casualties they have incurred. These casualties were due to a notable decrease in morale levels within Russian infantry units. This decline in morale subsequently resulted in inadequate unit cohesion and a lack of cooperation between different departments. Russia is reviewing its airpower strategy in the Russia–Ukraine war for utilising various elements of airpower to achieve its objectives. This integrated approach aims to gain a tactical advantage, pressurise Ukrainian forces and achieve operational and strategic goals.[37]

Ukraine's assistance from the West, NATO and USA was probably not anticipated and Russia thought it would capitulate. Russia after that changed its strategy to bomb/disrupt critical civil infrastructure, that is, electricity, water supply, communications, etc., leading to a large migration of Ukraine's population to other European countries.

## UKRAINE'S AIRPOWER STRATEGY

Ukraine's airpower strategy has focused on countering Russia's dominance by utilising international assistance, enhancing its AD capabilities and adapting its tactics to exploit vulnerabilities in Russian air operations. It aims to deter Russian aggression and protect its sovereignty.

The conflict in Ukraine is currently serving as a significant platform for evaluating new weapons technology. Although securing fighter aircraft for Ukraine is proving difficult, the same limitations do not appear to impede the deployment of advanced Unmanned Aerial Systems (UAS). Therefore, a variety of military and civil drones have been employed by the PSU.

Ukraine has faced significant challenges in countering Russia's airpower capabilities. Since the commencement of the invasion, the Ukrainian Air Force has incurred significant casualties, albeit the precise numerical data has not been disclosed.[38] However, it has formulated an airpower strategy focused on enhancing its defensive capabilities, deterring aggression and protecting its sovereignty. The actions of ground forces have had different outcomes based on how well Ukrainian forces cooperated. Even though close air support was restricted, the Ukrainian Army received sustainment and base-defence help from the ground forces around Kyiv and the north.[39] Ukraine has sought assistance from international partners, bolstered its AD systems and adapted its tactics to exploit vulnerabilities in Russian air operations.

## KEY LESSONS LEARNED

The nature of warfare continues to change from conventional to hybrid, wherein the means extend beyond the traditional air, maritime and land military assets. This also has lessons and implications for India, especially as we reorganise our force structures. The analysis of airpower utilisation in the conflict between Russia and Ukraine yields significant insights through a comparative study. The various applications of airpower and their outcomes encompass the importance of air superiority, the necessity for efficient AD systems, the significance of international collaboration and the flexibility of tactics in countering a more dominant opponent. The salient features of airpower exploitation observed during the conflict are given below:

(a) **Airpower is a Force Multiplier.** It has the potential to be a formidable force in both offensive and defensive operations. The conflict in Ukraine has provided evidence to support the notion that the utilisation of airpower, in conjunction with ground forces, can effectively enhance military capabilities. The Ukrainian Air Force was responsible for delivering close air support to ground forces and executing reconnaissance operations to gather strategic intelligence.

(b) **Valuable Counter-air Operations.** These operations are pivotal in contemporary military strategies as they prevent the adversary from engaging in air operations. The Russian Air Force exemplified the same. Missiles and drones should not be regarded as a panacea as fighters are crucial in conducting DEAD and SEAD operations within the contested airspace.

(c) **Always-ready Enablers.** Enabling assets such as AWACS and AEW&C play a vital role in supporting Air Defence Operations (AD Ops). They help alleviate line-of-sight limitations and offer crucial surveillance capabilities in extensive coverage.[40]

(d) **Disruptive Operations are Game Changers.** Disruptive operations upset the balance of military strength between rivals by using creative solutions that outdate the enemies' policies, doctrines and organisation. The Russian Air Force conducted extensive EW operations to disrupt Ukrainian communications and target acquisition capabilities.

(e) **UAVs Play a Crucial Role in Various Domains.** The utilisation of UAVs by both factions involved in the conflict exemplified their efficacy in reconnaissance and surveillance operations. The capacity to execute such missions without exposing human lives to potential harm is a notable benefit. Therefore, it is imperative to adopt a proactive stance to neutralise these assaults effectively. It is crucial to acknowledge that these unmanned aerial vehicles can also launch attacks within contested airspace.

(f) **The Significance of Integrated Air-ground Operations.** The offensive and AD operations are intricately intertwined and co-occur. Russia and Ukraine have recognised the significance of effectively integrating airpower with ground operations. The optimisation of collaboration between aerial resources and ground troops enhances operational efficiency, augments situational comprehension and maximises the potential of airpower capabilities.

(g) **AD Operations are Vital.** The conflict underscored the significance of deploying efficient AD systems to safeguard ground forces and critical infrastructure against hostile aerial assaults. Viable solutions encompass innovation, mobility and agility in employing modern, legacy, non-networked AD systems. The Ukrainian military initially incurred substantial casualties due to inadequate AD systems. The seamless integration of tri-service AD systems is paramount to facilitate collaborative target engagement during high-intensity, multi-domain military operations. The development of future AD capabilities and induction plans should consider the need to effectively detect and neutralise low Radar Cross-Section (RCS) threats.

(h) **AD Weapon Systems are Important.** Using innovation, mobility and agility in using modern as well as old non-networked AD systems result in a practical environment for the seamless conduct of air operations. Ukraine's strategic resource allocation towards procuring and deploying modern AD systems, such as SAMs, has proven crucial in deterring Russian aircraft strikes and defending critical infrastructure. The continued development and use of MANPADs are essential in air combat. MANPADS are a cost-effective and operationally viable AD technology. They are effective even in situations with no network access.

(i) **Equipment Doesn't Win Wars. People Do:** Russia's overall military expenditure has witnessed a moderate increase after its special operations in Ukraine in February 2022. SIPRI estimates its total military spending budget for 2023 to be 6,648 billion roubles.[41] However, Ukrainians' unequivocal demonstration of a strong will to face all odds has served as a pivotal factor that is likely to determine the outcome. In the face of formidable adversaries such as Russia, Ukraine has effectively implemented a parallel strategy to contend with the increased motivation of its citizens.

(j) **Investment in Training Pays Rich Dividends.** Training and interoperability are essential components that must be incorporated to enhance any weapon system's effectiveness and efficiency.[42] Training for non-networked AD operations, commonly called analogue warfare, is imperative because it can equip the workforce with the necessary skills to handle any contingency.

## CHALLENGES AND FUTURE PROSPECTS

### Technological Advancements

The progressive technological strides encompassing the evolution of sophisticated aerial platforms, precision weapons and autonomous systems will continue to persistently influence the pivotal function of airpower in forthcoming conflicts. Implications for future military confrontations as well as the prospective ramifications of these technological advancements may be readily ascertained in the ongoing Russia–Ukraine conflict.

### Evolving Strategies and Tactics

As the ongoing conflict stretches, it is anticipated that Russia and Ukraine will modify their strategies and tactics to secure a favourable position within the air domain. This will likely result in adaptations in procedures, development of new tactics and foster innovative counters to the ever-evolving array of threats.

### International Implications

The ongoing geopolitical dispute between Russia and Ukraine has garnered considerable interest and scrutiny from the global community. The international ramifications of using airpower, including heliborne operations within the context of the conflict, may also be visualised. It encompasses examining geopolitical factors, the consequential effects on regional security dynamics and the participation of external entities.

### Lessons for India

The Indian Air Force must re-evaluate its tactical approach, considering the increasing prevalence of shoulder-launched anti-aircraft and anti-tank missiles and stand-off weapons. The Su-30 MKI aircraft, procured from Russia, is pivotal in the Indian Air Force. At the same time, the Indian Army relies on tanks, artillery systems, rockets and ammunition of Russian origin. The Ukrainian military has gained prominence as a contemporary and proficient combat force mainly due to the substantial technological resources supplied by the United States and its NATO counterparts.[43] The conflict in Ukraine, therefore, provides a significant example of the decreasing significance of low-tech warfare, as observed during World War II, in modern military operations. Modernisation of weapon systems have only prolonged a war of attrition, lacking any clear victors.[44]

The imperative to allocate resources towards establishing a SEAD/DEAD entity equipped with dedicated platforms for dynamic targeting and Identification of Friend or Foe (IFF) is of utmost significance.[45]

The rapid increase in the use of drones, loitering munitions, man-portable stinger missiles and other technological advancements highlights the impressive capabilities of human innovation. It is crucial to allocate supplementary financial resources towards procuring cutting-edge assets, such as fifth-generation fighters, strategic bombers, encryption equipment, cyber systems, etc. Indigenous weaponry and equipment will probably continue to be employed in future conflicts. Therefore, it is crucial to cultivate self-reliance abilities.

Numerous studies have provided evidence that the widespread deployment of portable AD systems and anti-tank weapon systems can effectively hinder the progress of superior air forces and formidable armoured columns. The Ukrainian Armed Forces exhibit a notable disparity in the quantity of anti-tank weapons compared to the number of tanks held by the Russian military.

The prolonged Bakhmut operations are an indicator of the ineffectiveness of military leadership. At times, the substandard performance of troops within the Russian military has been observed as a significant factor contributing to its lack of success in its endeavours in Ukraine. Despite possessing advanced weapons, the enlisted personnel of this organisation demonstrated a lack of discipline, motivation and comprehensive training, thereby impeding their capacity to attain triumph in military engagements.

Considering the prevailing geopolitical context, India is confronted with the imperative of effectively tackling the obstacles a progressively assertive China presents. India acknowledges the necessity of allocating adequate time and resources to enhance and modernise its armed forces to address these challenges effectively. Therefore, it is crucial to engage in thorough training to proficiently handle diverse conflict situations and acquire proficiency in cross-domain operations. Similarly, we must be able to swiftly adapt our doctrines, equipment, training and tactics to counter emerging threats effectively.[46]

## CONCLUSION

The ongoing Russia–Ukraine conflict has resulted in a paradigm shift in the global understanding of inter-state war, the role of alliances such as NATO, the intricacies of diplomacy, intelligence gathering, national security, energy stability, economic diplomacy, the role of the United Nations Security Council and the role that media or information warfare plays in an increasingly interconnected, yet isolated world. The limited military operation launched by Russia on February 24, 2022, has its roots in the annexation of Crimea in 2014, NATO's expansion to Russia's borders and the independence of Donetsk and Luhansk. The conflict continues to rage even after 17 months, with little or no signs of an end in sight. Airpower has been utilised during the battle with mixed results despite the significant variations in force structures of Russia and Ukraine. The lack of success in Russia's utilisation of airpower during the conflict could be attributed to inadequate air campaign planning and execution, along with the effectiveness of the Ukrainian ground-based AD systems. The Russian Air Forces (VKS) endeavoured to carry out a 'Strategic Air Operation' with their extensively expressed 'non-contact' doctrine.

Missiles and drones have limited utility unless operations are planned with other air, land and maritime power elements. Mobile AD elements have their utility in ensuring air denial. Establishing air superiority remains an indispensable prerequisite, and the importance of SEAD/DEAD cannot be undermined. Military leadership, morale and combined arms training play a significant role, as it is not the equipment but the people who win or lose wars. Disruptive operations in the cyber and space domain and the use of commercial satellites would play an essential role in future conflicts. Information warfare is vital as strong narratives can have a global influence. With a reduced appetite for a worldwide rules-based world order, small nations unwittingly become pawns in great power rivalry with disastrous consequences.

The utility of hard power will remain, and without deft diplomacy and statesmanship, conflicts could rage forever, as witnessed in the Russia–Ukraine war. While the jury is out on the ongoing conflict, there are many lessons to learn on utilising airpower, which will continue to play an essential and inalienable role in any future conflict. Airpower and heliborne missions are debated in urban locations, where collateral damage and civilian deaths are a concern. Airpower and heliborne operations will become more crucial as battles get more complex and asymmetric. The assessment of the efficacy and constraints of airpower and specifically heliborne operations within the framework of the Russia–Ukraine conflict will also bear significance for present-day aerial warfare.

## NOTES

1 'War in Ukraine,' The Center for Preventive Action, June 26, 2023, at https://www.cfr.org/global-conflict-tracker/conflict/conflict-ukraine (Accessed July 9, 2023).

2 Viktoriya Fedorchak, *Understanding Contemporary Air Power,* 1st Edition, Routledge, 2020, at https://www.routledge.com/Understanding-Contemporary-Air-Power/Fedorchak/p/book/9781138393806 (Accessed July 9, 2023).

3 'The Role of Airpower in 21st Century Operations,' Second Line of Defense, October 4, 2013, at https://sldinfo.com/2013/04/the-role-of-airpower-in-21st-century-operations/ (Accessed July 9, 2023).

4 Jeremy Black, 'Air Power: Strength and Weaknesses,' Defence-In-Depth, at https://defenceindepth.co/2016/05/11/air-power-strength-and-weaknesses/ (Accessed July 9, 2023).

5 Kapil Kak, 'A Century of Air Power: Lessons and Pointers,' Strategic Analysis, March 2001 (Vol. XXIV No. 12), at https://www.tandfonline.com/doi/abs/10.1080/09700160108455344. (Accessed July 9, 2023).

6 Anil Chopra, 'Ukraine War. The War in the Air. An Analysis,' Air Power Asia (blog), March 9, 2022, at https://airpowerasia.com/2022/03/09/ukraine-war-the-war-in-the-air-an-analysis-air-marshal-anil-chopra-aadi-def-talks/ (Accessed July 10, 2023).

7 Justin Bronk, Nick Reynolds and Dr Jack Watling, 'The Russian Air War and Ukrainian

Requirements for Air Defence,' RUSI, Chapter-I, November 7, 2022, at https://rusi.org/explore-our-research/publications/special-resources/russian-air-war-and-ukrainian-requirements-air-defence (Accessed August 30, 2023).

8 Thomas R. McCabe, 'The Russian Perception of the NATO Aerospace Threat,' Air University, Fall 2016, at https://www.airuniversity.af.edu/Portals/10/ASPJ_Spanish/Journals/Volume-29_Issue-2/2017_2_09 _mccabe _s_eng.pdf (Accessed July 16, 2023).

9 Jon Jackson, 'Russia's Improved Combat Is Bad News for Ukraine: Report,' *The Newsweek*, May 19, 2023, at https://www.newsweek.com/russia-improved-combat-bad-news-ukraine-1801523 (Accessed July 11, 2023).

10 Global Firepower, 'Comparison of Air Forces of Russia and Ukraine As of 2023, By Type,' Statista, February 7, 2023, at https://www.statista.com/statistics/1293414/airpower-of-russia-and-ukraine-in-comparison/ (Accessed July 9, 2023).

11 Anil Chopra, no. 7.

12 'Air Force,' Ministry of Defense of Ukraine, at https://www.mil.gov.ua/ministry/ozbroennya-ta-texnika/povitryani-sili.html (Accessed July 11, 2023).

13 Anil Chopra, no. 7.

14 James Hackett, 'Russia and Eurasia,' The Military Balance 2023, International Institute for Strategic Studies, p.191 (Accessed July 12, 2023).

15 Chris Gordon, 'Ukraine Has Lost 60 Aircraft, Taken Down 70 in Russian Invasion, Hecker-says,' Air and Space Forces, March 6, 2023, at https://www.airandspaceforces.com/ukraine-has-lost-60-aircraft-taken-down-70-in-russian-invasion-hecker-says/ (Accessed July 11, 2023).

16 'Losses of the Russian Army in Ukraine,' MinFin, July 11, 2023, at https://index.minfin.com.ua/ua/russian-invading/casualties/ (Accessed July 11, 2023).

17 Steve Trimble, 'Russian Aircraft Losses Total 176 In Ukraine: RAF Chief,' *Aviation Week Network,* July 13, 2023, at https://aviationweek.com/defense-space/aircraft-propulsion/russian-aircraft-losses-total-176-ukraine-raf-chief#:~:text=By%20contrast%2C%20Ukraine%20has%20lost, according%20to%20the%20RAF%20estimates (Accessed August 30, 2023).

18 Justin Bronk, Nick Reynolds and Dr Jack Watling, no. 8, Chapter-II.

19 Ryan Pickrell, 'Russian Attack Helicopters Showed Up in Force on the Front Lines and Have Been Putting Dents In Ukraine's Armored Assaults,' *The Business Insider*, June 23, 2023, at https://www.businessinsider.in /international/news/russian-attack-helicopters-showed-up-in-force-on-the-front-lines-and-have-been-putting-dents-in-ukraines-armored-assaults/articleshow/101202361.cms (Accessed July 11, 2023).

20 Ibid.

21 AP, 'Deadly Secret: Electronic Warfare Shapes Russia-Ukraine War,' *The Economic Times*, Jun 03, 2022, at https://economictimes.indiatimes.com/news/defence/deadly-secret-electronic-warfare-shapes-russia-ukraine-war/articleshow/91984286.cms?from=mdr (Accessed July 11, 2023).

22 Chris Gordon, 'Cutting-Edge Drones Headed to Ukraine in Latest US Aid,' Air and Space Forces, February 26, 2023, at https://www.airandspaceforces.com/cutting-edge-drones-headed-to-ukraine-in-latest-us-aid/ (Accessed July 11, 2023).

23 Kerry Chávez, 'Learning on the Fly: Drones in the Russian-Ukrainian War,' Arms Control Association, January/February 2023, at https://www.armscontrol.org/act/2023-01/features/learning-fly-drones-russian-ukrainian-war (Accessed July 11, 2023).

24 Vijainder K Thakur, "New Offensive Tactics' To Degrade Ukrainian Air Defenses,' *The Eurasian Times*, April 27, 2023, at https://www.eurasiantimes.com/russia-adopts-new-offensive-tactics-to-decimate-ukrainian/ (Accessed July 9, 2023).

25 Ritu Sharma, "Super Killer' in Ukraine War, India Gets Its Own Anti-Radiation Missile That Can Be Fired From Both French & Russian Jets,' *The Eurasian Times*, July 25, 2023, at https://www.eurasiantimes.com/super-killer-in-ukraine-war-india-gets-its-own-anti-radiation/#:~:text=Kh%2D31%20is%20the%20best,to% 20 disable%20Ukrainian%20SAM%20radars (Accessed August 31, 2023).

26 Ashish Dangwal, '88 Anti-Radiation Missile Against Russia; US Air Force Pilot Questions Viral Video,' November 21, 2022, at https://www.eurasiantimes.com/ukrainian-mig-29-fighter-fires-agm-88-anti-radiation-missile-against-russia-us-air-force-pilot-debunks-viral-video/ (Accessed July 16, 2023).

27 Ritu Sharma, 'Ukraine's 'Cheap' Missile Outperforms World's Best S-400 Systems In Warzone, Wreaks Havoc On Russian Warplanes,' *The Eurasian Times*, June 27, 2023, at https://www.eurasiantimes.com/new-ukraines-cheap-missile-outperforms-worlds-best-s-400/ (Accessed July 9, 2023).

28 Chris, 22.

29 Carrington Malin, 'Counter UAS Becomes Top Priority in Ukraine War,' Armada International, May 11, 2023, at https://www.armadainternational.com/2023/05/counter-uas-becomes-top-priority-in-ukraine-war/ (Accessed July 12, 2023).

30 Dr Jack Watling and Nick Reynolds, 'Meatgrinder: Russian Tactics in the Second Year of Its Invasion of Ukraine,' RUSI, May 19, 2023, at https://rusi.org/explore-our-research/publications/special-resources/meatgrinder-russian-tactics-second-year-its-invasion-ukraine (Accessed August 31, 2023).

31 Dr V K Saxena, 'Why the Ukrainian Skies Are Still Contested - An Assessment,' Vivekananda International Foundation, March 24, 2022, at https://www.vifindia.org/article/2022/march/24/why-the-ukrainian-skies-are-still-contested-an-assessment (Accessed on July 12, 2023).

32 Joe Courtney, 'Moskva's Sinking, the Rise of Anti-Ship Cruise Missiles, and What That Means for the US Navy,' Houseman Joe Courtney, May 3, 2022, at https://courtney.house.gov/media-center/in-the-news/moskvas-sinking-rise-anti-ship-cruise-missiles-and-what-means-us-navy (Accessed July 12, 2023).

33 Parth Satam, 'Russian Fighter Pilot Admits Ukrainian Shoulder-Fired MANPADS Are Biggest Threat to Su-35, Su-34 Warplanes,' *The Eurasian Times*, October 1, 2022, at https://www.eurasiantimes.com/russian-fighter-pilot-admits-ukrainian-shoulder-fired-manpads-are-biggest-threat-to-su-35-su-34-warplanes/ (Accessed July 12, 2023).

34 Anil Chopra, no. 7.

35 Sean M Wiswesser, 'Potemkin on the Dnieper: The Failure of Russian Airpower in the Ukraine War,' Small Wars & Insurgencies, 34 (7), March 29, 2023, at https://doi.org/10.1080/09592318.2023.2187201 (Accessed July 10, 2023).

36 Jon Jackson, 9.

37 Jon Jackson, 9.

38 Abdujalil Abdurasulov and Zhanna Bezpiatchuk, 'Ukraine War: Jet Pilots Talk about the Air War with Russia,' *BBC*, May 9, 2022, at https://www.bbc.com/news/world-europe-65461405 (Accessed July 12, 2023).

39 Mandeep Singh, 'Fight to Win,' *The Force*, at https://forceindia.net/cover-story/fight-to-win/ (Accessed August 31, 2023).

40 'Airborne Early Warning and Control (AEW&C),' DRDO, July 12, 2019, at https://www.drdo.gov.in/airborne-early-warning-and-control-aewc (Accessed July 16, 2023).

41 Julian Cooper, 'Russia's Military Expenditure during Its War against Ukraine,' SIPRI, June 2023, at https://sipri.org/publications/2023/sipri-insights-peace-and-security/russias-military-

expenditure-during-its-war-against-ukraine (Accessed July 16, 2023).

42 Dr James Derleth, 'Enhancing Interoperability: The Foundation for Effective NATO Operations,' NATO Review, June 16, 2015, at https://www.nato.int/docu/review/articles/2015/06/16/enhancing-interoperability-the-foundation-for-effective-nato-operations/index.html (Accessed July 12, 2023).

43 Laura Jones, 'Lesson from a Year at War: In Contrast to the Russians, Ukrainians Master a Mix of High- and Low-end Technology on the Battlefield,' The Conversation, February 22, 2023, at https://theconversation.com/ lesson-from-a-year-at-war-in-contrast-to-the-russians-ukrainians-master-a-mix-of-high-and-low-end-technology-on-the-battlefield-197853 (Accessed August 31, 2023).

44 Hemant Mahajan, 'Russia Ukraine Air War: Lessons for India,' The Organiser, May 14, 2022, at https://organiser.org/2022/05/14/81094/opinion/russia-ukraine-air-war-lessons-for-india/ (Accessed July 6, 2023).

45 Ibid.

46 Ibid.

# 7

# Significance of Army Air Defence in the Ukraine Conflict

*Akhelesh Bhargava*

## INTRODUCTION

As war clouds loomed over Ukraine, it was anticipated that the Russian Air Force (AF) will be deployed in full force. The Russian AF with hundreds of fourth generation fighters was expected to establish air superiority/supremacy[1] over the Ukraine air space. Fearing the overwhelming advantage of Russian AF, North Atlantic Treaty Organisation (NATO)[2] countries provided Ukraine with thousands of short-range Man Portable Air Defence Systems (MANPADS) between February 22 and 28, 2022.[3] The Russia–Ukraine war commenced on February 24, 2022. The Russian air campaign started well and for the first three days was directed at Ukraine airfields, Air Defence (AD) weapons[4] and radars, ammunition dumps, command and control elements, other weapon systems, etc. It was expected that the Russian AF with its vast inventory of Migs and Sukhoi jets would be a deciding factor in the war. The Russian Army followed in quick time and made deep ingress into Ukraine. It was able to encircle Kyiv when the Ukraine resistance started.[5] The United States (US) provided Ukraine with precise intelligence[6] about the Russian targets and mode of attack, on the basis of which Ukraine took passive AD measures to disperse its AD systems and aircraft from permanent bases to satellite or alternate bases. Resultantly, the Ukrainian AD forces survived and largely remained intact to fight another day.

Both the opponents being offshoots of the erstwhile Union of Soviet Socialist Republic (USSR),[7] or Soviet Union, had similar legacy AD weapon systems and concept of deployment and employment. While Russia had upgraded its AD weapons and AF, Ukraine continued with the Soviet-era equipment. Russia was far ahead in numerical superiority and technology as compared to Ukraine. However, Ukraine was fighting a proxy war for the US, and it was assured all assistance by NATO allies. Before the war started, the first thing that Ukraine requisitioned from NATO was AD systems. The NATO alliance started supplying weapons to Ukraine including MANPADS just prior to the war. The advance variants, being technically complex, needed training for Ukrainian crews. Post training, these systems were supplied by NATO in a phased manner. Russia's over confidence on its numerical superiority was short lived. Its poor planning related to use of its AF and AD systems had a telling effect on its initial success. Thereafter, it decided to conserve its airpower and make do with only a part of it. What was expected to be a short, swift and punitive war has turned out to be a long-drawn affair. As of now more than 500 days have passed with no apparent end in sight. Even as Ukraine's AD missile and gun ammunition inventory is depleting at a high rate, Russia continues to have its AF intact and continues to use low-cost barrage firing of missiles, glide bombs[8] and loiter munitions.[9] Russia's idea to reduce cost of war, retain balance and yet ensure depletion of Ukraine's arsenal seems to be working until fresh AD munition supplies/ replenishment by NATO countries arrive.

The drone got added to the list of multi-spectral air threat to be countered by both Russian and Ukrainian AD. In the Russian–Ukraine war, drones have proliferated the battle zone in hundreds. To engage low-cost drones, alternate methods are being practiced and more are being tested.

On the technology front, Russia all along has been upgrading its technology but not much of it has been deployed for the Ground-Based AD Weapon Systems (GBADWS). NATO has been supplying Ukraine with advance technology in the field of drones, communications, Electronic Warfare (EW) and real-time processed intelligence inputs. The use of Artificial Intelligence (AI) and big data computing is being used extensively. Ukraine's troops and stream of volunteers are quick to adapt to the new technology being provided by the NATO allies including advanced AD systems and integrating them with the legacy equipment.[10]

The Russia–Ukraine war has lessons that India needs to learn. With the mass use of drones, the importance of AD has become significant. Low-cost countermeasures are the answer. Satellite-based communications, AI-based data handling and ingenuity-based ramping up of production line are essential for a long-drawn war.

## UNIQUE ASPECTS OF AD BATTLE

The GBADWS role is to defend a country's military and civilian assets from enemy air threat. The multi-spectral air threat includes fighter aircraft, bombers, helicopters, long-range Air to Surface Missiles (ASMs), long-range Surface to Surface Missiles (SSMs) (both ballistics and cruise), glide bombs, loiter munition, variety of drones including kamikaze, etc.

AD battle involves an integration of multiple functions which are essential to keep the assets safe from damage or destruction. In an AD battle, the engagement of a target is a matter of a few seconds. The targets, which pose air threat, have sub-, super- or hyper-sonic speeds. They, in turn, are engaged by guns and missiles systems with supersonic speeds. The unique aspects of an AD battle include:

- **Surveillance**. It involves keeping a defined air space under continuous observation using visual, electronic or satellite means. Thereafter integrating the observations into one picture and feeding it to the AD Control & Reporting System (ADC&RS) in real time. Though Russia scored on a better surveillance system, Ukraine got an edge when it got access to Starlink communication[11] and data link through US assistance.
- **ADC&RS**. In a defined air space there are multiple users, like aircraft, helicopters, drones, missiles, of both own and enemy. ADC&RS ensures control by placing varying degrees of restrictions or freedom on own air-space users or GBADWS. When enemy air threat is detected, ADC&RS reports its location to the deployed AD systems and give them the freedom to engage. In the Russia–Ukraine war, both sides have similar aircraft so the chances of fratricide increase exponentially. Electronic identification friend or foe (e-IFF) and visual identification plays a major role. An efficient ADC&RS must have good communication even when ranges get extended. While the US helped Ukraine to have an integrated ADC&RS, Russia made a strategic blunder and paid the price by not ensuring a reliable communication system during their march to Kyiv.
- **Weapon Systems**. The GBADWS are a mix of gun and missile family. Guns normally are multi-barrel with a very high rate of fire. The Surface to Air Missiles (SAMs) may be short- (less than 10 km), medium- (10 to 50 km) or long-range (beyond 50 km). The SAMs have different height coverage too. The GBADWS of both Russia and Ukraine cater to a multi-layered and multi-tiered deployment.[12] An asset is allocated point or area AD depending on its priority.

- **Electronic Warfare** (EW). The AD battle is all about 'who sees first gets to shoot first.' One way of ensuring this for GBADWS is by having a credible EW strategy in place. It is about denying the enemy from making effective use of the Electro-Magnetic (EM) spectrum and ensuring that their own troops are enabled to do so. Russia and Ukraine both had Soviet-era EW systems.[13] While Russia had continued to modernise its EW systems, Ukraine sought help from NATO countries to help it from Russian EW.[14] The NATO EW systems provided to Ukraine are much more robust and versatile in terms of power output and frequency coverage as compared to the Russian equipment.

## CONCEPT OF EMPLOYMENT

Russia and Ukraine are both offshoots of erstwhile USSR. The strategy and tactics employed in respect to GBADWS are basically the same. Both had good intelligence about each other's weapon dispositions due to continuous inputs from surveillance network and spies. Post the annexation of the Crimean Region by Russia in 2014, the US was actively involved and had been supporting Ukraine intelligence network.

The surveillance elements, command and control centres and EW related to GBADWS for both Russia and Ukraine have been similar. However, Ukraine AD is of more vintage origin and had, in terms of numbers, a fraction of what Russian had in its inventory. Obviously, both were aware of the operational capabilities and limitations of each other's equipment. The GBADWS asset allocation and deployment pattern were known to each other as well.

Input regarding stock availability of gun ammunition and SAMs with Ukraine was known to Russia as well as to NATO. Possibly due to this, Russia decided to go in for a limited air war, and not a classical 'air campaign', to gauge the preparedness of Ukraine's AD systems and the kind of support it was receiving from NATO.

Ukraine had learnt lessons from the Crimean War; it had kept its surveillance systems duly backed up by US intelligence on high alert. It had monitored activities of the Russian AF and took pre-emptive steps to disperse the bulk of its AD weapons to alternate locations or underground shelters and aircraft to air bases to its west. The US too had increased its surveillance, including by satellites, over the Ukraine–Russia border and provided Ukraine with intelligence inputs.[15] East Europe NATO countries also focussed on Russian activities. As the war broke out, NATO countries across Europe readily provided Ukraine with intelligence and financial aid.

There was dire need of GBADWS by Ukraine and NATO handed over MANPADS initially. As the war got extended, advanced AD systems[16] were gradually provided. The number of advanced AD systems available with European NATO countries are limited. They rely more on US air superiority over Russia.[17] Since AD systems are complex, their production line cannot be revived quickly, so fresh production in bulk is not possible. Since there is no alternative, NATO including the US are considering arming Ukraine with F-16s in the days ahead.

It is clear that Ukraine is fighting a US-led proxy war.[18] However, the NATO alliance does not want to escalate the war and accordingly is hesitant to admit Ukraine into NATO as a member immediately.

### Ukrainian AD Force

In 1992, on separating from erstwhile USSR there was a transfer of military assets including those related to GBADWS. The 28th AD Corps part of USSR 2nd AD Army was transferred under 8th AD Army of Ukraine. The Ukraine AD Force with 67,000 troops had three AD Corps as on February 01, 1992 – the 28th located at Lviv, the 49th at Odessa and the 60th at Dnipropetrovsk. The AD Forces were amalgamated with the Ukrainian AF in 2004 and thereafter known as Anti-Air Defence Missile Artillery (AADMA).[19]

Having been born out of USSR, the weapon profile of Ukrainian AADMA was very similar to that of Russia's. Prior to months before the war, Russian spies had been deployed in Ukraine to learn more about AD systems deployment among other things. Therefore, the intelligence available with the Russians about Ukraine's AADMA included:

- Weapon inventory and their initial dispositions
- Radars deployment and their coverage for surveillance and early warning
- Inventory of SAMs and gun ammunition
- Serviceability of equipment, Maintenance and Repair Organisation (MRO), including availability of spares

The original equipment profile of Ukrainian AD was of Soviet era and no new systems had been since acquired. It included:

- Zu-23 mm twin barrel gun
- Shilka-23 mm-quad barrel tracked gun
- Strela-2M - MANPADS – short-range SAM

- Strela-10 (SA 13) – short-range SAM
- OSA (SA 19) – short-range SAM
- Buk M1 (SA11) – medium- to long-range SAM
- S 300 (SA 10) – medium- to long-range SAM

The quantum of Ukraine AD assets available would have been sufficient for a short war but for an unexpected, prolonged war and Russia relying more on long-range missiles, Artillery rockets and multifarious drones (including the kamikaze ones procured from Iran), the Ukraine AD cover was inadequate to face the relentless attacks by Russia. Ukraine also had limited number of AD aircraft that included MiG-29s (37) and Su-27s (34). Before the war itself, Ukraine had requested NATO to provide it with as many GBADWS as it could. At the start of the war, Ukraine received MANPADS from NATO, which include:

- Strela-2M[20] from Germany (2,000) (ones supplied by the Soviet Union to East Germany) and the Czech Republic (700)
- Stinger[21] (US origin) from Denmark (300), Germany (500), Latvia (32), Lithuania (25), Netherlands (200) and USA (1,700)

### *Ukraine Counteroffensive*

As the days went by, Ukraine put in place its counteroffensive. However, its missiles inventory soon depleted, leading Ukraine to ask NATO to provide more AD weapon systems. NATO provided Ukraine with more MANPADS and advanced AD weapons. The NATO advanced systems have far superior radar coverage, better command and control systems, e-IFF, EW suite and precision strike capability. They are also equipped with terminal active homing guidance. These weapons included:

- MANPADS:
  - Mistral: France (50)[22]
  - Avenger: USA (12)[23]
- Star Streak: UK (85)[24]
- Piorun: Poland (1,000)[25]
- HAWK: UK (8)[26]
- Crotale: France (4)[27]
- Skynex: Italy (2)[28]
- Viktor: Czech Republic (15)[29]
- Gepard: Germany (37)[30]
- IRIS-T: Germany (2)[31]
- NASAMS: USA (8), Norway (3)[32]

- Aster 30 or SAMP-T: France–Italy (3)[33]
- Patriots: Germany (1), Netherlands (1), USA (2)[34]

## Russian AD

The Russian AD[35] is based on the erstwhile USSR AD Corps. To cover the entire Russian–Europe (NATO) frontage, Russia had deployed thousands of GBADWS. It was an impregnable wall with depth and altitude coverage, conceptually called a layered and tiered defence. As both Russia and Ukraine possessed a common AD ethos, they had a variety of weapons designed to intercept aircraft and missiles flying at different altitudes and varying ranges. They were designed to engage low-flying helicopters to high-altitude bombers and cruise missiles. The proliferation of drones and cruise missiles has led to these weapons being used to engage them as well. Russia has a family of AD equipment that no other country possess. This equipment includes:

- Short-range towed and tracked guns – Towed twin-barrel 23 mm Zu-23-2B, tracked four-barrel 23 mm ZSU-23-4B
- Short-range man portable and tracked missile system – Strela 2M, Igla, Strela 10M
- Mix Gun – Short-range missile – Tunguska
- Medium-range missile system – OSA, Pantsir, Sosna, Tor
- Long-range missile family – Buk 1M, S 75, S 125, S 200, S 300, S 350, S 400
- Anti-ballistic missile – A-35 ABM, Galosh

The Russian AD has been deployed in Russia, Belarus and occupied Ukraine. Being mostly mobile (towed/wheeled/tracked), they frequently change location, making it difficult for the Ukrainian AF to conduct operations freely. They have prevented the Ukraine airpower from causing any substantial damage to the Russian ground forces. The Russian AD, which was integrated with ground troops during the initial invasion, was soon out of communication coverage and without fuel. In the absence of ADC&RS and the promulgation of a controversial order that asked to 'consider all flying objects as Russian', Russian AD troops had little role to play. When the Russian retreat commenced, much of the AD equipment was captured or destroyed by the Ukrainian Army.

Presently the Russian AD weapons are deployed closer to their border and are more coordinated. During the counteroffensive operations, the Ukraine AF is finding its task more difficult. However, due to lapses three rogue drones have manged to sneak past the frontline AD surveillance towards Moscow.

## AIR THREAT

The air threat for both countries has been multi-faceted. Russia with its quantitative and qualitative superiority has had an upper hand. The composition of air delivered arsenal with both countries has been as follows:

- **RUSSIA**
  - * Fighter and AD Aircraft: Sukhois – SU-24, SU-25, SU-27, SU-30, SU-34, SU-35; Migs – Mig-29, Mig-31
  - * Helicopters:
    - – Attack Helicopters – Mi-24P, Mi-28N, Mi-35 Ka-52 Kamov
    - – Utility helicopters – Mi-8/17
  - * Surface-to-Surface Missiles (SSM):
    - – Ballistic Missiles – Kh-22, Kh-29, Kh-59, Kh-101, 9K79 OTR-21 Tochka, 9K720 Iskander
    - – Cruise Missile – 3M54-1 Novator Kalibr, 3M14 Biryuza, Kh-555
    - – Hypersonic Cruise Missile – Kh-47M2 Khinzal
  - * Unmanned Aerial Vehicles (UAVs)/Drones: Orlan-10/20/30, Forpost, Eleron 3 SV/ 28M, Zala Aero 421-16EM, Merlin; Iranian - Mohajer 6
  - * Loitering Munition: Shahed-–136
- **UKRAINE**
  - * Fighter and AD Aircraft: Sukhois - SU 24, SU 25, SU 27; Migs - Mig 29
  - * Helicopters:
    - – Attack Helicopters – MI 24, MI 28, H 225
    - – Utility Helicopters – MI 2, MI 8, MI 17, MI 14
  - * SSM: Ballistic Missile: Thunder, etc; Cruise Missile - R 360 Neptune, etc
  - * UAVs/Drones: A1 SM/AA1 SM/AV1A A1 CM Furia, Leleka 100, TU 141/143, etc; Turkish - Bayraktar TB 2 and a host of drones supplied by NATO countries

## DIFFERENCE IN APPROACH

### The Russian AF Edge and Initial Success

While the Ukraine AD systems may have been similar to what Russia had in its AD inventory, in terms of modernisation and upgradation Russia had an upper edge. Secondly, the intelligence of either side was known to the other but with Russia being the attacker, it had the advantage of surprise. Thirdly, in the EW aspect, Russia had the advantage of encircling East Ukraine from three sides,[36] due to which its jammers could act much more efficiently. However, to switch sectors, Ukraine troops and weapons had to travel much less. Fourthly, both Russia and Ukraine had similar radars and communication equipment operating at same frequency bands, which were subject to EW from both sides to include Electronic Counter Measures (ECMs) and Electronic Counter-Counter Measures (ECCMs). However, post separation from the Soviet Union, Russia had upgraded its EW capability.[37] Fifthly, since both sides were operating similar aircraft, the difficulty in visual identification was difficult, leading to relying more on e-IFF for which Russia is better equipped.

The Russian AF, with its superiority in numbers and quality of fighter aircraft (including 4$^{th}$ and 5$^{th}$ generation), bombers and helicopters, armed with guns, Air to Air Missiles (AAMs), Air to Surface Missiles (ASMs), rockets, unguided and guided bombs, etc had the advantage of the 'surprise factor' in terms of time, quantum and place of attack. Area of operations in Ukraine was surrounded by Russia on three sides: north (including an axis from Belarus), east (having pro-Russia population) and south (including from the Black Sea and Crimea, which had been annexed much before).[38] The key question was: 'What will be the weight of Russian attack from each direction?'

Before the war, Russia had employed its SU 24 maritime and electronic reconnaissance aircraft and IL-20 electronic intelligence aircraft to generate an electronic signature location map.[39] The process enabled Russia to identify the exact location of Ukrainian AD assets and surveillance radars. Their physical presence was ascertained by a battery of human spy network. The intelligence thus collated was used by the Russian AF to:

- Carry out EW on SAM sites. Ukraine equipment being of Soviet era made it easier for the Russian AF to take offensive EW actions
- Use fighters (SU 30SM and SU 35S fighters, SU 34 Bombers) to attack radar sites, AD guns and missile sites and ammunition storages
- Launch a series of missile strikes

The strategy adopted by the Russian ground forces was to head towards Kyiv with a purpose to destroy the Ukrainian government and force the Ukrainian Armed Forces to surrender. As the Russian troops moved deep inside Ukraine, capturing thousands of square kilometres of Ukrainian territory and surrounding

Kyiv, all seemed lost for Ukraine. The Russian AF, having pre-war collated intelligence (using Su-24MR and spy agents) about Ukrainian AD was successful to a large extent in destroying it over the first three days. The Russia AF carried out very effective suppression/destruction of enemy AD (SEAD/DEAD), rendering Ukraine AD virtually ineffective. Simultaneously the ground forces moved in.

By the end of first month, as the Russian AF bombed Ukrainian air bases and rained missiles on AD and other weapon concentrations, the Ukraine AF lost more than 40 aircraft, 15 helicopters and several drones and Unmanned Aerial Vehicles (UAVs). Many fixed assets of Ukrainian AD were completely/ partially destroyed. The Russians and the world thought that it would be a short, swift and a punitive kind of war.

### Ukraine's AD Battle

One of the terms of NATO's support to Ukraine included that Ukraine will not lead any offensive into Russian territory. As Russia attacked, it had the first-mover advantage while Ukraine had to adopt a reactive stance. Thus, Ukrainian AD was at a disadvantageous position. The Soviet-era surveillance radars had good medium- to high-level coverage, yet Ukraine had to rely on the early warning/ intelligence provided by NATO countries.

During the run up to the war there were many promises made by NATO about the supply of AD weapons, but the actual delivery commenced either just before or post February 24, 2022. As a result, Ukrainian AD was less coordinated with its AF.

In anticipation, Ukraine took passive AD measures and dispersed its AF and AD assets before the breakout of hostilities. With virtually no opposition, the Russian AF in the first three days of the war had distinct advantage. The Russian AF and missiles relentlessly attacked Ukrainian fixed AD weapons, radars and ammunition stores, causing much damage. Knowing the superiority of the Russian AF and the vulnerability of its AADMA, Ukraine adopted the following tactics:

- Operated its AD systems from multiple location to avoid its electronic signature being picked up by Russian Electronic Intelligence (ELINT) units.
- Wound up and moved to a new location in quick time post firing. The Russian retaliatory firing based on ELINT would find an empty space. This way the entire battery could never be destroyed/ damaged and most

of its AD systems continued to remain operational.

- Made good use of terrain folds as the Ukrainian AF had to fly in its own territory. Whereas if the Russian AF aircraft flew high, they became targets of Ukraine S-300 or Buk AD systems, and if they flew low to avoid radar detection, they became targets of MANPADS or AD gun fire.
- Trained its crews including in Maintenance and Repair Organisation (MRO), ably assisted by NATO allies.

Ukraine could salvage its equipment by resorting to passive AD measures. As the Russians virtually laid siege on Kyiv in double quick time, the resistive power of mobile Ukrainian AD and Ukraine's undaunting will to defend its territory slowed them down.[40]

Ukraine reorganised its mobile SAM batteries after the first three days of the war and shot down several Russian Su-34s and other attack planes, forcing Russia to keep much of its AF out of the fight.

As the Russian AF missed on accurate targeting repeatedly, it gave a ray of hope to the Ukrainian AD. Due to failed missions, the Russian AF resorted to undertaking additional missions to achieve desired effect on a given target. For more than a year, Ukrainian AD have proved their mettle by effectively destroying/ damaging/ warding off Russian AF fighters and helicopters. The Ukrainian AD, reinforced by NATO-supplied AD weapons, have imposed caution on the Russian AF.

For the first few months of the war, Ukraine relied heavily on the S-300 and the Buk, both mid- to long-range SAM systems, to target aircraft, cruise missiles and ballistic missiles. The infra-red seeking short-range missiles, MANPADS, were also used effectively. As Russian pilots became cautious, they seldom crossed the frontline and had to perforce resort to firing long-range artillery, using air- and ground-launched ballistic and cruise missiles and loitering munitions and drones.

## Russian AF: Lack of Strategy

The Russians for some reasons did not deploy their full strength of fourth and fifth generation aircraft. During the initial months of war and till date it has relied mostly on Su-24, Su-25, Su-30 and Su-34s. It flew Su-35 and Mig 31s only for special missions at high altitude as Combat Air Patrol (CAP). It extensively used Attack Helicopters (AH) Mi 24/35 – Hind, Mi 28 – Havok and Ka 52 – Alligator deep into Ukraine without achieving air superiority and suffered losses.[41]

Russian pilots lacked in strategy and training and took success for granted.[42] They considered each weapon fired (missiles, rockets, guns) as achieving a hit and relied less on Bomb Damage Assessment (BDA) reports. This confidence, as revealed later, proved to be a fatal mistake as very often they were way off the mark. Ukraine was quick to assess the situation as they were getting real time intelligence input from the NATO alliance, using satellite imagery and other modes.

As it moved deep into Ukraine, the Russian Army took little notice of communication breakdown, stretched logistics chain[43] and the exposed flanks. The jointmanship between the Russian AF and Army was found missing due to communication breakdown. Ground forces were without close air support. Russian AD elements were without proper ADC&RS and were briefed to consider every flying object as Russian. The other reasons why the Russian AF couldn't achieve optimum results against Ukraine are:

- The Ukrainian surveillance cover was further beefed up by the additional radars provided by the NATO allies. This forced the Russian pilots to fly low to avoid detection. However, thousands of MANPADS, AD guns and small arms weapons deployed across Ukraine caused great damage to them.
- The integration of the Ukrainian and the NATO command and control setup led to the availability of real-time satellite-based air picture, resulting in better decision making for the Ukrainian AF and AD units.
- The Ukrainian mobile AD systems were constantly being shifted after firing. The Russian AF couldn't take retaliatory measures against them.
- The Russian AF was forced to fly additional sorties/ missions due to inaccurate aiming. This resulted in Ukrainian AD troops achieving more kills.
- Russian pilots were fearful of the NATO-supplied Stinger and advanced AD systems, forcing them to be extra cautious and leading to inaccuracies while targeting.
- While Russian pilots seemed to have poor training standards, Ukrainian AF pilots fought valiantly.

### Ukraine's AD Counter Stroke

Ukrainian AD equipment that had taken passive AD measures was back in action. The ones that were lightly damaged were retrieved and repaired. Their MRO worked overtime to make maximum weapons serviceable. Whatever could be salvaged and cannibalised was done. By the third day of the war, Ukraine got its act together and struck back. The Ukrainian AF and ground forces, duly aided by US intelligence agencies, commenced to counter Russian forces. Simultaneously, the Ukrainian AD started to inflict casualty on the Russian AF.

## Effectiveness of the Russian AF

Instead of sending a package, constituting AD, EW and fighter aircraft for air attacks against priority targets, the Russian AF used single or a pair of aircraft randomly. Due to poor training standards and lack of confidence, the pilots flew their aircraft in daylight at medium to high altitude, thinking that the Ukrainian AD system has been decimated. As the war progressed, the Russian AF's aura of invincibility steadily kept diminishing and it turned out that most of the Russian pilots were playing safe. They would release weapons from standoff distances for fear of being engaged by the Ukraine AADMA. The Russian unguided bombs and ASMs were quite ineffective in terms of accurately hitting targets.

Due to poor communication[44] and consequently ADC&RS, the Russian AF suffered more than expected losses. As the Russian AF lost aircraft, it became cautious and started to fly at low levels. This put additional stress on pilots as they were engaged by thousands of Infra-Red (IR) homing MANPADS, which included Soviet-era Strela-2M and Igla and NATO-supplied Stinger missile systems. With losses surmounting, the Russian AF restricted their attacks from their own side of the frontline using the toss bombing technique[45] or standoff weapons.[46]

The Russian Attack Helicopter (AH) fleet initially conducted aggressive tank hunting sorties behind Ukrainian frontlines, with penetration depths of up to 50 km. The Russian helicopters were armed with the laser beam riding line of sight guidance system, which required considerable exposure time. The time available to Ukrainian MANPADS was sufficient to engage it effectively. Russian helicopters started to execute night attacks. As a result, Russia had to rely heavily on Ka-52s, which had better night vision devices and precision missiles.

The Ka-52s were armed with Missile Warning Receivers (MWR) and Infrared (IR) flare decoys to mislead the AD missiles. Each helicopter was equipped with a limited number of flares and when multiple missiles were launched, these would get quickly expended. Denuded of flares, the helicopters would become easy targets. This move resulted in the best Ka-52 crews being shot down early in the war. The new, less-skilled crews flew more cautiously, keeping their machines at the treetop level, whence they became prey to Anti-Tank Guided Missiles (ATGM) (such as

Javelin), rockets and even small arms fire. Russia lost the maximum number of Ka-52s.[47]

Other Russian helicopters decided to stay on their own side of the frontline and rarely closed in on their intended target. Russian helicopters were forced to use dumb bombs/ rockets, which were rarely accurate.

## Massed Missile Attack by Russia

On Oct 08, 2022, a bomb-laden truck attacked the Kerch Strait Bridge[48] (connecting Crimea to Russia), resulting in limiting logistics supplies to Russian troops in southern Ukraine. Besides, Ukraine had gained a sizeable portion of its lost territory. In retaliation, Russia changed tactics and started firing barrages of missiles and weaponised drones, including the Iranians Shahed-136. These barrages were fired at multiple targets repeatedly and at odd times, including at night. To counter them Ukraine had to use costly AD SAMs.

The first attack was on Oct 10, 2022[49] with a wave of 84 missiles and 24 drones at multiple targets in different regions with the main focus on Kyiv. Subsequently, Ukraine has been targeted by a large number of such wave attacks across regions.

Russia expanded the scope of its target to semi-military and civilian assets to include energy infrastructure (power-grid, power generation and distribution centres), industrial areas, railway infrastructure, bridges, shelters, university campuses and residential complexes. Ukraine, in turn, had to provision AD cover for these civilian assets as well. This meant thinning down the existing density of AD cover or providing area AD weapons such as Patriots. Besides, the rate of consumption of AD missiles and gun ammunition became very high. Stocks of missiles for Soviet-era S-300 and Buk AD systems, which made up more than 80 per cent of Ukraine's AD, started depleting fast.

The first missile attack was a success for Russia as it was unexpected. Subsequently, the missile barrage attacks were tracked. The flight data intelligence of these missiles was provided by NATO, which made it easier for Ukraine's AADMA to engage them with a high rate of success. In May 2023, multiple waves of missile–drone combination attacks were made by Russia on Ukraine. The Russian strategy was to distract the Ukrainian forces from its counteroffensive and keep Kyiv as the epicentre of these repeated attacks. Till May end, Kyiv was targeted by approximately 560 missiles/ drones; nearly 90 per cent of these were destroyed by Ukrainian AD. However, the strategy also involved the low-cost Iran-manufactured loitering munition, Shahed-136, being engaged by costly

Stinger or Patriot/NASAMS missiles. Russia succeeded in raising the overall cost of war for Ukraine (read NATO) exponentially. Simultaneously, there arose a concern regarding the replenishment of the AD missiles stock with no signs of what the source would be.

## Ukraine Deployment of Advanced AD Systems

When the Ukrainian Armed Forces launched its counteroffensive, Russia enlarged the spectrum of war by engaging civilian targets. In trying to protect civilian assets, the Ukrainian AD density reduced considerably, rendering AD cover inadequate. The need for additional AD system became a necessity.

To meet this challenge, Ukraine had to request the NATO countries to provide it with advanced AD systems[50] on priority. There was a decision dilemma amongst NATO countries as they had to handover their AD reserves. Besides, Ukrainian soldiers had to undergo intensive training on these complex systems as their operations were entirely different from the erstwhile Soviet-era systems. The advanced AD systems arrived in a trickle but nevertheless provided the Ukrainian Armed Forces with great succour and helped them to counter the Russian air threat.

The Ukraine AD soldiers were well trained on the NATO-provided advanced systems that were designed to intercept missiles. The Russian missiles could be detected, their trajectory tracked and the point of impact predicted with great accuracy. Ukraine was helped by US inputs and the location of mobile assets could be shifted in time and avoid being hit. Thus, Ukraine could keep its AD systems protected and were able to take offensive actions.

It is very creditable that Ukraine's AD has been able to destroy more than 70 per cent of Russian missiles including the hypersonic Kinzhal missile through the war. The Ukrainian AD shot down 73 out of 90 Russian cruise missiles (81 per cent) in November 2022 and 60 out of 76 (79 per cent) in December 2022.[51]

The success rate improved after Ukraine's AD created a tiered AD over Kyiv with its own and NATO advanced AD systems. As Kyiv was repeatedly attacked by missiles and drones, the AD troops remained ever vigilant.[52] On May 16, 2023, Ukraine's AD destroyed six Kh-47 Kinzhal hypersonic missiles fired at Kyiv. This was followed by attacks on May 24, 25 and 26, when Ukraine's AD shot down all drones and missiles. On May 28, Ukrainian AD shot down 40 Shahed-136 UAVs. On June 6, Ukrainian AD destroyed all 35 cruise missiles launched from Russia. The advanced AD systems provided by NATO countries proved their worth.

## HIGH-TECHNOLOGY ADVANCEMENT

The technologies being used during the Russian–Ukraine war and associated with GBADWS are as given in succeeding paragraphs.

### Artificial Intelligence (AI) Based Target Assessment and Engagement

Artificial Intelligence (AI) is increasingly being used in war for planning and execution and in weapon systems. AI and automation are indeed the future of war by making systems that are smarter, faster, more efficient and precise.

Throughout the war data has and is being collated using satellites, radars and drones. The sheer volume of data generated on daily basis is huge, making it humanly impossible to sift and filter usable data. Use of AI technology has enabled command centres to filter usable data. AI also helps in laying target priority, target designation, weapon selection and engagement. Precise commands are sent to the weapon to initiate action with pinpoint accuracy. In essence, AI is making the Observe-Orient-Decide-Act (OODA) loop cycle happen in near real time.

### Autonomous and Semi-autonomous Drones

The Bayraktar TB2 provided by Turkey to Ukraine contributed significantly towards the destruction of Russian armour stranded in the open enroute to Kyiv. The drone technology has made the job of AD warriors ever so difficult as it adopts the role of an 'Autonomous Weapon System (AWS)'.[53] On other hand, Russia employed the low-cost Iranian loiter munition Shahed-136, which were targeted and destroyed by costly AD missiles. Shahed-136 was simply fitted with a Global Positioning System (GPS) suite and could loiter over the target area, select, identify and attack the defined target.

The aerial AWS is a challenge for GBADWS. Drones are available the world over in different sizes, make, endurance, capacity, etc and are capable of being controlled in a fully or semi-autonomous mode. Drones, including the quadcopter/multi-copter variety, have the potential to be very dangerous. Their role may vary to include recce, EW, high explosives, kamikaze mode, etc. Some of the characteristics that makes them more challenging for GBADWS are:

- **Main Body.** The drone body is made of carbon fibre composite, which has low Equivalent Echoing Area (EEA) and is difficult to detect by radars. Troops have to be trained for visual detection, identification and reporting. Without timely detection, AD weapons may find it difficult to engage.

- **Autonomous Flight.**[54] GPS suites are readily available and these can be made to home onto pre-fed locations. Auto-pilots are available, which provide flight control capability to a drone/ loiter munition.
- **Endurance.** Varying endurance limits for drones can be achieved by using dual power source (fuel and battery), solar powered cells or enabling the drone with loiter capability after being released from mother aircraft. All this makes the task of GBADWS difficult.
- **Hovering and Flight Control.** The quadcopter's capability to hover at a point, fly nap of the earth, hide behind a tree/ building or pop up at a set time before carrying out an assigned task makes it a dangerous target for GBADWS apart from being difficult to detect. Drones are likely to be fitted with GPS-based automatic flight termination or return to home option, Radio Frequency Identification and Detection (RFID)-based tracking, radar/missile warning receivers, data links, etc. Many of its features make it a potent threat and a difficult target for GBADWS.

## Drone versus Drone Combat

Drones are being modified to carry out combat tasks. Besides recce and spying, dropping grenades or unguided bombs, they are being modified to simply ram into each other to destroy or damage the other.[55] In Ukraine, drone dogfights started using commercially available low-cost, low-altitude drones. Some are modified to act as virtual flying Improvised Explosive Devices (IEDs) that have the advantage of springing surprise on enemy drones. Sophisticated drones use advanced radars, backed by AI and aerospace technology, to precisely fire nets that trap enemy drones. Certain combat drones are suitably armed to fight in tandem with piloted mother aircraft that gives guidance command signals for greater accuracy. Due to their relative low cost, they are expendable but have the capability to cause substantial damage.

## Anti-Drone Technology

The war saw a multitude of drones being used for multiple roles. Both Ukraine and Russia are weary of them as they are a low cost means of waging a war but to defend against them can be very costly. Due to their small size, AD radars find it difficult to detect them. The possibility of improving AD radar's detection capability exists but it would result in too many false alarms as it will pick up bird signals as well.

They can be engaged by choosing between the costly hard-kill and the cheaper soft-kill option. Both options were employed during the war. For hard-kill, anti-drone guns, multi-barrel AD guns or MANPADS were used. However, a good drone controller is able to counter them easily by flying at the treetop level. On the other hand, by using jammers the drone control link can be jammed to deceive, manipulate, disable control or 'capture' control'. The jamming effect depends upon the power output of the jamming frequency. Anti-drone guns such as the Ukrainian KVS G-6[56] and the Lithuanian EDM4S[57] have been extensively used (in hundreds) by Ukrainians against Russia. The Russians used an elementary version of anti-drone guns to jam and capture Ukrainian drones.

Russia used Shahed-136 and Shahed-131[58] to attack both Ukrainian military and civilian power infrastructure. Ukraine often destroyed Iranian-made drones, which cost about USD 20,000 each, using a USD 500,000 AD missile. To deal with Shahed-136, the US has designed a c-UAS laser-guided rocket system that includes a M240 machine-gun mount and an EW system that can take control of a drone not equipped with advanced encryption.[59] This system costs just USD 30,000.

### Satellite-based Target Tracking Data Transfer

NATO countries together have hundreds of remote sensing and communication satellites. Starlink[60] communication of Space X has nearly 4,000 Low Earth Orbit (LEO) satellites. The US has permitted Ukraine to make use of it to connect shooters to sensors in real time. Based on the point of launch and corelating the missiles trajectory, the point of impact can be predicted with great accuracy. Data on approaching Russian missiles can be quickly processed and transmitted to Ukrainian AADMA C&R network. Once the NATO advanced AD systems were deployed every Russian missile fired has been effectively intercepted and the hit percentage has kept on improving.

### Electronic Warfare (EW)

One unique aspect of the AD battle is EW and its offensive capability. EW has the ability to make the opponents deaf (no communication) and blind (jammed radars). It is about frequency management over a wide band. The AD battle is fast paced as it takes just few seconds for aerial target engagement. Radio and wireless communication (operating in a 3–800 megahertz band) form an important function in passage of C&R orders. Radars detect and track targets and operate in frequencies ranging from 'P' band (800 megahertz) to 'Ku' band (40 gigahertz). Each AD weapon system has a unique operational frequency band. Therefore, every country ensures frequency diversity, which is achieved by having multiple AD equipment operating in different bands to avoid getting jammed across.

In EW, Russia had a clear edge over Ukraine, as seen in the Crimean War, and even over the US, as noted in the Syrian War. Russia is capable of jamming the GPS all along its border from Finland to the Black Sea. Ukraine expected a heavy dose of EW and it was ready for it with help of the NATO alliance. The Russian EW systems focused more on jamming recce drones to mislead them as well as on GPS receivers of enemy drones to locate their command & control links, etc. However, after the initial jamming of radars deployed at airbases and those of the AD equipment, the EW effect gradually reduced as Russian troops forayed deep into Ukraine. Russia made use of the EW/ recce drone, Orlan-10,[61] extensively. However, these were easy to track and many were shot down. It can be presumed that the Russian EW elements were not as effective as expected due to:

- Not being grouped with tac battle groups.
- The capture of two of Russian advanced systems, after which Russia took precautions. These systems were the 1RL257 Krasukha-4[62] (designed to jam drones, guidance systems, radar guided weapons from more than 250 km range) and the Borisaglebsk-2[63] (jam drone guidance).
- Over confidence of Russian commanders, who lost sight of EW units as an offensive weapon.
- Interference with their own equipment by high powered equipment, especially at longer ranges; evidence of the same being that many Russian troops started communicating in the clear. During the Ukraine counteroffensive in the east, the Ukraine troops again had to face the Russian EW challenge.
- Few well-trained soldiers on EW equipment.

To counter Russian EW, Ukraine took steps that included:

- Remaining more focussed on Russian EW activity after deciphering their equipment characteristics and accordingly taking countermeasures.
- Using Starlink commercial internet satellite services that were opened for Ukraine at the behest of the US. With hundreds of LEO satellites and thousands of ground stations to hook on to, it was impossible to jam each one.
- Using the EW protection equipment supplied by the US and UK.

- Using the encrypted communication equipment provided by US and Turkey.

### US Interface for Ukraine Command and Control Centres

Since Ukraine's AD equipment was of the Soviet era and the technology and frequency used in them were quite different from that of NATO's equipment, an interface had to be created in command-and-control centres to avoid interference and mix-ups. The US helped create and train the Ukrainians to operate the command-and-control centres, which were also enabled to receive satellite-based data.

### Tracking Cruise and Ballistic Missiles

The US continuously provided Ukraine with updated intelligence reports. An important facet of these reports was the accurate data on Russian missiles by monitoring their flight trajectory. Based on the point of launch and tracking of the flight path high speed computers could predict the point of impact. This data was relayed to Ukraine command and control centres via satellites. The data had a high degree of accuracy and based on it Ukraine dispersed its equipment to safe distances from the point of impact or engaged the missiles accurately with radar-controlled AD guns and SAMs. Ukraine's success rate in intercepting Russian missiles was more than 70 per cent.

### AI and Quantum Computing

The current Intelligence, Surveillance and Recce (ISR) capability based on visual, infra-red (IR) and electronic sensors have made battlefields transparent, irrespective of any camouflage and concealment. The proliferation of sensors such as recce drones and remote sensing satellites along with satellite data links have ensured foolproof coordination between sensors and shooters. No matter how voluminous the data is, AI and quantum computing has the capability to compress, filter and make it available in a 'ready for use format' within minutes. Anything that moves will be picked up by a sensor and can be hit. Defending troops, such as the Ukraine AD, have to remain well dispersed, concentrate quickly to act and again disperse before the enemy reacts. Attacking troops, on other hand, have to resort to saturation attacks using multiple modes simultaneously, as were undertaken by Russia. It requires a huge inventory of missiles to last for a prolonged battle.

As a corollary, when concentration of troops translates into attracting an aerial threat, decentralisation is the answer. To be effective as a whole, command and control elements have to synthesise the picture, using AI, of the entire war zone, update it in real time and engage the enemy simultaneously rather than sequentially. Long-range weapons will have an edge including Beyond Visual Range (BVR) capabilities, as available with the Russian AF.

## TAKEAWAYS FOR INDIA

The progress of the Russia–Ukraine war has been largely shaped by the Ukrainian AD. The quantum of high explosives that has been fired by Russia would have caused much more damage but for Ukrainian AD. Similarly, the Russian AF has been kept at bay by Ukrainian AD. Some of the key takeaways are as given in succeeding paragraphs.

**Layered and Tiered AD**: India is surrounded with enemies on its land frontiers. With China having a foothold in Sri Lanka and Pakistan, the Indian coastline is also exposed. There is a need to have a layered and tiered AD to meet the air threat. Since AD missiles are costly, a beginning has been made to create an AD shield.[64] This shield should cover the entire air space over India. It may include:

- An outermost layer of Ballistic Missile Defence (BMD) with a range beyond 250 km and altitude coverage of over 25 km
- A second layer of long-range SAM family with a varying range between 100 and 400 km and altitude coverage of up to 25 km
- A third layer of medium-range SAMs with a range between 50 and 100 km and altitude coverage of over 10 km
- A fourth layer of short-range SAMs with a range up to 25 km and altitude coverage of up to 10 km
- A fifth layer of very short-range SAMs and AD guns with a range up to 10 km and altitude coverage up to 3 km. This will also include the MANPADS family

**MANPADS**: The MANPADS proliferation, achieved by Ukraine across the war zone with the help of NATO enabled them to force the Russian AF to maintain a safe distance. The utility of MANPADS in the Russian–Ukraine war has been adequately exemplified by the number of aircraft, helicopters and drones shot down. India should gradually upgrade its limited inventory of MANPADS. India should develop indigenous capabilities to manufacture MANPADS since in the current air threat environment they are required in thousands. India should procure MANPADS in sufficient quantity till then.

**Radar Controlled Guns**: To engage low-cost drones with high-cost SAMs may not be a viable solution. Radar controlled guns such as the Germany

Gepard or Swiss Oerlikon (now manufactured by Italy) or the Czech Republic Viktor could be an answer. The target tracking radar technology needs to be fully indigenised and integrated with 30/ 40mm AD guns.

**Anti-Drone Weapons:** The Russian–Ukraine war and the earlier Azerbaijan–Armenia war have clearly highlighted that drones will be an important element of air threat. Their versatility in size, role, endurance, altitude coverage, all-up weight capability, type of body material, etc is so varied that it has become a potent threat that cannot be wished away. The drone threat has already manifested on India's borders. Therefore, an anti-drone policy encompassing all aspects is an urgent requirement. Anti-drone jamming guns for disabling control links and anti-drone laser guns for disablement of components are low-cost solutions. India also needs to mass produce MANPADS for hard-kill of larger drone versions. India needs to create an AD wing in each of the Central Armed Police Force (CAPF) for anti-drone operations in the hinterland.

**Radars:** India has a varied terrain all along its border and in its hinterland. Therefore, India needs radars with terrain specific capabilities. In addition, the radars must have drone detection capability as well. A pan India radar grid should be created with sufficient overlap, and it should be networked with control centres. There should be two-tier vertical coverage of space: one at low-level (below 1,500 m) and the other at medium- to high-level since the radar requirement is high.

**Satellite-based Communication and Data Links:** Just like the US made the Starlink satellite-based communication and data links available to Ukraine forces, our armed forces should also get access to OneWeb[65] India. Gradually, India should have its independent system. ADC&RS is an important function and it needs to be automated and made foolproof secure. Without it a coordinated AD battle cannot be fought successfully. It will involve integrating all sensors and shooters on one grid for optimum results.

**Electronic Intelligence (ELINT).** So far many of India's ELINT systems are being imported or simply assembled in India. There is a need to manufacture them indigenously. Public–private partnership in this field will ensure faster development. Automated ELINT systems backed with AI and data analytics will enable AD during a war to take effective countermeasures against the enemy and counter-counter measures to safeguard our own systems.

**EW Systems:** High-powered jammers with ranges beyond 250 km is the need of the hour. The soft-kill option of the enemy's drones and drone control systems is the best options. The system should have frequency agility and diversity to cater to all types of electromagnetic (EM) communication and non-communication frequencies.

## CONCLUSION

The Russian AF's inability to control the skies was an early surprise of the war. With many aircraft getting shot down, Russia pulled back its AF. Thereafter for much of the war, the Russian AF has concentrated on sorties along the frontlines, lobbing rockets and firing long-range missiles at Ukrainian positions. The Russian AF is rarely crossing the Forward Line of Troops (FLOT) even after 17 months of war. Even the Ukraine AF has kept its aircraft out of Russian SAM range. Both are relying more on long-range artillery to provide support to ground forces. So far Russia has lost 85 fighters and 65 helicopters while Ukraine has lost 100 fighters and 45 helicopters.

With more than 500 days of war and still counting, Russia has been relentlessly firing barrages of cruise and ballistic missiles, artillery and loitering munitions. Intercepting them with high-cost SAM missiles is escalating the cost of war for Ukraine. Ukraine continues to hold Soviet-era missile systems (S-300 and Buk M1) in large quantities as well as the NATO-supplied advanced systems. However, the missiles and gun ammunition are at an abysmally low level. The MANPADS and short-range SAMs (Strela-2m, Strela-10, OSA) seem to have gotten exhausted. The 23 mm guns (both tracked and towed) are still there but are not effective against missiles.

The Ukrainian AD by end 2022 was composed of a mix of Soviet-era weapons and more modern Western systems supplied by the US, Germany, France, Italy and UK. Each requires its own specialised training. Ukrainians have been able to effectively defend their airspace by deploying these weapons.

Post the end of the Cold War, NATO countries had mothballed their AD systems and new acquisitions did not take place as all countries were relying on the air superiority of the US AF and the Patriot system. Whatever little they had to spare has been handed over to Ukraine. As on mid-July 2023, European NATO members have very few GBADWS left to hand over to Ukraine, including expendable missiles and gun ammunition. To revive the production line will require months.

On other hand, despite NATO's sanctions, Russia has been receiving direct help from Iran and China, allowing it to maintain the tempo of its air threat throughout. It is unthinkable to continue with such a relentless aerial threat for any country. However, Ukrainian AD troops have stood their ground and have enabled the ground troops to fight back and wrest control of large tracts of lost ground.

Zelensky is disparately looking towards the US for multi-role F-16 Fighting Falcons. US President Biden has agreed to lift curbs on NATO members to lend or lease F-16s from their respective kitties to Ukraine with a condition that they shall be used to defend Ukraine territory and not escalate the war into Russia. Ukrainian pilots are currently being trained but can US risk the image of the F-16 taking a beating against the Russian Su-35 or Mig-31?

Ukrainian AD has managed to hold the Russian onslaught of missile and drone attacks as of mid-July 2023. Russia continues to attack Ukraine with waves of long-range missiles and loitering munitions. While defending against them, the Ukraine AD missiles and gun ammunition stocks have depleted. Russia is gradually wearing down Ukrainian AD including the ones provided by NATO allies. Low-density or absence of Ukrainian AD would create space for the Russian AF to cause unhindered damage to Ukrainian assets including civilian infrastructure. If this happens, Russian forces will have an opportunity to make significant gains on the battlefield. The world will have to wait to know the final outcome.

## NOTES

1 Chris Gordon, 'Lack of Airpower in Ukraine Proves Value of Air Superiority,' *Air & Space Journal*, March 22, 2023, at https://www.airandspaceforces.com/airpower-ukraine-air-superiority-hecker/

2 What is NATO at https://www.nato.int/nato-welcome/index.html

3 Alexandria, 'The West Needs to Keep Supporting Ukraine with MANPADS,' *GMF*, April 20, 2022, at https://www.gmfus.org/news/west-needs-keep-supporting-ukraine-manpads

4 'Russia Just Destroyed Ukraine's Air Defences in a Couple of Hours: Why Was it So Easy?,' *Military Watch Magazine*, February 24, 2022, at https://militarywatchmagazine.com/article/russia-just-destroyed-ukraine-s-air-defences-in-a-couple-of-hours-why-was-it-so-easy

5 Zach Beauchamp, 'Why the First Few Days of War in Ukraine Went Badly For Russia,' *Vox*, February 28, 2022, at https://www.vox.com/22954833/russia-ukraine-invasion-strategy-putin-kyiv

6 Ken Dilanian, Courtney Kube, Carol E Lee and Dan De Luce, 'US Intel Helped Ukraine Protect Air Defences, Shoot Russian Plane Carrying Troops,' *NBC News*, April 26, 2022, at https://www.nbcnews.com/politics/national-security/us-intel-helped-ukraine-protect-air-defences-shoot-russian-plane-carry-rcna26015

7 Dissolution of the Soviet Union at https://en.wikipedia.org/wiki/Dissolution_of_the_Soviet_Union

8 Sergio Miller, 'An Extremely Big Threat': Russian Glide Bombs Make Their Debut in the War,' *Wavell Room*, April 17, 2023, at https://wavellroom.com/2023/04/17/russian-glide-

bombs/#:~:text=Russian%20glide%20bombs%20emerged%20only,target%20at% 20a%20 greater%20distance.

9 Larry Dickerson, 'Loitering Munitions Will Change Warfare – Until Air Defence Catches Up,' *DSM*, April 24, 2023, at https://dsm.forecastinternational.com/wordpress/2023/04/24/ loitering-munitions-will-change-warfare-until-air-defence-catchup/

10 Jonathan Guyer, 'The West Is Testing Out a Lot of Shiny New Military Tech in Ukraine,' *Vox*, September 21, 2022, at https://www.vox.com/2022/9/21/23356800/us-testing-tech-ukraine-russia-war

11 'How Elon Musk's Starlink is Helping Ukraine in the Fight Against Russia,' *The Indian Express*, January 10, 2023, at https://indianexpress.com/article/explained/explained-global/how-elon-musks-starlink-is-helping-ukraine-in-the-fight-against-russia-8373736/

12 Lt Gen V K Saxena, 'Tiered Defence: Putting the SAM in Perspective,' *Indian Defence Review*, January 23, 2017 available at http://www.indiandefencereview.com/news/tiered-defence-putting-the-sam-in-perspective/

13 Daryna Antoniuk, 'How Electronic Warfare Is Reshaping the War Between Russia and Ukraine,' *The Record*, August 16, 22, at https://therecord.media/how-electronic-warfare-is-reshaping-the-war-between-russia-and-ukraine

14 Colin Demarest, 'US Sending Ukraine Electronic Jamming Gear in $150M Package,' *Defence News*, May 9, 2022, at https://www.defencenews.com/electronic-warfare/2022/05/09/us-sending-ukraine-electronic-jamming-gear-in-150m-package/

15 Tom Soufi BurridgeOleksiv Pshemyskiy, Dragana Jovanovic and Alesandro Pavone, 'US Surveillance Data Crucial For Ukraine, Top Commander Says,' *ABC News*, February 12, 2023, at https://abcnews.go.com/International/us-surveillance-data-crucial-ukraine-top-commander/ story?id=97059698

16 Alex Horton, Ruby Mellen, Samuel Granados and Arthur Galocha, 'These Are the Western Air Defence Systems Protecting Ukraine,' *The Washington Post*, May 19, 2023, at https:// www.washingtonpost.com/world/2023/05/19/ukraine-air-defence-systems-patriot/

17 Jacek Tarocinski, 'Safe skies? Air Defence on NATO's Northern, Eastern And South-Eastern Flank,' *OSW*, January 19, 2023, at https://www.osw.waw.pl/en/publikacje/osw-commentary/ 2023-01-19/safe-skies-air-defence-natos-northern-eastern-and-south

18 Niraj Srivastava, 'Leaked Papers Reveal Proxy War in Ukraine,' *The Tribune*, April 29, 2023, at https://www.tribuneindia.com/news/comment/leaked-papers-reveal-proxy-war-in-ukraine-502932

19 Ukrainian Air Defence Forces at https://en.wikipedia.org/wiki/Ukrainian_Air_Defence_Forces

20 'Strela 2m: Germany Approves the Delivery Of Ex-DDR SA-7 Grail Strela-2 Air Defence Missile Weapons To Ukraine,' *Defence News*, March 03, 2022, at https://www.armyrecognition.c om/defence_ news_march_2022_global_security_army_industry/germany_approves_ the_ delivery_of_ex-ddr_sa-7_grail_strela-2_air_defence_missile_weapons_to_ukraine.html

21 Anuj Tiwari, 'Stingers: Ukraine's Powerful Stinger Missiles That Wreaked Havoc on Russian Forces - All You Need to Know,' *India Times*, 08 Mar 2022, at https://www.indiatimes.com/ trending/social-relevance/stinger-missiles-ukraine-563850.html

22 Les Pa Norsk, Norway provides an air defence system to Ukraine, Norway MoD, 20 Apr 20, 2022, at https://www.regjeringen.no/en/aktuelt/air-defence-system-to-ukraine/id2908807/

23 Tanmay Kadam, '1st Batch Of US Avenger Activated in Ukraine; Expert Says Air Defence Vehicles Highly Vulnerable in War Zone,' *The Eurasian*, April 16, 2023, at https://www.eurasian times.com/us-made-avengers-provided-to-ukraine-vulnerable-in/

24 Jack Buckby, 'Starstreak, the Fastest Surface-To-Air Missile Ever Made, Is Bringing Down

Russian Helicopters in Ukraine,' *Business Insider*, May 11, 2022, at https://www.businessinsider.com/british-starstreak-missile-is-shooting-down-russian-helicopters-in-ukraine-2022-5?IR=T

25 Jerzy Reszcynski, 'Ukrainian Media Praise the Polish Piorun MANPADS,' *Defence 24*, August 5, 2022, at https://defence24.com/armed-forces/ukrainian-media-praise-the-polish-piorun-manpads

26 'US Considers HAWK Air Defence Equipment For Ukraine,' *Euractiv*, October 25, 2022, at https://www.euractiv.com/section/global-europe/news/us-considers-hawk-air-defence-equipment-for-ukraine/

27 Gaetan Powis, 'French Crotale in Ukraine: First Interception of a Russian Missile,' *Air & Cosmos International*, March 21, 2023, at https://aircosmosinternational.com/article/french-crotale-in-ukraine-first-interception-of-a-russian-missile-3734

28 'Skynex Anti-Aircraft Systems Are Designed to Strengthen Ukrainian Air Defences,' *E S & T*, April 27, 2023, at https://esut.de/en/2023/04/meldungen/41699/skynex-flugabwehrsysteme-staerken-die-ukrainische-luftverteidigung/

29 'Ukraine's Air Defence Fortified As Viktor System Enters Operational Service,' *Militarnyi*, June 11, 2023, at https://mil.in.ua/en/news/ukraine-s-air-defence-fortified-as-viktor-system-enters-operational-service/

30 dpa, 'Germany to Supply 45 More Gepard Tanks to Ukraine,' *Radio Free Europe Radio Liberty*, June 24, 2023, at https://www.rferl.org/a/germany-gepard-tanks-ukraine/32473632.html

31 'Germany Confirms Delivery Of Second IRIS-T Air Defence System to Ukraine,' *European Pravda* April 30, 2023, at https://www.pravda.com.ua/eng/news/2023/04/30/7400072/

32 'Ukraine Receives First NASAMS Air Defence Systems,' *DW*, July 11, 2022, at https://www.dw.com/en/updates-ukraine-receives-first-nasams-air-defence-systems/a-63667120

33 Astra 30 Best Europe Air Defence System Goes to War in Ukraine, YouTube video, at https://www.youtube.com/watch?v=ePbuthJPM54&ab_channel=WeaponDetective

34 Adam Pemble, 'US-made Patriot Guided Missile Systems Arrive in Ukraine,' *AP News*, April 20, 2023, at https://apnews.com/article/russia-ukraine-war-patriot-missile-system-4c79f91100899ca1880a61f2d1f328179

35 "Air Defense of Ground Troops (PVO Sukhoputnykh Voysk)" at Global Security.Org, at https://www.globalsecurity.org/military/world/russia/pvo-sv.htm

36 Steven Pifer, 'The Russia-Ukraine War at Three Months,' *Brookings,* May 23, 2022, at https://www.brookings.edu/articles/the-russia-ukraine-war-at-three-months/

37 Btyan Clark, 'The Fall and Rise of Russian Electronic Warfare,' *IEEE*, July 30, 2022, at https://spectrum.ieee.org/the-fall-and-rise-of-russian-electronic-warfare

38 Helene Cooper and Eric Schmitt, 'Russian's Assault in Ukraine Slows After an Aggressive Start,' *New York Times,* February 25, 2022, at https://www.nytimes.com/2022/02/25/us/politics/russia-attacks-ukraine.html

39 Justin Bronk, 'The Russian Air War and Ukrainian Requirements for Air Defence,' Royal United Services Institute, November 7, 2022, at https://static.rusi.org/SR-Russian-Air-War-Ukraine-web-final.pdf

40 'Battle for Kyiv: Ukrainian Valour, Russian Blunders,' *Washington Post* August 24, 2022, at https://www.washingtonpost.com/national-security/interactive/2022/kyiv-battle-ukraine-survival/

41 Dan Lamothe, 'Russia Invasion Begins With Precision Missiles But Weapons Are Changing As Siege War Begins,' *Washington Post,* March 1, 2022, at https://www.washingtonpost.com/national-security/2022/03/01/ukraine-invasion-russia-missiles-siege/

42 Sophia Ankel, 'Poor Training and Outdated Equipment Left Russia's Air Force Unable to

Help Much In the Invasion of Ukraine,' *Business Insider*, April 25, 2023, at https://www.businessinsider.in/international/news/poor-training-and-outdated-equipment-left-russias-air-force-unable-to-help-much-in-the-invasion-of-ukraine-study-finds/articleshow/99767288.cms

43 Denys Davydenko, Margaryta Khvostova, Dmytro Kryvosheiev and Olga Lymar, 'Lessons for the West: Russia's Military Failures in Ukraine,' *European Council of Foreign Affairs*, August 11, 2022, at https://ecfr.eu/article/lessons-for-the-west-russias-military-failures-in-ukraine/

44 Sergei Dobrynin and Mark Krutov, 'Communication Breakdown: How Russia's Invasion Of Ukraine Bogged Down,' *Radio Free Europe Radio Liberty* March 19, 2022, at https://www.rferl.org/a/communication-lapses-russia-invasion-failures/31761259.html

45 'Why Are Pilots in Ukraine Firing Rockets So Clumsily?,' *The Economist*, June 20, 2022, at https://www.economist.com/the-economist-explains/2022/06/20/why-are-pilots-in-ukraine-firing-rockets-so-clumsily

46 Col. Mark Gunzinger, USAF (Ret.), 'Stand In, Standoff,' *Air and Space Force*, July 01, 2020, at https://www.airandspaceforces.com/article/stand-in-standoff/

47 'Why Has Russia Lost So Many Ka-52s in Ukraine?,' *UK Defence Journal*, June 9, 2022, at https://ukdefencejournal.org.uk/why-has-russia-lost-so-many-ka-52s-in-ukraine/

48 Peter Beaumont and Emma Graham-Harrison, 'Key Bridge Linking Crimea To Russia Hit By Huge Explosion,' *The Guardian*, October 8, 2022, at https://www.theguardian.com/world/2022/oct/08/crimea-kerch-bridge-explosions-russia-ukraine

49 Max Hunder and Jonathan Landay, 'Russia Launches Biggest Air Strikes Since Start of Ukraine War,' *Reuters*, October 11, 2022, at https://www.reuters.com/world/europe/russias-ria-state-agency-reports-fuel-tank-fire-kerch-bridge-crimea-2022-10-08/

50 Justin Bronk, Nick Reynolds and Jack Watling, 'The Russian Air War and Ukrainian Requirements for Air Defence,' *Royal United Services Institute*, November 7, 2022, at https://rusi.org/explore-our-research/publications/special-resources/russian-air-war-and-ukrainian-requirements-air-defence

51 Joshua Thurston, 'Russia Launches 'Massive' Attack on Ukraine Cities With 120 Missiles and Drones,' *Times*, December 29, 2022, at https://www.thetimes.co.uk/article/russia-bombards-ukrainian-cities-with-120-missiles-v98qjl3wr

52 Adam Robinson and Kayleen Devlin, 'Kyiv Missile Strikes: Tracking the Rise of Russian Attacks,' *BBC*, June 3, 2023, at https://www.bbc.com/news/world-europe-65682618

53 Amitai Etzioni and Oren Etzioni, 'Pros and Cons of Autonomous Weapons Systems,' *Military Review*, May–June 2017, at https://www.armyupress.army.mil/Journals/Military-Review/English-Edition-Archives/May-June-2017/Pros-and-Cons-of-Autonomous-Weapons-Systems.

54 An autonomous flight is a flight which is under the control of automatic systems and needs no intervention from a human pilot.

55 David Hambling, 'Ukraine Wins First Drone Vs. Drone Dogfight Against Russia, Opening a New Era of Warfare,' *Forbes*, October 14, 2022, at https://www.forbes.com/sites/davidhambling/2022/10/14/ukraine-wins-first-drone-vs-drone-dogfight-against-russia-opening-a-new-era-of-warfare/?sh=37f8208119a5

56 'Ukrainian Company Kvertus "Supplying 180 KVS G-6 Drone Jammers to Ukrainian Forces",' *Unmanned Airspace*, February 20, 2023, at https://www.unmannedairspace.info/latest-news-and-information/ukrainian-company-kvertus-supplying-180-kvs-g-6-drone-jammers-to-ukrainian-forces/

57 NT Service UAB EDM4S (Sky Wiper), Military Factory, April 8, 2022, at https://www.militaryfactory.com/smallarms/detail.php?smallarms_id=1300

58 Shakshi Tiwari, 'Ukraine War: Iran 'Modified' Shahed-136 Kamikaze Drones For Russia to Cause Max Destruction on Ukrainian Infra,' *The Eurasian*, February 10, 2023, at https://www.eurasiantimes.com/ukraine-war-iran-modified-shahed-136-kamikaze-drones-for-russia/

59 "Drone Dome – C-UAS" at Rafael.co.il, at https://www.rafael.co.il/worlds/air-missile-defence/c-uas-counter-unmanned-aircraft-systems/

60 Amanda Macias and Michael Sheetz, 'Pentagon Awards Spacex With Ukraine Contract For Starlink Satellite Internet,' *CNBC*, June 1, 2023, at https://www.cnbc.com/2023/06/01/pentagon-awards-spacex-with-ukraine-contract-for-starlink-satellite-internet.html

61 Ibid, p. 33.

62 Ibid, p. 33.

63 Ibid, p. 33.

64 Shreershoo Deb, 'Full List of India's Air Defence Systems,' *Defence XP*, August 23, 2020, at https://www.defencexp.com/full-list-of-indian-air-defence-systems/

65 PTI, 'OneWeb Completes 618 Satellites Constellation For Global Internet Coverage,' *NDTV*, March 27, 2023, at https://www.ndtv.com/india-news/oneweb-completes-618-satellites-constellation-for-global-internet-coverage-3896072

# 8

# Maritime Theatre of the Ukraine War

*R Vignesh and Abhay Singh*

Ever since Russia initiated its so-called special military operations against Ukraine, the world has witnessed dramatic changes on the frontlines of this war. As the situation stands at the time of writing this chapter, these frontlines run along the eastern part of Ukraine, where pitched battles between the Russian and Ukrainian forces continue. While there has been a lot of focus on the progression of the land operations across these frontlines, there has been relatively lesser focus on naval operations that have unfolded in the maritime theatre of this war. The maritime theatre of the Ukraine conflict will play a vital role in shaping the outcome of this war and hence requires greater focus. Firstly, this chapter makes an assessment of the unique geography and complex geopolitical history of this maritime theatre. Secondly, the chapter chronicles the key events that shaped this maritime theatre before the outbreak of the war. Finally, the chapter lists the major engagements that have taken place so far in this maritime theatre and draws crucial inferences from them for understanding the emerging dynamics of naval warfare.

## THE STRATEGIC GEOGRAPHY OF THE MARITIME THEATRE

The maritime theatre of this war is confined to the Black Sea, which is a large enclosed sea situated between 40°56′ and 46°33′N and between 27°27′ and 41°42′E with a total surface area of around 4,32,000 sq km.[1] The Black Sea is roughly about the size of the US State of California.[2] It is surrounded by the coastlines of six littoral nations including Russia, Ukraine, Turkey, Bulgaria, Georgia and Romania. To the north, the Crimean Peninsula extends southwards from Ukraine's mainland into the Black Sea. The Kerch Strait situated east of the

Crimean Peninsula connects the Black Sea to the Sea of Azov. This strait is a significant maritime feature in the region as it separates the Crimean Peninsula from the Russian mainland. Both Russia and Ukraine share a disputed maritime boundary in the Black Sea. On the other hand, both nations signed a bilateral treaty in 2003 declaring the Azov Sea and the Kerch Strait as the internal waters of the Russian Federation and Ukraine.[3] Due to this, the Azov Sea, which has a surface area of 37,606 sq km between Russia and Ukraine, falls outside the purview of the United Nations Convention of the Law of the Sea (UNCLOS).[4] As per this treaty, Russia and Ukraine had mutually agreed that their respective commercial and military vessels would enjoy Unhindered Freedom of Navigation (FON) in the Azov Sea and the Kerch Strait. To the northwest of the Black Sea along the coast of Romania is the Danube Delta. This is a very important maritime feature as it connects the Black Sea to the Danube River, which is one of the longest navigable inland waterways in Europe.

In the south, the Black Sea is connected to the Marmara Sea through the Bosporus Straits. The Marmara Sea is the world's smallest inland sea and is connected to the Aegean Sea through the Dardanelles Strait. Both the Bosporus and the Dardanelles are collectively referred to as the Turkish Straits as they are part of the sovereign territory of Türkiye. This maritime route consisting of the Turkish Straits, Aegean Sea and Marmara Sea is the sole access to the Black Sea via the Mediterranean.[5] The maritime traffic passing through the Turkish Straits is governed by the 1936 Montreux Convention. This international agreement guarantees complete FON and passage to merchant and civilian vessels transiting along this vital maritime route.[6] During peacetime, this agreement ensures FON to military vessels albeit with certain restrictions based on their tonnage, class and nationality.[7] However, during times of war, the agreement bestows exclusive rights to Türkiye to regulate or even prohibit warships belonging to belligerent powers from using the Turkish Straits.[8] Also, the interpretation and implementation of these rights vary on basis of Türkiye's own status as a neutral or a belligerent party to the conflict.[9] Türkiye's geostrategic location combined with its exclusive rights to control maritime access to the Black Sea makes it one of the most vital actors in shaping the geopolitics of the region.

## ECONOMIC SIGNIFICANCE OF THE BLACK SEA

The Black Sea is the home to nearly 65 ports and major shipping routes that are critical for east–west and north–west connectivity across Eurasia. Among the major commercial ports in the region include Constana (Romania), Odessa (Ukraine),

**Map 8.1: The Black Sea Region**

© GIS Section, Manohar Parrikar Institute for Defence Studies and Analyses (MP-IDSA). Map not to scale.

Novorossiysk (Russia), Batumi (Georgia), Varna (Bulgaria) and Samsun (Turkey).[10] There are broadly three critical Sea Lanes of Communication (SLOC) in the Black Sea, which are as follows:

1. **The Black Sea–Mediterranean Sea Corridor:** This SLOC connects the Black Sea and the Mediterranean Sea through the Turkish Straits and the Aegean Sea. This can be considered as the most important SLOC in the Black Sea as it connects the region with the rest of the world. Pre-war data shows that over 50 per cent of imported containerised cargo that passes through the Turkish Straits originated from the Indo–Pacific Region.[11]
2. **The Black Sea–Adriatic Sea Corridor:** This SLOC links the Black Sea and the Adriatic Sea regions. As the Balkans and Western Europe are

connected with the Black Sea region via this route, it is also called the '*Trans-Balkan Transport Corridor*'.[12]

3. **The Danube–Black Sea Corridor:** This is an important corridor that connects Eastern European countries with the Black Sea via the Danube Delta in Romania. As the Danube River passes through 11 countries it is a very important transport artery connecting the Black Sea with the heart of Europe.[13]

In 2021, the total volume of container traffic transiting in the region was estimated to be around 3.1 million TEU, of which Ukraine accounted for over 1 million TEU.[14] The Turkish Straits being the sole access point to the region became amongst the busiest maritime routes in the world. Before the start of the war, approximately 40,000 commercial vessels transited through the Turkish Straits annually.[15] Over three million barrels of oil produced by Russia, Azerbaijan and Kazakhstan passed along this maritime route every day. This accounts for nearly three per cent of the daily global oil supply. Also, large volumes of iron, steel and agricultural products produced from the littoral states of the Black Sea are shipped through this crucial maritime passage.[16] The region is also the export route of three among the world's top 10 wheat exporting countries, which are Russia, Ukraine and Kazakhstan.[17] The war has endangered the safety of maritime transportation in the region, creating a cascading effect in the global supply chains. Due to the war, there has been a sharp drop in the volume of commercial shipping by 28.4 per cent (almost 6,90,000 TEU). Latest data have revealed that the region's overall laden import volumes fell by 25 per cent, while export traffic declined by 33 per cent.[18] Ukraine is a major exporter of grains; in 2021, it accounted for the supply of 11 per cent of world's wheat exports, 12 per cent of corn exports and 43 per cent of sunflower oil exports.

## GEOPOLITICAL HISTORY OF THE BLACK SEA

Given the geostrategic significance of the Black Sea to the Eurasian landmass, the region has always occupied a central position in Russia's strategic calculus. It must be understood that since the times of the Tsars, the episodic outset of Russian imperialism and irredentism in Eastern Europe have always centred around this region. The Russian perspective on the region has been influenced by its historical rivalry with the erstwhile Ottoman Empire and other European powers. The Russo–Turkish War (1768–74) was one of the first major wars fought between the Russian and Ottoman empires for securing access to the Black Sea. In this war, Russia decisively gained control of the Crimean Peninsula and forced the

Ottoman Empire to allow unrestricted passage of its ships through the Turkish Straits.[19] Almost a century later, a combined alliance of the Ottoman Empire, France and the UK defeated Russia in the Crimean War (1853–56). After this war, Russia's hegemony in the Black Sea diminished and maritime trade flourished in the region.[20] Many historians view that gaining control of the Turkish Straits were amongst the factors that motivated the Tsarist Russia to enter the First World War.

In 1936, much to Moscow's resentment the Montreux Convention legitimised and codified Türkiye's total control over the strategic straits. During the Second World War, Türkiye being a neutral power closed the straits to both the Allies and the Axis powers. During the Yalta Conference in February 1945, Joseph Stalin called for the revision of the Montreux Convention, which he described as an outmoded treaty. He stated that the treaty created a situation where in Türkiye had a hand on Russia's throat, which was unacceptable. He sought the renegotiation of the treaty in a manner wherein Russia has some degree of control over the straits along with Türkiye.[21] In April 1946, a crisis erupted when an American battleship arrived in the Turkish Straits and Moscow accused Türkiye of violating the Montreux Convention. Subsequently, the Soviet Union initiated a military buildup in the region in an attempt to coerce Türkiye to renegotiate the treaty. In response to this, the US and UK dispatched their naval task forces to the region in support of Türkiye. The Soviet Union subsequently disengaged and abandoned their call for renegotiation of the Montreux Convention in 1952 following the death of Joseph Stalin.[22] The Turkish Straits crisis is a watershed moment in the Cold War as it led to Türkiye's abandonment of its policy of neutrality and joining NATO.

After the dissolution of the Soviet Union, Moscow faced the possibility of losing control of Sevastopol naval base and Crimea as they now fell under the territorial jurisdiction of the newly independent Ukraine. The Sevastopol naval base is home to the Russian Navy's famous Black Sea Fleet. In Russia's national psyche, Sevastopol and Crimea have always been popularly associated with its rich naval history. In 1992, former Soviet Admiral Igor Kasatonov stated that Russia in any form cannot be imagined without its glorious Black Sea Fleet. He opined that to deprive Russia of the Black Sea Fleet and its Sevastopol naval base in Crimea would mean setting it back to an era before Peter the Great.[23] Due to this the continuation of Moscow's access to the Sevastopol naval base was an influencing factor in shaping the bilateral relations between Russia and Ukraine. In 1997, both nations signed an agreement known as the Partition Treaty on the

Status and Conditions of the Black Sea Fleet. This treaty allowed the Russian Navy to use the Sevastopol port for 20 years until 2017. Also, the treaty partitioned the fleet into an 80:20 ratio between Russia (338 vessels) and Ukraine (30 vessels). As a result of this, the Ukrainian Navy inherited a small fleet comprising fully of antiquated Soviet assets. Also, Russia was allowed to have 25,000 troops as well as other military assets in the Crimean Peninsula along with a commitment not to deploy nuclear weapons in the region.

In 2010, both nations signed the Kharkiv Pact to further extend this arrangement until 2042.[24] However, in 2014, the Euromaidan Revolution erupted across Ukraine and resulted in the ouster of the pro-Russian regime led by Viktor Yanukovych in Kyiv. This turn of events in Ukraine predictably made the Kremlin anxious about its continued access to Sevastopol. As a result, in early 2014, Russia brought Crimea under its control. Putin in his address made on April 17, 2014, stated that if Russia had not made the preempted move in Crimea then NATO ships would have ended up in the city of Russian navy glory, Sevastopol.[25] These historic events illustrate that the aim of successive regimes in Moscow to dominate this strategic maritime space stems from Russia's relentless pursuit of securing access to warm water ports.[26]

## BUILDUP TO THE MARITIME THEATRE

The events that unfolded after 2014 had a profound effect in shaping the balance of power between the Russian and Ukrainian navies in the Black Sea region. The annexation itself inflicted a devastating blow to Ukraine's maritime capabilities. The Ukrainian Navy lost two-thirds of its warships along with access to critical maritime infrastructure such as ports, repair docks and defence industries that were located in Crimea. Geographically, Ukraine lost access to a third of its Black Sea coastline and the strategic Kerch Strait.[27] Nearly 70 per cent of Ukrainian naval personnel either defected or were dismissed and most of its naval air assets were seized by Russia.[28] Post this, the Ukrainian Navy was left with a 'mosquito fleet' consisting of a sole frigate and few small vessels, which were only sufficient for protection of coastal waters.

On November 25, 2018, the Ukrainian Navy suffered another major setback when three of its small vessels (2 gunboats and 1 tugboat) were forcibly seized by Russia. The Kremlin claimed that these vessels violated Russia's territorial waters and did not seek prior permission to transit through the strait.[29] Prior to 2014, the eastern and western sides of the Kerch Strait were under the control of Russia and Ukraine respectively. But after 2014 both sides of the strait came under direct

Russian control. The European Parliament pointed out that Russia is bound by the 2003 bilateral cooperation agreement with Ukraine not to hamper or impede transit passage of Ukrainian vessels through the Kerch Strait and the Sea of Azov. Despite this since 2018 Russia has repeatedly obstructed the passage of other commercial and non-commercial vessels passing through the strait.[30] Russia's actions since 2018 have resulted in the drastic reduction of Ukraine's strategic presence in the Sea of Azov region.

Despite Russia's meticulous attempts to establish favourable strategic conditions in the region post 2014, it has faced the challenge of not having a land link to Crimea. To address this, in 2016, the Kremlin began the construction of the Crimean Bridge to connect mainland Russia with the Crimean Peninsula across the Kerch Strait. This bridge was constructed at a cost of 3.6 billion USD and spanned a length of 19 km, making it Europe's longest bridge. With four road lanes and two railway tracks, this bridge has become the integral route for both civilian and commercial movement since its inauguration 2018 by Vladimir Putin.[31]

Meanwhile, during this period the US and NATO became actively involved in building the capabilities of the Ukrainian Navy. Since 2017, Ukraine received eight new patrol boards and several former US Coast Guard vessels as part of the military aid from the West.[32] Apart from this, Ukrainian naval personnel received extensive training in the US for operating Western-origin ships, sensors and weapons. The Ukrainian Navy participated in a number of training exercises for planning and executing maritime operations in line with NATO standards and best practices.[33] As a result, Ukraine has developed robust coastal defence capabilities. This period also marked the Ukrainian Navy's transition from Soviet Naval Philosophy to that of the West. The comparative force levels of the Russian and Ukrainian navies in the Black Sea in early 2022 are as follows:

**Table 8.1: Comparative Force Levels of Russian and Ukrainian Navies in the Black Sea**

| *Russia (Black Sea Fleet)* | *Ukraine* |
|---|---|
| • 1 Guided Missile Cruiser (Moskva: Former Flagship of Black Sea Fleet) | • 1 Frigate (Hetman Sahaidachny: Former Flagship of the Ukrainian Navy) |
| • 4 Frigates (30th Surface Ships Division) | • 5 Patrol Craft |
| • 1 Corvette (30th Surface Ships Division) | • 1 Fast Attack Craft |
| • 6 Landing Ships (197th Assault Ship Brigade) | • 1 Minehunter |
| • 7 Diesel Electric Submarines (4th Independent Submarine Brigade) | • 1 Landing Ship |

| *Russia (Black Sea Fleet)* | *Ukraine* |
|---|---|
| • 3 Antisubmarine Corvette (149th Anti-submarine Ships Tactical Group) | • 31 Coastguard Vessels |
| • 5 Minesweepers (150th Minesweeper Tactical Group) | • Naval Aviation 2 Fixed Wing, 24 Rotary Wing |
| • 9 Missile Boats (41th Missile Boat Brigade) | |
| • 12 Coastal Defence Vessels (184th Coastal Defence Ship Brigade) | |
| • Naval Aviation 43rd Naval Assault Aviation Regiment (Sevastopol, Saki) – the mainstrike component of the Black Sea Fleet Aviation. The equipmentincludes Su-30SM, Su-24M and Su-24MR combat aircraft<br>318th Mixed Aviation Regiment (Sevastopol, Kacha) – the regimenthas, among others, Mi-8 and Ka-27 helicopters, An-26 transport aircraftand Be-12 flying amphibians | |

*Source:* Janes World Navies 2021- Issue 27.
KCHF.RU-Information Resource, at https://www.kchf.ru/eng/ship/today.htm (Accessed June 16, 2023)

## KEY NAVAL ENGAGEMENTS THUS FAR

In January 2022, Russia initiated the rapid buildup of its naval assets in the Black Sea. Six warships along with amphibious landing vessels (LSTs) and improved Kilo-class submarines of the Russian Navy entered the Black Sea through the Bosporus Straits. Several assault boats from Russia's Baltic fleet were transported to the Black Sea via road.[34] Simultaneously, naval strike groups were dispatched towards the Ukrainian coast from Russian bases at Novorossiysk and Sevastopol. While Ukraine and other Western nations raised alarm over this naval buildup, the Russian state media downplayed it as part of a pre-planned military exercise.[35] Despite these claims by Russia, on February 24, 2022 at 1800 hours local time the garrison of the Ukraine border guards received a radio broadcast from Moskva, Black Sea Fleet's flagship, demanding their surrender. The Ukrainian border guards defied the warning, in response to which Moskva and the patrol ship Vasily Bykov began the bombardment of Snake Island, marking the commencement of hostilities in the Black Sea. The subsequent key naval engagements have been sequenced thematically.

## The Snake Island Campaign

This 42-acre island marks the edge of Ukraine's territorial waters and is strategically significant as it is located in the shipping corridor to the Ukrainian port cities of Odessa, Mykolaiv and Kherson. After its bombardment on February 24, the Russian forces swiftly took control of the island. The following day, Russia announced the establishment of a Maritime Exclusion Zone (MEZ) over the entire Sea of Azov and in the northwest portion of the Black Sea north of 45° 212.[36] However by the first week of May, the Ukrainian military intensified its attacks on the Russian-occupied Snake Island. These attacks were primarily carried out to prevent the Russian military from setting up their long-range air-defence systems on the island. The setting up of such systems would have helped Russia to establish absolute control over the north-western part of the Black Sea and the southern part of Ukraine.[37]

But the Ukrainian military severely undermined Russia's ability to replenish its troops on Snake Island by constantly attacking its supply ships using Turkish Bayraktar TB2 drones and Western anti-ship missiles such as Harpoon and Brimstone. Throughout May and June 2022, the Ukrainian military released several videos of its drones and missiles hitting Russian vessels near the island. Due to this, Russia's attempts to resupply and reinforce its troops on the island became increasingly perilous and costly. Russia eventually withdrew its troops from Snake Island and abandoned the strategic outpost it had captured at the very beginning of the war. This event marked a tactical victory for Ukraine as it severely diminished Russia's ability to establish sea control in the north-western part of the Black Sea and impose a blockade of southern Ukrainian ports. The retaking of Snake Island and the Russian warships withdrawing from the north-western side of the Black Sea opened up possibilities for the Ukrainian military to launch attacks on Crimea. On July 8, 2023, as the war entered its 500th day the Ukrainian President Volodymyr Zelensky made a symbolic visit to Snake Island from where he enunciated his government's will to regain every inch of territory taken by Russia since the start of the war.[38]

## Ukraine's Loss of Surface Ships

By the first week of March 2022, Ukraine had lost most of its warships as they were either captured, sunk or scuttled since the war started. The most notable of these losses was Ukraine's scuttling of its flagship, Frigate Hetman Sahaidachny. This Soviet Era frigate was undergoing repairs in the port of Odesa and the Ukrainian government took this measure in order to prevent the ship from being captured by Russia. With the loss of Hetman Sahaidachny, the Ukrainian Navy virtually lost all its major surface ships with the exception of LST Yuri Olefirenko.[39] On May 29, 2023, Russia claimed that it had successfully destroyed this warship in a 'high-precision strike'. So far Ukraine has not confirmed Russia's claims but has declined to comment on the status of its last warship.[40]

## Closing of the Turkish Straits

On February 28, 2022, the Turkish foreign minister announced Ankara's decision to close the Turkish Straits for the transit of warships by exercising its rights as per the Montreux Convention.[41] This was a major setback to Moscow as the Russian Navy could no longer reinforce its Black Sea Fleet with warships from its other fleets. On the other hand, it must also be noted that since the closing of the Turkish Straits no NATO ships have transited into the Black Sea.[42] This makes any intervention in the maritime theatre of the war by any external actors in favour of Ukraine very difficult.

## Russian Amphibious Operations

On February 26, 2022, the Russian Navy carried out a successful amphibious landing of troops operation between the Ukrainian port cities of Melitopol and Mariupol. These amphibious landings in the Sea of Azov are believed to have played a crucial role in facilitating the Russian assault on these key Ukrainian port cities.[43] On March 24, 2022, a Russian Alligator-class LST berthed in the captured port city of Berdyansk was struck by a Ukrainian tactical ballistic missile. This led to the sinking of the LST and Russia suspended the use of the Berdyansk port as a point of reinforcement.[44] By mid-March, the Black Sea Fleet had carried out multiple amphibious demonstrations with its LSTs, minesweepers and other warships in the vicinity of Odessa.[45] The commercial satellite imagery of this fleet formation led to speculations that an amphibious Russian assault in the strategic Ukrainian port city of Odesa was imminent.[46] As a result, Odessa was heavily fortified by the Ukrainian military. Tank traps, mines and barricades were installed on the beaches of Odesa as preparations for an impending amphibious assault while half of the city's population was evacuated.

However, these operations never happened, and it has had a decisive impact in the course of the war. Had these amphibious landings happened in Odessa, it would have opened a new theatre in southern Ukraine, putting enormous pressure on Kyiv. Russia could have possibly cut off Kyiv's access to the Black Sea and also grossly undermined its ability to conduct operations in Eastern Ukraine. But some early assessments have pointed out to the limitations of Russia in conducting such large-scale amphibious operations. An article by a former US Marine officer published in January 2022 predicted these limitations due to the following factors:[47]

1. Weather and sea conditions of the Black Sea
2. Lack of landing sites due to the coast of Odessa's terrain
3. Russian military's inadequate amphibious lift capability
4. Challenge of maintaining air superiority over beachheads
5. Logistical challenges arising due to the distance between Crimean ports and Odessa

These factors possibly explain why Russia did not conduct amphibious landings in Odesa. On the other hand, these limitations have decisively allowed Ukraine to challenge Russian sea control of the Black Sea. Ukraine's success in the sinking of the Moskva, the retaking of the Snake Island and the attack on key targets in the Crimean Peninsula can all be attributed to these factors.

## Sinking of the Moskva

Commissioned in 1983 by the erstwhile Soviet Navy, the Moskva was a large, guided missile cruiser with a displacement of 11,500 tonnes and spanned 186 meters in length. The ship had indomitable firepower, consisting of 16 anti-ship missile launchers for P-1000 Vulkan missiles with a range of 700 km. In addition, the ship was armed with air defence missiles and gatling guns to provide three layers of protection. To counter distant aerial threats, the ship was equipped with S-300F Surface-to-Air Missiles (SAMs). To target short- to medium-range targets, Moskva had 9K33 Osa SAMs. Finally, for close-range protection, the ship was installed with several automated AK-630 gatling guns.[48] It was the largest and most powerful warship in the region and was described as the pride of the Russian Navy's Black Sea Fleet. In the ongoing war, the Moskva operated as a mobile air-defence umbrella for other Russian surface vessels and military assets operating in its vicinity. During the first two months of the war, the Moskva was positioned between the coast of Odesa and the Snake Island. The ship was instrumental in facilitating the Russian military operations in the north-western part of the Black Sea.

Meanwhile, shortly before the war, Ukraine unveiled its indigenously developed R-360 Neptune Anti-ship Cruise Missiles (ACMS). These shore based ACMS with a range of 200 km can skim as low as 10 metres above the surface of the water to avoid detection. On April 13, 2022, reportedly Moskva was struck by two of these ACMS. The warship supposedly sustained serious damage after the detonation of ammunition onboard caused by the missile strike. The following day Moskva sank due to hull damage while being towed to Sevastopol amid a storm.[49] While the Russian state media attributed Moskva's sinking solely to the onboard fire, Ukraine credited its Neptune missiles for inflicting the fatal blow to the erstwhile flagship of the Black Sea Fleet. Despite the differing accounts, the preponderance of circumstantial evidence substantiates Ukraine's assertions that the cruiser was indeed struck by its missiles.[50] This event marked a symbolic victory for Ukraine as it created a tremendous boost of morale for its war effort.

The sinking of Moskva can be regarded as an inflection point in the maritime theatre of this war. This is because with the loss of Moskva, the Black Sea Fleet lost its protective air cover and became vulnerable near the Ukrainian coast. As a result, the Russian surface vessels have been forced to operate at a range of 100–150 nautical miles away from the southern Ukrainian coasts.[51] The sinking of Moskva created a major challenge for Russia in its occupation of Snake Island as Ukraine increased its aerial attacks. This was certainly a contributing factor that led to the Russian withdrawal from the island. Moskva is the largest warship to be sunk since the sinking of Argentine cruiser ARA General Belgrano by the Royal Navy in 1982 during the Falklands War. This makes it a major event in the history of naval warfare and the incident is bound to be scrutinised in the years to come. However, several assessments attribute the following reason for Moskva's sinking.

1. Atmospheric conditions on the day of the incident may have helped Ukrainian radars to detect Moskva's position accurately. According to Ukrainian naval sources, low cloud cover on that day extended their radars' field of view beyond their normal range.
2. Observers have opined that Ukraine might have used an advanced over-the-horizon radar system. In October 2021, Ukraine unveiled a prototype of an advanced ground-based Beyond-Line-Of-Sight (BLOS) radar system called mineral-U. These radar networks were to be integrated with the Neptune ASCMS for searching and tracking targets. Although these systems were in their testing phases, Ukraine might have put them to use to track Moskva.
3. It is also probable that Ukraine received active support from US maritime-surveillance aircraft and satellite imagery in locating Moskva.
4. Moskva's outdated and non-functional weapons, radars and targeting

systems may have led to its crew being unable to detect and intercept the incoming missiles.

5. Failing to control the onboard fire after the missile strike may have been due to Moskva's crew lacking well-trained personnel. Observers have noted that over half of the crew were conscripts who had served only a year.

A combination of these factors may have helped the depleted Ukrainian Navy to achieve the remarkable feat of sinking a large and powerful warship such as the Moskva.

## UKRAINIAN ATTACK ON SEVASTOPOL

On July 31, 2022, the Black Sea Fleet's headquarters in Sevastopol was struck by Ukrainian Unmanned Aerial Vehicles (UAVs). Due to this incident, Russia cancelled its Navy Day ceremony.[52] This attack was the first in the series of attacks on Sevastopol carried out by Ukraine using UAVs and Unmanned Surface Vessels (USVs). On October 29, 2022, seven Ukrainian USVs penetrated the harbour defence of Sevastopol and struck two warships including Frigate Admiral Makarov, which had assumed the role of flagship of the Black Sea Fleet after Moskva. Although this attack failed to inflict any major damage, it forced the Russian Navy to increase the defences to secure Sevastopol and their most powerful warships were tied up to the port. Hence, the attack was successful in effectively reducing and restricting the activity of the Black Sea Fleet.[53] Also, the Black Sea Fleet began to relocate some of its warships to the port of Novorossiysk situated on the southern coast of the Russian mainland. This attack set the precedent of Ukraine challenging Russia's conventional naval superiority through the use of USVs.

But the biggest attack on Sevastopol took place on September 13, 2023, when three Ukrainian cruise missiles penetrated the Russian air defence grid over Crimea and struck two vessels that were undergoing repairs in dry docks. Ukraine carried out this attack using Storm Shadow cruise missiles, which it acquired from the United Kingdom in early 2023. The two vessels that were hit included an improved Kilo-class submarine called the Rostov-on-Don and a large LST named Minsk.[54] In the attack, one missile hit the submarine and two missiles struck the LST. After the attack, Russia claimed that the two ships would be soon repaired and put back to service. But photos of the damaged vessels have revealed that the two ships have sustained irreparable damage. The damaged hull of the submarine reveals that the missile had managed to penetrate the outer hull and the warhead had exploded inside the pressure hull. This means that all the key systems inside the submarine have been completely destroyed.[55] On the other hand, the two missiles that struck the LST have completely destroyed its upper deck. Therefore, it would be safe to assume that both these important assets of the Russian Navy are most likely to be written off from service. Hence, this attack has been the biggest loss for the Russian Navy in the war since the sinking of Moskva. This attack has demonstrated Ukraine's ability to penetrate Russian air defence grids and strike key military targets inside Crimea with devastating effect.

This became evident with satellite imagery confirming that the 744th Communication Centre of the Black Sea Fleet in Crimea had been struck by Ukrainian missile on September 20, 2023. These attacks on Sevastopol had far-reaching implications for the maritime theatre of the Ukraine War. The Russian Navy is most likely to shift its key assets to Novorossiysk from the Sevastopol base, which has been the nerve centre of Russian naval operations since the beginning of the war. This will result in overstretching the Operation Turnaround (OTR) and the supply chains of Russian warships and submarines, making them less efficient and more vulnerable.[56] But shifting the Black Sea Fleet to Novorossiysk does not ensure the complete safety of Russian naval assets. The USV attack on Novorossiysk carried out on August 4, 2023, points out that the Ukraine Navy has the ability to strike even on the coast of the Russian mainland.

### Attacks on the Crimean Bridge

On October 8, 2022, a huge explosion occurred on the Crimean Bridge. Although Ukraine has not directly claimed responsibility for this attack, Russian investigations revealed that the explosion was carried out by a truck bomb. Putin in his address on the following day claimed that the attack was planned and carried out by the Ukrainian Special Services.[57] With the crucial connectivity with the Crimean Peninsula severed, Russia extensively made use of LSTs for transportation. The bridge was reopened on February 23, 2023, after extensive repairs and the security around the bridge was further strengthened by the Russian authorities. Despite this, once again two explosions occurred on the bridge that killed two people and caused traffic disruptions on July 17, 2023. In August, satellite images revealed that Russia has installed barges south of the Crimean Bridge to protect it against attacks by Ukrainian naval drones.[58] However, the attack on Sevastopol in September 2023 is an indicator that Ukraine now has the capability to attack the bridge with cruise missiles with a potential to inflict damage on a larger scale. Therefore, it will become more difficult for Russia to protect this 19-kilometer-long bridge in the forthcoming days and months of the war.

## The Black Sea Grain Initiative (BSGI)

As brought out earlier in this chapter, Ukraine exported large quantities of wheat and grain through the Black Sea from its key southern seaports that include Odesa, Chornomorsk and Pivdennyi. The conflict and the subsequent naval blockade by Russia severely constrained Ukraine's ability to export these grains. Due to this the global grain prices had drastically increased and created food insecurity, particularly in the developing countries.[59] On April 25, 2022, the UN Secretary-General António Guterres met the Turkish President Recep Tayyip Erdoðan for brokering negotiations with the two belligerents to allow the export of food grains through the Black Sea. In the following months, the UN Secretary-General met with both Putin and Zelensky for the establishment of a safe maritime corridor to export grains and fertilisers from the Southern Ukrainian Ports. On July 27, 2022, Russia and Ukraine signed the Black Sea Grain Initiative (BSGI) agreement in Istanbul to provide a safe passage for ships with grain-laden cargo. The BSGI is a unique maritime treaty signed between two belligerents during the war. This is due to the fact that usually in a war a belligerent with superior maritime capability aims to deny seaborne trade of its opponent. However, the BSGI has effectively lifted the blockade of Odesa, thereby enabling Ukraine to export its agricultural produce. The loss of Snake Island may have influenced Russia's decision to accede to BSGI.

The BSGI expired on July 17, 2023, after which Russia warned that it could no longer guarantee the safety of ships exporting grain through the Black Sea. In the following days, Russia attacked port and grain facilities in the Odessa region in retaliation for the attack on Crimean Bridge that occurred on the same day the BSGI expired. President Zelensky in a statement claimed that a Russian missile attack destroyed a large storage facility in Odesa holding 60,000 tonnes of grain on July 19, 2023.[60] Following the suspension of BSGI, global wheat prices experienced their biggest increase since the beginning of the war. However, Kremlin spokesperson Dmirty Peskov has implied that Moscow would consider resurrecting the BSGI provided its terms are renegotiated as per its demands. Hence, Moscow has made it clear that it seeks to secure better terms for the export of its own food grains and fertilisers.[61] In the UN Security Council meeting held on July 21, 2023, American representatives remarked that Russia is using the BSGI as a bargaining chip and has been holding humanity hostage by weaponizing food.[62] As uncertainty over the future of BSGI continues, it is clear that Russia would seek to leverage the situation to secure a better position for itself in any potential negotiations to reinstate the deal.

## MAJOR INFERENCES FROM NAVAL OPERATIONS THUS FAR

From the naval operations that have happened thus far in this war, certain broad inferences can be drawn about the application of sea power by the belligerents.

### Russian Naval Operations

As brought out in the comparative force levels earlier, Russia enjoys overwhelming naval superiority over Ukraine. But the Russian Navy has suffered some serious losses and Ukraine continues to challenge Russia's dominance in the Black Sea. The enclosed geography and restricted access to this maritime theatre has limited the scope of application of sea power by Russia due to the following factors:

- **Limited Utilisation of Available Warships:** The Russian Navy is amongst the largest and most powerful navies in the world. It has four operational fleets that includes the Black Sea, Baltic, Northern and Pacific fleets. But due to the closure of the Turkish Straits, the Russian Navy is solely reliant upon the assets of its Black Sea Fleet and cannot employ warships from its other fleets.
- **Limited Firepower:** The Montreux Convention prohibits warships above 15,000 tonnes from passing through the Turkish Straits. Due to this, the Russian Navy even before the war was not in a position to deploy its larger and more powerful warships such as its nuclear-powered battlecruiser or its sole aircraft carrier in the Black Sea.
- **Limited Undersea Capabilities:** Despite possessing nuclear submarines, it is very difficult for the Russian Navy to deploy them in the Black Sea because of its shallow waters and the narrow passage of the Turkish Straits. Due to this, the Black Sea Fleet's undersea capability is restricted only to conventional submarines with limited firepower and endurance.

Overall, the Russian naval operations thus far gives the impression that the war planners in the Kremlin did not envisage a clear role for its navy before initiating their special military operation. Also, ambiguity in Russia's war objectives has resulted in its navy's failure to make optimum use of its resources. Unlike in Syria, the effectiveness of the Russian Navy's ground strike capability has been undermined by Ukraine's robust air-defence grids & coastal defence networks. While in Syria, the Russian Navy's Kalibr cruise missile strikes had a devastating effect against ISIS, which is a non-state actor. But in the case of the ongoing war, these strikes have had very limited effect as Ukraine possesses advanced Western manufactured air-defence missile systems such as the American Patriot and German IRIS-T.

## Ukrainian Naval Operations

Since the start of the war, the naval operations of Ukraine have focused on keeping the superior Russian Navy as far away as possible from its southern coasts. To a great extent, the Ukrainian Navy has succeeded in this objective through the application of the mosquito fleet strategy. The term mosquito fleet is used to describe a naval fleet consisting predominately of small, fast and cheap platforms such as gunboats, mines and coastal defence ships. Such fleets are often raised by a lesser naval power to deny command of the sea to a superior naval power through the use of asymmetrical tactics.[63] The advantage of such mosquito fleets over the larger conventional fleets is their ability to mount surprise attacks, flexibility to be relocated by land and capability to operate on rivers. In November 2018, Kyiv released its naval strategy that identified the raising of a mosquito fleet as the most realistic and cost-effective solution for countering Russian naval supremacy.[64] This strategy brought out that the Ukrainian Navy aims to gradually increase the combat potential of its mosquito fleet by incorporating advanced weaponry, niche technologies, innovative tactics and well-trained crew.[65] From the naval engagements that have happened thus far it can be inferred that the Ukrainian Navy has effectively put this strategy into practice. Ukraine's mosquito fleet has successfully demonstrated the ability of long-range missiles, USVs and UAVs to act as potent instruments of naval asymmetry.

In the course of the war, one of the major successes of the Ukrainian Navy has been its ability to consistently expand its maritime strike range. In the initial months of the war, Russian warships operated with impunity on the Black Sea and Ukraine's maritime strike capability was largely confined only to its coastal waters. By April 2022, it was seen how the Ukrainian Navy's shore-based missiles and UAVs played a decisive role in the sinking of Moskva and the Russian withdrawal from Snake Island. By October 2022, the continuous attacks on Sevastopol and the Crimean Bridge indicated that the Ukrainian strike range had expanded up to Crimea. The attack on Novorossiysk further indicated that the Ukrainian strike capability has expanded up to Russia's southern coasts as illustrated in Map 8.2.[66]

Also, since Ukraine has demonstrated its capability to strike Novorossiysk and penetrate Russian air defence grids over Crimea, it is in a better position to interdict and disrupt Russian supply chains and communication networks across the Black Sea. In September, Ukraine gained control of several offshore oil drilling platforms close to Crimea. These platforms can be potentially used by Ukraine to track movements and mount attacks on Russian warships in the Black Sea.[67]

**Map 8.2: Expanding Ukrainian Maritime Strike Range in the Black Sea**

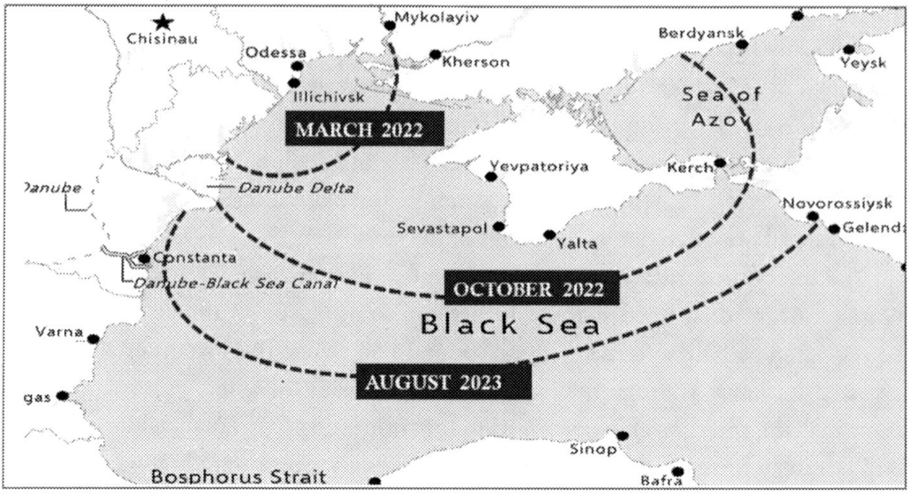


*Source:* GIS Section, Manohar Parrikar Institute for Defence Studies and Analyses (MP-IDSA)

These developments have indicated that the Ukrainian Navy now possesses the capability to pose serious challenge to the Russian Navy's dominance of the Black Sea and its ability to protect Crimea in the forthcoming months.

## CONCLUSION

As the hostilities in the Black Sea continue to rage on with no end in sight, it is very difficult to speculate about the future course of this war. However, what has become clear from the naval engagements thus far is that despite suffering considerable losses Russia continues to dominate the critical SLOCs in the Northern Black Sea. On the other hand, Ukraine despite virtually not having any significant naval assets has managed to resiliently challenge Russia's naval supremacy by means of asymmetric warfare. Due to the constraints imposed by geography and resources, Russia despite being the superior naval power has so far failed to secure any decisive victories in the maritime theatre. The enclosed geography and the restricted access to this maritime theatre makes it very difficult for any external factors to influence the course of this war. As a result of this, it is very difficult to draw comparison with any past or future naval engagements taking place in any other part of the world. As a chapter written while the war is still ongoing the major naval engagements and the inferences drawn from them are neither exhaustive nor comprehensive. But in the decades to come every key engagement in the maritime theatre of this war is bound to be subjected to critical scrutiny by scholars and will have a lasting influence on the history of naval warfare.

## NOTES

1 International Legal Materials, *International Court of Justice: Maritime Delimitation in the Black Sea (Romania V. Ukraine)*, Cambridge University Press, Cambridge. 2009, p. 698.

2 Manoj Babu Buraga, 'Black Sea Geography in Competitive Maritime Space, European Union and India,' *World Focus*, 43 (10), 2022, p. 45.

3 Vladimir Socor, 'Azov Sea, Kerch Strait: Evolution of Their Purported Legal Status (Part One),' *Eurasia Daily Monitor*, 15 (169), 2018.

4 "Brief Description of the Sea of Azov," Water Database, at https://www.waterdatabase.com/seas/sea-of-azov/ (Accessed May 5,2023).

5 International Legal Materials, no. 1.

6 Ministry of Foreign Affairs, *Convention Relating to the Régime of the Straits*, Republic of Türkiye.

7 Ibid.

8 Nilüfer Oral, "To Close or Not to Close the Turkish Straits Under Article 19 of the 1936 Montreux Convention Regarding the Regime of the Straits," National University of Singapore, 2022, at https://cil.nus.edu.sg/to-close-or-not-to-close-the-turkish-straits-under-article-19-of-the-1936-montreux-convention-regarding-the-regime-of-the-straits/ (Accessed May 6, 2023).

9 Ministry of Foreign Affairs, "Convention Relating to the Régime of the Straits," Republic of Türkiye.

10 Soumyajit Dasgupta, '8 Major Black Sea Ports,' *Marine Insights*, February 14, 2022, at https://www.marineinsight.com/know-more/major-black-sea-ports/ (Accessed May 6, 2023).

11 'How the Black Sea Container Market is Changing in 2022?,' *Hellenic Shipping News Worldwide*, 2022, at https://www.hellenicshippingnews.com/how-the-black-sea-container-market-is-changing-in-2022/ (Accessed May 6, 2023).

12 N. Güler, "Black Sea Maritime Transport Corridors in Relations with EU Projects", in R. Marcet I Barbe, C.A. Brebbia and J. Olivella (eds.), *Maritime Heritage and Modern Ports,*: Wessex Institute of Technology, Southampton, 2005, pp. 293–300.

13 Ibid. p. 297.

14 Hellenic Shipping New Worldwide., no. 11.

15 N. Güler, no. 12.

16 Deutsche Welle, 'What Is the Montreax Convention and Can Turkey Use It to Block Russian Warships?,' *Indian Express*, 2022, at https://indianexpress.com/article/explained/turkey-russia-black-sea-7795658/

17 "The World's Top Wheat Exporters in 2021," U.S. Department of Agriculture (USDA), 2022, at https://www.rferl.org/a/top-10-wheat-exporters-russia-ukraine/31871594.html (Accessed May 6, 2023).

18 Vassiliy Vesselovski, Daniil Meclnychenko and Alexander Khromov, 'Invasion of Ukraine Caused Steep Drop in Black Sea Container Traffic,' *The Maritime Executive*, 2023, at https://maritime-executive.com/editorials/invasion-of-ukraine-caused-steep-drop-in-black-sea-container-traffic (Accessed May 7, 2023).

19 "The Russo-Turkish War of 1768-1774 Broke Out," Boris Yeltsin Presidential Library, at https://www.prlib.ru/en/history/619605 (Accessed May 8, 2023).

20 "The Treaty of Paris Signed," Boris Yeltsin Presidential Library, at https://www.prlib.ru/en/history/619130 (Accessed June 9, 2023).

21 "Truman Papers," No. 679 Memorandum by the Assistant to the President's Naval Aide (Elsey), Foreign Relations of the United States: Diplomatic Papers, The Conference of Berlin (The Potsdam Conference), 1945.

22 Chris Carter, '7 August 1946: Turkish Straits Crisis Reaches its Climax,' *Moneyweek*, 2020, at https://moneyweek.com/332694/7-august-1946-turkish-straits-crisis-reaches-its-climax (Accessed June 12, 2023).

23 Serhii Plokhy, 'The City of Glory: Sevastopol in Russian Historical Mythology,' *Journal of Contemporary History*, 35 (3), 2000, pp. 369–83.

24 Tatiana Zonova 'Mediterranean Trends in the Russia's Foreign Policy,' *Revista di Studi Politici Internazionali*, 2015, at https://www.jstor.org/stable/pdf/43785687.pdf?refreqid= excelsior %3A54a07612 befd84ac4973a2927c41e96b&ab_segments=&origin=&initiator =&acceptTC =1 (Accessed June 13, 2023).

25 'Putin Says Annexation of Crimea Partly a Response to NATO Enlargement,' Reuters, 2014, at https://www.reuters.com/article/us-russia-putin-nato-idUKBREA3G22A20140417 (Accessed June 9, 2023).

26 Manoj Babu Buraga, 'The Black Sea Geography in Competitive Maritime Space, European Union and India,' *World Focus*, 2022, p. 45.

27 Deborah Sanders, 'Rebuilding the Ukrainian Navy,' *Naval War College Review,* 70 (4), 2017, pp.61–77.

28 Megan Eckstein, 'After 2014 Decimation, Ukrainian Navy Rebuilds to Fends of Russia,' *Defense News*, 2021, at https://www.defensenews.com/naval/2021/08/09/after-2014-decimation-ukrainian-navy-rebuilds-to-fend-off-russia/ (Accessed June 14, 2023).

29 Dmitry Gorenburg and Michael Kofman, 'Russia and Ukraine had a Short Naval Battle. Here's What you Need to Know,' *The Washington Post*, 2018, at https://www.washington post.com/news/monkey-cage/wp/2018/11/28/russia-and-ukraine-had-a-short-naval-battle-heres-what-you-need-to-know/ (Accessed June 14, 2023).

30 Alexander Lott, 'The Passage Regimes of the Kerch Straits- To Each Their Own?,' *Ocean Development & International Law*, 2021, at https://doi.org/10.1080/00908320.2020.1869445 (Accessed June 15, 2023).

31 Elena Teslova, 'Why the Kerch Bridge is Important for Russia,' *Anadolu Ajansi*, 2022, at https://www.aa.com.tr/en/russia-ukraine-war/why-the-kerch-bridge-is-important-for-russia/ 2706341 (Accessed June 15, 2023).

32 Andrew Strike, "Former U.S. Coast Guard Patrol Boats to Serve Again in the Ukrainian Navy," US Department of State, 2021, at https://www.state.gov/dipnote-u-s-department-of-state-official-blog/former-u-s-coast-guard-patrol-boats-to-serve-again-in-the-ukrainian-navy/ (Accessed June 16, 2023).

33 Megan Eckstein, 'After 2014 Decimation, Ukrainian Navy Rebuilds to Fend Off Russia,' *Defense News*, 2021, at https://www.defensenews.com/naval/2021/08/09/after-2014-decimation-ukrainian-navy-rebuilds-to-fend-off-russia/ (Accessed June 16, 2023).

34 HI Sutton, "Timeline of 2022 Ukraine Invasion: War in the Black Sea," 2023, at http:// www.hisutton.com/Timeline-2022-Ukraine-Invasion-At-Sea.html (Accessed July 6, 2023).

35 Paul D Shinkman, 'Russia Deploys Warships to Black Sea in Dangerous Escalation Near Ukraine,' *US News*, 2022, at https://www.usnews.com/news/world/articles/2022-01-26/russia-deploys-warships-to-black-sea-in-dangerous-escalation-near-ukraine (Accessed July 14, 2023)..

36 Raul Pedrozo, "Ukraine Symposium – Maritime Exclusion Zones in Armed Conflicts," Lieber Institute West Point, 2022, at https://lieber.westpoint.edu/maritime-exclusion-zones-armed-conflicts/ (Accessed July 7, 2022).

37 'Ukraine War: Snake Island and Battle for Control in Black Sea,' *BBC*, 2022, at https://www.bbc.com/news/world-europe-61406808 (Accessed July 11, 2022).

38 Thomas Mackintosh, 'Zelensky Visits Snake Island on Ukraine War's 500 th Day,' *BBC*, 2023, at https://www.bbc.com/news/world-europe-66141701 (Accessed July 12, 2022).

39 David Axe, 'The Ukrainian Navy Still Has One Big Amphibious Ship. She'd be Pretty Useful Right About Now,' *Forbes*, 2022, at https://www.forbes.com/sites/davidaxe/2022/11/23/the-ukrainian-navy-still-has-one-big-amphibious-ship-shed-be-pretty-useful-right-about-now/?sh=3ec800da6329 (Accessed July 9, 2022).

40 Ellie Cook, 'Why Russian Sinking of Ukraine's 'Last Warship' Wouldn't Matter,' *Newsweek*, 2023, at https://www.newsweek.com/russia-destruction-ukraine-last-warship-yuri-olefirenko-1803858 (Accessed July 12, 2023).

41 Tayfun Ozberk, 'Turkey Closes the Dardanelles and Bosporus to Warships,' *Naval News*, 2022, at https://www.navalnews.com/naval-news/2022/02/turkey-closes-the-dardanelles-and-bosphorus-to-warships/ (Accessed July 7, 2022).

42 Mark Nevitt, 'Assessing Military Operations in the Black Sea a Year Into Russia's Full-Scale Invasion of Ukraine,' *Just Security*, 2023, at https://www.justsecurity.org/85181/assessing-military-operations-in-the-black-sea-a-year-into-russias-full-scale-invasion-of-ukraine/ (Accessed July 17, 2023).

43 Tayfun Ozberk, 'Russia's Amphibious Operation Dilemma,' *Naval News*, 2022, at https://www.navalnews.com/naval-news/2022/03/russias-amphibious-operation-dilemma/ (Accessed July 9, 2022).

44 Tayfun Ozberk, 'Ukraine Strikes Russia's Alligator Class LST with Ballistic Missile,' *Naval News*, 2022, at https://www.navalnews.com/naval-news/2022/03/ukraine-strikes-alligator-class-lst-with-ballistic-missile/ (Accessed July 9, 2022).

45 HI Sutton, "Timeline of 2022 Ukraine Invasion: War in the Black Sea,"2023, at http://www.hisutton.com/Timeline-2022-Ukraine-Invasion-At-Sea.html (Accessed July 9, 2023).

46 Joseph Trevithick, 'Amphibious Assault on Odesa Could Be Imminent According to Satellite Imagery (Updated),' *The Drive*, 2022, at https://www.thedrive.com/the-war-zone/44758/amphibious-assault-on-odesa-could-be-imminent-according-to-satellite-imagery (Accessed July 9, 2022).

47 Philip G Wasielewski, 'The Feasibility of Russian Amphibious Operations Against Ukraine,' *Marine Corps Gazette*, 2022, at https://mca-marines.org/wp-content/uploads/The-Feasibility-of-Russian-Amphibious-Operations-against-Ukraine.pdf (Accessed July 18, 2023).

48 Wendell Steavenson and Marta Rodionova, 'How Ukraine's Virtually Non-Existent Navy Sank Russia's Flagship,' *The Economist*, 2023, at https://www.economist.com/interactive/1843/2023/07/27/how-ukraines-virtually-non-existent-navy-sank-russias-flagship (Accessed August 9, 2023).

49 'Moskva Cruiser Sank While Being Towed in a Strom – Russian Defense Ministry,' *TASS Russian News Agency*, 2022, at https://tass.com/russia/1438045 (Accessed July 10, 2022).

50 Douglas Barrie and Nick Childs, 'The Moskva Incidents and Its Wider Implications,' *International Institute for Strategic Studies*, 2022, at https://www.iiss.org/online-analysis//military-balance/2022/04/the-moskva-incident-and-its-wider-implications (Accessed July 10, 2022).

51 'How Oceans Became New Technological Battlefields,' *The Economist*, 2023, at https://www.economist.com/special-report/2023/07/03/how-oceans-became-new-technological-battlefields#:~:text=The%20project%20showed%20how%20technology,Offence%20is%20another%20matter (Accessed August 9, 2023).

52 'Drone Hits Russia's Black Sea Fleet Headquarters in Sevastopol,' *Voice of America*, 2022, at

https://www.voanews.com/a/ukraine-attacks-russia-s-black-sea-fleet-in-sevastopol/6680894.html (Accessed July 11, 2023).

53 HI Sutton, 'Why Ukraine's Remarkable Attack on Sevastopol Will Go Down in History,' *Naval News*, 2022, at https://www.navalnews.com/naval-news/2022/11/why-ukraines-remarkable-attack-on-sevastopol-will-go-down-in-history/ (Accessed July 11, 2022).

54 'Satellite Images Show Damage to Russian Naval Vessels Struck in Ukraine Attack,' *Reuters*, 2023, at https://www.reuters.com/world/europe/satellite-images-show-damage-russian-naval-vessels-struck-ukraine-attack-2023-09-14/ (Accessed October 19, 2023).

55 R. Vignesh and Abhay K. Singh, 'Attack on Sevastopol: Key Takeaways,' IDSA, 2023, at https://www.idsa.in/issuebrief/Attack-on-Sevastopol-RVignesh-AKSingh-041023 (Accessed October 20, 2023).

56 Ibid.

57 'Putin Blames Ukrainian Special Services for Crimea Bridge Explosion,' Radio Free Europe Radio Liberty, 2022, at https://www.rferl.org/a/crimean-bridge-blast-divers-investigate-kerch/32071969.html (Accessed July 12, 2022).

58 Ukrayinska Pravda, 'Satellite Shows Barricade Barges Against Ukrainian Drones Near Crimean Bridge,' 2023, at https://news.yahoo.com/satellite-shows-barricade-barges-against-130800937.html (Accessed August 30, 2023).

59 Arvin Donley, "Odesa Official: Ukraine Grain Exports to Begin Soon," World Grain.Com, 2022, at https://www.world-grain.com/articles/17231-odesa-official-ukraine-grain-exports-to-begin-soon (Accessed June 7, 2023).

60 Clyde Hughes, 'Russia Continues Deadly Missile Assault on Odessa, Grain Facilities,' *United Press International*, 2023, at https://www.upi.com/Top_News/World-News/2023/07/21/Ukraine-Russia-Odesa-grain-Putin-Zelensky/8311689957113/ (Accessed July 23, 2023).

61 Julian Borger, 'Russia 'Holding Humanity Hostage' Over Black Sea Grain Deal, UN Hears,' *The Guardian*, July 21, 2023, at https://www.theguardian.com/world/2023/jul/21/russia-holding-humanity-hostage-over-black-sea-grain-deal-un-hears (Accessed July 23, 2023).

62 "Russian Federation Attacks on Ukrainian Ports Risk Far-Reaching Impacts for Food in Developing Countries, Under-Secretary-General Tells Security Council," United Nations, July 21, 2023, at https://press.un.org/en/2023/sc15362.doc.htm (Accessed July 23, 2023).

63 Deborah Sanders, 'Rebuilding the Ukrainian Navy,' *Naval War College Review*, 70 (4), 2017, pp.61–77.

64 'Strategy of the Naval Forces of the Armed Forces of Ukraine 2035,' Ukrainian Navy, 2018, at https://navy.mil.gov.ua/en/strategiya-vijskovo-morskyh-syl-zbrojnyh-syl-ukrayiny-2035/ (Accessed July 23, 2023).

65 Ibid.

66 R. Vignesh and Abhay K. Singh, no. 55.

67 Ibid.

## APPENDIX – I

### Timeline of Key Naval Engagements in the Ukraine War

| *Date* | *Engagement* | *Outcome* |
|---|---|---|
| Feb. 24–22 | Bombardment of Snake Island by Russia | This engagement marks the beginning of hostilities in the Black Sea |
| Feb. 25–22 | Russian troops land on Snake Island | Russia takes control of Snake Island located just 35 km from the southern Ukrainian coast |
| Feb. 25–22 | Russia announces establishment of MEZ | The Russian MEZ encompasses the entire Sea of Azov and the north-western part of the Black Sea |
| Feb. 26–22 | The Russian Navy carries out amphibious landings of troops in the eastern Ukrainian coast | These landings play a vital role in bringing key Ukrainian port cities in the Sea of Azov such as Melitopol and Mariupol under Russian control |
| Feb. 28–22 | Türkiye announces the closure of the Turkish Straits to warships as per the provisions of the Montreux Convention | The closure of the Turkish Straits means that Russia can no longer bring its warships to the Black Sea, making the possibility of any external intervention in the maritime theatre unlikely |
| Mar. 03–22 | Ukraine scuttles its largest warship and the flagship of its navy, Frigate Hetman Sahaidachny, which was undergoing repairs in Nikolaev to prevent it from being captured by Russia | Most of the Ukrainian Navy's surface ships are either sunk, scuttled or captured by the Russian Navy with the exception of an LST named Yury Olefirenko |
| Mar. 15–22 | The Black Sea Fleet carries out amphibious demonstrations near Odesa | These demonstrations indicates an imminent Russian amphibious assault on Odesa. This leads to the amassment of Ukrainian troops and defences in Odesa to protect the city against possible Russian seaborne assault |
| Mar. 24–22 | A Russian Navy LST berthed in the eastern Ukrainian port city of Berdyansk is sunk by a missile attack by Ukraine | After this attack Russia suspends the use of Berdyansk port as a point of reinforcement in the Russian-controlled eastern Ukrainian coast along the Sea of Azov |
| Apr. 03/04–2022 | The Black Sea Fleet's flagship Moskva is reportedly hit by two Ukraianian missiles. This leads to the ship sinking the following day while being towed to Sevastopol | Moskva was the largest and most powerful warship of the Black Sea Fleet. It played a vital role in providing air defence cover to Russian military assets operating in the north-western part of the Black Sea. With its sinking, Russian military assets lose their protective umbrella. In addition, Moskva's sinking boosts Ukrainians' morale |
| Apr. Jun. 2022 | Between April and June 2022, Ukraine begins targeting Russian resupply ships to Snake Island using drones and missiles | Russia loses several of its resupply & patrol boats in these attacks. As a result, sustaining its hold on the Snake Island becomes increasingly difficult. |
| Jun. 30–22 | Russia withdraws from Snake Island | The Russian withdrawal from Snake Island is a |

| *Date* | *Engagement* | *Outcome* |
|---|---|---|
| | | tactical victory for Ukraine. It diminishes Russia's ability to exercise sea control in the north-western part of the Black Sea. The retaking of Snake Island also opens up opportunities for Ukraine to mount attacks eastwards towards Crimea and Sevastopol |
| Jul. 27–22 | Russia and Ukraine sign the UN brokered BSGI deal to establish a safe maritime corridor in the Black Sea to facilitate the transit of grain-laden cargo | The BSGI effectively lifts the blockade of Odesa and mitigates the shortage of wheat exports to developing countries |
| Jul. 31–22 | Ukraine successfully carries out its first-ever attack on the Crimean Peninsula. The attack is carried out using an UAV that strikes the headquarters of the Black Sea Fleet situated in Sevastopol | Russia cancels its Navy Day ceremony and security around the Sevastopol base is increased |
| Oct. 08–22 | A huge explosion damages a section of the Crimean Bridge, causing serious disruption to Russia's connectivity with the Crimean Peninsula. Putin claims that the attack was planned and carried out by the Ukrainian Special Services by using a truck bomb | The bridge is rendered out of service for four months until it's reopened for traffic after extensive repairs. During this time, the Russian Navy uses its LSTs to transport military personnel and civilians to the Crimean Peninsula |
| Oct. 29–22 | Seven Ukrainian USV's penetrate the harbor defence of Sevastopol and reportedly damage two Russian warships, including the Black Sea Fleet's flagship frigate Admiral Makarov | Despite failing to inflict any major damage to the ship, the attack demonstrates Ukraine's ability to strike port infrastructure in Sevastopol. As a result, the Russian Navy increases defences in Sevastopol and restricts the activity of the Black Sea Fleet. Also, Russia begins to relocate some of the ships of the Black Sea Fleet to the port of Novorossiysk situated in the Russian mainland |
| May 29–23 | Russia claims that the Ukrainian Navy's last combat ship LST Yury Olefirenko has been destroyed by a high precision missile strike | Despite Ukraine not confirming the sinking, it is likely that the ship has been sunk |
| Jul. 17–23 | Crimean Bridge is attacked by two Ukrainian USVs. The attack results in the killing of two Russian civilians and injuring one | Russia begins to restrict civilian traffic on the Crimean Bridge. Russian authorities issue an advisory to its citizens travelling in and out of Crimea to use an alternative route. This route goes through southern Ukrainian territory currently under Russian control |
| Aug. 04–23 | The port of Novorossiysk is attacked by Ukrainian USVs that reportedly damage Russian warships | The attack indicates that the maritime strike range of Ukraine has further expanded eastwards, reaching the Russian mainland |

| *Date* | *Engagement* | *Outcome* |
|---|---|---|
| Aug. 12–23 | Ukraine again targets the Crimean Bridge using both missiles and USVs. Russia claims to have neutralised all the missiles and USVs | Satellite images show that Russia has begun installing protective barges along the southern side of the Crimean Bridge to protect it from USV attacks. Also, Russia increases its air defence installations over the bridge |
| Sep. 13–23 | Ukraine mounts the largest ever attack on Sevastopol through the use of cruise missiles and USVs. In these attacks three cruise missiles penetrate Russian air defence grids and hit a Kilo-class submarine Rostov-on-Don and a LST Minsk. Both ships were undergoing repairs in the dry docks | The attack demonstrates Ukraine's ability to penetrate Russian air defence grids over Crimea. Photos of the damaged submarine and LST indicate that these vessels are most likely to be written off from service. This loss is the Russian Navy's biggest loss since the loss of Moskva |
| Sep. 20–23 | Satellite imagery confirms that the 744th Communication Centre of the Black Sea Fleet in Crimea has been struck by Ukrainian missiles | This attack will likely disrupt Russian Ground Lines of Communication (GLOCs) in Crimea |
| Sep. 23 | Throughout September Ukrainian forces gain control of several offshore oil drilling platforms near Crimea | Ukraine can use these offshore oil drilling platforms to disrupt the Black Sea Fleet's supply chains and communication networks |
| Oct. 13–23 | Ukraine attacks and damages two Russian vessels with USVs and likely UUVs | The nature of damage sustained indicates that fully submersible unmanned attack boats have been used for the first time since the beginning of the war |

# 9

# Salient Lessons Learnt in Operational Logistics in Russia–Ukraine War 2023

*Anil Kapoor*

*Counting tanks before the war was a necessary but insufficient exercise. It didn't tell you what you needed to know for assessing the net strength of each side in the conflict. What impressed me about the '73 war was how asymmetric it was. Israel was not only much better prepared to recover and repair its tanks, it also dominated the battlefield, making recovery possible. Superior force, by standard measures, did not win. The number that truly counted was the one that revealed a tank's likely longevity.*

**—Andrew Marshall's Lessons in Yom Kippur Arab Israel War 1973**

## INTRODUCTION

February 24, 2022, marked the tipping point in global affairs when Russia attacked Ukraine, ending speculations on the why, when, what, where and how Russia would respond to the impasse with an unrelenting Ukraine. Russia was confident that it would end the conflict on its terms in an acceptable timeframe and expand beyond Crimea to force Ukraine to remain aligned to Russian interests. Ukraine, on the other hand, has displayed psychological resilience in its resolve to withstand the invasion.

The slower than expected progress by Russians in Ukraine is often attributed to failing logistics.[1] Analysis of the Russian logistics planning and execution in the war makes for an extremely interesting case study. Sometimes failing logistics slowed down the military operations and at other times operational plans had to be modified when these could not be logistically sustained. This was evident in a number of battles in the Russian Course of Action (COA) for the capture of Kyiv. When the COA failed, the contingency operational plans were ineffective since they did not take into consideration the logistical challenges to support the revised plan. The southeast thrust line could not be effectively sustained by the logistics echelons. Both the aforesaid operations were stalled by the successful interdiction of the Russian logistics supply chains by Ukrainian forces. That said, this analysis and assessment is based on openly accessible information about the Russian War.

## THE BIG STRATEGIC PICTURE

### The Resources Balance Sheet

#### *Impact of Sanctions*

Post the annexation of Crimea in 2014, Russia came under heavy United States-led sanctions. However, despite these sanctions, Russia's economy continued to surge ahead on its oil, gas and resources revenues. Be that as it may, the major United States (US) sanctions post the Russian invasion in February 2022, were more widespread and designed to put a squeeze on the entire economy. Russia was barred from the Society for Worldwide International Financial Telecommunications (SWIFT), which made it difficult for Russian banks to conduct seamless real time international financial transactions. Further, Russian assets of USD 640 billion held in the US and Western banks were frozen, adversely affecting the Russian economy and the invasion. Other consequences of the sanctions impacting strategic economic issues with global implications were on energy security and food security.

#### *Energy Insecurity*

Russia supplies over 40 per cent of Europe's energy requirements. This is particularly important in winters when Russian oil and gas heats up homes and keeps factories running in the European Union (EU). Energy, oil and gas are what kept the engine of the Russian economy running. Russian oil, refined oil products and coal imports were banned from the US and Western nations with a caveat that nations dealing with Russia would also come under US sanctions. The G7 decided to impose a price cap on Russian oil at USD 60 per barrel, which was aimed at keeping the oil supplies from Russia available, but denying its real value revenue adds to Russia. Russia responded to the decision by halting the supply of fuel and gas into Europe by shutting down the Nord Stream 1 gas pipeline. With subsequent underwater explosions in both Nord Stream 1 and 2 pipelines, the complete supply chain to Europe was disrupted. Russia concurrently increased oil supplies to China in Yuan, India in Rupees and created a oil supply hub through Turkey. Despite these actions, the sanctions did affect the Russian economy, which funded the war.

#### *Food Insecurity*

Russia and Ukraine together provide 27 per cent of the world's market for wheat, 16 per cent of corn, 23 per cent of barley and a whopping 53 per cent of sunflower oils. With sanctions imposed, Russia responded by blockading Ukrainian wheat and grain in its ports, causing a global food scarcity. The Black Sea ports of Odesa, Mariupol, Melitopol and Kherson accounted for 95 per cent of Ukraine's grain exports, after February 2022 these were either under Russian control or blocked by Russian ships. With the disruption of supplies from the two major producers, global shortages raised food inflation worldwide and food shortages hit the world, striking nations as far as Ethiopia, Mexico and Bangladesh. This disruption was further accentuated when Ukrainian farmlands and grain warehouses were damaged when Russian tanks rolled in. The impact of war on farmlands and the major damage to the Nova Kakhovka Dam affected water security and agriculture, spiralling into food insecurity. The war has raised the Food Price Index by over 30 per cent and the shortages created puts over 500 million people at a risk of food insecurity.[2]

#### *Economy*

The global economy was still recovering from the catastrophic impact of the COVID pandemic when the war commenced. The plummeting economic growth, global dependence on energy resources from Russia, food grains from Ukraine have taken the biggest hit due to erratic global supply chains. Global growth is expected to drop from 4.5 per cent to just 3 per cent, and a major threat of recession looms over most economies. With shortages of fuel and grain, prices have risen, leading to world-wide inflation in the region of 9 per cent, which will push the global economy into recession. The Kenyan proverb *When two elephants fight, it is the grass that gets trampled*, epitomised by the Russia–Ukraine war, reflects the state of affairs of the world today.[3]

## THE WAR ZONE LOGISTICS

### Military Logistics Principles

An integral part of a nation's deterrence is a trustworthy national logistics base and infrastructure composed of an industrial base, transportation resources, secure storage facilities and linkages from the hinterland to the Tactical Battle Area (TBA). Military logistics is designed to sustain military capability, and the military supply chain connects the industrial base to troops in the TBA. At the strategic level, warfighting needs and surge requirements are integrated with national industrial capacities. However, logistics in the TBA are integrated at the operational level. Hence, logistics planning at the operational level must ensure that the tempo of military operations is maintained in all contingencies. At the operational level, the logisticians' plan, prioritises and distributes resources to logistics hubs from where resources are transferred to tactical logistics units. Military logistics at tactical levels is tailored to establish supply hub-and-spoke networks to sustain combat units in the area of operations. Total quality logistics management must ensure that the material assets of combat capability merge at the right place, at the right time, in the right quantity and in the right condition to maintain the tempo of operations.

## Logistics Planning and Preparations

### *Rail, Roads in Ukraine and Russia and Logistics Capabilities*

The rail, road and air transportation infrastructure plays a vital role in operational logistics and sustenance support of ground forces. Ukraine and Russia share a compatible rail and road infrastructure as Ukraine has Soviet-era broad gauge railway lines. Thus, Russia has the advantage of exploiting the railroad infrastructure in Ukraine. In contrast, Ukraine's western neighbours have medium gauge rail lines. Hence, any logistics support into Ukraine from its neighbours involves transhipment and double handling of freight at the border railhead, which is both a time-consuming and cost-prohibitive process.[4] During the Second World War this difference in the gauge of the railway lines had also disrupted German logistics during their invasion of the Soviet Union. The medium gauge railway lines, engines and rolling stock could not be used on the Soviet broad gauge rail lines, thus forcing the Germans to send their logistics supplies by road or aira factor that contributed to their ultimate defeat.

### *Russian Principles of Logistics*

Since the Soviet era, the Russian concept for offensive operations was based on the leap frogging of echelons, wherein when one echelon fought, the other was ready to be deployed to the frontline when the first echelon was exhausted. Once replaced, the first echelon would reorganise and be refitted with personnel, equipment and logistics supplies to be combat ready for deployment. The echelon principle was built on army groups supported by Material Technical Support (MTS) brigades. The fighting units had limited organic capacity to retrieve supplies from the MTS for operational logistics.[5] The Russian Armed Forces' operational concept, inherited from the Soviet era, was modernised to a lean logistics during a major transformation in 2009. Though successfully tested in Crimea, Russia's lean logistics system was not designed for a long-haul war.

### *An Analysis of the Russian Offensive's Operational Logistics Capabilities*

The Russian Army logistics forces are not designed for a large-scale deep-strike ground offensive far from rail and road heads. As per an RAND analysis, the Russian Army does not have enough integral load carriers to meet its logistics requirement more than 150 Km beyond supply dumps. To reach a 300 Km range, the Russian Army would have to double its vehicle allocation for each of the material-technical support brigades. To gain familiarity with Russian logistics requirements and lift resources, a useful starting point is the Russian Combined Arms Army. They all have different force structures. Each combined arms army is assigned a material–technical support brigade. Each material–technical support brigade has one tactical pipeline battalion and two truck battalions with a total of 150 general cargo trucks with 50 trailers and 260 specialised trucks. The Russian Army makes heavy use of tube and rocket artillery fire, and rocket ammunition is very bulky. Each army has 56 to 90 multiple launch rocket system launchers, which have huge rocket replenishing requirements. As per a staff check, in case the combined arms army fires a single volley, it would require 56–90 trucks just to replenish rocket ammunition, which amounts to about a 75-cargo-truck force in the material–technical support brigade just to replace one volley of rockets. There are also from six to nine tube artillery battalions, air defence artillery battalions, mechanised and recon battalions, infantry battalions and three to five tank battalions with their replenishment requirements for mortar, anti-tank missiles and small arms ammunition. In addition to ammunition, food, fuels, oils and lubricants (FOL), engineering and medical supplies and other operational stores also need to be transported. Thus, the potential resupply requirements are substantial. Hence, the Russian Army combat force needs a large number of vehicles for ammunition and dry cargo replenishment. Replenishment of fuel and water is established by a tactical pipeline battalion. Until then, FOL and water trucks are required for operational logistics. In an overall analysis, the load-carrying capability falls grossly short of the need for supplies, FOL, ammunition and other operational stores.[6]

### *Exercise Zapad-2021: Planning and Preparing Logistics for a War*

It would be pertinent to analyse and understand the build-up of the Russian forces during the exercises conducted along the Ukrainian border prior to the commencement of the war. Exercise Zapad-2021, a joint Russian–Belarusian exercise on the Ukraine border was a follow-up of the Spring 2021 military exercise in which a substantial amount of equipment was left behind. In effect, these exercises helped the Russians build-up along the border and continue to augment the deployments there with more equipment. These large-scale exercises were based on a detailed exercise plan, including a logistics plan for supply, maintenance, medical services and transportation. Logistics units for Zapad-2021 were deployed as a part of the preparatory activities in July and August of 2021. It is conjectured from the US and NATO open intelligence reports that this surge was actually in preparation for the impending war. That said, transitioning from exercise to war for combat battle groups is a hot start, changing the dynamics of logistics. Operational logistics is a function of plans, revised plans, depth of thrust lines for selected objectives, tempo of operations and the dynamics of the fog of war. A full-scale war over vast distances is replete with logistical Volatility, Uncertainty, Complexity and Ambiguity (VUCA) due to unpredictability in the replenishment of supplies, FOL and ammunition deep inside enemy territory. In addition, tactical engagements add to the attritional losses in terms of both troopcasualties and damaged equipment, leading to increased demands for transportation, maintenance and repair and medical evacuations and treatment.[7] For these exercises, major logistics hubs were located at strategic railheads, close to but at a safe distance from the Ukrainian border. It was planned that based on the Russian progress of operations, from the railheads supplies would be distributed by road and rail transportation systems to establish fresh distribution hubs across the areas of operations in Ukraine. Given the sheer volume and velocity of logistics requirement, this transition from an exercise to an invasion could have resulted in a logistics vacuum, which, in turn, had a negative impact on the Russian military capability in the first phase of the war.

## Russian Invasion of Ukraine

### *The Balloon Goes Up*

On February 24, 2022, Russians launched the military operation in Ukraine. Kremlin had planned a short blitzkrieg type of operation in which Russian forces would capture and depose the Ukrainian President and leadership. The war was launched on two fronts with two different operational objectives. While the northwest thrust had to capture Kyiv, the thrust in the east and southeast was aimed at capturing the Donbas region to establish a land corridor between the Donbas and Crimea.

### *Russian Operations and Logistics Support in the Kyiv Region*

The Russians had planned a short, quick offensive in Kyiv by initially seizing terrain and then quickly consolidating gains. The first step was to capture the Antonov Airport in Hostomel near Kyiv through an airborne operation. This operation was crucial to build a logistics hub at the airport for the anticipated short, intense operation pulse. The airhead would then become a hub for the beefing up of equipment and requisite mission logistics. The follow-up logistics would have been coordinated from Hostomel once the Russian troops had gained control of the area. However, this break in operations to secure the airhead failed, and logistics became a challenge. Russian forces normally carry supplies for three to five days.[8] Thereafter, sustenance support of supplies, FOL and ammunition are big volume drivers and a logisticians' nightmare. The Russians could neither secure the airhead at Hostomel nor the railhead at Chernihiv in the north. When these courses of action failed, the infamous 40-mile-long convoy north of Kyiv was unleashed, either as a part of the operational logistics plan or a contingency plan, to establish a log base on wheels and since the ground was wet and slushy the Russian vehicles had to stick to the roads. The convoy consisted of a reduced MTS brigade, reinforced with a mechanised battalion for convoy protection, comprising trucks, fuel tankers, ammunition, spare parts and food and supplies as a tactical logistics hub for the next phase of the operations. The convoy halted for want of orders for deployment. Given the tyranny of distance and inordinately high turnaround time from the Russian strategic and operational hubs, pushing forces and logistics in the north on narrow roads became a challenge. The situation was further impacted by lack of air superiority in the early stages of the war. Russians lacked protection against the agile Ukrainian forces using drones, artillery and mortars and launching special operations to inflict damage on the logistics convoy. This attrition significantly reduced the Russian logistics' robustness and stamina, leading to Russian withdrawal from the Kyiv area. The Kyiv campaign was thus a failure.[9]

### *The Operations and Logistics Support in Donbas*

The Russian forces had planned operations in the eastern and southern regions of Ukraine in the Donbas region. Since the annexation of Crimea in 2014, Russia had commenced the build-up of military and logistics capability to make it sufficient to fight a war against Ukraine. Russians preferred to move troops and supplies by railroad transportation systems after seizing Kherson and Melitopol and securing a crossing over the Dnieper River, but despite this, the Russian forces gained terrain in eastern and southern Ukraine extremely slowly. This was due to Ukraine's operational focus on effectively targeting the Russian logistics echelons and supply lines, thereby retarding the offensive. While the Russian Army definitely had the combat power to achieve value objectives in depth but it neither had the requisite operational logistics endurance nor any pragmatic contingency plans to support these operations. The logistics vacuum imposed restrictions, leading to operational pauses.

### *Ukraine's Targeting of Russian Logistics*

A major highlight of the Ukrainian operations was the targeting of Russian logistic echelons at all levels as priority targets. Ukrainian forces combined old and new technologies including drones and special operations to attack the Russian supply lines, thus shrinking Russian logistics capability. Continuing the quest for attrition, Ukraine destroyed railways infrastructure and bridges and ambushed Russian supply convoys and force protection tank columns. They also killed a number of commanders including generals. This imposed a logistics and decision vacuum, eventually retarding the progress of Russian offensive operations.

### *Russia's Tryst with the Latest Technologies*

Russia deployed HESA Shahed 136, an Iranian loitering munition, with a 40-kg payload, as long-range autonomous pusher-prop drone to conduct tactical strikes and degrade Ukraine's infrastructure. Building on this success, Russia pulverised the battlefield with its own ZALA Lancet drone to effectively target and destroy Ukrainian tanks, artillery and air defence systems. A striking trend observed in the war is that Russia is able to produce better and cheaper weapon systems than its NATO opponents. The Geran-2 and Lancet drones cost about $15,000 each in contrast to the US Reaper drone, which costs $32 million. The Russians also designed, developed and deployed one-and-a-half-ton payload glide bombs upgraded with a precision-controlled GPS system and wings that allow the bomb to 'glide' to the target. Glide bombs effectively conducted precision strikes from Su-34 and 35 jets outside the range of Ukrainian air defence networks. The planes could not be targeted, and the bombs wreaked havoc on the high-rise buildings Ukraine was using as defensive strongholds. Glide bombs further showcased

Russian ingenuity in developing a weapon system at a very little cost from the hardware they already had in stock.[10] Currently, the FAB-500M-62 is the most used munition as a glide bomb platform. The Russians also designed, developed many more weapon systems that are examples of Russia moving from prototype to battlefield use in a phenomenal timeframe.

(a) **IB75 Penicillin Counter Artillery System**. The Penicillin has been effectively detecting and neutralising Ukrainian mortar, artillery and Multiple Launch Rocket Systems (MLRSs) with pinpoint accuracy and delivering a precision retaliatory strike. Unlike the US ANTPQ37, Penicillin does not use radar to track projectiles, it uses sound waves. An array of thermoacoustic sensors and optical and infrared cameras are set up around the Penicillin unit to detect even small targets such as mortar shells.

(b) **Kinzhal Missiles.** Russia conducted a series of strikes on Ukraine's infrastructure in an endeavour to degrade the Ukrainian air defence system by using drones, loiter munitions and glide bombs. Russia also used its conventional Iskander and first-generation hypersonic missile, the Kinzhal. Recently the world witnessed a spectacular footage of a US-supplied Patriot missile battery attempting to intercept a Kinzhal missile. The Patriot launched 30 missiles into the air over a period of 90 seconds, unable to find and bring down the Kinzhal before being struck and destroyed. Though Ukraine claimed that it had shot down a Kinzhal, these claims are not confirmed. Kinzhal is a first-generation Russian hypersonic missile; two more systems are in the prototype stage.

(c) **Innovative Assault Guns.** Russia adapted and focused on using tanks in an assault gun role by innovatively upgrading large stockpiles of previous generation T-62 and T-54/55 tanks. Russians deployed the T-62s and T-54/55s and attacked entrenched Ukrainian positions from over two kilometres. The tank assault guns also provided close fire support to infantry battle groups.

### *The US and NATO Support for Ukraine*

Ukraine has been supported with state-of-the-art equipment by the US and NATO including the training of troops to use and sustain these systems. Ukraine has acquired advanced tanks Leopards, Challengers, Abrams, Stryker AFVs, Bradley Fighting Vehicles, Patriot and Starstreak AD missile systems, M777 and M142 Artillery Systems, Bayraktar TB2 Turkish Drone Systems, F 16 aircraft to name a few big tickets for the conduct of offensive operations including a major counteroffensive that commenced with effect from June 2023. The problems Ukrainians face is managing the technology transition and sustenance support of the high-tech equipment. The gestation period in learning how to operate the equipment under combat pressure and maintaining their operational capabilities to include the training of operators, technicians and the management of spares, tools and test equipment has resulted in the suboptimal exploitation of the weapon system platforms.

### *Casualties and Refugee Management*

War has resulted in huge devastation of infrastructure in Ukraine, notably the nuclear power plants and the Khakhova Dam. The war has also created massive humanitarian and human rights challenges. As per the latest UNHCR Report Update 48 of June 09, 2023, there are over 1300,000 refugees and 500,000 internally displaced Ukrainians. The Russia–Ukraine war casualties have been heavy and the management of the over 20,000 civilians injured and the over 10,000 civilian dead has been a major challenge. Though the exact number is a challenge, a bigger challenge has been the combatant casualties and prisoners of war management and the transportation of the injured and the dead, especially for Russia. Russia was not adequately prepared for war casualty management in the TBA and casevac for the resuscitation of casualties.

## SALIENT LESSONS LEARNT IN OPERATIONAL LOGISTICS

### Major Lessons Learnt

The sheer size of Ukraine, one of the largest countries in Europe, and the Russian attempt to 'demilitarize and denazify' it was ambitious and replete with problems. That said, the Russia–Ukraine war reflects poorly on the Russian operational and operational logistics planning. Russian operational logistics is not fully integrated with the planning process. Logistics planning seems to have taken place after a COA had been decided. Russians were surprised not only by the size of Ukraine but also by the sheer intensity of Ukrainian resistance. Lessons learnt from a war are best evaluated by analysing the Principles of War. The key principles impacting war from a logistics perspective are administration, sustenance, flexibility, adaptability, economy of effort and cooperation including whole of nation and international support. Salient logistics support lessons learnt from this conflict are explained in the paragraphs below.

### *Administration*

If logistics cannot keep up with the operational pace, logistics vacuum leading to logistics culmination occurs, warranting a logistics pause. Russian administration to sustain its force through matching logistics stamina was lacking. A logistics vacuum at critical stages stalled the freedom of action of application of combat power at decisive points. This led to thwarted maintenance of momentum and concentration of force at a critical operational juncture thereby failing to capture planned value objectives, adversely affecting the morale of troops.

(a) **Effective Logistics Management.** Russia deployed over 150,000 troops in Ukraine, organised into various formations. This called for deliberate operational planning in sync with mission logistics planning. Russians should have planned a deliberate invasion with slow and steady advances, setting up secure small logistics footprints every 40Km approximately they captured territory. Each base should have had a repair depot, medical station and dumped stocks so that supplies were within less than a six-hour turnaround timeframe with adequate air defence and local protection. The choice to go light on logistics may work in a quick, limited military offensive but not in this kind of long protracted operations. Effective management of logistics support is imperative when planning combat mission pulses. Impacts from the conflict are forcing logistics companies to recalibrate and, in some cases, wholly reconsider their long-standing supply chain and partner ecosystems.[11]

(b) **Lack of Favourable Air Situation and Adequate Convoy Protection.** Logistics convoys moving along supply lines need protection, especially in enemy territory with a few predictable roads. Russian troops violated the basics of logistics convoy escort, making them vulnerable. The Ukrainians had identified that the Achilles' heel on the Russian effort was logistics. Most logistics convoys were attacked by drones and ambushed even by civilians after the Ukrainian military advised them to do so on social media. These ambushes forced Russia to divert troops to defend their supply lines, thereby affecting operations.

(c) **Resources Management for War Readiness.** War is an alchemy. It is contingent upon weapon systems readiness and soldier readiness. A mere military exercise cannot be scaled up to a war effort without major surge efforts. Most supply chain models assume a steady state, which is not applicable for redesigning something that is in transition. When designing supply chain networks, decision makers should adopt systems thinking approach to define logistics goals, objectives, key related activities and Key Performance Indicators (KPIs).[12] Contingency planning in logistics is important. There is a need for combat ready soldiers and combat ready support crew—mechanics, paramedics, engineers, truck drivers, labour and other crew. The needs of soldiers fighting a modern long-drawn war are enormous. A Russian soldier goes through about 4 kgs of supplies a day, in addition to fuel, ammunition, medical support and other. The Russian troops in the conflict were self-contained for three days after which lack of logistics supply adversely affected their combat readiness, leading to looting and acts of indiscipline that affected their morale and the will to fight. Some Russian soldiers suffered frostbite because they lacked extra cold weather clothing. Further, the recovery and repair of equipment requirements were humungous and inadequacy in sustenance support affected equipment availability in the hands of troops, leading to combat pulse exhaustion. The Ukrainian Armed Forces were equally affected by the induction of high-tech equipment with minimum essential training, minimum crew and crew support, which resulted in suboptimal exploitation.

(d) **Lack of Medical Support.** A vital aspect of military logistics planning is dedicated medical support in the golden first hour, prompt casevac, medical care and the recycling of troops. Russians were not adequately prepared to support their soldiers in terms of their medical needs. Ukrainians had to be prepared on multiple fronts for casevac and found it difficult to manage the surge in civilian and combatant casualties. There is a dire need to cater for casevac including air ambulances and medical facilities to support war-wounded casualties and respectable last rites of the dead.

(e) **Lack of Equipment and Ammunition.** As admitted by Mr Putin, Russia had severe shortages in state-of-the-art tanks, small arms and precision munitions including guided missiles. Russia exports plenty of weapon systems to the Middle East and Asia, however Mr Putin's revelation highlighted the hollowness of the Russian defence industry to meet the surge needs of the long-drawn war. Ukraine, on the other hand, packed a punch by inducting state-of-the-art tanks from Germany and the US, drones and other essential military hardware for a subdued counteroffensive.

(f) **Combat Force Regeneration (CFR).** Russia lacked CFR capabilities despite the fact that their industries were the Original Equipment Manufacturers (OEMs). They lost over 3,000 vehicles and over 500 tanks. Some of the tanks were over 50 years in vintage and unreliable; the tempo of military operations was tough on these tanks. Also, the logistics for the exercises were only partially coordinated with the planning of the invasion. The interval between the military exercises and the war did not permit necessary maintenance and refurbishment, severely reducing operational availability. The maintenance shortcomings were compounded by the fact that the troops had been in exercises for two months before crossing into Ukraine. Resources for recovery and repair were grossly inadequate, affecting CFR, recycling of equipment and consequent shortages in mission critical equipment, thereby impacting the combat pulse effectiveness of battle groups.

(g) **Lean Logistics Support.** Post reorganisation and transformation of its armed forces in 2009, Russia planned for a manoeuvre-based lean effective combat force but did not cater for matching logistics. In fact, the lean thinking resulted in the downsizing of organic logistics units and outsourcing of logistics, thereby reducing the punch on integral logistics capabilities and capacity with dependencies on external logistics resources—consequence that were neither foreseen nor factored during the war planning. The invasion was planned as a short campaign with only minor logistical needs, hence the quality and quantity of logistics assets were lower than anticipated.

(h) **Targeting the Weaknesses.** The Ukrainian forces understood the importance of targeting the Russian supply lines. They combined both high- and low-tech assets, regular forces and civilians to effectively ambush logistics units and convoys. There is, therefore, a dire need to plan defensive tactics to protect supply lines, define small logistics footprints and deploy new logistics technologies to minimise damage to one's own logistics.

(j) **Revisit Logistics Doctrines**. Given the transparency, deep look, deep strike capabilities of air assets including drones and the new type of warfare based on high-tech systems and precision munition, there is a dire need for the armed forces to deliberately plan logistics doctrines for offensive and defensive operations. The shortcomings of Russian logistics were due to not well thought through logistics reductions, insufficient maintenance, an untested logistical system and the fact that logistics is not an integrated part of Russian decision-making at every level. Flexibility through agile and responsive logistics support and the ability to readily adapt to meet changed circumstances through air maintenance must be deliberately planned. Also, cooperation between air and land forces for sharing of risks and opportunities must form a part of joint and integrated operational logistics planning.

(k) **Protection of Key Installations as VAs/VPs.** Nuclear power plants and dam were interdicted with massive damage and loss to life and property. There is a need to nominate vulnerable areas (VA) and vulnerable points (VP) and have a formalised plan for the security of such installations.

In Russia, the **Military–Industrial Commission of the Russian Federation** established in March 2006 is a permanent functional body responsible for supervising defence and military affairs. Directly under the President of Russia, the Commission coordinates and implements programmes in concert with the Defence Ministry of the Russian Federation, the Armed Forces of the Russian Federation and the defence industry.[13] Given their focus on defence technology and status as a global net weapon systems provider, Rosoboron, the export wing of Russia, has been providing aircraft, tanks and missile systems globally as well as providing life cycle sustenance support to Ukraine, Poland and other erstwhile USSR allies. However, despite a strong military and industrial base, Russia had reached a stage when it sought weapon systems from its allies to maintain the momentum in war. The Russia–Ukraine war has huge lessons on the deliberate and realistic strategic planning of National infrastructure and allied support for a full-scale long-drawn war.

Ukraine has also developed a manufacturing sector with special reference to defence. In fact, tank engines and power pack engines have been its strong point. On February 24, 2022, the Ukrainian military was still dependent on Russian-made military equipment with mutual dependence on technical spares support. That notwithstanding, the Ukraine Armed Forces have emerged as a modern, effective fighting force during the course of war due to the abundance of technology and equipment support provided by the US and its NATO allies. This is an apt example of how favourable diplomatic alliance can integrate technologies and weapon systems to create combat superiority by facilitating adaptability and agility.

Nations build resilient capacities and capabilities through infrastructure development, revamping manufacturing sector through industrial corridors comprising public and private enterprises. Original Equipment Manufacturers

(OEMs), Micro, Small and Medium Enterprises (MSMEs) and ancillary low-tech support tiers, defence industrial bases must be developed to meet long-term capabilities for weapon systems and Maintenance, Repair and Operations (MRO) life cycle sustenance support. In addition, allied sectors to include agriculture sector, energy and services support sector must be organised to cater for regular and surge requirements of the nation during crisis and calamities. India's present stature in the comity of nations is an opportunity for it to create synergies to gain the required technology catalysts by creating consortiums for achieving a technological edge and taking huge strides to lay strong foundations for Atmanirbharta and technology sovereignty. China Plus One initiative is a supply chain strategy that encourages OEMs to minimize their supply chain dependency on China by diversifying to other countries of their choice. Itis an opportunity that India must seize and gear up to have a manufacturing boom in its industrial corridors and defence industrial complex is to scale up to a global manufacturing hub.

National security strategy and technology strategy are two inseparable DNA strands. Despite being one of the vanguards of technology and its weaponization, Russia has been found wanting in terms of its technological superiority, employment and sustenance of resources in this long-drawn war. Western technologies and weapons in the hands of Ukrainians has created a tech imbalance in favour of Ukraine. Technology forecasting, planning, development and upgrade is a continuous exercise in nation building and helps in creating disruption, something that is so important in warfare. The war has seen escalated employment of information warfare, cyber warfare and Artificial Intelligence (AI). Technology management must be based on a well thought through technology strategy, which should be factored in operational strategy at the macro theatre and operational levels; merging technology with tactics must become the standard in the TBA for best impact. All technology strategy for defence has to have a focus on the cutting edge of technology development–quantum computing, 5G, 6G, augmented Reality, virtual Reality, Artificial Intelligence, big data analytics, blockchain for C7I2S2R,[14] (command and control communication, computer, cybertronics, cognition, combat, intelligence, information, surveillance, security and reconnaissance)-based Decision Support System (DSS). The key technology drivers for defence preparedness are lethality, sensor tech and internet of battlefield things (IoBT), Internet of Things (IoT), information, protection, stealth, adaptive camouflage, precision, positioning, automation and autonomy.

Once a battle is joined, offensive operations by design tend to be intense in consumption of critical resources and hence replenishment—ammunition, missiles, spares and assemblies, FOL, supplies and other resources—is vital to consolidate territorial gains. The fog of war, ad hoc infrastructures and weak lines of communications, vulnerability of feebly guarded logistics supply chains to enemy action and ever-increasing lines of communication resulting in a high turnaround time need detailed contingency planning and backup plans for operational effectiveness. Ambitious operations plans will be contingent on well-orchestrated operational logistics plans. There have been gross inadequacies in Russian operational planning, leading to logistics vacuums and hence, operational pauses. Due to lack of matching logistics stamina the tenuous lines of communication with the progress of operations inhibited the combat potential of the Russian forces in Ukraine. Russian forces were found wanting as they carried the offensive beyond the Russian borders into Ukraine. Lack of basic food supply to troops once the battle was joined resulted in mass plundering of meagre local resources, causing problems in good order and military discipline. Replenishment of ammunition and missiles could not happen in time, resulting in frequent logistics pause. In addition to inadequate FOL refill supply, load carrier vehicles were woefully short to meet operational logistics requirements. The turnaround time was also inordinately high to sustain the large combat force. Russian forces appeared unprepared for the war beyond their borders into the depths of Ukraine.

Victory is measured by foot and an army marches on its stomach are age-old home truths. The crux of war fighting and victory in the TBA is to a great measure soldier dependent. Hence, guaranteeing logistics support to the troops on ground is of paramount importance in war. Soldier readiness comprises sustenance support to troops in the TBA with food, water, other supplies and ammunition, clothing based on climatic conditions, billets for rest and refit, timely medical attention leading to casevac based on the nature of the casualty and also communication with families back home whenever there is a lull, to name a few big ticket items. There is also a need to cater for labour in the TBA, displaced civilians, soldier stragglers and prisoners of war, all of which put an additional burden on logistics. Gati Shakti India, the multifaceted National Master Plan complemented by the roll out of 5G, eGovernance initiatives under Digital India, UDAN-RCS, BharatNet and Ayushman Bharat are some big ticket programmes that have given India a global technological dominance and promoted ease of living in the country. These local for global outreach programmes and many others have created ripples globally, but the impact is yet to be felt in the Armed Forces Information and

Decision Support System. There are obviously some dots that need to be connected to create net-centric armed forces.

Russia has been a global arms and weapon systems supplier and net exporter driven by Rosoboron. As of Feb 2022 Ukraine with a large number of equipment of its own as well as Russian equipment that was antiquated in technology. However, as the war progressed, the support from the US and NATO countries changed not only the technology threshold but also gave Ukraine adequate combat potential to blunt Russian offensive, notwithstanding the initial Russian superiority in numbers. This real-time induction of technology by Ukraine has been a challenge in technology absorption and training of users and maintenance personnel, which require in-depth knowledge and more expertise. This technology upgrade in war has been an uphill task for maintenance agencies of Ukraine, adversely affecting optimal exploitation. The Russian Armed Forces also epitomise mismanagement of resources, poor operational logistics and contingency planning, lack of logistics support in the TBA despite formidable technology, adequate supplies in the hinterland and a robust industrial base. In effect, in this crisis, Russia has demonstrated lack of adequate foresight, planning and professional incompetence at all levels of command to orchestrate the war effort. Ukraine also was adversely affected due to shortage of equipment and faced the challenges of high tech weapon induction in the war zone during the active war.

Equipment readiness defines the operational effectiveness of combat formations and units. The management of technology transition was a weakness demonstrated by the Russians. Despite an elaborate military industrial complex, the CFR of military equipment was suboptimal. The repair and maintenance cover was inadequate for want of adequately trained manpower, gross shortages in spares support, specialised tools and test equipment in the TBA.[15] Ukraine displayed better CFR preparedness and not only restored its own weapon platforms and exploited the commonality of equipment but also repaired the captured Russian equipment. This was achieved despite the Russian forces having destroyed a large portion of the military industrial complexes at Kharkiv and Kiev.[16]

Timely repair, major interventions and maintenance in situ as far forward as possible ensures equipment sustenance support. The pillars of equipment support comprise skilled trained manpower, availability of specialised tools and test equipment, essential infrastructure and spares. Total quality equipment management guarantees that the right equipment is at the right place at the right time in the right condition. The armed forces must be prepared for effective CFR in war. In this regard, the combat ratio at the beginning of war is a necessary condition but is not sufficient, CFR is a necessary and sufficient condition for maintaining combat superiority. It is not the teeth to tail ratio but CFR that is the most appropriate matrix as a KPI in war. It brings to the fore a major lesson in strategic planning, that is, while combat ratios are essential reasonable matrix during peacetime, in war the matrix that is necessary and sufficient is the ability to sustain high combat ratios through CFR. This was also the lesson learnt in the Yom Kippur War of 1973, as highlighted in the quote by Andrew Marshall, stated as a preamble to this chapter. There is a need to factor in management of technology transition and CFR in war by generating best practices and good planning in peace. The Army Technology Centre and Corps Technology Centres were created with this precise intent in mind and must be revamped as Tri Service Technology Centres. Formations and units would do well in case all troops (all ranks) undergo a formal annual technology and technical inoculation for better technology absorption in line with the annual medical examination and a tri service annual battle inoculation.

A sequel to effective CFR is creating systems enabled with sensors and IoT for effective Human Machine Interface (HMI). This technology facilitates humanising weapon systems assets, which can monitor their health and indicate potential failures well in time, just like humans, and assess residual life. The Torsional Vibration Sensor with HMI, for example, can give the precise condition of engines and the residual useful life of the complete power pack. The age-old problem of Armoured Fighting Vehicles (AFVs) engine residual life and fear of failure prior to major exercises and military operations often results in periodic and preventive maintenance, premature change of engines for want of precise information. In the absence of condition monitoring systems, equipment maintenance becomes a major exercise prior to deployments. The efforts and huge cost of maintenance notwithstanding, the confidence in equipment continues to be a cause for concern of commanders at all levels. This technology for humanising weapon system assets for condition monitoring is the cornerstone of reliability centric mission planning and a major departure from the erstwhile periodic preventive maintenance to predictive prescriptive maintenance. The tardy CFR observed in the Russia-–Ukraine war, especially by Russian forces, adversely affected the operational combat stamina, progress of offensive, prolonged operations and, of course, the morale of troops.

The Indian Armed Forces must take steps to upgrade legacy critical equipment with condition monitoring systems for effective CFR. This shall ensure mission oriented integrated battle groups, are well poised for a sustained seamless offensive.

The cost-prohibitive periodic preventive maintenance would be replaced by cost-effective reliability centric predictive prescriptive maintenance with a visibility into residual life.

## CONCLUSION

The Russia–Ukraine war is a window into the future of warfare. Future wars will hinge on combat forces that are better organised in command and control, better prepared to meet the operational logistics needs of the forces in the TBA. Forces that are better prepared with the wherewithal for adequate CFR and not only use all levels of technology but are also able to integrate them into a coherent military strategy will be at an advantage. Operational plans duly supported by matching operational logistics plans must be tied in with an integrated C7I2S2R-based DSS. Short or long-drawn wars, this DSS recipe enabled by technology will be a game changer and will more or less favour, if not decide, the victor.

War is a whole of nation approach supported by friendly nations, especially when it comes to war stamina and logistics support. The importance of logistics becomes profound in war with its multifaceted surge needs. This is especially so when it comes to long-drawn multi-dimensional campaigns, as is being witnessed in the Russia–Ukraine war. Therefore, the key drivers for seamless integrated sustenance support are soldier readiness, equipment readiness, stamina for an effective and efficient supply chain to support operational plans and the deployment of enabling technologies. The lessons learnt in the Russia Ukraine War are pertinent and encompass the complete spectrum of strategic, operational and tactical levels.

## NOTES

1 Bonnie Berkowitz and Artur Galocha, 'Why the Russian Military Is Bogged Down by Logistics in Ukraine – An Analysis,' *The Washington Post*, March 30, 2022.

2 Col Ajay Singh (Retired),The Russia Ukraine War, Chapter 12 Gas, Grain and Sanctions: the Economic Effects of the War,',

3 Ibid.

4 Alex Vershinin, 'Feeding The Bear: A Closer Look At Russian Army Logistics And The Fait Accompli,' War on the Rocks, November 23, 2021.

5 Per Skoglund, Tore Listou and Thomas Ekstrom, 'Russian Logistics in the Ukrainian War: Can Operational Failures be Attributed to logistics?,' Scandinavian Journal of Military Studies, 5 (1), September 08, 2022, pp. 99–110.

6 Ibid.

7 Ibid.

8 Patrick J McDonnell, 'Russia Lost the Battle for Kyiv With Its Hasty Assault on a Ukrainian Airport,' *Los Angeles Times*, Apr 10, 2022.

9 Ibid.
10 Tanmay Kadam, 'Russian Su-34, Su-35 Jets 'Checkmate' Ukraine's Air Defense Systems; Fires 20 'Crudely Built' Guided Bombs Daily,' *The Eurasian Times*, April 07, 2023.
11 Beth Stackpole, 'Ripple Effects from Russia-Ukraine War Test Global Economies,' MIT Management Sloan School, June 28, 2022.
12 Ibid.
13 'Military-Industrial Commission of Russia,' Wikipedia.
14 Lt Gen Dr Anil Kapoor (Retired), 'Six Strategic Lessons from Russia-Ukraine War,'Bharat Shakti, June 15 2023.
15 Lt Gen NB Singh (Retired), 'Strategic Readiness: Revisiting Close and Deep Engineering Support,' *Indian Defence Review*, 38 (2), July 12, 2023.
16 Ibid.

## BIBLIOGRAPHY

Beth Stackpole, 'Ripple Effect from Russia-Ukraine War Test Global Economies,' MIT Sloan School, June 28, 2022.

Col Ajay Singh (Retired), The Russia Ukraine War, Chapter 12 'Gas, Grain and Sanctions: The Economic Effects of the War,'

James McBride, Noah Berman and Andrew Chatzky, 'China's Massive Belt and Road Initiative,' Council on Foreign Relations, February 02, 2023.

Lester W Grau and Charles K Bartel, 'The Russian Way of War,' Foreign Military Studies Office, US DoD, 2016.

Lt Gen Dr Anil Kapoor (Retired), 'Six Strategic Lessons from Russia-Ukraine War,' Bharat Shakti, June 15, 2023.

Paul Sandle, 'Catastrophe: UK Households Face Fuel Poverty as Energy Bills Jump,' *The Indian Express*, September 09, 2022.

Sara Brown, 'Russia-Ukraine War, Social Media Stokes Ingenuity, Disinformation, Why It Matters,' MIT Sloan School, April 06, 2022.

Surojit Gupta, 'Europe Faces Winter Chill as Russia Halts Gas Flows,' *The Times of India*, September 11, 2022.

'As Europe Falls into Recession, Russia Climbs Out,' *The Economist*, October 13, 2022.

'United Nations Needs to be More Democratic and Representative, Says Rajnath Singh,' *The Hindu*, June 13, 2023.

'Ukraine's Flash Update No 48,' UN Refugee Agency, June 09, 2023.

Vitaly Sergeev, Igor Ilin and Alexey Fadeev, 'Transport and Logistics Infrastructure in the Arctic Zone of Russia,' Trans Siberia 2020 Conference.

'How War in Ukraine is Reverberating Across World Regions,' https://www.imf.org, March, 15 2022.

'What Are the Sanctions on Russia and Are They Hurting it's Economy', *BBC News*, https://www.bbc.com, May,25, 2023.

# 10

# Civil and Militia Mobilisation

*Jason Wahlang*

## INTRODUCTION

A regional conflict with mass global implications is one way to describe the Russia–Ukraine conflict. The conflict, which has crossed the one-year mark, has seen large-scale destruction, loss of life and restructuring of the global order. There has been a change in the shaping of alliances and the recalibration of various existing partnerships. The once less fragmented and closely connected Europe and Russia now have opposing aspirations in the region.

The conflict also has regional implications for the post-Soviet space, which in addition to already suffering from internal conflicts, disputes and frozen conflicts is witnessing a significant outbreak of war in its backyard. In its perception, Russia is the leading security provider and its preoccupation with Ukraine has led to a changed mentality within the region.

## MOBILISATION

The two warring nations' mobilisation of individuals differs in its ideas, execution and needs. It has not been limited to the civilian and reservist population, instead it includes private military companies, militia groups and even various ethnic groups. The conflict has also seen the movement of many foreign fighters willing to join the fight. In Ukraine, by March 2022, the number of fighters was approximately 20,000 from 52 different countries, while Russia announced that 16,000 West Asians had joined its ranks.[1] This mobilisation of various groups and individuals is seen as one that could shape the conflict for both sides.

## Ukrainian Mobilisation

The application of the martial law to defend its land was enough for Ukraine to mobilise individuals across society. In the beginning, Ukrainian President Volodymyr Zelensky requested all citizens to assist the armed forces to save Ukraine. This was followed by the declaration of the martial law on February 24, 2022, per clause 20 of Article 106 of the Constitution of Ukraine,[2] which was still in place until August 8, 2023. Under the law, all males between 18 and 60, with certain exceptions, must be present in Ukraine and serve the Ukrainian military.[3] This can be seen as a general mobilisation; even conscripted men were kept from leaving the country. This is the second time martial law has been declared in Ukraine's history post the collapse of the Soviet Union, the first being in 2018 due to Russian action.[4]

## Vladimir Putin's Partial Mobilisation

With regard to mobilisation, this is the first mobilisation in Russia's history since the collapse of the Soviet Union in support of wartime troops in the field of action.

On October 21, 2022, Russian President Vladimir Putin announced a 'partial mobilisation' of up to 3,00,000 military reservists aged 18–50 in the Russian Armed Forces to contribute to the battlefield in Ukraine. This necessity of calling the reservists could have been due to the unpredictability of the time and extent of the conflict, given how this call was made seven months into the war.

The idea of partial mobilisation was to accommodate a more significant force after the major Russian miscalculation regarding the extent the conflict had weakened the fighting force. One more reason could be that preceding the call Russia had conducted referendums in the conflicted region of Donbas. The call could be about expanding the scope of the Russian Armed Forces' jurisdiction. Such situations may have compelled the Russian leadership to mobilise to an extent.

The mobilisation process ended on October 31, 2023, with Vladimir Putin announcing that the Ministry of Defence has proposed the completion of the mobilisation.[5] Russia has an estimated military reserve of over 2 million men, including conscripts, retired officers and those who have left active duty.[6] The mobilisation, as per the address of the Russian president on September 21, 2022, clearly stated that 'only military reservists, primarily those who have served in the armed forces and have special military occupational specialties and corresponding experience, will be called up'.[7]

Though the eligibility was explicitly mentioned, there have been reports of the migrant population, including those from Central Asia, being asked to join the fight in Ukraine.[8]

Additionally, the signing of a decree to fast-track citizenship for foreigners and stateless people if they respond to the mobilisation call[9] and join the Russian Army adds to the argument that the process was not limited to reservists.

Several recruitment centres were established for the mobilisation process all over the country, however, the mobilisation has resulted in some reaction from the domestic population, particularly in the form of protests.[10] One of the main points of the protestors has been that the focus of the mobilisation has been limited to the minorities-based regions and far away from the supposed Slav-dominated areas of Moscow and St Petersburg. This was visible in the North Caucasus and its adjoining republics of Russia. The protesting population also began a mass exodus to other post-Soviet countries, mainly Central Asia and Georgia.[11] A vast number was also headed towards Europe through these states, using them as transit points. This caused a domino effect within these post-Soviet nations, eventually leading to various issues with their populace.

## IMPACT OF MOBILISATION

The mobilisation of reservists from the Russian side and the migration of people hoping to evade participating in the war has caused domestic reverberations. There was anxiousness among the host nations' leadership when the dissidents fled; while some welcomed them to an extent, others chose stoic silence. The movement of Russians to various countries has caused a regional economic slowdown, rising inflation and food shortages, leading to large-scale discontentment.[12] This has led to the development of Russophobia across the nations where the Russian defectors shifted. The mobilisation has also led to questions of whether the Russian war machinery can handle an all-out conflict, given the time taken to handle the situation and the conflict extending with no clear victory. With the initial Russian expectation being that the conflict would only take weeks to end to it needing to mobilise troops to continue offensives has given rise to questions of whether Russia and its army's narrative is correct.

In Ukraine, the rise in nationalistic feeling and the quest to protect its integrity and sovereignty ensured that any individual eligible for mobilisation to the army was ready for the ultimate sacrifice. There have been limited reactions to Ukraine's call for mobilisation, mainly due to it being a martial law applied during the period of war. However, this has changed recently, with some Russian reports stating that President Zelensky hinted that Ukrainian refugees in Europe could have an unfavourable reaction if aid to Ukraine was curbed.[13] This shows that though there are no regional effects in the short term when it comes to reactions from Ukraine, there could be some adverse effects in the long run.

## TRAINING, INTEGRATION AND PERFORMANCE

Since most other militias are fighting alongside the Ukrainian Army, their successes are interconnected with the Ukrainian military. However, there are groups in which the Ukrainian Army has denied having any stake, such as the Russian-populated militia groups fighting against the Russian regime. These groups are said to be trained and have no prior connection to the Ukrainian war effort. There is also the Ajnad al Kavkaz, another group that has no connection to the Ukrainian Army but it has old Islamic State links and, therefore, has prior training from its expeditions in Syria. The same can be said of the two other groups of Chechens involved in the conflict from the Ukrainian side; both are old, established groups with proper training and fighting experience mainly from the wars in Chechnya. All these groups are fighting alongside the Ukrainian Army, so their deployment is with the army, and therefore, their successes are connected to that of the Ukrainian Army.

The Azov Battalion is part and parcel of the Ukrainian National Guard, making it one of the few militia groups directly connected to the Ukrainian Army. The battalion has seen limited success in its defence of Mariupol, with members of the group being part of the recent prisoners' exchange. There have been some reports of Azov's achievements in the latest counteroffensive. It fought alongside the military as part of the 12th Brigade, which focused on the east and southern sides of the counteroffensive.[14] This highlights the battalion's importance and expresses the group's successful integration within the Ukrainian Armed Forces.

Russian militia training and deployment differs slightly from that of Ukraine. The Russian militia, notably the Wagner Group, preferentially works on training and deployment this has been visible in its Africa and Syrian campaigns. The Kadyrovsty is under the command of Ramzan Kadyrov and is considered his private militia group. Since his close connections to the Russian state are explicitly visible, the group works alone as well as within the Russian establishment. While the Wagner Group works under the umbrella of Private Military Company (PMC) and functions separately, which is visible in how it handled the Bakhmut campaign, the Kadyrovsty has been known to support the Russian Army in its operations. The Kadyrovsty has worked alongside the Russian Army in Syria and even taken up army assignments such as the ones in Bakhmut, where it replaced the Wagner Group once its objectives were achieved.

These groups have had different results in the current conflict, with the Wagner Group, until its miscalculated coup attempt, being one of the most successful groups fighting in the conflict. The coup and its long-term repercussions, including the loss of its leader and the return of heavy arms to Russia, has ensured that the Wagner Group has lost its ability to repeat its success in Bakhmut. The Kadyrovsty, however, is yet to report any major achievement in its contribution towards the Russian war effort. This has led to the question whether the Kadyrovsty's reputation as brutal warriors is a reality or mere propaganda. The main reason for this could be that since its creation, the group's primary purpose has been to counter terrorism compared to the Wagner Group's military operations ability. This highlights the loophole between trained militias for conflict and those associated with counterterrorism.

## MILITIA AND CIVILIAN GROUPS AND THE IDEATIONAL CONNECT

Apart from the population that has mobilised within the nations, foreign fighters have also been mobilised within the conflict. One such example is that of militia and civilian groups that are mainly fighting from Ukraine's side. These groups have their own objectives and ideology and the conflict in Ukraine could, for most of them, be a short-term goal to achieve their long-term territorial and ideological purposes. Ideology plays a vital role in any conflict and is a point of connect among various groups within disputes. Any group fighting in a war must draw some inspiration from an idea or ideology.

In the current clash with Ukraine, from the Russian side the idea stems from the Novorossiya (New Russia) concept. Novorossiya is a concept that is part of Russian society and history; the term has existed over various annals of Russian history, from Catherine the Great to the Soviet Union to the current leadership.

The Ukrainians, on the other hand, have only one objective, which is to protect the ideas and ideals of democracy, which have been framed in the West. Though the leadership in Ukraine espouses the concept of liberty, equality and fraternity, certain elements within the state and from outside do not overtly agree with it. The conflict and, particularly in Ukraine, the rise of the far right and its long-term involvement could create a long-term issue for the defenders of democracy.

Some groups have been established with the singular purpose of defending Ukraine and they do not stand for what the Ukrainians are fighting for. One such example is the International Legion for the Territorial Defense of Ukraine, comprised of foreign fighters whose sole purpose is the protection of Ukraine and its identity. Groups such as the Freedom of Russia Legion and the Russian Volunteer Corps consist of Russians who have come with the sole idea of destroying the regime of Russia. These groups feel the need for change in the ideological structure of Russia and include those who are disillusioned with the Russian leadership under Vladimir Putin. The commonality between the three groups mentioned can be their connection with the far right; all three groups, including the International Legion, have a strong far right base. Another ideology that has crept up during the conflict is the rise of Islamist groups. Ajnad Al Kavkaz is one such example; this ISIS-linked Chechen group is fighting from the Ukrainian side with the long-term objective of the secession of Chechnya from Russia.

### International Legion for Territorial Defense of Ukraine

Two days after Russia launched a special military operation in Ukraine, President Volodymyr Zelensky requested foreign friends of Ukraine to fight the Russian aggression. This led to the establishment of International Legion for Territorial Defense of Ukraine, a separate subdivision created for foreigners who want to fight for Ukraine. This subdivision is part and parcel of the Regulation of Military Service in the Armed Forces of Ukraine, approved by the Decree of the President of Ukraine on June 10, 2016, which allowed citizens of different countries and stateless people to serve voluntarily.[15] A week into the subdivision's formation, approximately 20,000 people from 52 countries volunteered to fight to ease the pains of the Ukrainian population.[16] This was countered by Russia, which stated that 16,000 foreign individuals were ready to fight for Russia and its cause in the disputed territories.

The International Legion division includes veterans who have served in the US Army, Marine Corps and the British Army[17] as well as many from across Europe. There are reports of a few Indians also wanting to join the fight for Ukraine, with one individual from Tamil Nadu reportedly joining the volunteer army.[18] The volunteers are free to leave at any time; however, a mass of the population remains a part of the fight against Russia. On the first anniversary of the conflict Volodymyr Zelensky applauded the International Legion division for its assistance and sacrifice.[19] According to Vera Mironova, an expert on foreign fighters, the big question is why there are no checks and balances on foreign fighters and whether these individuals will become assets or liabilities to the Ukrainian cause.[20] While there has been some success in the division experiment in the one year, there has also been a loss of lives.

Like the many foreigners fighting for the Ukrainian cause, there have been recent reports of Nepalese Gurkhas joining the fight on the Russian side and are training in Russian military camps against Ukraine.[21] This adds to the list of foreign fighters in the conflict, with Russians gaining assistance after the mobilisation decree where the Russian State Duma passed an amendment on September 20, 2022. The decree allows any foreign fighters to gain from a reduced timeline for citizenship, possibly within a year, alongside monetary assistance.[22]

## Freedom of Russia Legion and Russian Volunteer Corps

In May 2023, coming from the north of Kharkiv two groups attacked the Russian territory of Belgorod. There was an immediate denial from Ukraine regarding the two groups; it was later discovered that they were Russian groups—The Freedom of Russia Legion and the Russian Volunteer Corps. These two groups are volunteer groups of Russian citizens and ethnic Russians who are disgruntled with the Russian regime and want a change in the leadership. Though the groups failed to capture the city, they came into the limelight primarily because it was a direct attack on Russian territory.

The **Russian Volunteer Corps** is a far-right group, similar to the Azov Battalion, and was founded in August 2022 after the start of the Ukrainian conflict.[23] The group is small in number and said to have 30–150 members; one of its leaders is Denis Kapustin, a far-right businessman from Russia. The group is also part of the Civil Council, a Russian emigrant association founded in Warsaw.[24] Before its tie-up with the Civil Council, the group entertained Russians who had lived abroad and even those who fought with the Azov Battalion in 2014; now, the Civil Council acts as a recruitment centre for the group.

Regarding the leadership of the group, Denis Kapustin, or White Rex, is one of the most connected neo-Nazis and has maintained links with two famed neo-Nazis of America: Robert Rundo and Christopher Pohlhaus.[25] A famous face in the European far right, Kapustin gained prominence in the United States after collaborating with Rundo, an individual connected to the Charlottesville antisemitic riots, for his podcast.

The group has claimed responsibility for the attacks on Belgorod and in the Bryansk region in May.[26] Concerning its connection to the Ukrainian government,

Ukraine denies any linkage to the group but also stresses that while it does provide the group with information and intelligence it does not provide any military equipment.[27] The group has since been quiet on the war front and a couple of attacks are considered its most extensive contribution towards the conflict.

Like the other Russian groups fighting for Ukraine, the **Freedom of Russia Legion** is comprised of Russians who are fighting against Moscow's establishment and political leadership. It was also formed in the spring of 2022 after Russia's operations in Ukraine and has asked fellow Russians to fight the establishment in the country. The group comprises former prisoners of war and is said to have approximately 2,000 fighters.[28] The group, is also active in the disputed territories. It is said to be more connected to the Ukrainian Defence Ministry than the Russian Volunteer Corps.

The group is led by Maximillian Andronnikov, also known as Caeser, who according to the Russian media has links to the far right in Russia. Caeser was once a member of the Russian Imperial Movement, an ultranationalist group that opposed Vladimir Putin's leadership and even fielded soldiers during the Crimean Crisis.[29] The group was designated as a terror group in Russia when the Supreme Court on March 16, 2023, passed a bill highlighting the same.[30]

There are, however, reports of the group threatening to repeat its escapades of Belgorod in the next month or so.[31] The group feels that the turmoil created by Wagner and its leader, Yevgeny Prigozhin, and its attempted coup could benefit the group. In its understanding, the rising conflict within Russia could be exploited and therefore it would be the perfect situation to attack the already distracted establishment.

## Ajnad al Kavkaz (Soldiers of the Caucasus)

Amidst the continuous conflict in Ukraine, one of the vital pieces of information that was confirmed was that of the jihadi leader of Chechen origin fighting alongside the Ukrainians. Rustam Azhiev, known as Abdul Hakim al-Shishani, is a Chechen jihadi and emir of Ajnad al Kavkaz. The group comprises of exiled Chechen fighters who left Russia after the Second Chechen War and fought in Syria against the country's leader Bashar al Assad, mainly focusing on Latakia where a Russian airbase is located.[32] There are other reports that the once dormant jihadi group that had suffered losses in Syria travelled to Ukraine from Idlib to seek revenge from Vladimir Putin and Ramzan Kadyrov.[33] The group has a history of fighting against the Russians in Syria, with it being one of three groups, including

Junnad al-Sham and Tarkhan's Jamaat, all comprised of Chechens. The Act of the Ukrainian parliament further fuelled the group into joining the Ukrainian side. On October 18, 2022, the Ukrainian parliament brought a resolution stating that Ukraine would recognise the Chechen Republic of Ichkeria, temporarily occupied by Russia, and condemn the genocide of the Chechens by Russia.[34] This is significant mainly because the groups that are fighting against Russia are especially fighting for the creation of the Chechen state. This has been the age-old demand of Chechens who had supported the idea of secessionism from Russia, which led to the two Chechen wars.

## PRIVATE MILITARY COMPANIES AND GROUPS

Mercenary groups and PMCs have played a pivotal role in the conflict in the past. Western groups have been dominating this field: the Blackwater Group's (Academi) involvement in the Iraq and Afghanistan wars is one example. The West has used these groups as versatile tools for reconnaissance, intelligence gathering, detainment and interrogation operations. The West has successfully implemented these groups for its objectives, and the success of such groups is evident; the same can be said in the current conflict in Ukraine.

The Wagner Group's achievements for the Russians are apparent from its territorial gains and claim on Bakhmut (Artemivsk) and the recent successes on the battlefield. Various groups in the United States and Europe, including human rights groups, have been critical of the Wagner Group and its modes of operation and personnel. For Ukraine, a similar role is played by the Azov Battalion, a group that has gained notoriety for an alleged controversial ideological stance, a supposed linkage to neo-Nazis.

### The Wagner Group

The name Wagner Group has been synonymous with recent decisive victories for Russia on the battlefield. The Wagner Group, with its leader Yevgeny Prigozhin, popularly called 'Putin's Chef', may have been in the headlines during the conflict. However, the group is an old company that gained its name and fame due to its exploits in Africa and Syria. Though the group is important to the Russian state, it is not registered within Russia because it is illegal to register mercenary groups. The group, which had remained clandestine in its connection with the Russian establishment till 2022, came into the limelight after media reports of its escapades for the Russian motherland. The group contains mostly retired military men aged between 35 and 55; however, there are reports of prisoners being recruited to add to the manpower.[35] This is unsurprising since Prigozhin was once a convict and part of the Russian prison system.

When it comes to Ukraine, Wagner has been a mainstay in the successes of Russia, but there have been some miscommunication issues between the state and the group. Recently, there was mistrust and misunderstanding between Wagner and the Russian Ministry of Defence (MoD). The leader who was seen berating MoD policies to express the group's dissatisfaction had become popular. The videos produced by Wagner during their Bakhmut expedition particularly focused on Sergei Soigu (Russia's Defence Minister) and Valery Gerasimov (Chief of General Staff) for the lack of supplies, notably weapons, and food, showing that there was some friction between the state establishment and the PMC. Despite all the challenges, Wagner managed to win over Bakhmut, which ensured that it attained hero status for Prigozhin and his troops.

Wagner's presence has also inspired other private enterprises to form their own PMCs or military services, one such example being Gazprom. Gazprom's success has even prompted the Russian leadership, such as the Russian Prime Minister on February 4, 2023, allowing the creation of Gazprom Neft, a subsidiary of Gazprom, to give energy companies permission to form their own PMCs.[36]

There have been alleged statements that the Gazprom PMC is involved in Ukraine as well. Some groups linked to Gazprom include Potok (heavily linked to Gazprom), Fakel and Redut. They are said to be involved in supporting Wagner in securing Bakhmut. This shows that Wagner has ensured the creation of more PMCs in Russia, and its influence has ensured further changes in the PMC culture in Russia.

The recent attempts, however, at creating disruptions within the Russian state and society, mainly critical of the leadership and MoD, have impacted Wagner's influence. The coup and occupation of Rostov and constant anti-state messaging have caused the Kremlin's leadership to react. The revolt had long-term consequences with Wagner reportedly told to move out to Belarus after the peace talks orchestrated by Belarussian President Aleksandr Lukashenko. Nonetheless, the coup attempt benefited the Russian establishment and the president; the swift handling of the coup ensured that Putin gained popularity of approximately 90 per cent—the highest since the beginning of the conflict.

## The Azov Battalion

Since its establishment in 2014, Azov has been popularly seen as Ukraine's most famed battalion, particularly after the Crimean Crisis (2014). The main purpose for its formation was to counter Russian 'separatists' in the Donetsk and Luhansk regions. The battalion is integrated into the Ukrainian National Guard as a Special Purposes Regiment and has its political wing named the National Corps and its paramilitary wing, the National Militia.[37] The group came into the limelight for its military escapades against the Russians in Mariupol and Kharkiv.

The primary debate, however, with Azov has not been its military-like behaviour but its ideology. Before dwelling deep into the Azov, it is essential to note that most of the Ukrainian far-right collective exists in the western side of Ukraine. The Azov Battalion can be traced back to the 'Patriots of Ukraine', a militant organisation of the past in Ukraine with strong white nationalists, anti-immigrant and extreme right ideas. The other association Azov has is to the neo-Nazi group Social-National Assembly (SNA). The SNA is a derivative of the ultra-far-right group called Svoboda; the Patriots of Ukraine also link themselves to SNA as an armed wing. These groups that are connected by ideological narratives and strong supremacist thinking have combined to form the Azov Battalion. Another connection that Azov has to these two groups is that its founder, Andriy Biletsky, is a member of both the Patriots of Ukraine and SNA.[38] However, he is not the only Azov leader connected to the Patriots and SNA, Ihor Mykhailenko, who took over from Biletsky, is another example. Apart from meeting with the Ukrainian right, the group's political wing head from 2016 to 2021, Olena Semenyaka, has met with various far-right group leaders in Europe. Additionally, Azov has even eulogised far-right individuals. One example is Dominique Venner, a French far-right icon of the 'Nouvelle Droite' (New Right). After he died in 2015, Azov members mourned his death outside the French embassy in Kiev.[39] Politically connected to the Ukrainian establishment, with some of its former members becoming part of the Ukrainian parliament, Azov has strong political influence. Andriy Biletsky exited the group after he was elected to the Ukrainian parliament and, in 2016, founded the National Corps Party, a party that is considered to have emerged from Azov.[40] With its strong far-right tendencies, the party has many former Azov members becoming a part of it.

Though far right, Azov garners the support of the local Ukrainian populace, mainly due to the group's victory in Mariupol during the Crimean Crisis of 2014. The group gained prominence after Russia's special military operations in Ukraine last year. Azov's highly nationalistic sentiments attracted the local populace, particularly during wartime. In the past it has been instrumental in protecting many districts of Ukraine, especially Mariupol (Azovstal), which it considers its home ground however, in the current conflict it has since lost to the Russians. While its popularity due to the war will help create a solid space for it, its ideology in the long term could be harmful to the Ukrainian nation. A nation that has crafted an image of being a defender of democracy, if it falls in the hands of the far right it will only prove Russia right in its quest to denazify Ukraine.

## ETHNIC DIVISION IN MOBILISATION

Division regarding the conflict is not restricted to ideology and within PMCs, there are also divisions regarding ethnicity. Some members of the same ethnic groups still have a solid tie-up with either front in the war. One such example is the presence of two Chechen groups on either front: the loyal to the Russian establishment the Kadyrovsty group and the other drawing its inspiration from the former Chechen secessionist leader Dzhokhar Dudayev, the Dudayev group. The two groups have already fought one another in the past in Ukraine. The presence of a third group, the Sheikh Mansur Battalion, shows that even history's complexities can supersede identical genealogical connections. Such differences are further complicated by the presence of the Chechen jihadi group Ajnad al Kavkaz, another Chechen group fighting in the conflict.

Chechens fighters have been connected to Russia and its conflicts in the past. The Chechens themselves have waged wars against the Russian state. After the two wars, the Chechens were divided into two groups: one that supported the rule of Moscow and the other of guerrilla insurgency. These historical grievances of dispossession and suppression by Russia have made the resistance towards Russia a top priority for most Chechen groups, regardless of location or fight.[41]

### The Kadyrovsty/Kadyrovites

The Kadyrovsty or the Kadyrovites are special forces of Chechen origin. The group has exceptional status in the Russian military establishment; it is known as the 141st Specialised Motorised Regiment and though considered a part of the Rosgvardia (Russian National Guard) it is commanded by Ramzan Kadyrov.[42]

Popularly known as Moscow's North Caucasian Battalion, the group did not always have the same relationship it now has with the Russian state. The Kadyrovsty was once part of the Chechen secessionist struggle during the 1990s under its founder Akhmad Kadyrov,[43] the current leader's father. Akhmad Kadyrov eventually left the secessionist forces and joined hands with the Russian state until his assassination.

Post his death, the power was transferred to his son, Ramzan Kadyrov. Under his leadership the Kadyrovsty has become one of the most loyal forces of Grozny and Moscow. In the Kadyrovsty, clan and family bonds are of utmost importance and its inner circle comprises members of its clan (teip) or related clans.[44] This shows how closely connected the group is to the Kadyrov family, which provides it with Moscow's validation.

The Kadyrovsty has gained acclaim from the Kremlin, particularly for its methods to neutralise the threat and spread of the jihadi group linked to the Islamic State, the Vilayat Caucasus. The jihadi group, whose focus was the Northern Caucasus, was brought in direct contention with the Kadyrovsty. The Russian state has been heavily dependent on the Kadyrovsty for handling the affairs of the North Caucasus,[45] and the same continued when it came to handling the ISIS affiliate. This dependence of the Russian state has ensured that the group has a strong connection to Moscow, as seen in the current conflict.

Apart from handling the domestic security apparatus of the Northern Caucasus, the group has been involved in other regional and international conflicts in Russia as well. The Kadyrovsty has been involved in the conflict in Georgia, Crimea, Lebanon and Syria.[46] Given the experience it already has regarding fighting conflicts in Ukraine, it is no surprise when it comes to the group's involvement in Ukraine since 2022.

When it comes to the current conflict, it has played a significant role since the beginning, both in fighting and spreading of propaganda. The Kadyrovsty had been trained and been preparing for an attack on Ukraine years before the special military operations. In fact, Ramzan Kadyrov has been signalling an attack on Ukraine since 2021 and has been demanding Ukraine's reunification with Russia.[47]

Reports have alleged that the Kadyrovsty was sent into Ukraine with the significant agenda of eliminating various Ukrainian personalities, including the Ukrainian President Volodymyr Zelensky.[48] The Kadyrovsty and other troops from the Chechen republic have been deployed in Ukraine since the beginning of the conflict. Kadyrov has insisted that Russia make further advances into Ukrainian territory and even demanded the uprooting of the leadership in Ukraine.[49] The other objective of the group is to eliminate all the mercenary groups within the disputed Russian territories of Donetsk and Luhansk. From the data garnered from reports, the Kadyrovsty is predicted to be approximately 1,200–21,000 strong, depending on the sources.[50]

The presence of a tech-savvy leader also has its advantages, with the Chechens being very well-versed in using social media to spread propaganda. Specific examples include videos of Chechens praying in the forest before battle, playing cards with the names of their intended targets and Kadyrov's constant threats to Kiev.[51] In the past, Kadyrov has used social media to highlight victories over the Chechen groups fighting in support of Ukraine and offered advice to Chechens within Russia to not defect from Russia or to accept their fate.[52] The same is done in the current conflict, where he uses social media to simultaneously rile up the population against Ukraine and spread the propaganda of Russian victories within Ukraine.

Conflict within the various Chechen groups has grown so Kadyrov has taken it upon himself to target the other two Chechen groups. Recently, the Chechen leader put up a bounty of $1 million for information on both groups operating on the Ukrainian side.[53]

### Sheikh Mansur Battalion

Another important battalion fighting against the Russians in Ukraine is the Sheikh Mansur Battalion. It is one more battalion comprised of Chechens who oppose Ramzan Kadyrov's rule and have stuck to demands of independence of the Chechen republic. It joins the Dudayev Group and Ajnad al Kavkaz as yet another Chechen group fighting in support of Ukraine.

The Sheikh Mansur Battalion derives its name from a historical figure, Sheikh Mansur, an Islamic leader and military commander who fought against the Russians in the 18th century. The name's significance is that Sheikh Mansur ensured the unification of Caucasus against Russia's growing presence in the 1700s, mainly against the famed Catherine the Great.[54] The battalion is primarily composed of veterans of the two Chechen wars against Russia,[55] hence they still harbour animosity against the Russian state. However, there are some issues with the group, with both the Russian and Western media bringing up its linkages with the Islamic State.[56]

What is significant about the group is that it has been functioning since 2014. It was disbanded after 2019 but revived after Russia's special military operation commenced in 2022. The main reason for the recommissioning was that, in the long run, it believes that the fight in Ukraine is an extension of the battle for the independence of Chechnya and a war against a common enemy, Russia.[57] The group, similar to its adversary Kadyrovsty, is known for its guerrilla-style warfare and is well suited for urban conflicts, mainly due to the experiences in the two Chechen wars. The group even believes that Russian tactics are reminiscent of the tactics used during the Chechen expeditions of the 1990s.[58]

Compared to other foreign legions of Chechens who support Ukraine, this battalion is the only one without Ukrainian funding. The group seeks donations and volunteers and uses the equipment it manages to capture.[59] The group has been stationed in Mariupol, Kiev, Zaporizhzhia, Soledar and Bakhmut in the current conflict. Though active in the conflict, the group has just been in the crosshairs of the Kadyrovsty.

## The Dzhokhar Dudayev Battalion

Another influential Chechen group involved in Ukraine is the Dzhokhar Dudayev Battalion. Like the Sheikh Mansur group, this group has been named after a famed Chechen leader. Dzhokhar Dudayev was the first leader after the collapse of the Soviet Union to take up arms against the newly established Russian Federation. He spearheaded the secessionist movement and the quest for Chechnya's independence in the First Chechen War. He is credited with victory over the Russian forces in the first war, which was against Yeltsin's Russia.

The group views Vladimir Putin's Russia, the victor in the Second Chechen War, as the sworn enemy and Ramzan Kadyrov and his Kadyrovsty as traitors to the cause and thus also as enemies.[60] Like the Sheikh Mansur Battalion, the group members also belong to the Chechens affected by the two wars within the republic, hence the animosity towards Russia. Members of the group mainly constitute Chechens from Europe and Turkey and include outsiders from the post-Soviet Caucasus such as Azerbaijan and Georgia. Unlike the Mansur Battalion, it does not rally under the flag of the named leader; it is said to have flown the Chechen Republic of Ichkeria flag—the proposed flag of an independent Chechnya.

The group was formed in 2014 during the Crimean Crisis and was recently engaged in the battle of Bakhmut.[61] While the Sheikh Mansur Battalion operated within the city walls, the Dudayev Battalion was preoccupied with reconnaissance work on the city edges. Given its experience in the Chechen wars, the group is highly trained in the art of intense urban battles and, therefore, important to the Ukrainian forces, who lack urban battle experience.[62]

One unique aspect of the two groups opposing the Kadyrovsty in Ukraine is that while the Kadyrovsty is closely linked to the Chechen idea of clanship and is relatively Chechen to the core, the other two groups welcome the addition of non-Chechens. This could be either to garner more support for the idea of independent Chechnya from the outside world or the lack of manpower to support its ideas post-Ukraine.

## CONCLUSION

Overall, it can be seen that mobilisation has been possible not just through the means of law, which was visible in both nations' mobilisation and martial law decrees, but also through the protection of ideas and long-term objectives. In the short term, mobilisation has succeeded and ensured vital assistance for both nations in their quests. The importance of the troops and their constant involvement on both sides show that the experimentation, particularly on the militia side, has been a success. The most important example of this success is the exploits of the Wagner Group when it came to Bakhmut. Russia has seen some significant success with regard to the use of the militia. However, regarding the Russians fighting from its side, Ukraine was unsuccessful in its attempts to capture Belgorod, and most of these attempts were quashed almost immediately.

Collectively, the groups are fighting for the idea of Ukraine and Russia, but individually their objectives may have some long-term implications. While one of the groups fighting for the Ukrainian cause is tied up with the far-right movement internationally, the other group is connected to the more significant jihadi movement. This, however, shows that during the fog of war, ideological grounds are covered by a common enemy, Russia. In the long term, the bigger question is that when the situation changes and the fog of war lifts, then ideology will become an essential core of the groups, who then will be the new enemy after Russia?

Regarding the International Legion for Territorial Defense of Ukraine, its ideological connection to the conflict is, in its members' minds, the protection of the three principles espoused during the French Revolution, that is, 'liberty, fraternity, and equality'. This is the leading cause for it, along with a tinge of defence of democracy. Its ideological connection is more towards a Western liberal order, which is common in the Western world.

Wagner and its ambitious leader attempted to change the structure; the same is not valid for other PMCs. Gazprom and its subsidiaries are considered close loyalists of the Russian state; they are also more focused on protecting their financial assets. Therefore, considering that such groups' aims and objectives are limited, any rebellion, such as Wagner's, cannot be predicted. The expectation of new coup attempts from the other PMCs may be less than imagined.

Azov's strong connection to the far right has been one of the reasons for Russia's quest to denazify Ukraine. Russia's criticism of Azov is based on three main points: symbolism, ideology and organisational structure.[63] This is where Russia tries to bring the neo-Nazi connection to Azov, and since it has such solid far-right links, the accusations, to an extent, have some truth to them. On the other hand, Azov is more focused on the tasks for which it was established in the first place: an anti-Russian regiment with the sole purpose of protecting Ukraine from the ambitions of Russia.

The objectives of all Chechen groups are similar to an extent: they are all established for the wants and demands of the state. The major difference being the state they are fighting for. If one is fighting for the Russian state and its members are close to the Kremlin, the other is seeking to alter the Russian geographical and demographical situation, the Chechen republic. While one group's objective is limited to Ukraine, the other two groups have aspirations further than Ukraine and see Kiev as a pitstop to their aims and objectives.

## NOTES

1 Egle E Murauskaite, 'Foreign Fighters in Ukraine: What Concerns Should Really Be on the Agenda?' *Russia Matters*, Harvard Kennedy School Belfer Center for Science and International Affairs, 2022.

2 Volodymyr Zelensky, Decree of The President of Ukraine No. 64/2022, President of Ukraine, 2022, at https://www.president.gov.ua/documents/642022-41397 (Accessed June 23, 2023).

3 'Ukraine's Parliament, Votes to Extend Martial Law,' *The Kyiv Independent*, 2022, at https://kyivindependent.com/ukraines-parliament-votes-to-extend-martial-law/ (Accessed June 22, 2023).

4 Alesya Pavlynska, 'Martial Law in Ukraine,' American Bar Association, 2022, at https://www.americanbar.org/groups/labor_law/publications/labor_employment_law_news/spring-2022/martial-law-in-ukraine/ (Accessed June 22, 2023).

5 'Putin Will Consult With Lawyers About the Need For a Decree on the End of Partial Mobilization,' *Tass News Agency*, 2022, at https://tass.ru/politika/16210087 (Accessed August 3, 2023).

6 James Beardsworth, 'Explainer: What Does Russia's 'Partial Mobilization' Mean?,' *The Moscow Times*, 2022, at https://www.themoscowtimes.com/2022/09/21/explainer-what-does-russias-partial-mobilization-mean-a78854 (Accessed August 3, 2023).

7 Vladimir Putin, Address by the President of the Russian Federation, President of Russia, 2022, at http://en.kremlin.ru/events/president/news/69390 (Accessed August 3, 2023).

8 Rivniak Siuzanna, 'Russia May Be Recruiting Migrants From Central Asia to Fight Against Ukraine,' *Svidomi*, 2023, at https://svidomi.in.ua/en/page/russia-may-be-recruiting-migrants-from-central-asia-to-fight-against-ukraine (Accessed September 5, 2023).

9 'Putin Eases Citizenship for Foreigners in Russian Army,' *The Moscow Times*, 2022, at https://www.themoscowtimes.com/2022/09/30/putin-eases-citizenship-for-foreigners-in-russian-army-a78942 (Accessed August 4, 2023).

10 'Over 1,300 Detained as Russians Protest Mobilization,' *The Moscow Times*, 2022, at https://www.themoscowtimes.com/2022/09/21/over-1300-detained-as-russians-protest-mobilization-a78859 (Accessed June 22, 2023).

11 'Fact box: Where Have Russians Been Fleeing to Since Mobilisation Began?,' *Reuters*, 2022, at https://www.reuters.com/world/europe/where-have-russians-been-fleeing-since-mobilisation-began-2022-10-06/ (Accessed June 22, 2023).

12 Yunis Sharifli, Chia-Lin Kao and Bermet Derbishova, 'Russia's War in Ukraine and Its Impact on Central Asia,' *The Diplomat*, 2022, at https://thediplomat.com/2022/10/russias-war-in-ukraine-and-its-impact-on-central-asia/ (Accessed on 22 June 2023).

13 'Zelensky Threatened Europe With Problems With Ukrainian Migrants If Aid to Kyiv Was Cut,' *Reporter*, September 11, 2023, at https://en.topcor.ru/39153-zelenskij-prigrozil-evrope-problemami-s-ukrainskimi-migrantami-v-sluchae-sokraschenija-pomoschi-kievu.html?ysclid=ln7bckcxi591659771 (Accessed September 30, 2023).

14 'Ukraine Reports Some Successes in Counteroffensive Against Russian Forces,' *Reuters*, September 8, 2023, at https://www.reuters.com/world/europe/ukraine-reports-some-successes-counteroffensive-against-russian-forces-2023-09-08/ (Accessed October 1, 2023).

15 Volodymyr Zelenskyy, Appeal to Foreign Citizens to Help Ukraine in Fighting Against Russia's Aggression, President of Ukraine, 2022, at https://www.president.gov.ua/en/news/zvernennya-do-gromadyan-inozemnih-derzhav-yaki-pragnut-dopom-73213 (Accessed June 14, 2023).

16 Lisa Abend, 'Meet the Foreign Volunteers Risking Their Lives to Defend Ukraine—and Europe,' *Time*, 2022, at https://time.com/6155670/foreign-fighters-ukraine-europe/ (Accessed June 14, 2023).

17 Isacc Chakyan Tang, 'The Latest in a Long Line: Ukraine's International Legion and a History of Foreign Fighters,' *Harvard International Review*, 2022, at https://hir.harvard.edu/the-latest-in-a-long-line-ukraines-international-legion-and-a-history-of-foreign-fighters/ (Accessed June 14, 2023).

18 Rezaul H Laskar and Divya Chandrababu, 'Tamil Nadu Student in Ukraine Joins Voluntary Military Force to Fight Russia,' *The Hindustan Times*, 2022, at https://www.hindustantimes.com/india-news/tamil-nadu-student-in-ukraine-joins-voluntary-military-force-to-fight-russia-101646728268979.html (Accessed June 14, 2023).

19 Volodymyr Zelenskyy, Address by President of Ukraine Volodymyr Zelenskyy "February. The Year of Invincibility", President of Ukraine, 2023, at https://www.president.gov.ua/en/news/zvernennya-prezidenta-ukrayini-volodimira-zelenskogo-lyutij-81213 (Accessed June 14, 2023).

20 Mark Mackinnon, 'Ukraine's Foreign Legion, Offers a Shot at Redemption for Fighters from Around the Globe,' *The Globe and Mail*, 2022, at https://www.theglobeandmail.com/world/article-russia-ukraine-war-foreign-legion/ (Accessed on June 14, 2023).

21 Sanjib Chaudhary, 'Russia's Foreign Fighters: Geolocating the Nepalis Training in the Russian Army,' *Bellingcat*, 2023, at https://www.bellingcat.com/news/2023/06/23/russias-foreign-fighters-geolocating-the-nepalis-training-in-the-russian-army/ (Accessed June 25, 2023).

22 The State Duma, Foreign Citizens Serving in the Russian Army under Contract to Be Able to Obtain Citizenship of Russia under a Simplified Procedure, The Federal Assembly of the Russian Federation, 2022, at http://duma.gov.ru/en/news/55276/ (Accessed June 20, 2023).

23 'Who are the Freedom of Russia Legion and Russian Volunteer Corps?,' *Reuters*, 2023, at https://www.reuters.com/world/europe/who-are-armed-fighters-russias-belgorod-region-2023-06-05/ (Accessed June 14, 2023).

24 Sergey Satanovskiy, 'Who Are the Russian Volunteers Fighting for Ukraine?,' *DW News*, 2023, at https://www.dw.com/en/who-are-the-russian-volunteers-fighting-for-ukraine/a-65722771

(Accessed June 15, 2023).

25 Ben Makuch, 'Russian Militia Has Links to American Neo-Nazi and Anti-Trans Figures,' *The Intercept*, 2023, at https://theintercept.com/2023/07/08/american-neo-nazis-ukraine-war/ (Accessed July 9, 2023).

26 Sergey Satanovskiy, no. 24.

27 'Ukraine's Defence Intelligence, Claims It Provides Information to Russian Volunteer Corps But Not Military Equipment,' *Ukrainska Pravda*, 2023, at https://www.pravda.com.ua/eng/news/2023/05/24/7403695/ (Accessed June 15, 2023).

28 Sebastian Sebit, 'A Look At The Free Russia Legion, The Pro-Ukrainian Group That Attacked Belgorod,' *France 24*, 2023, at https://www.france24.com/en/europe/20230524-what-is-the-free-russian-legion-the-pro-ukrainian-group-that-attacked-russia-s-belgorod (Accessed June 23, 2023).

29 Harding Luke, "'We Have Ambitious Plans': Anti-Putin Forces Plan Fresh Attacks inside Russia,' *The Guardian*, 2023, at https://www.theguardian.com/world/2023/jul/08/anti-putin-forces-plan-fresh-attacks-inside-russia (Accessed July 9, 2023).

30 'Russian Supreme Court Deems Freedom of Russia Legion Terrorist Organization,' *The Moscow Times*, 2023, at https://www.themoscowtimes.com/2023/03/16/russian-supreme-court-deems-freedom-of-russia-legion-terrorist-organization-a80516 (Accessed June 22, 2023).

31 'Freedom of Russia Legion Announced New Raid on Russian Territory,' *Defence Express*, 2023, at https://en.defence ua.com/news/freedom_of_russia_legion_announed_ on_ new_ raid_ on _ russian_territory-7257.html (Accessed July 9, 2023).

32 Michael Starr, 'Why is an Ex-Syria War Jihadist Fighting for Ukraine Against Russia?,' *The Jerusalem Post*, 2023, at https://www.jpost.com/international/article-728127 (Accessed June 22, 2023).

33 Sultan al-Kanj, 'Chechen Fighters Leave Syria to Battle Russians in Ukraine,' *Al-Monitor*, 2022, at https://www.al-monitor.com/originals/2022/10/chechen-fighters-leave-syria-battle-russians-ukraine#ixzz86hrhjl7m (Accessed June 22, 2023).

34 Verkhovna Rada of Ukraine, Draft Resolution on the Statement of the Verkhovna Rada of Ukraine on the recognition of the Chechen Republic of Ichkeria as temporarily occupied by the Russian Federation and condemnation of the genocide of the Chechen people, 2022, at https://itd.rada.gov.ua/billInfo/Bills/Card/40676 (Accessed June 22, 2023).

35 Kristaps Andrejsons, 'Russia's Convict-Soldiers Have Their Own Brutal Rules,' *Foreign Policy*, 2023, at https://foreignpolicy.com/2023/05/16/russia-prisons-wagner-group-ukraine-crime-culture/ (Accessed July 1, 2023).

36 "Decree of the Government of the Russian Federation dated February 4, 2023 No. 240-r", Official Publication of Legal Acts, at Распоряжение Правительства Российской Федерации от 04.02.2023 № 240-р, Официальное опубликование правовых актов (pravo.gov.ru) (Accessed June 27, 2023).

37 Mapping Militant Organizations, "Azov Movement", Stanford University, 2022, at - MMP: Azov Battalion (stanford.edu) (Accessed June 27, 2023).

38 Al Jazeera Profiles, 'Who Are Ukraine's Far-Right Azov Regiment?,' *Al Jazeera*, 2022, at https://www.aljazeera.com/news/2022/3/1/who-are-the-azov-regiment (Accessed June 27, 2023).

39 Michael Colborne, "There's One Far-Right Movement That Hates the Kremlin", *Foreign Policy*, 2019, at https://foreignpolicy.com/2019/04/17/theres-one-far-right-movement-that-hates-the-kremlin-azov-ukraine-biletsky-nouvelle-droite-venner/ (Accessed June 27, 2023).

40 Kate Baklitskaya, 'National Corps: Why Ukraine's Far-Right Party Is Enjoying Growing Support,' *euronews*, 2019, at https://www.euronews.com/2019/03/03/national-corps-why-

ukraine-far-right-party-is-enjoying-growing-support (Accessed July 2, 2023).

41 Haid, 'With Russia in Their Sights, Chechens Depart Syria for Ukraine,' *The Arab Weekly*, 2023, at https://thearabweekly.com/russia-their-sights-chechens-depart-syria-ukraine (Accessed July 2, 2023).

42 Katharina Miriam Heß, Leveraging Islam and Internal Conflict Strategies and Consequences in Russia's War Against Ukraine, The German Council of Foreign Relations, 2023.

43 Munira Mustaffa, 'The Kadyrovtsy: Putin's Force Multiplier or Propaganda Tool,' *Newsline Institute*, 2022, at https://newlinesinstitute.org/state-resilience-fragility/authoritarianism/the-kadyrovtsy-putins-force-multiplier-or-propaganda-tool/. Accessed on July 5 2023.

44 Tomas Šmíd and Miroslav Mareš, 'Kadyrovtsy': Russia's Counterinsurgency Strategy and the Wars of Paramilitary Clans,' *Journal of Strategic Studies*, 2015.

45 Elena Pokalova, 'The Islamic State Comes to Russia?,' *War on the Rocks*, 2015, at https://warontherocks.com/2015/07/the-islamic-state-comes-to-russia/ (Accessed July 6, 2023).

46 Alexey D Muraviev, 'How the Russian Military Remade Itself Into a Modern, Efficient and Deadly Fighting Machine,' *The Conversation*, 2022, at https://theconversation.com/how-the-russian-military-remade-itself-into-a-modern-efficient-and-deadly-fighting-machine-178014 (Accessed July 6, 2023).

47 'Amid War on Ukraine, Video From Aircraft With Kadyrov's Voice Appears on Internet,' *Caucasian Knot*, 2022, at https://eng.kavkaz-uzel.eu/articles/58339/ (Accessed July 7, 2023).

48 Cahal Milmo, 'Russian Special Forces Have Entered Kyiv to Hunt Down Ukraine's Leaders, Says Volodymyr Zelensky,' *I News*, 2022, at https://inews.co.uk/news/russia-special-forces-kyiv-ukraine-leaders-mercanaries-behind-lines-1483303 (Accessed July 7, 2023).

49 Tuqa Khalid, 'Chechen Leader Kadyrov Calls For Expanding Russia's Invasion 'In All Directions',' *Al Arabiya*, 2022, at https://english.alarabiya.net/News/world/2022/02/27/Chechen-leader-Kadyrov-calls-for-expanding-Russia-s-invasion-in-all-directions- (Accessed July 7, 2023).

50 Katharina Miriam Heß, no. 42.

51 Justin Ling, 'Russia Tries to Terrorize Ukraine With Images of Chechen Soldiers,' *Foreign Policy*, 2022, at https://foreignpolicy.com/2022/02/26/russia-chechen-propaganda-ukraine/ (Accessed July 7, 2023).

52 Simon Shuster, 'Why Chechens Are Fighting Chechens in Ukraine's Civil War,' *Time*, 2015, at https://time.com/3893066/chechens-ukraine-war/ (Accessed July 7, 2023).

53 'Chechnya's Leader Offers $1-Mln Reward For Information on Two Ukrainian Battalions,' *Tass Agency*, 2023, at https://tass.com/society/1443103 (Accessed July 7, 2023).

54 Igor Kossov, 'Chechen Veteran Battalion Fighting Russia: 'When Chechens Are Independent, They Pick This Side',' *Kyiv Independent*, 2023, at https://kyivindependent.com/chechen-veteran-battalion-fighting-russia-when-chechens-are-independent-they-pick-this-side/ (Accessed July 7, 2023).

55 Ibid.

56 Monir Ghaedi, 'Chechen, Tatar Muslims Fight For Ukraine,' *DW News*, 2022, at https://www.dw.com/en/chechen-and-tatar-muslims-take-up-arms-to-fight-for-ukraine/a-61174375 (Accessed July 8, 2023).

57 Olivia Gibson, 'Sheik Mansur Battalion: Chechen Force Multiplier for Ukraine,' London Politica, 2023, at https://londonpolitica.com/intelligence-department-articles/politicalriskexplained-5 (Accessed on July 8, 2023)

58 Dominic Waghorn, 'The Chechen Fighters Taking on Putin's 'Empire Of Evil' in Ukraine Who Say Russian Troops Are Like 'Cattle For Slaughter',' *Sky News*, 2022, at https://

news.sky.com/story/ukraine-war-chechens-fighting-for-kyiv-say-russian-troops-are-like-cattle-for-slaughter-leaving-the-ground-covered-with-corpses-12773194 (Accessed July 8, 2023).

59 "We'll Liberate City After City' In Their Own Words, Chechen Soldiers Fighting For Ukraine Explain What Drives Them,' Meduza, 2023, at https://meduza.io/en/feature/2023/03/07/we-ll-liberate-city-after-city (Accessed July 8, 2023).

60 Andrew Kravchenko and Derek Gatopoulos, 'Rival Chechen Fighters Take War to Battlefields of Ukraine,' *Associated Press*, 2022, at https://apnews.com/article/chechen-fight-on-both-sides-of-ukraine-war-6c663cbbc506c198ce14fa2266a826be (Accessed July 8, 2023).

61 Neil Hauer, 'Fighting Russia From Chechnya to Ukraine – And Back Again,' *bne Intellinews*, 2023, at https://www.intellinews.com/fighting-russia-from-chechnya-to-ukraine-and-back-again-276439/ (Accessed July 8, 2023).

62 Ibid.

63 Анастасія Кондрат, 'Azov Brigade is Nine Years Old: How Russian Propaganda Discredited the Unit and What Consequences It Had During the Defence of Mariupol,' *Свідомі*, 2023, at https://svidomi.in.ua/page/azov-brigade-is-nine-years-old-how-russian-propaganda-discredited-the-unit-and-what-consequences-it-had-during-the-defence-of-mariupol (Accessed July 1, 2023).

# SECTION III

# Advent of Disruptive Technologies

# 11

# Lessons Learned from the Russia–Ukraine Conflict: Unmanned Systems and Missiles

*Akshat Upadhyay*

## INTRODUCTION

Every war is a laboratory—for ideas, operational concepts and weapon systems—and the ongoing Russia–Ukraine conflict adheres loyally to the norm. In fact, as this chapter shows, one can trace an unbroken, though broad, line from the Soviet operational doctrines of the Cold War right down to the current one. On the other hand, due to the non-essentiality of Ukraine as an analysable military actor till 2014, the lessons gleaned will be ahistorical and relevant only from the start of the Ukrainian resistance to Russian actions post the Crimean crisis. The aim of the chapter is to detail the Russian and Ukrainian use of unmanned systems and missiles during the ongoing conflict, including the concept of employment by both sides, shifts with respect to previous wars, technological advances creating paradigm shifts and finally to eke out takeaways and lessons for India. Interestingly, while the employment of both these weapon systems may seem separate and distinct, they have been used together on multiple instances, especially by Russians against Ukrainian targets.[1] As of writing this chapter, Ukraine has just received the initial consignment of long-range Storm Shadow Air-Launched Cruise Missiles (ALCMs) from the United Kingdom (UK),[2] Russia has been using a combination of ALCMs, Ship-Launched Cruise Missiles (SLCMs), Short-Range Ballistic Missiles (SRBMs) and certain repurposed Surface to Air Missiles (SAMs) such as S-300s to attack ground targets[3] in Ukraine in a visibly chronological manner.[4]

Both sides have witnessed the advantages of technology diffusion and have rushed to take advantage of the proliferation of commercial drones, attempting to integrate them within their targeting philosophies and operational doctrines. While Russia's perspective on drones skews towards the conventional, Ukraine has been more adventurous and innovative in its employment of drones and other niche technologies such as 3D printing[5] and artificial intelligence (AI),[6] especially data fusion in utilising the unique attributes of drones. Russian attempts have recently emulated Ukraine's entrepreneurial spirit in using drones and a slew of Russian volunteers and private players are churning out drone and payload prototypes, expediting the '*blueprint to battleground*' cycle. Whether this approach has granted them a long-term advantage over the Russians remains to be seen. Finally, the war has witnessed an increasing and direct role of civilians on both sides in the warfighting realm—drone pilot volunteers, crowdfunding, and private companies—all introducing a novel dimension in the prosecution of the war and how International Humanitarian Law (IHL) needs to be revamped in order to take into account these realities.

## CONCEPT OF EMPLOYMENT ON BOTH SIDES

The chapter will initially focus on the employment of unmanned systems by Russia followed by Ukraine. Both missiles and unmanned systems provide hypervisibility,[7] the drone through its 'God's-eye-view'[8] and the missile systems through their attendant tracking and targeting systems such as satellites. By seemingly providing technical and collateral-free solutions to what is essentially a social phenomenon, that is, war, they not only facilitate sustained combat operations but also make it difficult for either side to come to the negotiating table, keeping the chimaera of 'victory' alive. The usage of aerial drones (used interchangeably with unmanned systems) in the current conflict bears witness to the fact that as of date, they may provide a new dynamic to the conflict—in the larger context they still have to prove their worth as 'game changers'.[9]

### Russian Reconnaissance Complexes: Shot from the Past

The Russian use of unmanned systems against Ukraine, especially Unmanned Aerial Vehicles (UAVs) and long-range missiles in the current conflict can be considered as an extension of the Soviet-era Reconnaissance-Strike (RSC) and Reconnaissance-Fire Complex (RFC), collectively termed Reconnaissance-Destruction Complex (RDC). The system is conceptualised as a functional grouping involving four subsets: an automated system of reconnaissance and vectoring, fire control centre (usually mobile), high-precision weaponry and a system for precise location determination.[10] Unlike regiments and battalions, this system is not envisaged as a permanent or fixed body but changes in response to the adversary, tasking and/or availability of assets. An RSC differs from an RFC in the use and range of firepower to be used. While an RFC is the usage of firepower at a tactical level (up to a division) involving tube and multiple rocket launcher artillery, the RSC is envisaged as its operational level peer, comprising strikes using tactical aviation, helicopters, tactical and operational-tactical missiles—the last term indicating usage of missiles that fall in the intermediate range as per global categorisation norms. The RDC, as a whole, was designed as a counter to the consistent improvements in mobility, range and destructive power of weapon platforms used by the North Atlantic Treaty Organisation (NATO) later augmented by the AirLand Battle (ALB) and the Follow-on-Forces Attack (FOFA) doctrines.[11] The intention of both doctrines was to overcome the numerical superiority of the Warsaw Pact using precision weapons targeting second and third echelon forces, preventing a major battle from being joined. Ironically, the Soviets came up with a counter to this counterstrategy: the RDC. Automated linking of dispersed assets was used to achieve twin aims: detection avoidance and destruction. This was helpful during operations against the adversary's mobile armoured and artillery forces. A major theoretical innovation in RDC was that the command post of the strike complex was capable of integrating reconnaissance assets from different domains such as maritime, space and air. The use of Remotely Piloted Vehicles (RPVs) for reconnaissance, intelligence, target acquisition and surveillance (ISTAR) has already been acknowledged in Soviet military literature of the 1980s and 90s.[12] Along with platforms such as counterbattery radars, 'new munitions' and command and control (C2) subsystems, the RDC formed a complex system of systems with computation forming the hub of data fusion and target designation.

## Russian Military Theory

Certain Russian military theorists have provided a doctrinal scaffolding on which the current avatar of RDC has been used in Ukraine. Soviet Marshal Nikolai Ogarkov was a proponent of using conventional 'high-precision' weapons as a means of establishing non-nuclear deterrence, especially in pursuit of Russian foreign policy objectives.[13] Imbibing lessons from the United States' (US) use of Precision-Guided Munitions (PGMs) in Vietnam and RPVs by Israel against Syria during the 1982 invasion of Lebanon,[14] he realised the importance of integrating long-range missiles with emerging technologies for C2, Electronic Warfare (EW), precision-strike capabilities and weapons based on 'new physical principles'. Together these capabilities could have the same effect on an enemy nation-state's decision-making processes as nuclear weapons without the need to resort to nuclear warfighting or committing ground forces. Major General Vladimir Slipchenko furthered these ideas by advancing the notion of sixth generation warfare where offensive aerospace operations would be preceded by EW and led by UAVs with minimal role for ground forces.[15] Again, the idea was to preclude the use of nuclear weapons, as well as boots-on-ground, since all operational and strategic objectives could be accomplished using conventional PGMs.[16] In fact, the usage of high-precision weapons is considered as part of Russia's asymmetric warfare strategy, in addition to their own understanding of Network-Centric Warfare (NCW), which they call non-contact warfare (*bezcontaktnaia voina),*[17] and the 'strategic concept of reflexive control'.[18] Reflexive control, Low Intensity Conflict (LIC) and NCW are combined to create a type of 'new generation warfare', which is all-encompassing in terms of targeting political, diplomatic, informational, economic, military and other indirect forms of targets at the same time.[19] The Russians believe that the use of these attributes will make occupation of enemy territory unnecessary. This type of warfare has been waged in stages in Ukraine. Initially the seizure of Crimea and Donbas region in 2014 involved precision attacks, militias, disinformation campaigns and referendums.

The ongoing 'special military operation' used conventional attacks across Ukraine in conjunction with the use of special forces to seize the Hostomel airbase in Kyiv,[20] evoking memories of Operation Market Garden. When this failed, long-range missiles were used to attack a multitude of targets (civil and military) in phases. Reflective control—proactively providing the opponent with information to make him or her voluntarily take a predetermined action desired by the controller—has been attempted using missiles to target Ukraine's electricity grid system in order to deprive the Ukrainian populace of electricity during the winter season[21] and hence, increase discontent against the Ukrainian authorities. Reflective control has also been used to implicate Ukraine's government in conducting false-flag attacks against its own citizens using common missiles held in both countries' inventories, especially the Tochka-U (RS-SS 21 Scarab).[22] Again, due to prompt efforts by certain think-tanks, these efforts have so far not yielded the desired results.[23] It is, however, in the conventional use of UAVs as part of the Russian RDC where maximum strategic results have been achieved.

## Russian Use of UAVs

One of the primary uses of UAVs by Russia is to serve as links in real-time intelligence fusion and rapid target acquisition and destruction of Ukrainian military and civilian target.[24] Additionally, they are being used for artillery spotting, vertical reconnaissance (platoon level), intelligence gathering, targeting Ukrainian electricity grid (homing onto sub-stations) and other civilian infrastructure, dogfighting drones as part of counter-drone systems,[25] improving accuracy of missile systems,[26] reducing sensor-to-shooter time window for mobile targets, forcing Ukraine to expend valuable Air Defence (AD) ammunition, as Loitering Munitions (LMs), Suppression/destruction of Enemy Air Defences (SEAD/DEAD)[27] and finally as crucial cogs of a 'unified information space' that emphasises a detailed understanding of the battle space, later distributed across its entirety and accessible to relevant units. As an example, the Russians have paired UAVs with artillery systems, missiles and tanks, enhancing the range of the latter using indirect observation and providing a pseudo-Beyond Visual Range (BVR) mode extending up to 12 kilometres. This mode has been theorised in a number of Russian military publications including using tethered UAVs as range enhancers for the T-14 Armatas.[28]

So far, the Russians have used UAVs in a conventional role, that is, as part of their existing C2 setup. Innovations observed during multiple battles have been about replacing humans in certain tactical roles but the roles themselves remain defined and fixed. UAVs have been used in lieu of human operators in Listening and Observation Posts (LPs and OPs), ahead of the Russian defensive line. As per a report, close to 25–50 UAVs from both sides operate in the area between Forward Line of Own Troops (FLOT) and Forward Line of Enemy Troops (FLET) per 10 kilometres of frontage.[29] UAVs such as Orlan-10 and Orlan-30, with maximum ranges of 120 and 300 kilometres respectively, have been used for target designation for Krasnopol 152 mm laser-guided rounds. The original range of the Krasnopol ammunition is 20 kilometres[30] with an option of extending it up to 43 kilometres,[31] however, the laser designators initially being used were limited to only a few kilometres. These drones use off-the-shelf Canon cameras, specifically the OS 750 D version,[32] and laser designators to provide Russian artillery with footage and designation beyond the range of conventional designators. Additionally, Orlan-30s have also designated targets for 240 mm Smelchak mines from Tyulpan mortars,[33] and in certain cases have been found to be equipped with 80-megapixel cameras with image stabilisation systems and electronic intelligence equipment for detecting communication devices.[34] Russia has allotted multiple UAVs to the commanders of their artillery batteries enabling long-range fires on Ukrainian positions in a compressed time frame—close to three to five minutes.[35]

## Case Studies of UAV Integration

The example of Russian assault on the village of Artemiviske in December 2022 highlights the technique through which drones are integrated into the kill chain. Several UAVs were involved in the assault and were used in four kinds of tasks. One group of UAVs conducted reconnaissance outside the village for Ukrainian artillery positions, the second on possible routes for reserves, the third preceded the assault group to identify Ukrainian ambushes and firing positions and the fourth flew above the assault group itself, providing the assault group commander with real time tactical information and a bird's eye view of the area.[36] The feed from the UAV was being given to the assault group commander for calling artillery and also to the higher commanders for reinforcing the position with additional artillery, if required. All these engagements were managed by the Strelets system, an automated data fusion and C2 system. In another engagement, a Twitter video shows a Russian drone team guiding an assault team on the ground to enemy firing positions, pinpoint available cover and alert them about incoming vehicles, even micromanaging their entry into a building.[37] The dictum that a soldier on ground knows far more about the combat environs than the command element in the rear seems to be turning on its head.

Fixed wing UAVs have been supplemented with heavy quadcopters such as Sibir-1 (Siberia-1 on some sites)[38] and Griffon (Griffin/Grifin on some websites) carrying repeaters, to extend the range of communications, enabling better C2 over far-flung and dispersed assets. Sibir-1 can stay in the air up to three days at a stretch.[39] The payload in the form of a repeater and a dome video camera is carried by a special equipment lifting system 'Quasimast'.[40] Some drones are also being used for EW such as the Leer-3 EW modification on the Orlan-10 UAV to jam Ukrainian communications.[41]

## Syria as an Experimental Battlefield

Russia has perfected its RDC system in a number of multinational exercises and its operations in Syria, where it coordinated cross-domain ground strikes using naval and air launched cruise missiles, used UAVs for ISTAR, both for artillery as well as missile platforms, and performed Post-Strike Damage Assessment (PSDA). Syria and deployments practised in subsequent military district level exercises have been executed with a view to evolving, calibrating and strengthening the

Russian version of Multi-Domain Operations (MDO)—the Russian version of mosaic warfare. The Syrian intervention came almost immediately after the Crimea and Donbas episodes of 2014. Subsequent exercises and the current special military operation have proven that Russian NCW capabilities have evolved significantly. A quick look at the intended aims and lessons of the various district-level exercises will provide a more holistic understanding of the evolution of NCW in the last 10 years.

Starting with Kavkaz 2016, the exercise focused on two aspects: testing the improved automated tactical-level joint C2 system called YeSU TZ T3, which improved communication and increased the speed of commanders' decision-making. Orlan-10s made their first appearance in the form of the Leer-3 (*Lieer-3)* modification, which could be used to gather Global System for Mobile Communications (GSM) data and jam communications.[42] These are now being used regularly in Ukraine. Zapad 2017 focused on integrated manoeuvres comprising drones and EW, as well as counter-UAV systems. The exercise was divided into two phases with the second phase depicted as a full-scale conventional war featuring integration of Russian forces across domains and involving the coordinated use of drones, missiles, anti-submarine warfare and EW.[43] Vostok 2018 involved more than 1,000 aircraft including UAVs and featured Chinese People's Liberation Army (PLA) troops for the first time. The exercise was used to fine-tune and officially imbibe operational concepts learnt during the Crimean and Syrian interventions. There were three main objectives of the exercise, out of which two included training for EW as a new type of warfare and use of UAVs and robotic technologies.[44] During Tsentr 2019, a special squad comprising UAVs of various types was created to focus on kinetic operations[45] rather than being limited to ISTAR. Kavkaz 2020 focused on combating the threat of unmanned systems and cruise missiles while also grouping together Forpost, Orlan-10 and Eleron-3 drones into a single combat formation.[46] The final military exercise before the commencement of the special military operation on February 24, 2022 was the Zapad 2021, which involved the proliferation of new EW, drones and reconnaissance units down to the company level and measures to protect against LMs and drone swarms.[47] Russia also field-tested drone swarm capabilities in a joint anti-terrorism exercise with Kyrgyzstan called Issyk-Kul in 2018 where it utilised Forpost, Orlan and Takhion models in swarm mode and also simulated a 'vertical envelopment' of adversary forces.[48]

Most operational concepts have been tried out in Syria, especially related to EW, robotics and the use of UAVs integrated with long-range fires. Sergei Shoigu,

Russia's defence minister has consistently argued from 2017 that the role of robotics on the battlefield has assumed prime importance.[49] By July 2018, the Russian Ministry of Defence (MOD) was claiming that UAVs in Syria had clocked 140,000 hours comprising 23,000 missions.[50] Syria also provided an opportunity for the Russian Army to test the resilience of their UAVs against adversary EW platforms by undertaking actions such as 'activating specialized frequency/radio channels'.[51] Russia also acknowledged the importance of Unmanned Combat Aerial Vehicles (UCAVs), a deficiency that still needs redressal. In addition, Russia tested Korsar in Syria, a multi-function UAV capable of targeting human forces, armoured vehicles and other infrastructure. Korsar has a flight time of 12 hours, range of 200 kilometres and carries the Ataka missile (range six kilometres) and multi-task fixed grenade launchers.[52]

## Operations in Ukraine (2022)

There was an initial absence of UAVs when Russia launched the special military operation in February 2022. This could be attributed to an excessive confidence in a swift victory over Ukraine and toppling of the government in Kyiv. However, as the conflict dragged on and certain locations became operationally and geographically stalemated, the Russians increasingly starting using UAVs, both in aforementioned conventional roles and as part of a psychological campaign. UAVs in Russia's Armed Forces are brigaded, that is, all the UAVs in a fleet for a brigade are grouped into a single company, which is then divided into platoons based on the size and range of the UAVs being operated. A mini platoon, for example, operates the hand-launched Granat-1 and the short-range platoon, Orlan-10 and Granat-4. Training for the UAVs is imparted through the UAV operator course at the Inter Branch Center for Training of Specialists for Ground Troops at Kolomna, where only contract Non-Commissioned Officers (NCOs) operate the UAVs and the conscripts perform auxiliary tasks. Officers from all three services are also being given UAV training at the Russian Air Force Academy with preference given to officers from the artillery.[53]

Iranian-made Shahed-131 and Shahed-136s (both LMs), in conjunction with cruise and ballistic missile attacks[54] targeted Ukrainian civilian areas to pressure Kiev into capitulating. Mohajer-6 was used in tandem with the Shahed series LMs, with the former undertaking DEAD and allowing the Shaheds to go further and destroy Ukrainian targets in depth.[55] This trend continues till date. However, the Russians have been hamstrung by a deficiency of readily available Russian-made UCAVs, though certain volunteer groups inside Russia are attempting to make high-speed drones with First Person View (FPV) using minimal imported components.[56] Another challenge, which is now being rectified, is the integration of commercial quadcopters and drones into the Russian military's C2 structure. The Russians have been slow to use commercially available technology and initially suffered significant casualties due to their inability to utilise commercially available quadcopters and drones as 'personalised air reconnaissance' vehicles, something the Ukrainians have excelled at. Even in June 2022, Russian soldiers were complaining that they were like 'blind kittens' due to lack of UAV coverage[57] and by December 2022, the state-sponsored newspaper TASS reported demand by front-line soldiers for more quadcopters[58] since domestic industry could not scale rapidly enough to supply UAVs down to the company and platoon level. Some Telegram channels have praised junior and mid-level Russian officers' understanding of these new platforms and the speed at which FPV drones and quadcopters are collected and their training organised but claim that the senior hierarchy is still not competent enough to appreciate their utility.[59]

Russian industry efforts at fast-tracking production of drones and LMs have not borne fruit so far. Altius and Okhotnik, two of the most highly anticipated Russian UCAVs have still not made their battlefield appearance over Ukraine.[60] As a result, the Russians have modified Orlan-10, Korsar (Corsair), Lastochka, Forpost-R and Orion drones to carry out strikes, albeit with unguided munitions or dumb bombs such as OFAB-100-120,[61] though some variants of Orion can fire Kornet Anti-Tank Guided Munitions (ATGM) or the Kh-BPLA and KAB-20 guided bombs.[62] Russia is trying to increase its drone production through two parallel tracks: indigenisation and imports from trusted partners such as Iran (Shahed-129, Shahed-131, Shahed-136, Shahed-191 and Mohajer-6 drones and LMs[63]) and China (DJI series quadcopters such as the Mavic 2 Enterprise Advanced, Mavic 2 Pro/Zoom, Mavic 3 and Air 2S;[64] Autel Evo II and Evo Max 4T[65]). Chinese companies have, however, vehemently denied their involvement in enabling the Russian war machinery publicly. The challenge with the first track, that is, indigenisation is scaling up the production of military grade drones[66] since the commercial ones are being shot out of the sky in the thousands and there is a constant need to replace them. Commercial drones still keep appearing on the battlefield as they are either being routed through third countries or procured by volunteers through crowdfunding and donations.

As per one estimate, since there are vague descriptions within export data, it is hard to verify whether any of the drone components form part of export controls by the US or other countries, China has shipped close to $12 million in drones and drone parts to Russia between February 2022 and 2023.[67] Out of this, the majority has been by DJI while close to $2 million have been exported by Autel.[68] Russia's own efforts at innovating trial, evaluation and procurement of smaller and commercially procured drones have rapidly increased and they have managed to create innovation clusters similar to Ukraine. The Tsar's Wolves, a semi-military organisation filled with military technology experts and headed by Dmitry Rogozhin, has been tasked with getting the latest technologies to front-line soldiers in an accelerated time frame.[69] Private LM creators, such as Oko and Archangel, have received extensive backing from the group and are said to be in the process of creating competitor LMs to the Shahed series.[70]

Russia is reportedly also looking at Iranian drones, namely the Ababil and Arash series; the former being used for ISTAR and combat and the latter as a kamikaze drone or LM. Russia and Iran have already coordinated plans for a joint venture inside Russia (plant in Alabuga Special Economic Zone)[71] that will produce Shahed series drones. The Russians have also used LMs such as Lancet-3M (or Product 52) and Zala KYB (or KUB-BLA). Russia's use of KUB-BLA also ignited a debate about the LM's autonomous capabilities, which were later contested by multiple publications.[72] Most LMs are being used to target Ukrainian gun batteries in a counter-battery mode.[73] One can even argue that pinpointed attacks on gun emplacements using LMs is a much more efficient way to preserve artillery ammunition for major battlefield attacks rather than expending them on futile artillery duels. Russia's use of unmanned systems, though, is not limited to the aerial domain. Some innovations have also been attempted on the ground, portending similar systems to be made available in future conflicts and testing the capabilities of these systems in a comparatively more cluttered environment.

## Russian Use of Unmanned Platforms in other Domains

Though aerospace and specifically the air littoral—airspace between the ground forces and high-end fighters and bombers—has been the major focus for unmanned platforms, both Russia and Ukraine have made efforts at using Unmanned Ground Vehicles (UGVs) and Unmanned Underwater Vehicles (UUVs) and Underwater Surface Vehicles (USVs) to counter perceived weaknesses of the other side. These efforts have proceeded slowly on ground due to the presence of a complex environment with significant obstacles as compared to air. Ukraine, however, has evolved a way to use USVs for both Aden-style attacks on large Russian surface vessels and utilising them for propaganda attacks. Three major attacks involving these so-called kamikaze drone boats in October 2022, March 2023 and April

2023 have been observed so far, the last two coming in quick succession and involving up to three USVs.[74] Russia has applied lessons learnt from Syria in the use of Galtel UUVs and the Diamant mine detection/destruction system. This reflects an evolving unmanned maritime capability, though yet untested in actual combat.[75]

On land, Russia has been using Uran-6 and Uran-14 UGVs for demining operations in the Donbas, similar to what the Russians did in the disputed area of Nagorno–Karabakh in the aftermath of the Armenia–Azerbaijan War, in their role as peacekeepers.[76] Russia has also introduced a new 'Marker' robot UGV, which is being tested in the Donbas region for autonomous combat missions though the publicised capabilities are still far from being advanced enough to label them fully autonomous operations. As per Dmitry Roghozin, head of the 'Tsar's Wolves' military advisor group, the Marker will target West-supplied Abrams and Leopard tanks using advanced AI-based image cataloguing system in the visible and infrared (IR) ranges.[77] Some Western analysts feel that the announcements are mere hyperbole and the results on ground may not play out as expected. The Russian use of unmanned systems, therefore, has a mix of the orthodox and the unconventional, with the former dominating. With a larger military, Russia's use of unmanned systems in innovative ways is slow and gradual, unlike the Ukrainians. They have used a limited budget, infrastructure and materials to cobble together a more than expected resistance during the Russian attack phase.

### Ukrainian Use of UAVs

Ukraine has gone in for major tactical level innovations in the use of UAVs. Analysis of these UAVs and their impact on operations, however, suffers from four major drawbacks: most reportage and literature are heavily skewed towards the Ukrainians and hence, shortcomings are difficult to pinpoint. Secondly, due to the opaque nature of Ukrainian access to reporters on the ground, one has to really read between the lines to separate the grain of objective lessons from the chaff of fluff pieces. Thirdly, and this is a challenge in reporting in any contemporary conflict, the impact of Ukrainian innovations in the use and deployment of unmanned systems is hard to gauge due to conflicting numbers and lack of any quantifiable or comparable data of casualties, for example. Finally, Ukraine's military has been in conflict only with Russia since its breakaway from the Soviet Union and therefore lessons from previous wars are limited by the time period, that is, 2014 till date. In this time, Ukraine's military has rapidly integrated

UAVs within its folds, absorbed private volunteers and undergone a cost-effective modernisation in certain areas.

One of the major successes of the Ukrainian Armed Forces in using UAVs is the effective weaponization of the air littoral. The 'thickness' of the air littoral can vary from army to army, but a standard norm broadly is the volume of airspace between the infantry and fighter planes. The air littoral is the site of maximum engagements by the Ukrainians and where maximum innovation in UAVs have taken place. For a force with a very limited starting defence budget of $500 million[78] in 2014—conventional military aid from the West such as Javelin ATGMs, Stinger SAMs and other military-grade equipment had still not arrived—the Ukrainians, at least the younger officers and soldiers adapted niche technologies. Innovation efforts are now led by private militias, civilian volunteers and mid- and junior-level officers and men of the Ukrainian Armed Forces in parallel and coordination with each other. The senior hierarchy, like the Russians, still finds it difficult to appreciate the countervailing power of certain emerging technologies. The Ukrainian government has supplemented the efforts of the armed forces with two broader aims in mind: make Ukraine a major digital power after the end of the war[79] and use social media platforms to strengthen their influence operations—gain sympathy for Ukraine, maintain the West's interest and support and denigrate Russian 'psyops'.[80] One of the major areas of innovation by Ukraine and which has reaped disproportionate rewards for them is unmanned systems—UAVs and USVs. Entrepreneurship and low-level military innovation has, to a large extent, achieved two major aims: create compatible payloads for drones using commercially available sensors such as cameras, gyroscopes, infrared (IR) sensors etc and exploit international standards for different software and hardware to piece together modular systems capable of taking on multiple roles.

Starting in 2014, the Ukrainians used crowdfunding initiatives such as the People's Project[81] for seeding money to procure commercial drones. These were initially used for Intelligence, Surveillance and Reconnaissance (ISR) purposes and later evolved to conduct harassment attacks at a tactical level targeting individual gun positions, Russian infantry sections, tanks and mechanised vehicles. Most of them were and are still designed to carry strap-on grenades and anti-personnel mines and act as crude variants of LMs. A host of companies such as Ukrspecsystems (PD-1[82]), Athlone Air (A1-CM Furia[83]) and even the Kiev Polytechnic (Spectator[84]) sprouted in the late 2014 and fielded small privately funded and designed drones, supplying them directly to either the soldiers or militias. In certain cases, they were and still are piloted exclusively by civilian volunteers, creating a new category of combatants whose treatment as per IHL remains undefined.

The US supplied limited quantities of RQ-11 Raven drones in July 2016, but they were quickly brought down by the Russians using their superior EW capabilities.[85] Ukraine's state-run defence conglomerate UkrOboronProm designed a multifunctional unmanned aerial 'complex' AN-BK-1, which is being tested for the last six years[86] but hasn't been produced at scale. Similar efforts by defence contractor Luch to produce Sokil-300, a long-range multi-use UAV, have also not shown much success either.[87] An 'Army of Drones' initiative by the Ukrainian government aims to produce close to 200,000 drones by the end of 2023 and Minister for Digital Transformation Mykhailo Federov is personally leading the group. The aim is to conduct studies, organise competitions and try and fast-track the delivery of various drones to the frontline.[88] Estimates of the number of drone startups in Ukraine vary between 30[89] and 80,[90] all having been birthed in the last six to 10 months. Ukraine has attempted to bring the war to the Russian doorstep by engaging in some high-profile attacks on Engels air base (twice: December 05 and 26, 2022[91]), Moscow (May 30, 2023[92]), oil refinery in Krasnodar (May 31, 2023[93]) and injuring 10 Russian soldiers at a military training ground in the Voronezh region on May 10, 2023. UJ-22, Tu-141 and 'Beaver' drones are most likely suspected to be used in these attacks.[94] These high-profile attacks form only a small proportion of the approximately 60 attacks conducted inside Russia and Russian-occupied territories.[95] The Moscow attack started with eight drones but only three were able to make contact with civilian infrastructure as the other five were shot down.[96] Some of the drones used featured long-range flying capabilities. The audacity of the attack rankled the Russian government as they served two purposes: create fear psychosis amongst Russian citizens and put pressure on the government to end the special military operation and use these as part of shaping operations to pull valuable Russian AD assets away from the frontline towards depth areas to protect civilian facilities and infrastructure.

The tactical use of drones by Ukraine includes a number of innovations. Ukrainian civilians have relied on 3D printing for creating various drone parts, in addition to piecing together makeshift drones using materials such as foam plastic, mounting foam and Chinese spare parts.[97] These are mostly expendable and as per one report, Ukraine is losing close to 10,000 commercial drones a month.[98] The rate of expenditure is so rapid that drones are being viewed as flying ammunition, rather than aircraft. Initially, Ukraine used Turkish-supplied Bayraktar TB-2s to target Russian logistics and armoured convoys but after a period of time when they started getting shot down using EW and SAMs by the Russians, the TB-2s had to be shelved, their main use being propaganda for the Ukrainians.[99] Another factor prohibiting the use of TB-2s in the later phase of the conflict is their high cost. One of the highest publicised uses of the TB-2 was its support role in sinking Moskva, Russia's missile cruiser and the flagship of the Black Sea fleet.[100]

Longer-range drones with more potent weapon systems have been a challenge for the Ukrainians though there are a few projects in the pipeline, especially that the BRAVE1 technology cluster has been created to marry the military, defence sector and private startups together.[101] In the interim, the Ukrainians have absorbed a number of West-supplied UAVs and LMs such as the US Switchblade[102] and Phoenix Ghost[103] LMs and Puma ISR UAVs,[104] Norwegian PD-100 'Black Hornet' nano UAVs,[105] Chinese DJI Mavics and Polish Warmate LMs into certain organisations.

Till the time Starlink was not geofenced and speed locked, Ukrainian soldiers were using the satellite-based communication system for operating their UAVs and avoiding Russian EW systems.[106] As observed by members of a training team imparting combat lessons to Ukrainian soldiers, they are poor at combined arms warfare.[107] This means that UAVs may not be adequately integrated into the Ukrainian military structure as the Russian RFCs and RSCs, but aim to augment artillery shells and rockets in terms of pinpoint targeting of small bodies of troops and armour. They are also being used by Ukrainian Special Operation Forces (SOFs), volunteer reconnaissance battalions and militias[108] as part of a larger resistance movement. Ukrainian tank-hunting teams use UAVs to find and target Russian armour, consumer quadcopters are used for ISR and dropping anti-personnel grenades directly into trenches and racing drones or FPV drones have been converted into LMs that target Russians inside bunkers.[109] A number of these accounts have been uploaded on social media platforms and coupled with a blanket ban on pro-Russian material, seem to project an image of Ukrainian invincibility. But the almost nine-month long stalemate at Bakhmut[110] that finally resulted in a Russian victory has proved this notion wrong, though one could also infer that the Ukrainians have managed to stall a larger military for a considerable amount of time.

These engagements have served as laboratories where both countries have experimented with different platforms and tactics. In terms of drones, one can see the smooth diffusion of technology and expansion of drone use: initially handled by armed forces exclusively and now with militias and volunteers. If integrated within the Ukrainian military structure, they can be used to offset major Russian military advantages, till that time they will remain hindered by a small-war mentality that favours long-term resistance over a decisive outcome. Now that the counteroffensive has started, it remains to be seen how effective Ukrainian UAV operational innovations are while on the offensive.

### Ukrainian Use of other Unmanned Systems

Ukrainian use of USVs or drone boats to target conventional Russian vessels have not yielded any operational success so far but provide the operators with invaluable operational experience. Ukraine is also mulling designing its own UUV to target the Russian fleet. For the time being, videos by onboard cameras provide excellent propaganda material and may prove to be a template for other state and non-state actors to take on bigger adversaries. Ukraine has also used UGVs in innovative ways such as mobile mines, firefighting and in demining operations.[111]

## RUSSIAN USE OF LONG-RANGE MISSILES

Russia has used long-range ballistic and cruise missiles (air, ground and ship-launched) to attack Ukraine's military and civilian infrastructure since the opening phase of the conflict. There was an expectation that the opening phase of the Russian special military operation will lead to the obliteration of Ukraine's fledgling Air Force and AD systems and airfields through a combination of missiles and aircraft. However, this did not happen.[112] Some likely factors include dispersion, mobility and deception on part of the Ukrainians, a slow targeting cycle, an inadequate number of explosives catered for each target and abysmal PSDA. Resultantly, Russia's targeting priorities using missiles have shifted, displaying planning flexibility. The first wave of missile strikes attacked airfields, AD and ammunition storehouses. Around 160 missile and air strikes were carried out in the first two days of the conflict, far too less for the number of critically important targets that Ukraine presented.[113] The second wave, around April 2022, shifted to targeting Ukraine's fuel and transportation sectors including roads and railway lines.[114] The next wave till date has focused on civilian infrastructure, electricity grid and has placed a special emphasis on Kiev.[115]

The attacks in the last wave have two peculiarities: they are carried as part of a hybrid attack using a mix of Iskander-M, Kalibr, Kh-101, Kh-55 missiles and S-300 SAMs in ground attack mode as well as Shahed-136s and they seem to have become large in scale but infrequent. Some analysts attribute this to a dwindling stock of missiles due to Western sanctions,[116] though these remain unproven. There are speculations that Russia had stockpiled microchips years before[117] and is being covertly assisted by China.[118] Russia has also ramped up its missile production capacity and may be keeping certain quantities of missiles in reserve for the just-begun Ukrainian counteroffensive. Russian missile attacks, though, have forced Ukraine to expend precious AD missiles and ammunition in countering them and forcing it to prioritise between civilian and combat areas. Russia is at a clear advantage here since Ukraine lacks any major missile production capacity apart from the Tochka-U ballistic missiles.[119] Russia has also stripped some of its nuclear capable missiles such as the Kh-55 cruise missiles and fired them into Ukraine armed only with ballast to waste Ukraine's AD ammunition.[120]

As mentioned previously, use of precision-strike using missiles and drones was seen by Russia as a new and improved way of conducting foreign policy in its neighbour precluding boots on ground. In the current conflict, Russia hoped for a quick victory, which was belied by Ukrainian resistance, Western aid and Russian lack of coordination in logistics and air and ground operations. As a result, the lack of air superiority is being supplanted by missile strikes by Russia. Drones are also being used for pinpointing locations and conducting PSDA missions post the missile strikes. At multiple occasions, LMs, suicide drones and missiles are used to launch hybrid attacks to overwhelm Ukrainian AD and cause civilian damage.

All these techniques have been perfected in the Syrian theatre of operations during which Russia tested its new precision strike weapons such as long-range cruise missiles and air and ship launched missiles and guided bombs. Syria was also used for testing Russia cross-domain targeting capabilities along with advanced ISR, using the Kalibr SLCM (range 1500 kilometres)[121] and P-800 Oniks/Yakhont (range 600 kilometres)[122] for attacking ground targets. Back to back strikes were conducted first by the Russian Navy in October 2015 using Kalbr cruise missiles[123] followed by the VKS in November 2015 using ALCMs such as Kh-101 and Kh-555s from Tu series bombers such as Tu-95MS and Tu-22M3.[124] Russia also tested the Kh 59 Mk 2 cruise missiles from an Su-57 in Syria in 2018 with the final aim being the integration of a hypersonic missile into the same aircraft.[125] Interestingly, one of the UCAVs under development in Russia, the S-70 Okhotnik can reportedly carry similar munitions as the Su-57, functioning as a loyal wingman in a manned-unmanned teaming (MUM-T) format.[126] In this case, there is a possibility of merging of two unique technologies in a single platform: unmanned system and hypersonic missiles. Russia also tested its first helicopter-based 'fire-

and-forget' missile called the lightweight multirole guided missile (LMUR/ Izdeliye 305) in Syria from Mi-28M helicopters in late 2016.[127]

Currently, against Ukraine, apart from the above-mentioned missiles, Russia uses a mix of ALCMs (Kh-101 and Kh-555) from Tu-95 and Tu-160 bombers at standoff distances.[128] As per some Ukrainian sources, Russia fired close to 2700 ALCMs in the first five months of the war,[129] leading some military officials and commentators to believe that they had expended a significant quantity of their stock. Russia has also launched a number of air-to-ground guided missiles from tactical aircraft such as Su-24 and Su-25.[130] These missiles include Kh-29[131], Kh-31[132], Kh-58[133] and Kh-59.[134] Out of these, the Kh-31 and Kh-58 are Anti-Radiation Missiles (ARMs) meant to take out Ukrainian mobile AD assets. Russia has also repurposed its air launched anti-ship missiles such as Kh-22 and Kh-32 for land-attack missions.[135] Finally, the much-touted Kinzhal missile with a hypersonic capability has also been used, though it seems for a performative purpose.[136] The intent is to signal the possession of a functional capability to the West since there was no specific need for the use of the missile in the Ukrainian theatre. This signalling has had mixed results as the Kinzhal has been reportedly intercepted by a US-supplied Patriot SAM system. Reinforcing the centrality of missiles and especially precision strike weapons, the Russian President approved the State Armaments Programme (SAP) 2018–27,[137] allotting 20 trillion rubles ($313 billion) to focus on procuring nuclear systems, hypersonic missiles and laser systems, apart from precision strike weapons and UAVs. The importance given to the use of missiles in its various uses by Russia seems to be increasing in the coming years. Ukraine's use of missiles is not being covered since, at the time of writing this chapter, it has just procured air-launched Storm Shadow missiles from the UK and not much has been reported on their use.

## LESSONS FOR INDIA

The use of unmanned systems and missiles has many lessons for India that are enumerated below:

(a) The centrality of conventional war itself, for the purpose of achieving political aims has become suspect. For both sides, conventional warfare does not form a critical part of their strategic and political aims. One can argue that well-trained soldiers, armoured formations and advanced aircraft will always be critical for warfighting, however, the truth is that contemporary warfare has become non-contact in nature. The initial onslaught of missile and air strikes failed to achieve the desired effect of SEAD/DEAD and achieve air superiority. On the Russian side, inadequate intelligence, lack of planning and dissemination, opaque war plans, insufficient integration and miscalculating the number of explosives required for target destruction are to blame for the lukewarm results. The subsequent strikes on Ukraine's civilian infrastructure such as agriculture sector, transportation networks and electricity grid have brought the war directly to the people, rather than being limited to the Ukrainian geographical periphery such as Donbas or Crimea. Apart from the civilians, Russian missile strikes have targeted military installations in depth, bypassing the almost stalemated frontline. Compared with the quick capitulation of Crimea and the comparatively easier takeover of the Donbas using means other than conventional combat makes the role of this type of warfighting suspect in the achievement of a country's political goals. At best, if conventional war is to be fought, it has to be fought as a combined-arms manoeuvre on ground, integrated with an air, missile and maritime offensive across domains. Anything less may lead to sub-optimal outcomes, the first sparks of which are evident from the way the Ukrainian counteroffensive is progressing.

(b) Non-contact warfare has been made possible due to a confluence of technology diffusion, increased computing power and network effects. Precision-strikes have supplanted dumb bombs and rockets. The current conflict has shown that with cheaply available ISTAR capabilities in the form of commercial UAVs, one can produce near-precision effects without expending heavy sums on precision ammunition. UAVs, with their ubiquity and persistence, have ensured a pinpoint targeting capability down to an infantry section and in Ukraine's case, private militias and ordinary citizens. Use of dumb bombs, rockets and even grenades dropped directly on top of trenches and use of LMs has created exponential tactical effects on the battlefield. These have been amplified by the use of SRBMs, Ground-Launched Cruise Missiles (GLCMs), SLCMs and ALCMs. Taking cognisance of the operational impact of battlefield missiles, India has taken steps towards operationalising an Integrated Rocket Force (IRF) by commissioning Pralay missiles.[138] Long-Range Land Attack Cruise Missiles (LR-ALCMs) and SLCMs may be added to this tri-services organisation later. The challenge of target mapping and calculating the number of explosives required for each target need to be kept in mind and production capacity ramped up as per requirement.

(c) Three main platforms have played an outsized role in this conflict so far. These are artillery guns/batteries (mobile and static), UAVs and missiles. All three have been networked through a number of automated platforms such as Strelets for the Russians, and Diia for the Ukrainians,[139] the latter repurposed from being a civic amenities geo-tagging app based on the internet. The role of UAVs has already been discussed in detail. Future warfighting will increase the degree of automation of disparate and dispersed assets for concentration of fires rather than concentration of mass. All these three platforms will continue to play disproportionate roles.

(d) Data integration and fusion have become critical. The chaotic and dispersed nature of the battlefield and the commingling of own and enemy assets necessitates the use of data fusion, integration and deconfliction algorithms. Companies such as Palantir have provided a unique Graphic User Interface- (GUI) based data solution to the Ukrainian Armed Forces, which integrates data from US satellites, human intelligence (HUMINT), drones and social media feeds to create a Common Operating Picture (COP) segregated by data classification protocols in order to ensure that relevant actors receive information.[140]

(e) Counter-UAV, anti-missile and AD systems will be crucial in future wars, one of the primary reasons being the weaponization and democratisation of the air littoral. A multi-layered cross-domain interoperable AD network is the need of the day. This includes anti-aircraft guns, Man-Portable AD Systems (MANPADS), tracked and wheeled AD systems combined with adequate EW capability. The issue of cost also needs to be factored in. For example, it is financially imprudent to use expensive AD missiles to target Do It Yourself (DIY) drones made by volunteers in their basement. As a result, EW capabilities must be integrated with the AD structure and should devolve down to the section level in the form of portable platforms. The ineffectiveness of armour without AD protection in the current conflict is clear to everyone. Integral AD of individual tanks will not be effective without the necessary long-term identification, which is only possible with the integration of the identification 'stack', that is, a COP that is visible to all. A closer integration of the Army Air Defence (AAD) both with the Indian Air Force (IAF) and mechanised formations along with its expansion is necessary. The Ukrainian conflict has also shown the need for data compatibility and hence the need for common data standards. For example, AD systems, donated by Germany and other countries, such as NASAMS and IRIS-T have automated systems that integrate data from its own and nearby radars and data sources,[141] providing the operator with an identification range much beyond the capability of the equipment's organic radar.

(f) Intra-complementarity between weapon systems is very important and India's move towards Atmanirbhar Bharat is the right step in this direction. A comparison between Ukraine and Russia's firepower systems shows that while Russia has improved its integration across platforms and domains—the various military district level exercises and operations in Syria prove this—and strengthened its RFC and RSC complexes using automation, UAVs and long-range missiles, Ukraine is still struggling to piece together coherent combined arms manoeuvres. One of the major reasons behind this is Ukraine's reliance on platforms from multiple countries, which may not be compatible with each other. Russia, on the other hand, has produced every system domestically apart from advanced microelectronics and LMs for which it is dependent on countries such as Iran and China. For Atmanirbhar Bharat to be a success, there is a requirement to ensure that standards be designed and disseminated in time to private vendors and startups, so that scaling up of crucial items can be done in parallel during crises.

(g) One of the major lessons from this conflict and contemporary ones is the democratisation of the air littoral. It is presumed that air superiority by contesting sides will be difficult to achieve. This aero stalemate enables the use of UAVs of all types and payloads. For near-peer adversaries, this assumes critical importance. Many academics have correctly pointed out that the 'game-changing' nature of drones has been made possible due to the absence of either integrated AD systems or effective air cover.[142] Achievement of air superiority now seems like a distant task and many air forces have repurposed their tasks to that of air denial to the adversary. The air littoral is filled with drones that bypass the bureaucratic and rather lengthy route of accessing real-time operational information—a task which earlier used to take a considerable amount of time and for the soldier on the ground was in an audio rather than visual format. Now, every platoon and section have the ability to be aware of their environs, conduct real-time Identification of Friend and Foe (IFF), see their adversaries in real time and pinpoint exact targets that require additional attention from bigger weapons. The air littoral is also the site of precision kills—tanks, artillery guns and soldiers—all vulnerable to drones, LMs, quadcopters and other unmanned systems.

(h) The role of private players in operations of conventional armies in the current conflict has shifted from the facilitation to the conduct phase. Apart from militias and mercenary groups such as the Wagner Group (Russia) or the Azov Battalion (Ukraine), private companies have directly taken part in operations of these countries by providing data fusion products (Palantir), facial recognition software (Clearview),[143] satellite communication and navigation (Starlink)[144] and similar products. Volunteers and students on either side have created multiple startups for producing drones and UAVs in order to ship them to the soldiers on the frontline or in many cases, operating the platforms themselves, especially in the case of FPV drones (fast flying small drones that can reach speeds up to 250 kmph and act as LMs to target personnel). The participation of these civilians raises questions regarding the updation of IHL. In India's case, drone pilots are being trained in significant numbers.[145] These form a potential pool from which recruits for armed forces can be selected in the future. Indian defence startups, telecom and defence-adjacent companies need to be integrated further into the Indian national security setup. The example of Starlink showcases the reliance on foreign companies for critical functions such as communication, navigation and ISTAR. For these functions, Indian companies need to be further integrated within the national security setup. In the case of UAVs, though bigger and sophisticated UAVs seem to offer much more functional options, smaller and varied UAVs by small startups with single payloads have their own utility.

(j) Russian and Ukrainian innovation clusters such as BRAVE1 (Ukraine),[146] Era Military Innovation Technopolis[147] and Tsar's Wolves (Russia) have sprung up to marry up public defence enterprises, startups and operators to quickly create and design products, send them to the frontline, get them battle-tested, perform A/B testing and then ship an improved product in an accelerated time frame at scale. This has enabled the development of multiple startups in both countries, which have truly bypassed the red-tapism of bigger defence industries and created niche products using locally made components. This blueprint-to-battlefield strategy has led to the production of hundreds of thousands of drones and UAVs that have saturated the air littoral. In India's case also, the slow pace of central acquisition of technologies through the conventional setup has hampered the modernisation of the forces since technologies get outdated very quickly as compared to industrial-age products. A sector/theatre command-based approach wherein local clusters may be created based on terrain and threat analyses and then handheld by the respective formations, products designed and tested in that very theatre may be a good option for a vast country such as India that has diverse threats and terrains.

(k) The use of USVs by Ukraine against Russian surface vessels has not yielded any results so far but due to propaganda effects will be studied and analysed by multiple state and non-state actors across the globe. These Aden-style tactics, if complemented by LTTE-style kamikaze swarms[148] can overwhelm the defences of Carrier Battle Groups (CBGs) or target individual ships. Bigger navies will have to monitor these developments. In India's case, facing a far bigger adversarial navy, mass-production of drone boats along with swarming algorithms can be a cost-effective way of establishing deterrence.

## CONCLUSION

The use of drones in all three domains has seen exponential growth in the current conflict. Augmented with the use of missiles, these two unmanned systems have created battlefield effects within minutes and hours, which older militaries or more conventional ones would have struggled to produce in weeks and months. The ability to bring to bear accurate and devastating firepower repeatedly on specific targets through use of cross-domain missile launching platforms, using UAVs for ISTAR and PSDA and LMs for destruction—all these integrated within an overarching complex that also integrates information, political and social effects—has led to redefining total war for the modern age.

## NOTES

1 AFP, 'Ukraine Says Downed All Missiles, Drones in New Attacks on Kyiv,' *The Moscow Times*, June 2, 2023, at https://www.themoscowtimes.com/2023/06/02/ukraine-says-downed-all-missiles-drones-in-new-attacks-on-kyiv-a81375 (Accessed June 6, 2023)

2 James Gregory, 'UK Confirms Supply of Storm Shadow Long-range Missiles in Ukraine,' *BBC News*, May 11, 2023, at https://www.bbc.com/news/world-europe-65558070 (Accessed June 5, 2023).

3 Thomas Newdick, 'Russia Now Firing S-300 Surface-To-Air Missiles at Land Targets In Ukraine: Official,' *The Drive*, July 9, 2022, at https://www.thedrive.com/the-war-zone/russia-now-firing-s-300-surface-to-air-missiles-at-land-targets-in-ukraine-official (Accessed June 5, 2023).

4 Ian Williams, 'Putin's Missile War: Russia's Strike Campaign in Ukraine,' Centre for Strategic and International Studies, May, 2023, at https://www.csis.org/analysis/putins-missile-war (Accessed June 5, 2023).

5 'Baguette-sized Flying Bombs Are About to Enter Service in Ukraine,' March 26, 2022, at https://www.economist.com/science-and-technology/baguette-sized-flying-bombs-are-about-to-enter-service-in-ukraine/21808317 (Accessed June 5, 2023).

6 D. Ignatius, 'How the Algorithm Tipped the Balance in Ukraine,' *Washington Post*, December 19, 2022, at https://www.washingtonpost.com/opinions/2022/12/19/palantir-algorithm-data-ukraine-war/ (Accessed June 5, 2023).

7 J. Knight, 'Decentering Anthropos: Insights from New Materialism,' *E-International Relations*, March 28, 2023, at https://www.e-ir.info/2023/03/28/decentering-anthropos-insights-from-new-materialism/ (Accessed May 21, 2023)

8 'The Drone: God's Eye, Death Machine, Cultural Puzzle – Naief Yehya,' *Culture Machine*, December 13, 2015, at https://culturemachine.net/vol-16-drone-cultures/the-drone-gods-eye/ (Accessed May 9, 2023)

9 A. Calcara, A. Gilli, M. Gilli, R. Marchetti and I. Zaccagnini, 'Why Drones Have Not Revolutionized War: The Enduring Hider-Finder Competition in Air Warfare,' *International Security*, *46*(4), 2022, pp. 130–71, at https://doi.org/10.1162/isec_a_0043.1

10 Vego, 'Recce-Strike Complexes in Soviet Theory and Practice,' *DTIC*, June 1, 1990, at https://apps.dtic.mil/sti/citations/ADA231900 (Accessed June 6, 2023).

11 L.A. Brisky, 'The Reconnaissance Destruction Complex: A Soviet Operational Response to Airland Battle,' *The Journal of Soviet Military Studies*, *3*(2), June 1990, pp. 296–306, at https://doi.org/10.1080/13518049008429985.

12 Ibid.

13 Watts, 'The Maturing Revolution in Military Affairs,' *CSBA*, June 2, 2011, at https://csbaonline.org/research/publications/the-maturing-revolution-in-military-affairs/publication/1 (Accessed June 6, 2023).

14 McDermott, 'Russia's UAVs and UCAVs: ISR and Future Strike Capabilities,' Jamestown.org, March 23, 2022, at https://jamestown.org/program/russias-uavs-and-ucavs-isr-and-future-strike-capabilities/ (Accessed June 6, 2023).

15 R. McDermott and Bukkvall, 'Russia in the Precision-Strike Regime – Military Theory, Procurement and Operational Impact,' Academia.edu, at https://www.academia.edu/33924504/Russia_in_the_Precision_Strike_Regime_Military_theory_Procurement_and_Operational_Impact (Accessed June 6, 2023).

16 J.W. Kipp, Russia's Nonstrategic Nuclear Weapons, Foreign Military Studies Office, May 2001, at https://ciaotest.cc.columbia.edu/cbr/cbr00/video/cbr_ctd/cbr_ctd_06.html (Accessed June 6, 2023).

17 R. McDermott and Bukkvall, no. xv.

18 J. Berzins, 'The Theory and Practice of New Generation Warfare: The Case of Ukraine and Syria,' *The Journal of Slavic Military Studies*, *33*(3), July 2, 2020, pp. 355–80, at https://doi.org/10.1080/13518046.2020.1824109.

19 Ibid.

20 O. Mitzer and Oliemans, ‚Destination Disaster: Russia's Failure At Hostomel Airport,' Oryx. April 13, 2022, at https://www.oryxspioenkop.com/2022/04/destination-disaster-russias-failure-at.html (Accessed June 6, 2023).

21 Yaffa, 'The Impact of Russian Missile Strikes on Ukraine's Power Grid,' *The New Yorker*, February 20, 2023, at https://www.newyorker.com/culture/photo-booth/the-impact-of-russian-missile-strikes-on-ukraines-power-grid (Accessed June 6, 2023).

22 Williams, 'Putin's Missile War: Russia's Strike Campaign in Ukraine,' Centre for Strategic and International Studies, May 2023, at https://www.csis.org/analysis/putins-missile-war (Accessed June 5, 2023).

23 L. Freedman, 'False Flag Attacks Are Usually Just That — False,' *New Statesman*, May 4, 2023, at https://www.newstatesman.com/world/europe/ukraine/2023/05/false-flag-attacks-lawrence-freedman (Accessed May 16, 2023)

24 Bendett and Edmonds, (2023, March 31). 'Russia's Use of Uncrewed Systems in Ukraine,' CNA.org, March 31, 2023, at https://www.cna.org/reports/2023/05/russias-use-of-drones-in-ukraine (Accessed June 7, 2023).

25 'How Drones Dogfight Above Ukraine,' at https://www.economist.com/the-economist-explains/2023/02/07/how-drones-dogfight-above-ukraine (Accessed Mar 22, 2023)

26 Bendett and Edmonds, no. xxiv.

27 V.K. Thakur (2023, April 27). 'Russian Aerospace Forces Using "New Offensive Tactics" To Degrade Ukrainian Air Defenses,' *EurAsian Times*, April 27, 2023, at https://eurasiantimes.com/russia-adopts-new-offensive-tactics-to-decimate-ukrainian/ (Accessed May 1, 2023)

28 L.W. Grau and C.K. Bartles, *The Russian Way of War: Force Structure, Tactics, and Modernization of the Russian Ground Forces* (1st ed.). Mentor Enterprises, Inc., Jan 1, 2018.

29 J. Watling and N. Reynolds, N. 'Meatgrinder: Russian Tactics in the Second Year of Its Invasion of Ukraine,' Royal United Services Institute, May 19, 2023, at https://rusi.org/explore-our-research/publications/special-resources/meatgrinder-russian-tactics-second-year-its-invasion-ukraine (Accessed June 7, 2023).

30 W. Williams, Threat Update Krasnopol – A Laser-Guided Projectile for Tube Artillery, Foreign Military Studies Office Publications - Red Thrust Star, Federation of American Scientists (FAS), at https://man.fas.org/dod-101/sys/land/row/krasnopol.htm (Accessed June 7, 2023).

31 S. Bryen, 'US-made Parts Keep Russia's Artillery Firing in Ukraine,' *Asia Times*, June 3, 2022, at https://asiatimes.com/2022/06/us-made-parts-keep-russias-artillery-firing-in-ukraine/ (Accessed June 7, 2023).

32 D. Hambling, 'Russia's Deadly Artillery Drones Have a Strange Secret,' *Forbes*, April 11, 2022, at https://www.forbes.com/sites/davidhambling/2022/04/11/russias-deadly-artillery-drones-have-a-strange-secret/ (Accessed June 7, 2023)

33 'Russian Army to Get Orlan-30 Drone in 2020,' airrecognition.com, October 3, 2019, at https://www.airrecognition.com/index.php/focus-analysis-photo-report-aviation-defence-industry/aviation-defence-industry-technology/5503-russian-army-to-get-orlan-30-drone-in-2020.html (Accessed June 9, 2023)

34 Bendett and Edmonds, no. xxiv.

35 J. Watling and N. Reynolds, no. xxix.

36 Ibid.

37 The Bazaar of War [@bazaarofwar], A recent video of a Russian drone team guiding an assault shows, April 27, 2023, Twitter. https://twitter.com/bazaarofwar/status/1651619485923659777 (Accessed May 28, 2023)

38 'Russian Multifunctional UAVs "Siberia-1" and "Griffin" Are Actively Used in the NVO

Zone,' November 3, 2022, Военное Обозрение at https://en.topwar.ru/204452-rossijskie-mnogofunkcionalnye-bpla-sibir-1-i-grifon-aktivno-ispolzujutsja-v-zone-svo.html (Accessed May 28, 2023)

39 Lamp of Knowledge, Russia Uses New Drones Sibir-1 and Griffin [Video], November 7, 2022, YouTube, Retrieved June 7, 2023, at https://www.youtube.com/watch?v=pD1L6ackd70 (Accessed June 7, 2023).

40 Минобороны РФ показало кадры применения беспилотников ЦВО в зоне спецоперации, ТАСС, at https://tass.ru/armiya-i-opk/16234817.

41 Leer-3 Electronic Warfare and Reconnaissance Systems Continue Tasks in Special Military Operation Area, Ministry of Defence of the Russian Federation, April 6, 2023, at https://eng.mil.ru/en/news_page/country/more.htm?id=12463043@egNews (Accessed June 7, 2023).

42 M. Dura, Electronic Warfare: Russian Response to the NATO's Advantage?, Defence24.com, May 5, 2017, at https://defence24.com/electronic-warfare-russian-response-to-the-natos-advantage-analysis (Accessed June 7, 2023).

43 M. Tennis, Russia Showcases Military Capabilities, Arms Control Association, November 2017, at https://www.armscontrol.org/act/2017-11/news/russia-showcases-military-capabilities (Accessed June 7, 2023).

44 S. Sukhankin, Vostok-2018: An Alternative Analysis, ICDS, November 28, 2018, at https://icds.ee/en/vostok-2018-an-alternative-analysis/ (Accessed June 7, 2023).

45 Sukhankin, S. (2019, October 24). *What Did Russia's Strategic Military Exercise Tsentr-2019 Reveal? - ICDS*. ICDS. at https://icds.ee/en/what-did-russias-strategic-military-exercise-tsentr-2019-reveal/, ((Accessed May 28, 2023)

46 S. Sukhankin, Kavkaz-2020 Exercises: A Preliminary Analysis, ICDS, October 7, 2020, at https://icds.ee/en/kavkaz-2020-exercises-a-preliminary-analysis/ (Accessed June 7, 2023).

47 M. Kofman, Zapad-2021: What to Expect from Russia's Strategic Military Exercise, War on the Rocks, September 8, 2021, at https://warontherocks.com/2021/09/zapad-2021-what-to-expect-from-russias-strategic-military-exercise/, ((Accessed May 28, 2023)

48 S. Sukhankin, Syrian Experience Provides New Impetus for Russia's UAV Strategy (Part Two), Jamestown, February 20, 2019, at https://jamestown.org/program/syrian-experience-provides-new-impetus-for-russias-uav-strategy-part-two/ (Accessed June 7, 2023).

49 Российские беспилотники ведут круглосуточный контроль в Сирии, заявил Шойгу, РИА Новости, at https://ria.ru/20171027/1507669571.html.

50 Bendett and Edmonds, no. xxiv.

51 S. Sukhankin, no. xlviii.

52 Сокирко, *Беспилотник «Корсар»: в чем главные достоинства уникальной новинки*, Телеканал «Звезда», May 28, 2018, at https://tvzvezda.ru/news/201805281031-psxq.htm

53 L.W. Grau and C.K. Bartles, no. xxviii.

54 R. McDermott and Bukkvall, no. xv.

55 M. Eslami, 'Iran's Drone Supply to Russia and Changing Dynamics of the Ukraine War,' *Journal for Peace and Nuclear Disarmament*, *5*(2), July 3, 2022, pp. 507–18, at https://doi.org/10.1080/25751654.2022.2149077.

56 P. Satam, 'Russia's New UAV With 'Do-It-Yourself' Feature, 3D Printed & Strapped With RPG-7 Aims To Hunt Ukraine's Tanks,' *EurAsian Times*, May 14, 2023, at https://eurasiantimes.com/russias-new-uav-with-do-it-yourself-feature-3d-printed-strapped-with-rpg-7-aims-to-hunt-ukraines-tanks/ (Accessed May 28, 2023)

57 O. Gerasimenko and K. Khinkulova, 'The Russian Soldiers Refusing to Fight in Ukraine,' *BBC News*, June 3, 2022, at https://www.bbc.com/news/world-europe-61607184 (Accessed

June 8, 2023).

58 Bendett and Edmonds, no. xxiv.

59 Samuel Bendett [@sambendett]. (2023, May 21). *A Telegram post from one of the pro-Kremlin channels once again discusses initiative as a way to get what is most needed, including quadcopters and FPV drones…* Twitter. https://twitter.com/sambendett/status/1660277760919588866 (Accessed May 28, 2023)

60 Ibid.

61 R. Perkins and S. Leo, 'Syria's "Dirty Dozen": The OFAB 100-120,' AOAV, September 23, 2013, at https://aoav.org.uk/2013/syrias-dirty-dozen-ofab-100/ (Accessed June 7, 2023).

62 A. Dangwal, 'Russia Says Its Orion UAV Has Fighter-Like Capabilities; Can Shoot Down Drones in Air-To-Air Combat,' *EurAsian Times,* December 22, 2021, at https://eurasiantimes.com/russia-says-its-orion-uav-has-fighter-like-capabilities-can-shoot-down-drones-in-air-to-air-combat-watch/ (Accessed June 23, 2023)

63 M. Chulov and D. Sabbagh, 'Iran Smuggled Drones into Russia Using Boats and State Airline, Sources Reveal,' *The Guardian*, February 12, 2023, at https://www.theguardian.com/world/2023/feb/12/iran-uses-boats-state-airline-smuggle-drones-into-russia (Accessed June 28, 2023)

64 Bendett and Edmonds. no. xxiv.

65 D. Hambling, 'Russia Wants a Pretext for War and These Drones Could Supply It,' *Forbes*, February 18, 2022, at https://www.forbes.com/sites/davidhambling/2022/02/18/russia-wants-a-pretext-for-war-and-these-drones-could-supply-it/ (Accessed June 28, 2023)

66 "Алмаз -Антей" планирует выпускать 2-3 тыс. беспилотников в месяц с июля., ТАСС, at https://tass.ru/ekonomika/17751575.

67 P. Mozur, A. Krolik and K. Bradsher, 'As War in Ukraine Grinds On, China Helps Refill Russian Drone Supplies,' *The New York Times*, March 21, 2023, at https://www.nytimes.com/2023/03/21/business/russia-china-drones-ukraine-war.html (Accessed June 8, 2023).

68 Ibid.

69 D. Hambling, 'Russia Taps Power Of Tech Startups For New Kamikaze Drones, Aiming For 'Cruise Missile For The Price Of A Washing Machine,' *Forbes*, June 8, 2023, at https://www.forbes.com/sites/davidhambling/2023/06/08/russia-taps-power-of-tech-startups-for-new-kamikaze-drones/ (Accessed June 9, 2023)

70 Ibid.

71 P. Iddon, 'Tailor-Made Shaheds: Iranian Drones Are Being Modified To Russian Specifications,' *Forbes*, February 12, 2023, at https://www.forbes.com/sites/pauliddon/2023/02/12/tailor-made-shaheds-iranian-drones-are-being-modified-to-russian-specifications/ (Accessed June 9, 2023)

72 W. Knight, 'Russia's Killer Drone in Ukraine Raises Fears About AI in Warfare,' WIRED, March 17, 2022, at https://www.wired.com/story/ai-drones-russia-ukraine/ (Accessed June 7, 2023).

73 E.T. Desk, 'Ukraine War: Russia Says 45% Of NATO Artillery, Inc M777s, Single-Handedly Destroyed By Lancet-3 Kamikaze Drones,' *EurAsian Times*, April 10, 2023, at https://eurasiantimes.com/ukraine-war-russia-says-45-of-nato-artillery-inc-m777/ (Accessed June 8, 2023).

74 P. Satam, 'Ukraine's "Killer" Sea Drones With Low Visibility, High Maneuverability Pose Permanent Threat to Russian Navy,' *EurAsian Times*, April 25, 2023, at https://eurasiantimes.com/ukraines-killer-sea-drones-with-low-visibility-high/ (Accessed May 28, 2023)

75 S. Bendett and J. Edmonds, 'Russian Military Autonomy in a Ukraine Conflict,' CNA, February 2, 2022, at https://www.cna.org/reports/2022/02/russian-military-autonomy-in-a-ukraine-

conflict (Accessed June 8, 2023).

76 'Russian Peacekeepers Use Uran-6 Mine Clearing Robot in Nagorno-Karabak,' TASS, at https://tass.com/defense/1233857?utm_source=google.com&utm _medium= organic&utm _ campaign=google.com&ut (Accessed May 30, 2023)

77 *Рогозин: первые роботы "Маркер" прибыли в зону СВО*, Радио Sputnik, February 2, 2023, at https://radiosputnik.ria.ru/20230202/marker-1849284193.html.

78 J. Pike, Ukrainian Military Budget, at https://www.globalsecurity.org/military/world/ukraine/budget.htm (Accessed June 7, 2023)

79 G. Tett, 'Ukraine Is Already Looking to a Postwar Digital Future,' *Financial Times*, May 25, 2023, at https://www.ft.com/content/2c73dfbc-a25f-420b-bf2b-41fbb17e5ddb (Accessed June 9, 2023).

80 K.D. Atherton, 'How Drones in Ukraine Help Fuel Propaganda and Shape Perception,' Center for Public Integrity, March 26, 2022, at http://publicintegrity.org/national-security/ukraine-in-crisis/how-drones-in-ukraine-help-fuel-propaganda-and-shape-perception/ (Accessed June 9, 2023).

81 Ukrainian Nationwide Volunteer Center, People's Project.com, November 3, 2022, at https://www.peoplesproject.com/en/ (Accessed June 3, 2023)

82 'The Ragtag Drone Air Force Ukraine Built to Fight Russia,' *Popular Mechanics*, February 20, 2017, at https://www.popularmechanics.com/flight/drones/a25281/ukraine-makeshift-drones/ (Accessed May 28, 2023)

83 *Беспилотный комплекс Фурия. Революция возможностей*, Крылья - Все Об Украинской Авиации, at https://www.wing.com.ua/content/view/16941/38/.

84 'Second Batch of Ukraine-made Spectator Drones to Be Supplied to Army,' UNIAN, January 13, 2016, at https://www.unian.info/economics/1235546-second-batch-of-ukraine-made-spectator-drones-to-be-supplied-to-army.html (Accessed June 9, 2023).

85 P. Stewart, 'U.S.-supplied Drones Disappoint Ukraine at the Front Lines,' *Reuters*, December 22, 2016, at https://www.reuters.com/article/us-usa-ukraine-drones-exclusive-idUSKBN14A26D (Accessed June 9, 2023).

86 Popular Mechanics, no. lxxxii.

87 I. Kossov, 'Ukrainian Drones Threaten Russia But Production Scarcity Is an Issue,' *The Kyiv Independent*, December 9, 2022, at https://kyivindependent.com/ukrainian-drones-threaten-russia-but-production-scarcity-is-an-issue/ (Accessed June 9, 2023).

88 Vasco Cotovio, Tim Lister, Frederik Pleitgen, William Bonnett and Daria Tarasova, ,Inside Ukraine's Secretive Drone Program,' *CNN*, June 3, 2023, at https://www.cnn.com/2023/06/03/europe/ukraine-secretive-drone-program-russia-war-intl/index.html (Accessed June 9, 2023)

89 Ibid.

90 D. Hambling, no. lxix.

91 V. Melkozerova, 'Drone Attack Hits Russia's Engels Airbase for Second Time in a Month,' *POLITICO*, December 26, 2022, at https://www.politico.eu/article/russia-ukraine-war-vladimir-putin-drone-attack-hits-russias-engels-airbase-for-second-time-in-a-month/ (Accessed June 9, 2023).

92 A. Roth and P. Sauer, 'Large-scale Drone Attack Hits Moscow For First Time in Ukraine War,' *The Guardian*, May 30, 2023, at https://www.theguardian.com/world/2023/may/30/moscow-drone-attack-mayor-reports-minor-damage-to-buildings (Accessed June 5, 2023)

93 J. Horton, O. Robinson and D. Palumbo, 'What Do We Know About Drone Attacks in Russia?,' *BBC News*, May 31, 2023, at https://www.bbc.com/news/world-europe-65475333 (Accessed June 9, 2023).

94 D. Hambling, 'Drone Attack On Moscow: Why It May Not Have Been the Ukrainian Government,' *Forbes*, May 30, 2023, at https://www.forbes.com/sites/davidhambling/2023/05/30/ukraine-has-a-growing-arsenal-of-drones-able-to-hit-moscow/ (Accessed June 29, 2023).

95 J. Horton, O. Robinson and D. Palumbo, no. xciii.

96 Ibid.

97 D. Hambling, 'Bargain Basement Bombers: Ukraine's Homemade Drones Hit Russian Forces,' *Forbes*, January 24, 2023, at https://www.forbes.com/sites/davidhambling/2023/01/24/bargain-basement-bombers—ukraines-homemade-drones-hit-russian-forces/ (Accessed May 28, 2023)

98 J. Watling and N. Reynolds, no. xxix.

99 S. Tiwari, 'Russia "Shot Down" Over 100 Bayraktar TB2 Drones in the Ukraine War & Kicked Them Out Of Action – Moscow,' *EurAsian Times*, April 11, 2023, at https://eurasiantimes.com/russia-shot-down-over-100-bayraktar-tb2-drones-in-the-ukraine/ (Accessed June 9, 2023).

100 S. Tavsan, 'Turkish-made Drones Likely Involved in Moskva Sinking,' *Nikkei Asia*, April 18, 2022, at https://asia.nikkei.com/Spotlight/Most-read-in-2022/Turkish-made-drones-likely-involved-in-Moskva-sinking (Accessed June 9, 2023).

101 H. Arhirova, Ukraine Launches 'BRAVE12 Tech Cluster to Boost Military Capability, C4ISRNet, April 26, 2023, at https://www.c4isrnet.com/unmanned/2023/04/26/ukraine-launches-brave1-tech-cluster-to-boost-military-capability/ (Accessed June 7, 2023)

102 Baguette-sized Flying Bombs Are About to Enter Service in Ukraine at https://www.economist.com/science-and-technology/baguette-sized-flying-bombs-are-about-to-enter-service-in-ukraine/21808317 (Accessed June 10, 2023)

103 S. Atlamazoglou, 'The US Has Sent Hundreds of Phoenix Ghosts to Ukraine, But There Have Been Few Glimpses of the "Kamikaze" Drones in Action,' *Business Insider*, September 8, 2022, at https://www.businessinsider.in/international/news/the-us-has-sent-hundreds-of-phoenix-ghosts-to-ukraine-but-there-have-been-few-glimpses-the-kamikaze-drones-in-action/articleshow/94085128.cms (Accessed June 9, 2023).

104 RQ-20 Puma UAVs Arriving in Ukraine with the Latest U.S. Assistance Package: What Are These Drones?,'Technology Org, February 4, 2023, at https://www.technology.org/2023/02/04/rq-20-puma-uavs-arriving-in-ukraine-with-the-latest-u-s-assistance-package-what-are-these-drones/ (Accessed June 8, 2023)

105 T. McMillan, 'Ukrainian Army to Receive "Black Hornet" Military Micro-Drones,' *The Debrief*, August 25, 2022, at https://thedebrief.org/ukrainian-army-to-receive-black-hornet-military-micro-drones/ (Accessed May 28, 2023)

106 'How Elon Musk's Satellites Have Saved Ukraine and Changed Warfare,' *The Economist*, at https://www.economist.com/briefing/2023/01/05/how-elon-musks-satellites-have-saved-ukraine-and-changed-warfare (Accessed June 6, 2023)

107 E. Kramer and P. Schneider, 'What the Ukrainian Armed Forces Need to Do to Win,' War on the Rocks, June 2, 2023, https://warontherocks.com/2023/06/what-the-ukrainian-armed-forces-need-to-do-to-win/ (Accessed June 9, 2023)

108 'How Consumer Drones Are Changing Warfare,' *The Economist*, at https://www.economist.com/the-economist-explains/2022/06/29/how-consumer-drones-are-changing-warfare (Accessed May 28, 2023)

109 'How Racing Drones Are Used as Improvised Missiles in Ukraine,' *The Economist*, at https://www.economist.com/the-economist-explains/2023/03/24/how-racing-drones-are-used-as-improvised-missiles-in-ukraine (Accessed May 28, 2023)

110 S. Sy and T. Aranda, 'Longest Battle of Ukraine War Leaves City of Bakhmut in Ruins,' *PBS*

*NewsHour*, May 22, 2023, at https://www.pbs.org/newshour/show/longest-battle-of-ukraine-war-leaves-city-of-bakhmut-in-ruins (Accessed June 9, 2023).

111 Z. Kallenborn and M. Plichta, ‚Release the Robot Hounds: Providing Unmanned Ground Vehicles to Ukraine,' Centre for Strategic and International Studies, at https://www.csis.org/analysis/release-robot-hounds-providing-unmanned-ground-vehicles-ukraine (Accessed June 10, 2023)

112 Williams, (2023, May) 'Putin's Missile War: Russia's Strike Campaign in Ukraine,' Centre for Strategic and International Studies,' May, 2023, at https://www.csis.org/analysis/putins-missile-war (Accessed June 5, 2023).

113 A. Segal, 'Russia Has Launched "More Than 160 Missiles," US Senior Defense Official Says,' *CNN*, February 24, 2022, at https://edition.cnn.com/europe/live-news/ukraine-russia-news-02-24-22-intl/h_6b42ef21fbc2684426583983fdd94d8e (Accessed June 9, 2023).

114 B. Surk, 'Why Is Russia Attacking Ukraine's Railway System?,' *AP NEWS*, May 4, 2022, at https://apnews.com/article/russia-ukraine-europe-migration-4129b6c37dfff07ec 63ebdbb 05ef 37a2 (Accessed June 9, 2023).

115 P. Polityuk and A. Perun, 'Russia Kills Civilians in First Huge Missile Wave for Weeks,' *Reuters*, March 9, 2023, at https://www.reuters.com/world/europe/pro-ukraine-group-sabotaged-pipelines-intelligence-suggests-nyt-2023-03-08/ (Accessed May 28, 2023)

116 C.A. Research, Dating Newly Produced Russian Missiles Used in Kyiv Attacks,' ArcGIS StoryMaps, April 21, 2023, at https://storymaps.arcgis.com/stories/81bc6b71fdc64361a05a 21020c3d6d5e (Accessed June 8, 2023)

117 L. Jakes and M. Santora, 'How Was Russia Able to Launch Its Biggest Aerial Attack on Ukraine?,' *The Japan Times*, November 19, 2022, at https://www.japantimes.co.jp/news/2022/11/19/world/russia-missile-stockpile-ukraine/ (Accessed May 28, 2023)

118 B. Kot, 'Hong Kong's Technology Lifeline to Russia,' Carnegie Endowment for International Peace, May 17, 2023, at https://carnegieendowment.org/2023/05/17/hong-kong-s-technology-lifeline-to-russia-pub-89775 (Accessed June 9, 2023).

119 'Russia Says It Destroyed Ukrainian Factory Producing Tochka-U Missile Parts,' *National Post*, July 16, 2022, https://nationalpost.com/pmn/news-pmn/russia-says-it-destroyed-ukrainian-factory-producing-tochka-u-missile-parts (Accessed June 9, 2023).

120 M. Mirovalev, 'Russia Using Old Ukrainian Weapons Sent in Goodwill on Front Line,' *Al Jazeera*, January 11, 2023, at https://www.aljazeera.com/news/2023/1/11/kyiv-once-sent-weapons-to-moscow-now-its-used-on-the-frontline (Accessed May 28, 2023)

121 'Russia Enhances Navy's 3M14 Kalibr Missiles Based on Operational Experience in Syria,' *Military Watch Magazine*, September 28, 2019, at https://militarywatchmagazine.com/article/russia-enhances-navy-s-3m14-kalibr-missiles-based-on-operational-experience-in-syria (Accessed June 9, 2023) (Accessed June 8, 2023)

122 M. Dahlgren, 'P-800 Oniks/Yakhont/Bastion (SS-N-26 Strobile),' *Missile Threat*, August 12, 2021, at https://missilethreat.csis.org/missile/ss-n-26/ (Accessed May 28, 2023)

123 Kalibr Cruise Missiles Strike IS Targets in Syria [Video]. YouTube, October 8, 2015, at https://www.youtube.com/watch?v=tMfGtaQZJ2s (Accessed June 9, 2023).

124 Guy Plopsky, 'The Kh-101 and Syria: Maturing the Long-Range Precision-Strike Capabilities of Russia's Aerospace Forces,' Balloons to Drones, October 18, 2017, at https://balloonstodrones.com/2017/10/18/the-kh-101-and-syria-maturing-the-long-range-precision-strike-capabilities-of-russias-aerospace-forces/ (Accessed June 8, 2023)

125 Williams, 'Putin's Missile War: Russia's Strike Campaign in Ukraine,' Centre for Strategic and International Studies, May 2023, at https://www.csis.org/analysis/putins-missile-war (Accessed

June 5, 2023) (Accessed June 7, 2023)

126 'Russia's New Su-57 Fighters to Each Command Four Stealthy Okhotnik Attack Drones,' *Military Watch Magazine*, June 5, 2021, at https://militarywatchmagazine.com/article/russia-s-new-su-57-fighters-to-each-command-for-four-stealthy-okhotnik-attack-drones (Accessed June 9, 2023).

127 A. Petrenko, 'Army-2021: Izdelie 305 Sees the Light of Day,' *Shephard Media,* August 31, 2021, at https://www.shephardmedia.com/news/air-warfare/army-2021-izdelie-305-sees-light-day/ (Accessed June 9, 2023).

128 V.K. Thakur, 'Russian Decoys Trick Ukrainian Air Defense While Kh-101 Stealth Missiles Deliver a Painful Blow,' *EurAsian Times*, May 2, 2023, at https://eurasiantimes.com/russian-decoys-trick-ukrainian-air-defense-while-kh-101-stealth-missiles-deliver-a-painful-blow/ (Accessed June 9, 2023).

129 Williams, no. cxxv.

130 P. Satam, 'Su-24 Fencer, Storm Shadow Missiles & the Western Hack! Expert Says Kyiv "Pre-Programs" ALCMs to Strike Russia,' *EurAsian Times*, May 27, 2023, at https://eurasiantimes.com/ukraine-is-pre-programming-storm-shadow-missiles-before/ (Accessed June 9, 2023).

131 V.K. Thakur, 'Russia Relies Heavily on Kh-29 Missiles For Precision Strikes on Ukraine Amid Claims Of Production Upswing,' *EurAsian Times*, October 25, 2022, at https://eurasiantimes.com/russia-relies-heavily-on-kh-29-for-precision-attacks-amid-war/ (Accessed June 9, 2023).

132 'Russian Kh-31PD Missile Can Win Duel With US Patriot Air Defense System — Tech Firm,' TASS, January 26, 2023, at https://tass.com/defense/1567263 (Accessed June 9, 2023).

133 J. Bronk, N. Reynolds and J. Watling, 'The Russian Air War and Ukrainian Requirements for Air Defence,' Royal United Services Institute, November 7, 2022, at https://rusi.org/explore-our-research/publications/special-resources/russian-air-war-and-ukrainian-requirements-air-defence (Accessed June 9, 2023).

134 T. Martin, B. Defense and M. Marrow, 'Weapons Tracing Shows Russia Firing New Cruise Missiles at Ukraine Just Weeks After Production,' *Breaking Defense*, May 10, 2023, at https://breakingdefense.sites.breakingmedia.com/2023/05/weapons-tracing-shows-russia-firing-new-cruise-missiles-at-ukraine-just-weeks-after-production/ (Accessed June 9, 2023).

135 D. Barrie and J. Dempsey, 'Russia's Missile Inventories: KITCHEN Use Points to Dwindling Stocks,' International Institute for Strategic Studies, July 8, 2022, at https://www.iiss.org/online-analysis/military-balance/2022/07/russias-missile-inventories-kitchen-use-points-to-dwindling-stocks/ (Accessed June 9, 2023).

136 P. Mitchell, 'Hypersonic Hype? Russia's Kinzhal Missiles and the Lessons for Air Defense,' *Modern War Institute*, May 23, 2023, at https://mwi.usma.edu/hypersonic-hype-russias-kinzhal-missiles-and-the-lessons-for-air-defense/ (Accessed May 28, 2023)

137 'Analysis: The Russian State Armament Programme 2018 – 2027,' *Navy Recognition*, December 12, 2019, at https://www.navyrecognition.com/index.php/focus-analysis/naval-technology/7791-analysis-the-russian-state-armament-programme-2018-2027.html (Accessed April 29, 2023)

138 A. Upadhyay, 'Integrated Rocket Force: A Timely Idea,' Manohar Parrikar Institute for Defence Studies and Analyses, January 24, 2023, at https://www.idsa.in/issuebrief/Integrated-Rocket-Force-AUpadhyay-240123 (Accessed June 11, 2023).

139 At Diia in DC Event, U.S. Highlights U.S.-Ukraine Innovation Partnership and Launches First Phase of Countries in Digital Transformation Initiative, U.S. Agency For International

Development at https://www.usaid.gov/news-information/press-releases/may-23-2023-diia-dc-event-us-highlights-us-ukraine-innovation-partnership-and-launches-first-phase-countries-digital-transformation-initiative

140 D. Ignatius, 'How the Algorithm Tipped the Balance in Ukraine,' *Washington Post*, December 19, 2022, at https://www.washingtonpost.com/opinions/2022/12/19/palantir-algorithm-data-ukraine-war/ (Accessed June 2, 2023)

141 T. Kiek, 'Why Ukraine Wants Iris-T SLM and Nasams Air Defence Systems,' *The National*, June 11, 2023, at https://www.thenationalnews.com/world/europe/2022/10/12/explained-the-iris-t-slm-and-nasams-air-defence-systems-ukraine-needs/ (Accessed June 8, 2023)

142 A. Calcara, A. Gilli, M. Gilli and I. Zaccagnini, 'Will the Drone Always Get Through? Offensive Myths and Defensive Realities,' *Security Studies*, 31(5), October 20, 2022, pp. 791–825 at https://doi.org/10.1080/09636412.2022.2153734.

143 P. Dave and J. Dastin, 'Ukraine Has Started Using Clearview AI's Facial Recognition During War,' *Reuters*, March 14, 2022, at https://www.reuters.com/technology/exclusive-ukraine-has-started-using-clearview-ais-facial-recognition-during-war-2022-03-13/ (Accessed April 23, 2023)

144 K. Ray, 'Starlink's Role in Ukraine: Portent of a Space War?,' Manohar Parrikar Institute for Defence Studies and Analyses, March 1, 2023, at https://www.idsa.in/jds/17-1-2023-Starlink-Role-in-Ukraine (Accessed June 11, 2023).

145 'Moca & FICCI Drone Mela at IIT Kanpur (H),' *India Science*, at https://www.indiascience.in/videos/moca-and-ficci-drone-mela-at-iit-kanpur-h-1 (Accessed May 28, 2023)

146 H. Arhirova 'Ukraine Launches 'BRAVE12 Tech Cluster to Boost Military Capability,' C4ISRNet, April 26, 2023, at https://www.c4isrnet.com/unmanned/2023/04/26/ukraine-launches-brave1-tech-cluster-to-boost-military-capability/ (Accessed June 7, 2023)

147 A. Nikolsky, 'Era Technopolis Is the Russian Army's Most Ambitious R&D Project,' *Force*, June 11, 2023, at https://forceindia.net/cover-story/lofty-goals/ (Accessed June 11, 2023).

148 A. Carter and D. Fernando, 'The Rise of the Small Boats,' Daniel K. Inouye Asia-Pacific Center for Security Studies, 2018, at https://apps.dtic.mil/sti/pdfs/AD1056724.pdf (Accessed June 11, 2023).

# 12

# Understanding Cyberwarfare Dynamics: Insights from the Russia–Ukraine Conflict and Implications for Indian Cybersecurity Strategy

*Krutika Patil*

## INTRODUCTION

The initiation of the Gulf War era flagged a revolutionary phase in warfare history with Information and Communication Technologies (ICT) becoming integral in battle tactics and strategies. However, the dilemma that raises is: Are cyber capabilities overshadowing traditional military forces or are they merely complementary? The appeal of cyberwarfare largely stems from its covert nature and lower costs, granting a strategic advantage by fostering power dynamics under the veil of anonymity. The worldwide spread of the internet further inflates this virtual battleground, magnifying the race to acquire and control information.[1]

In the current conflict landscape, it is critical to understand the boundaries, strengths and limitations of cyberwarfare. In this context, the Russia–Ukraine cyber conflict presents itself as a complex yet enlightening case study. Although rooted in a unique historical context and undergoing continual evolution, this conflict underlines the complex relationship between traditional and cyber warfare and offers essential lessons on contemporary conflict dynamics.

A significant shift in this digital warfare environment is the increasing role of non-state actors, including hacktivists, private enterprises and cybercriminals. Operating with considerable autonomy, these entities often navigate the battlefield beyond the grasp of state control.[2] While seemingly minor, this shift raises pertinent questions about the nature of warfare and the concept of state sovereignty.

The inability of states to regulate the actions of these cyber actors highlights an immediate need for an international legal framework for cyberwarfare. Without such a consensus, we risk empowering these actors to reshape the contours of global conflict in ways never seen before. Furthermore, contemporary warfare has increasingly integrated cyberattacks as precursors to traditional combat, with cyberspace evolving from a passive backdrop to an active conflict theatre, exemplified by the Russia–Ukraine situation. This domain offers nations the advantage of discreetly probing or damaging adversaries' systems, often under cover of plausible deniability, thus acting as force multipliers that weaken foes before troop mobilisation. The challenges of attribution in cyber engagements and the use of proxies and false-flag operations can hinder timely international responses. As cyberattacks become central to broader conflict strategies, they blur the lines between digital and physical warfare, necessitating that strategists recognise and adeptly navigate this confluence for holistic defence planning.

Thus, this chapter aims to critically examine the different aspects of the Russia–Ukraine cyber conflict, including the strategies employed, the role of non-state actors, the changing nature of conflict and the implications for the international community.

## UNFURLING THE RUSSIA–UKRAINE CONFLICT

The escalating cyber conflict between Russia and Ukraine, which grabbed international headlines in January 2022,[3] encapsulates the stark reality of warfare in our digital age. The inaugural attack on Ukraine's financial institutions and defence ministry triggered a swift, multi-dimensional response, signalling the onset of a significant cyber conflict.[4] Even though Ukraine initially absolved Russia, later pinning the blame on Belarus, the narrative eventually evolved and Russia was ultimately held responsible.[5] This elicited international condemnation, and NATO's decision to fortify Ukraine's cyber defences highlighted the global ramifications of this conflict.[6]

In tandem, the global hacker collective 'Anonymous' initiated a digital war against Russia, a move reciprocated by the pro-Russian 'Killnet' hacking group, setting the stage for the unpredictable and rampant role of non-state actors in this conflict.[7] Such non-state actors, either pro-Ukrainian or pro-Russian, were reported to reach numbers as high as 300,000 on a given day.[8] An important event was the attack on the German subsidiary of Russian oil company Rosneft, orchestrated by a group of pro-Ukrainian cyber activists pejoratively labelled 'cyber–ISIS' by Russian authorities.[9]

Although the origins of the Ukraine–Russia conflict precede 2014, the 2022 invasion of Ukraine prominently highlights cyberwarfare. Contrary to initial expectations, the onset of the conflict didn't witness significant large-scale disabling cyber operations by Russia against Ukraine's critical infrastructure.[10] Russia instead concentrated its cyber efforts on softer targets within Ukraine's national infrastructure.[11] Despite initiating the largest-ever wave of destructive cyberattacks against Ukraine's networks at the war's inception, Russia's subsequent attacks have fallen short of the initial disruption.

Simultaneously, Ukraine has been drafting legislation to legitimise its hacker brigade as a 'cyber reserve' military group, signifying the emergence of the digital soldier. This move forms part of a broader trend of countries formalising cyberwarfare units and strategies, as seen in the recent digital safety agreement signed between Russia and Belarus.[12]

The cyber conflict hasn't been restricted to cyberspace but has infiltrated traditional media platforms. The successful hacking of radio and television systems by Ukraine, which resulted in fake air raid alerts in Moscow, is a big victory for the country on the information front.[13] Interestingly, social media platforms have also become a battlefield, revealing the increasingly blurred line between tech corporations and state actors.[14]

As the war has evolved, Russia claims to be the most cyberattacked country, and has found itself playing defence, repelling an alleged 50,000 hacker attacks on its infrastructure in 2022 alone.[15] Such revelations underline the vulnerability of even a powerful nation's cybersecurity framework. This evolving Russia–Ukraine conflict has rung warning bells about the imminent threat to critical infrastructure from state and state-sponsored cyber actors.[16]

In conclusion, beyond its immediate geopolitical implications, the still-unfolding Russia–Ukraine cyber conflict is reshaping warfare. In this new era, alliances go beyond traditional military cooperation and extend into the digital realm, and the battlefield spans from physical territories to the vast expanse of cyberspace. This global, multi-dimensional conflict underscores the necessity for innovative strategies to protect the digital integrity of nations and underscores the potent force of cyberwarfare in today's world.

## CYBER TACTICS EMPLOYED BY BOTH SIDES

The ongoing Russia–Ukraine war illuminates the critical nature of cyberwarfare, with both nations exercising innovative tactics in their digital arsenal.[17] Ukraine, despite initial apprehensions, has proven to be a resilient cyber combatant, swiftly transitioning its crucial functions to the cloud and enhancing its software and hardware across key sectors, thereby solidifying cyber resistance as an integral part of its post-reconstruction identity.[18] Simultaneously, Russia's state-sponsored cyber activities extend beyond the Ukrainian borders, with widespread network intrusions and espionage attempts targeting 128 entities across 42 nations, emphasising the necessity of robust cyber defence mechanisms.[19]

Upon the initiation of the conflict, a discernible shift emerged in the cybercrime ecosystem, particularly towards Ukrainian targets. This shift illustrates the evolution in cyberwarfare, with traditional territorial boundaries blurred and replaced by a globally reaching digital battlefield. The Ukraine IT army, a volunteer force, masterfully targeted Russian state-sponsored media outlets and countered disinformation campaigns, effectively highlighting the evolving roles of non-state actors in cyberwarfare.[20] Furthermore, the Russian government has harnessed advanced technologies such as Artificial Intelligence for its offensive operations, highlighting the strategic advantage of cyberspace in hybrid warfare.[21] In this increasingly complex and evolving cyber conflict, it's essential to understand the strategies employed by Ukraine and Russia, the shifting targets and the global implications of their actions. This paper seeks to delve into these facets, comprehensively exploring the cyber tactics in the Russia–Ukraine conflict.

### Russia's Cyber Tactics

Russia, for over 15 years, has been honing its offensive cyber capabilities, building an information operations capability that subverts its adversaries' information spaces and asserting control over its own.[22]. The ongoing war has, however, spotlighted weaknesses in Russian cyber strategies, notably its inability to seamlessly coordinate cyber and conventional military operations and its lack of capabilities required for precisely impairing military units and systems.[23] The war demonstrated that Russia instead zeroed in on softer targets—Ukraine's critical national infrastructure, including power plants, water plants and vital information infrastructure.[24]

A significant aspect of Russia's cyber strategy is the engagement of proxies, allowing Russia to maintain a veneer of plausible deniability.[25] As the conflict escalated into open warfare, the employment of cyber proxies became increasingly conspicuous, pushing the boundaries of credibility. However, the impact of Russian cyber operations diminishes in relevance during larger, longer wars. For sustaining potent cyberattacks during warfare, military forces might need to expand their cyber capabilities, enhance their recovery speed and experiment with patterns of intense, brief cyber onslaughts followed by rest intervals.[26]

Russia's cyber operations have often been accused of causing global disruption, aggressively targeting vast networks and pursuing political objectives through digital intrusions.[27] Yet, during the conflict, Russia's pace of cyber operations demonstrated a level of endurance that could only last a few weeks, signifying either its reluctance or incapacity to execute warfare in the data-informed, accurate approach ideal for cyber manoeuvres. It showed an unexpected level of restraint, seemingly avoiding widespread international impact through cyberattacks.[28]

Russia's alleged 'massive campaign of cyber aggression' signals a more active secret cyber frontline than what is visible to the public eye. Its persistent cyber espionage and exploitation of Ukrainian networks suggest a shift in priorities, with cyber espionage playing a more significant role than disruptive or degradative cyberattacks. However, the tangible, lasting effects of Russian-sponsored cyber operations were limited and not strategically significant, suggesting potential challenges in planning and implementation.[29]

The synchronization of cyber and kinetic operations was crucial to Russia's cyber strategy. Cyber threat groups consistently aligned with their military's objectives, often overlapping cyber and kinetic military operations geographically and targeting the same sectors. This strategic alignment contributed to the degradation of targeted organisations, disrupting citizens' access to reliable information and essential services and shaking confidence in the country's leadership. The potential expansion of destructive cyberattacks outside of Ukraine, in response to increased international support for Ukraine, reflects the evolving nature of this cyberwarfare.[30]

Without assessing the specific systems aimed at and the implementation of 'cyber fires'—cyber operations designed to confuse, annihilate or tamper with data or systems—a holistic study of Russia's cyber strategy in Ukraine would remain incomplete. A case study of a cyberattack on a local government agency in Dnipro demonstrated the tactical, operational and strategic impacts of cyber-kinetic strikes, underscoring the ongoing challenge of coordinating cyber and kinetic operations.[31] The evolving Russian cyberwarfare scenario underscored the need for comprehensive intelligence assessments to inform strategic planning, revealing the complexities of waging war in the digital age.

## Ukraine's Cyber Tactics

Ukraine has embarked on a wide array of cyber operations aimed at Russian targets to neutralise Russian cyber undertakings, obstruct Russian military manoeuvres on Ukrainian soil and impede activities supporting the war in Russia. Given Russia's cybersecurity weak spots, these manoeuvres are presumed to have created a certain level of disruption. It's also reported that Ukraine's state allies, predominantly the United States (US) and United Kingdom (UK), have executed successful intelligence operations against Russia both prior to and amid the conflict.[32]

Ukraine's efforts are supported by its 'IT Army', a hacktivist collective conducting destructive attacks on Russian civilian 'critical infrastructure'. The role of technological platforms in the ongoing conflict is significant. Companies providing telecommunication and data services, among others, have emerged as key players, both on the information scene and the cyber battleground, with substantial power over the cyber confrontation.[33]

Digital services in Ukraine have functioned as a lifeline throughout the invasion. Apps such as 'Diia' and 'eVorog' have enabled millions of displaced people to cross borders with digital IDs, receive government updates and report Russian troop movements. The cyber support received from Western tech companies has been instrumental for Ukraine to sustain its network and continue offering services.[34]

Ukraine's cyber defence capabilities and endurance have been bolstered by a robust digital infrastructure, long-term investments in cybersecurity and significant cyber backing from international bodies. The role of commercial entities has shifted from mere vendors to vital agents of defence and foreign policies. This poses different priorities among Western allies and raises questions about the scalability of such an ad hoc coalition, especially against potential Chinese threats to Taiwan.[35]

Ukraine's cyber capabilities, despite benefiting from Western assistance, have struggled due to various political and economic challenges, including governmental infighting and rampant corruption. The maintenance of communications and web services has been successful thus far, albeit with uncertain contribution from Ukrainian–Western cooperation.[36]

Ukrainian military equipment, primarily consisting of Soviet-era artefacts, seemed immune to direct cyber disruptions. As Ukraine procured more modern foreign-provided weapons and equipment, no credible claims of successful cyberattacks on Ukrainian military systems have been put forward. Ukrainians have also leveraged foreign messaging apps for communication and information sharing, with these platforms doubling up as tools for propaganda by Russia. The 'constant synergy' between the Ukrainian government, US Cyber Command and the NSA in securing Ukrainian networks signifies the strong defensive and counter-cyber operations in place, although the details remain undisclosed.[37]

## ASCENDANCY OF NON-STATE ENTITIES IN THE CYBER DOMAIN

The recent global surge in cyber activities has highlighted the ascent of non-state entities in the cyber domain. Their increased involvement has brought about changes to the landscape of cyberwarfare and has led to the evolution of novel strategies in this arena. Several themes emerge from the actions of these entities during recent international conflicts, particularly the Russian–Ukrainian war.

One of the pivotal elements has been the increased prominence of cybercrime groups. These groups, previously motivated by financial gain, have now started to align themselves with state interests, often engaging in cyber operations aimed at specific political or strategic targets. The example of the CONTI group, a Russian-based cybercrime group, stands out.[38] It shifted its operations to act against state not supporting Russia's interests, showcasing a significant transformation in the cybercrime ecosystem.

At the same time, there has been an explosive growth in volunteer affiliates and hacktivism. The Ukrainian IT army, for instance, composed of around 215,000 volunteers, played a significant role in disrupting Russian state-sponsored media outlets.[39] These non-state actors blurred the conventional boundaries of warfare, broadening the conflict beyond physical territory into global cyberspace. Furthermore, the influence of hacktivism, driven by social media, brought a new dimension to the war, engaging hundreds of thousands of individuals globally.

The cyberwarfare landscape has also been marked by a multitude of hybrid threats. These pose a risk to not just the digital assets, but to the economy, politics and critical infrastructure as well.[40] The use of ransomware attacks by groups such as CONTI to disrupt key sectors in Ukraine is a potent illustration of these threats.[41] The involvement of such non-state actors introduces an element of unpredictability and escalation potential, as seen by the extensive cyber vigilantism witnessed during the Russia-Ukraine War.

Notably, the involvement of commercial technology and cybersecurity companies has emerged as another major theme. Companies such as Amazon, Cloudflare, Google and Microsoft played crucial roles in defending Ukrainian cyberspace.[42] These entities have demonstrated their capacity to provide automated protection for massive networks, migrate government data to distributed cloud servers and offer real-time threat intelligence. Their involvement has highlighted the benefits of collaboration between public and private sectors, potentially shaping future strategies for international alliances in cyber defence.

However, the rise of non-state actors in the cyber domain is not without concern. The blurring lines between state and non-state actors pose significant challenges regarding attribution and legal responsibility.[43] As noted during conflict, cyber operations often involved hackers with murky relations to states, masking state involvement and thereby allowing plausible deniability.

This accentuates the urgent need for a global legal structure to control cyber operations. Cyber activities seen during the Russia–Ukraine conflict underlined the current lack of any enforceable international laws governing cyberspace.[44] The absence of regulation allows violations of sovereignty in cyberspace. Consequently, digital sanctions have surfaced as a new kind of global punitive measure, capable of immobilising services and significantly undermining military access.

The ascendancy of non-state entities in the cyber domain is reshaping the dynamics of cyberwarfare. From cybercrime groups aligning with state interests, the surge in volunteer affiliates and hacktivism, to the collaborative involvement of commercial technology companies, non-state actors are playing increasingly significant roles. While this phenomenon brings about novel strategies and alliances, it also raises urgent legal and regulatory issues that must be addressed internationally. As such, states, academics and civil society must clarify and enforce legal rules applicable to high-end and grey-zone-like cyber operations.

## WHAT HAS CHANGED? COMPARISON WITH PREVIOUS CONFLICTS AND TECHNOLOGICAL PARADIGM SHIFT

The landscape of modern warfare has witnessed a seismic shift over the past few decades, moving from traditional battlegrounds to the intricate corridors of cyberspace. Various cyberattacks, espionage operations and strategic disinformation campaigns have punctuated this shift. With the recent conflict between Russia and Ukraine throwing light on the extensive use of cyber weapons, there arises a need to analyse the historical precedent. Specifically, Estonia and Georgia are classic examples that elucidate Russia's prolonged engagement in cyberwarfare.

In 2007, Estonia experienced one of the first instances of what can be defined as state-sponsored cyberwarfare.[45] Following a political dispute with Russia over the relocation of a Soviet-era statue in Tallinn, Estonia suffered extensive Distributed Denial of Service (DDoS) attacks. These attacks targeted Estonian banks, ministries, newspapers and broadcasters, virtually crippling the country's digital infrastructure. Given the immediacy of the attacks following the statue's relocation, fingers were inevitably pointed at Russia. While concrete attribution was challenging, the incident echoed a potential prototype for state-backed cyberattacks.

Similarly, during the Russo–Georgia War in 2008, Georgia experienced debilitating cyberattacks that disrupted several websites, including government, banks and media outlets.[46] Again, suspicions regarding Russian involvement were strong. The synchronicity between the cyber onslaught and ground offensive led many to believe that this was a coordinated strategy by Russia, blending traditional military operations with cyber tactics. These incidents can be seen as precursors to the strategies Russia would later employ in its confrontation with Ukraine.

The omission of these crucial events in discussions related to Russia's historical cyber engagements represents a significant gap in understanding the full spectrum of the nation's cyber strategies. It's not merely about acknowledging these events but understanding their relevance in shaping Russia's cyber doctrine.

Drawing parallels between these historical events and the recent Russia–Ukraine conflict offers illuminating insights. Over the years, Russia has finetuned its approach to cyberwarfare, evolving from blatant DDoS attacks to more sophisticated strategies encompassing false-flag operations, proxies and misinformation campaigns. The utilisation of non-state actors, hacktivists and cybercriminals has allowed for a degree of deniability, further complicating attribution efforts. However, this modus operandi is not entirely novel, traces of it can be discerned in the events of Estonia and Georgia.

The Russia–Ukraine cyber conflict underscored the significance of preparation and foresight in executing digital warfare strategies. The use of advanced cyber weapons, targeting critical infrastructure and the propagation of disinformation suggest a high degree of premeditation and planning. This wasn't a spur-of-the-moment campaign but a culmination of years of experience and a deep understanding of cyberwarfare's mechanics.

Russia's prolonged engagement in cyber activities has served dual purposes. Firstly, these operations have been employed as force multipliers, augmenting conventional military efforts by sowing discord, disrupting communications and demoralising the adversary. Secondly, they have acted as tools of geopolitical influence, enabling Russia to exert power, destabilise regions and shape narratives without resorting to overt military action.

The incidents involving Estonia and Georgia offer a glimpse into Russia's cyber playbook. Analysing these events can help comprehend Russia's motivations and tactics during the Ukraine conflict. For instance, while the Estonia and Georgia cyberattacks were primarily disruptive, the operations against Ukraine were more expansive, involving espionage, data manipulation and sabotage. This suggests a progression in capabilities and objectives. Furthermore, the prior attacks served as testing grounds. The cyberattacks on Estonia and Georgia provided Russia with a sandbox environment to test tools, gauge international reactions and study the effectiveness of their strategies. This iterative process has undeniably contributed to refining their tactics in subsequent engagements.

The transformation of warfare from conventional battle spaces to the digital domain represents a paradigm shift in how conflicts are conducted in the 21st century. One salient feature of this shift is the increased prevalence of Cyber Threat Intelligence (CTI). However, due to the abundance and variability of data, research highlighted the limitations of collecting consequential CTI through social media (SOCMINT). Strategies such as the careful pre-selection of influential users posting sincere cybersecurity content and employing graph and network theory for analysis can help refine the methodologies for collecting CTI.[47]

Cyberspace has become an arena for warfare where nations, regardless of their physical military strength, can carry out operations. The use of cybercrime groups targeting Ukraine and its supporters represents a departure from their traditional targeting methodologies, indicating a change in the cybercrime ecosystem. Besides, creating a Ukrainian IT army of volunteer affiliates is a novel example of the population mobilisation for cyberwarfare, showing that this conflict is borderless and has a global dimension.

The integration of advanced technologies such as AI and automation in Russia's offensive operations, along with its attempt to isolate its internet from the global one, marks a strategic shift in leveraging cyberspace for hybrid warfare. A shift in targets to specifically target Ukraine indicates a modification of strategies in response to the changing geopolitical scenario.[48]

The transition from physical to informational domains reflects the evolving objectives of modern competitors, with information acquisition and control becoming critical, especially in the era of global internet connectivity. Despite theories suggesting that cyber operations directly complement or substitute conventional warfare, these operations are used independently due to coordination difficulties and their disparate political purposes. The idea of 'indirect substitution' proposes that increased internet access can lead to more cyber conflicts and fewer conventional conflicts.[49]

The post-9/11 period has seen Western intelligence agencies increasingly adopt sharing, integrated Intelligence, Surveillance, and Reconnaissance and Open Source Intelligence collection and analysis, contrasting Russia's emphasis on Committee for State Security (KGB) legacy tasks. Developments in great-power offensive cyber campaigns have been significant, with noteworthy advancements in Russian information warfare tactics such as reflexive control and offensive cyber operations.[50]

The role of electronic warfare in the conflict and the use of proxies, such as the 'IT Army of Ukraine', indicate the diversification of warfare tactics. The influence of technological platforms on cyberwarfare has been transformative, with their policies significantly impacting the cyber-conflict scenario.

The likelihood of offensive cyber operations persisting after the cessation of kinetic operations and the prominence of false-flag operations and extensive employment of proxies such as state-sponsored hacktivists, technology companies, and cybercriminals all demonstrate the evolving nature of cyber warfare. This transformation necessitates the effective coordination and synchronisation of kinetic and cyber operations, which, despite being challenging, is crucial for achieving desired effects.

The use of early warning and situational awareness tools powered by AI and data fusion technologies has significantly improved the understanding and anticipation of conflict situations. In the Ukraine conflict, Ukraine and its Western allies outperformed Russia in the competition over cyber defence, early warning and battlefield situational awareness.[51] These developments illustrate the continuing evolution of warfare tactics and the rising importance of cyberspace in modern conflicts.

## IMPLICATIONS FOR INDIA: DECIPHERING LESSONS FROM THE RUSSIA–UKRAINE CYBER CONFLICT

The Russia–Ukraine conflict serves as an exemplar of modern warfare's intertwining complexities, where cyberwarfare transitions from the sidelines to the forefront. As India charts its path in an increasingly digitised world, the conflict's implications, particularly its cyber dimension, warrant rigorous examination tailored to India's strategic environment.

India's digital horizon is ever-expanding, and with it comes a heightened vulnerability to cyber threats. The Russian–Ukrainian conflict starkly highlighted this vulnerability, bringing to the fore several key considerations for India's cybersecurity strategy. The conflict has underscored the urgency for India to bolster its cybersecurity infrastructure. Considering the alarming 18 per cent spike in weekly cyberattacks on Indian organisations during Q1 2023, it's paramount to strengthen defences across both public and private sectors.[52] The framework established by CERT-In under the IT Act exemplifies a move in the right direction, but the journey is arduous and demands consistent commitment.[53] Prioritising the detection and neutralisation of advanced cyberattacks from various actors is indispensable for India's cybersecurity apparatus.

The Ukraine conflict has brought to light the instrumental role that private tech enterprises can play in bolstering national cybersecurity. India, poised to witness its cybersecurity market burgeon past the $15 billion mark by 2023, stands to benefit immensely by fostering robust public–private collaborations.[54] Such symbiotic associations can offer enhanced threat intelligence, bolstering defensive capabilities and ensuring comprehensive protection of India's burgeoning digital assets.

However, cyber resilience isn't just about grand alliances or vast infrastructure, it's equally about the individual. The emergent phenomenon of hacktivism delineates the potential power of individual actors in the digital arena. With India's IT sector contributing a formidable 7.4 per cent to the national GDP in 2022, there lies a latent force waiting to be harnessed.[55] Through initiatives that promote cyber literacy and security awareness, India can catalyse a digital transformation, pivoting from vulnerability to resilience.

Moreover, the multifaceted nature of cyber threats necessitates a legal scaffolding robust enough to deter potential adversaries while providing avenues for redressal. The Russia–Ukraine conflict accentuates the need for comprehensive cyber laws. For a nation such as India, with its vast digital landscape, legal frameworks that elucidate the responsibilities and punitive measures for all digital stakeholders, be they state or non-state entities, become indispensable.[56]

Another dimension that the Russia–Ukraine conflict has brought to prominence is the arena of international cooperation in cyberspace. India, given its stature, needs to be more than just a spectator. Engaging proactively in global dialogues, particularly with entities such as the UN, provides an avenue for India to advocate its perspective and influence the evolving paradigms of cyber governance.[57]

The spectre of digital sanctions, as observed in the Russian scenario, necessitates foresight and preparedness on India's part. Aligning with the vision of self-reliance, or Atmanirbhar Bharat, India must prioritise domestic technological advancements. This ethos is consistent with the perspective of former National Cyber Security Coordinator, Lt Gen (Dr) Rajesh Pant, emphasising the indispensable nature of indigenous cybersecurity products in the larger tapestry of national security.[58]

Furthermore, in an era punctuated by cyber conflicts, the sanctity of India's defence sector's digital infrastructure emerges as a non-negotiable. This entails not only the integration of indigenous cybersecurity technologies but also an evolution in strategic doctrine. Recognising the dual nature of cyber tools, India must seamlessly integrate defensive postures with potential offensive cyber strategies to deter adversaries effectively.[59]Acknowledging the escalating complexity of cyber threats, India must substantially invest in cyber intelligence capabilities, focusing on developing advanced early warning systems to assure timely alerts and swift response to potential threats. Despite the slow government action, the country's vibrant startup culture and expansive talent pool have enabled the private sector to move faster in advancing national cybersecurity. Nonetheless, India must not overlook its reliance on international partners for broader cyber-intelligence insights.[60]

To effectively counter accelerating cyber threats, India must fuel research and development in cybersecurity. Strategic collaborations between academic institutions, such as the Indian Institute of Technology and the Indian Statistical Institute, industries and the government should be incentivised.[61] This interdisciplinary approach, focusing on areas such as coding security, hardware safety and security for automated systems, could significantly bolster our digital world's security. At its core, cybersecurity isn't just about sophisticated tools or intricate algorithms, it's about a collective mindset. With India being the recipient of a staggering 59 per cent of global cyberattacks in Q4 2022, there's an unmissable clarion call for a nationwide cultural shift.[62] This revolves around not just enhanced cybersecurity education but also widespread campaigns that underscore the essence of cyber hygiene.

The international cyber landscape is no longer just about data breaches or monetary theft. It's about power, influence and geopolitics. The Russia–Ukraine conflict showcased this paradigm shift vividly. As cyberattacks increasingly become precursors to or integral components of traditional warfare, nations must evolve their strategies accordingly. For India two critical dimensions emerge. First, the challenge posed by non-state actors. The blurred lines between hacktivists, state-sponsored cyber mercenaries and independent rogue entities add layers of complexity. Given India's historical tensions with neighbours such as China and Pakistan, the nation must remain vigilant against asymmetric cyber threats that such entities could deploy. The plausible deniability these actors offer to states can obfuscate accountability, making pre-emptive defence and rapid response even more critical. Second, there's the dimension of infrastructure resilience. As India continues its ambitious digital journey, its critical infrastructure becomes an attractive target. Power grids, communication networks and even satellite systems present potential vulnerabilities. Leveraging lessons from the Ukraine conflict, India must prioritise securing these assets, anticipating potential choke points and ensuring redundancy.

In the face of escalating geopolitical tensions, India must be acutely aware of the role cyberspace plays in modern conflict, particularly considering Pakistan and China. The Russia–Ukraine conflict underlined the integration of cyberattacks as precursors to traditional warfare. If India were to experience cyber offensives from Pakistan and China just before an overt war, an immediate and calibrated response would be paramount. This response should prioritise securing and restoring compromised critical infrastructure, especially power grids, communication networks and satellite systems. At the same time, India must discern the lines of attribution, cognisant of the fact that blurred boundaries between state actors, hacktivists and cyber mercenaries make pinpointing responsibility complex. Rapid engagement with international allies for collective diplomatic and strategic counteraction can help dilute the aggressors' advantages. Additionally, India must employ its own cyber capabilities to gather intelligence, anticipate further attacks and potentially counteract. It's essential for India not just to defend but also to showcase its resilience and readiness, converting this digital confrontation into an opportunity to demonstrate its robust cyber capabilities and strategic agility in the face of multi-pronged threats.

To encapsulate, as the shadows of the Russia–Ukraine cyber conflict linger, India finds itself at a critical juncture. The lessons from this confrontation offer invaluable insights. However, their effective translation into actionable strategies requires an astute understanding of India's unique geopolitical, technological and socio-cultural dynamics. An informed, strategic approach in this realm can transform challenges into opportunities, enabling India to navigate the digital future with resilience and vision. In sum, as global cyber dynamics evolve, so must India's strategies. The nation stands at a crossroads, with the potential to either emerge as a global cyber powerhouse or become a victim of its digital vulnerabilities.

## CONCLUSION

An in-depth dissection of the cyber warfare in the Russia–Ukraine conflict reveals a labyrinth of implications, tactics and lessons that stretch beyond the confines of conventional warfare. The prevalent use of misinformation campaigns and intermediaries throughout the confrontation showcases the exploitation of the digital domain to mask culpability and incite conflict. Indeed, the cessation of physical warfare does not equate to an end of hostilities in the digital sphere. By taking into account Russia's historical perspective on information warfare, we can circumvent common pitfalls such as false mirror imaging and skewed expectations that often occur in discussions around offensive cyber operations.

The conflict also magnified the vital role that multinational technology and cybersecurity corporations play in cyber defence. It's clear that the geopolitics of the world significantly influences cyberspace dynamics, with shared values and government involvement acting as the main drivers for a coordinated defence approach. In terms of legal aspects, the war pointed out the urgent need to clarify and enforce rules surrounding cyber operations. Whether it's defining what constitutes an 'attack' in the context of international humanitarian law or attributing responsibility to non-state actors, there's an explicit demand for robust legal frameworks to be in place. This remains true even in situations where violations of international law occur.

The Russia–Ukraine conflict saw a significant component of cyberwarfare. Despite the absence of anticipated destructive cyber operations at the onset of the war, Russia's cyber strategies soon reverted to their familiar pre-conflict form.

This exposed limitations in their arsenal, revealing weaknesses in coordination, security and targeted capabilities. Within the public sectors, the deployment of digital tools, especially in the realm of national security, is imperative. The conflict emphasised the importance of transparency, accessibility to information and efficient feedback mechanisms during times of conflict. A noticeable power dynamic shift is occurring at societal and global levels, which illustrates the increasing politicisation of the cyber environment. As the level of threat transitions from individual to national, strengthening cyber defences becomes paramount, especially against state and state-sponsored actors.

Insights from large corporations, such as Microsoft, demonstrated the convergence of military operations and cyber intrusions. These revelations underscored the necessity for comprehensive security measures and layered defences. The Russia–Ukraine conflict serves as a prime example of the powerful influence online public sentiment can wield over the course of warfare. The advent of social cognitive warfare, facilitated by cyberspace, is emerging as a potent force that deserves further investigation. Yet, the challenge of attributing responsibility for cyberattacks persists. The blurred lines between state-sponsored and non-state actions, coupled with the need for effective global cooperation and attribution strategies, underline the intricate nature of modern cyberwarfare. In conclusion, the Russia–Ukraine conflict underscores the importance of reassessing norms in cyberspace, enhancing global cooperation and understanding the motivations behind cyber operations. The insights gleaned from this cyber conflict will undoubtedly shape future strategies in the continually evolving arena of cyberwarfare.

## NOTES

1 N. Kostyuk and E. Gartzke, 'Why Cyber Dogs Have Yet to Bark Loudly in Russia's Invasion of Ukraine,' *Texas National Security Review*, 2022.

2 Jon Bateman, J., Gavin Wilde and Nick Beecroft, 'What the Russian Invasion Reveals About the Future of Cyber Warfare,' 2022, at: https://carnegieendowment.org/2022/12/19/what-russian-invasion-reveals-about-future-of-cyber-warfare-pub-88667 (Accessed on April 14, 2023)

3 Jonny Tickle, 'Ukraine Hit by Huge Cyberattack,' *RT News*, January 14, 2022, at https://www.rt.com/russia/546026-ukrainian-government-agencies-massive-cyberattack/ (Accessed April 14, 2023).

4 'Ukraine Reports Massive Cyberattack,' *RT News*, February 15, 2022, at https://www.rt.com/russia/549486-ukraine-cyber-attack-banks-government/ (Accessed April 14, 2023).

5 'US Blames Russia for Cyberattacks on Ukrainian Banks,' *RT News*, February 18, 2022, at https://www.rt.com/russia/549928-us-blames-russia-ukraine-hacks/ (Accessed April 14, 2023).

6 'NATO Touts Ukraine Deal After Massive Cyberattack,' *RT News*, January 14, 2022, at https://www.rt.com/russia/546075-nato-ukraine-deal-cyberattack/ (Accessed April 14, 2023).

7 Ariel Levite, 'Integrating Cyber Into Warfighting: Some Early Takeaways From the Ukraine Conflict,' Carnegie Endowment for International Peace, 2023, at: https://carnegieendowment.org/2023/04/18/integrating-cyber-into-warfighting-some-early-takeaways-from-ukraine-conflict-pub-89544 (Accessed on May 30, 2023)

8 Marcus Willett, 'The Cyber Dimension of the Russia–Ukraine War,' *Survival*, 64(5), pp. 7–26, 2022, at: https://doi.org/10.1080/00396338.2022.2126193 (Accessed on May 30, 2023)

9 'Ukrainian 'Cyber ISIS' Will Backfire on West – Russia,' *RT News*, March 23, 2022, at https://www.rt.com/russia/552541-ukraine-it-army-threat/ (Accessed April 14, 2023).

10 K. Eichensehr, 'Ukraine, Cyberattacks, and the Lessons for International Law,' *AJIL Unbound*, 2022, at https://doi.org/10.1017/aju.2022.20 (Accessed on May 30, 2023)

11 Jon Bateman, J., Gavin Wilde and Nick Beecroft, no. 2.

12 'Ukraine Wants to Legalise Controversial Hacker Brigade,' *RT News*, March 15, 2023, at https://www.rt.com/russia/573039-ukraine-volunteer-hacker/ (Accessed April 14, 2023).

13 'Air Raid Alert Broadcast in Moscow by Hackers – Officials', *RT News*, March 9, 2023, at https://www.rt.com/russia/572700-moscow-fake-air-alert/ (Accessed April 14, 2023).

14 M. Albakjaji, 'The Impact of Digital Technology on International Relations: The Case of the War between Russia and Ukraine,' *Access to Justice in Eastern Europe*, 2023, at: https://doi.org/10.33327/ajee-18-6.2-a000203 (Accessed on May 30, 2023).

15 'NATO State 'Modeling Cyber Strikes' on Russian Infrastructure – Moscow,' *RT News*, January 28, 2023, at https://www.rt.com/russia/570605-uk-training-hack-russia/ (Accessed April 14, 2023).

16 Henry Durojaye and Oluwaukola Raji, 'Impact of State and State Sponsored Actors on the Cyber Environment and the Future of Critical Infrastructure,' *arXiv.org*, 2022, at https://doi.org/10.48550/arxiv.2212.08036 (Accessed April 14, 2023)

17 Brad Smith, 'Defending Ukraine: Early Lessons from the Cyber War,' Microsoft, 2022, at: https://query.prod.cms.rt.microsoft.com/cms/api/am/binary/RE50KOK (Accessed April 14, 2023).

18 Nelson, A. and Wilde, G. 'How Cyber Support to Ukraine Can Build Its Democratic Future,' *CyberScoop*, April 18, 2023, at https://cyberscoop.com/ukraine-cyber-aid-russia-war/ (Accessed May 30, 2023).

19 Brad Smith, no. 17.

20 Claudia–Alecsandra Gabrian, 'How The Russia–Ukraine War May Change the Cybercrime Ecosystem,' *Bulletin of 'Carol I' National Defence University*, 2023, at https://doi.org/10.53477/2284-9378-22-92 (Accessed June 15, 2023)

21 Ibid.

22 Marcus Willett, no. 8.; Ariel Levite, no. 7.

23 Marcus Willett, no. 8.

24 Ariel Levite, no. 7.

25 Ibid.

26 Jon Bateman, J., Gavin Wilde and Nick Beecroft, no. 2.

27 Ibid.

28 Ibid.

29 N. Kostyuk and E. Gartzke, no.1.

30 Digital Security Unit, 'An Overview of Russia's Cyberattack Activity in Ukraine,' Microsoft, 2022, at https://query.prod.cms.rt.microsoft.com/cms/api/am/binary/RE4Vwwd (Accessed April 14, 2023).

31 Jon Bateman, 'Russia's Wartime Cyber Operations in Ukraine: Military Impacts, Influences,

and Implications,' 2022, Carnegie Endowment for International Peace, at https://carnegieendowment.org/2022/12/16/russia-s-wartime-cyber-operations-in-ukraine-military-impacts-influences-and-implications-pub-88657 (Accessed April 14, 2023)

32 Marcus Willett, no. 8.

33 Ariel Levite, no. 7.

34 Nelson, A. and Wilde, G., no. 18.

35 Jon Bateman, J., Gavin Wilde and Nick Beecroft, no. 2.

36 N. Kostyuk and E. Gartzke, no.1.

37 Jon Bateman, no. 31.

38 Claudia–Alecsandra Gabrian, no. 20.

39 Ibid.

40 Ibid.

41 Marcus Willett, no. 8.

42 Nick Beecroft, 'Evaluating the International Support to Ukrainian Cyber Defense,' Carnegie Endowment for International Peace, 2022, at https://carnegieendowment.org/2022/11/03/evaluating-international-support-to-ukrainian-cyber-defense-pub-88322 (Accessed April 14, 2023).

43 K. Eichensehr, no. 10.

44 M. Albakjaji, no. 14.

45 Damien McGuinness, 'How a Cyberattack Transformed Estonia,' *BBC News*, April 27, 2017, at https://www.bbc.com/news/39655415 (Accessed August 14, 2023).

46 Sarah White. 'Understanding Cyberwarfare: Lessons from the Russia Georgia War,' Modern War Institute, March 20, 2018, at https://mwi.westpoint.edu/understanding-cyberwarfare-lessons-russia-georgia-war/ (Accessed August 14, 2018).

47 Bipun Thapa, 'Applying Socmint to Extract Cyber Threat Intelligence from the Russia–Ukraine Conflict,' *IADIS International Journal*, 2023, at: https://doi.org/10.33965/ijwi_202220204 (Accessed June 15, 2023).

48 Claudia–Alecsandra Gabrian, no. 20.

49 N. Kostyuk and E. Gartzke, no.1.

50 Gavin Wilde, 'Cyber Operations in Ukraine: Russia's Unmet Expectations,' Carnegie Endowment for International Peace, 2022, at: https://carnegieendowment.org/2022/12/12/cyber-operations-in-ukraine-russia-s-unmet-expectations-pub-88607 (Accessed April 14, 2023).

51 Ariel Levite, no. 7.

52 Pihu Yadav, 'India Sees 18% Increase in Weekly Cyberattacks in Q1 2023: Report,' *CNBC TV18*, May 5, 2023, at India sees 18% increase in weekly cyber attacks in Q1 2023: Report (cnbctv18.com) (Accessed July 1, 2023).

53 Anirudh Suri, 'Public-private Cooperation: A Key Pillar in Creating a Cyber-secure India,' *Hindustan Times*, June 2, 2023, at https://www.hindustantimes.com/opinion/publicprivate-cooperation-a-key-pillar-in-creating-a-cyber-secure-india-101654166844685.html (Accessed July 1, 2023).

54 Tanushree Basuroy, 'Value of Cyber Security Market in India from 2018 to 2021, With Estimates Until 2023,' *Statista*, December 2021, at https://www.statista.com/statistics/1197074/india-cyber-security-market-size/ (Accessed July 1, 2023).

55 Shangliao Sun, 'IT Industry in India - Statistics & Facts,' *Statista*, August 24, 2022, at IT industry in India - statistics & facts | Statista (Accessed July 1, 2023).

56 Shiv Raman and Nidhi Sharma, 'Cyber Terrorism in India: A Physical Reality Orvirtual Myth,' Indian *J Law Hum Behav*,5(2), 2019, pp. 133–140, at https://journals.indexcopernicus.com/

api/file/viewByFileId/783266.pdf (Accessed April 14, 2023).

57 Nikhil Sud, 'For Cybersecurity, India Must Look to International Law', *Forbes India*, September 28, 2021, at https://www.forbesindia.com/blog/legalese/for-cybersecurity-india-must-look-to-international-law/ (Accessed July 1, 2022).

58 'Cybersecurity Sector Requires Indigenization, Industry Should Invest To Make It Atmanirbhar – National Cyber Security Coordinator,', *India Education Diary*, October 21, 2020, at https://indiaeducationdiary.in/cybersecurity-sector-requires-indigenization-industry-should-invest-to-make-it-atmanirbhar-national-cyber-security-coordinator/ (Accessed July 1, 2023).

59 Kartik Bommakanti, 'India and Cyberspace: Balance between Offence and Defence,', Observer Research Foundation, June 18, 2021, at https://www.orfonline.org/expert-speak/india-and-cyberspace-balance-between-offence-and-defence/ (Accessed July 1, 2023).

60 'Cyber Power - Tier Three', The International Institute for Strategic Studies, June 28, 2021, at https://www.iiss.org/research-paper/2021/06/cyber-power—tier-three/ (Accessed July 1, 2023).

61 Debdeep Mukhopadhyay, 'Cybersecurity in India,' *Communications of the ACM*, 65(11), November 2022, pp. 98-–102, 10.1145/3554910 (Accessed April 14, 2023).

62 Anupriya Chatterjee, 'India's Had Its Worst Year of Cyberattacks, But 2023 Will See Govt & Firms Ramp Up Defences,' *The Print*, December 30, 2022, at https://theprint.in/india/indias-had-its-worst-year-of-cyberattacks-but-2023-will-see-govt-firms-ramp-up-defences/1286441/ (Accessed July 1, 2023).

# 13

# War of Narratives: Weaponisation of Information

*Rajorshi Roy*

## INTRODUCTION

The war in Ukraine continues to rage as one of modern era's most prolonged conflicts. With differences between the adversaries seemingly irreconcilable, the proverbial light at the end of tunnel appears distant. In fact, it is widely anticipated that the situation could turn worse[1] before a solution to this festering confrontation is found.[2]

However, as the saying goes, in every crisis there is an opportunity to assess, analyse and incorporate the lessons learnt. And the war in Ukraine is no exception. Two years of a full-blown conflict provide insights into the tactics and strategies deployed.

As a sign of the evolving nature of warfare, one of the vital tools of this conflict has been the increasing weaponisation of information with the new battleground being in the realm of digital space. This includes the social media, internet, electronic media and cyber domains. The scale of reach and speed of dissemination of these arenas set this conflict apart.

In this, shaping public opinion, morale and reputation has been a key *modus operandi* of the stakeholders. Winning hearts and minds have, perhaps, never had a more relevant connotation, anchored to each side trying to outdo the other to make themselves heard. In fact, the perception of which side is winning the war is being increasingly shaped by whose message is being heard the most.

This emphasis on an effective communication strategy has, unsurprisingly, seen the emergence of competing narratives. These include the entire spectrum of information related to a war—from casualty figures to potential use of nuclear, chemical and biological weapons, regime change and even the destruction of precious art, among others.

The target has not only been the domestic but also the global audience. This stems from the need to rally the local electorate as well as canvass support of the international community in a globalised world. The latter has, inevitably, polarised the global community[3] amidst the war in Ukraine being a *de-facto* proxy war between Russia and the United States.

The warring sides have sought to leverage the reach of social media to make themselves heard. Their toolkit includes videos, photographs, podcasts, memes and influencers. This has also brought to light the prominent role of Open-Source Intelligence (OSINT) in dispelling several existing perceptions.

In this shadow boxing of information contestation, the adage 'smart phones being as potent as guns'[4] aptly sums up the new warfare dynamics.

Notably, the fog of war has provided a fertile ground for the spread of disinformation and misinformation. Insidious propaganda, fabricated evidence and censorship—hallmarks of a psychological warfare playbook—have been aimed at eroding morale and unsettling the rival. Incidentally, the growing role of spin doctors blends in with Sun Tzu's articulation of 'war being based on deception' and 'truth being sacrificed at the altar of war'.[5]

Against the backdrop of these dynamics, this chapter will seek to address the following questions:

(i) What are the key information strategies being deployed by the stakeholders?
(ii) How successful have these strategies been?
(iii) What are the lessons that can be learnt from this conflict?

## RUSSIAN STRATEGY

### Genesis

It would appear that Russia has had a head start in weaponising information. While the roots of acknowledging the role of information in a conflict dates back to the Bolsheviks in 1923 (which led to creation of the Disinformation Bureau),[6] it is the Colour Revolutions[7] in Russia's immediate periphery in the new millennia that appears to have spurred Russia into action.

This was reflected in the words of the Russian Chief of General Staff Valeryi Gerasimov that highlighted, in 2013, the growing unconventional nature of warfare and the need for Russia to overcome increasing asymmetry in power with its rival, the United States (US), through similar unconventional means. He stated:

> In the 21st century we have seen a tendency toward blurring the lines between the states of war and peace. Wars are no longer declared and, having begun, proceed according to an unfamiliar template… subversion, disinformation, and sabotage prepare the ground for eventual kinetic operations, and the role of non-military means of achieving political and strategic goals… in many cases, they have exceeded the power of force of weapons in their effectiveness.[8]

As such, the Russian hybrid model of warfare involved prioritising information campaign to shape the conflict's outcome. In this, 'distracting, dividing and demoralising' the opposition emerged as a vital part of the Russian stratagem.[9] The model, inevitably, was put to test during Ukraine 1.0 in 2014. The arrival of the 'little green men', who were Russian special forces in disguise but officially renounced by the Kremlin, in Crimea as well as a deluge of information discrediting the ruling Ukrainian regime marked the incipient implementation of Russia's hybrid model of warfare strategy.[10]

Meanwhile, the emphasis on improving the efficiency of the hybrid model was institutionalised with the adoption of the Doctrine of Information Security of Russian Federation in 2016.[11] The doctrine calls for a whole of government approach in achieving information security across the information spectrum. Similarly, Russian strategic thinkers such as Aleksandr Dugin[12] and Igor Panarin[13] sought to provide legitimacy to the hybrid model through their conceptualisation of a 'net-centric war' and 'information warfare' respectively. These inherently justified the growing allocation of resources for inculcating the hybrid model as a pillar of Russia's defence and deterrence.

### Ukraine 2.0: Pre-Invasion Narrative

It appears that Russia sought to build an elaborate public case for its invasion of Ukraine by highlighting its grievances much prior to its tanks and jets crossing into Ukrainian territory on February 24, 2022. This involved a publicity blitz through social, print and electronic media.

Notably, President Putin led from the front by discrediting Ukraine's credentials as an independent country.[14] This narrative was picked up by several high-ranking officials as well. Similarly, allegations were levelled against the growing clout of 'neo-Nazis' in Kiev and perceived genocide of ethnic Russians.[15] The call for a referendum flowed out of the need to protect the Russian minorities.

Meanwhile, Ukraine's aspiration of NATO membership and alleged development of Weapons of Mass Destruction (WMD) in conjunction with the US was projected by Russia as an existential threat.[16] The Russian Ambassador to the United Nations (UN) even accused the US–Ukraine tandem of deploying migratory birds to spread viruses in Russia and its neighbourhood.[17] On the day of invasion, several Ukrainian officials received en-masse text messages imploring them to surrender to prevent bloodshed.[18]

## Post-Invasion: Two-Pronged Strategy

Russia appears to have adopted a two-pronged information strategy aimed at domestic and global constituencies. The former is particularly relevant amidst the incipient protests[19] over the Kremlin's 'special military operation' in a neighbourhood that Russians have traditionally viewed as part of their civilisational and spiritual yolk.[20]

Notably, foreign policy aimed at restoring Russia's Great Power status remains a key source of domestic legitimacy. It, therefore, has become imperative for the Russian regime to justify its operations in Ukraine amidst unprecedented Western economic sanctions. These sanctions have led to painful readjustments in the Russian way of life. High inflation, unemployment and shortages have become a recurring phenomenon.[21]

Similarly, the flow of body bags from the war and conscription have created much heartburn.[22] There have been several reports of mothers of deceased soldiers staging protests. Moreover, punitive action against Russians fleeing conscription[23] has put at risk the carefully crafted social contract between the state and people—that the state would create conditions for citizens to achieve their human and intellectual potential in return for political stability.

As such, the usual Russian *modus operandi* of rallying its people around the flag by tapping the famed Russian resilience, inevitably, has needed recalibration.

Russia has responded by tightly controlling the information that its citizens are exposed to. Censorship, particularly of the Western media, has been prioritised. This has led to a ban on most Western electronic, print and social media platforms. This includes Meta, Twitter, LinkedIn and Instagram.[24] Meanwhile, Google and Telegram have been labelled anti-Russian. These could be next in line of being purged from the Russian waves.

Pertinently, Russia's banning of these platforms, which enjoy immense popularity among the politically vibrant younger Russian generation, could be a double-edged sword. While a ban may prevent political activism, it could lead to protests over widespread disruption to peoples' social lives. Perhaps, this explains Moscow making an exception for WhatsApp and Telegram—Russia's two most popular social messaging platforms—to continue operations in the country.

However, indications are that the government is biding its time to ban WhatsApp amidst its recent launch of a one-way broadcasting tool. Russian state legislators believe that this is a precursor to the spread of Western propaganda.[25]

Incidentally, Telegram is seen as the lesser of the two evils given that the reins of the organisation are in the hands of Pavel Durov—a Russian-born Emirati entrepreneur. While Durov has gone on record to dispel apprehensions of government interference yet Telegram's blocking of jailed opposition leader Alexey Navalny's smart voting bot during regional elections in 2021 possibly highlights a behind-the-scenes collusion.[26]

Meanwhile, the government has sought to promote locally developed alternatives such as Vkontakte (VK) and Yandex. These platforms have a reputation of regulating content at the behest of the state. In fact, a number of VK users have been fined for posting 'fake information' on the war on this platform. Interestingly, these same platforms are also being utilised to advertise army recruitment.[27]

Crucially, the state-run Russian media too appears to be toeing the official position. This includes justifying Russia's 'military intervention' as existential in order to deter Ukraine's Westward drift and to purge Kiev of the violent neo-Nazis.[28] These right-wing groups have been painted as perpetrators of violence who have used civilians as human shields to fortify their urban positions.

Similarly, the Russian media has pushed the government narrative of the West collaborating with Ukraine to develop WMD that would target Russia.[29] It is also not uncommon for the media to highlight Russia's accusation of the Ukrainian government targeting its own citizens to pin the blame on Moscow. Interestingly, these state-run companies have been prohibited from using the terms 'war' and 'invasion' in their reportage.

In the same vein, Russian media have sought to discredit[30] the West in the eyes of the Russian people by highlighting the growing fissures in the Western support to Ukraine. Reports of the US Senate withholding additional funding for Ukraine and protests in Europe about continuing support to Kiev have received widespread coverage.[31] The underlying theme has been of the West's tactical ploy of containing Russia and not genuinely caring about Ukraine's plight.[32] This argument has also been used to justify the narrative of a 'rightful' war.

In fact, President Putin and other senior officials' statements aimed at rallying the Russian population in this moment of crisis have been given prime time news coverage. President Putin's New Year's address[33] to the nation on the eve of 2023 was one of the most widely reported events.

Meanwhile, the new media narrative of the Russian President enjoying more than 70 per cent approval[34] for the ongoing military action is undoubtedly timely amidst the growing cracks in the carefully crafted narrative. This includes the much-publicised protest by a state-run Channel One employee[35] apart from the mass resignation of journalists on the RT channel. With Presidential elections due in Russia in March 2024, strategic communication with the Russian electorate appears to have gone into an overdrive. Russian officials have been taking recourse to state media to appreciate and acknowledge peoples' sacrifices in Russia's war time recovery.[36] This is seen as an attempt to repair the frayed social contract between the state and the people.

Amidst the strengthening of the iron curtain, independent media houses in Russia too have come under Russian censorship. Being labelled as a 'foreign agent' has hung like the proverbial Damocles' Sword. This would restrict their access to private funding and invite greater governmental oversight.

TV Rain and the radio station Ekho Moskvy have already ceased operations.[37] Novaya Gazeta, whose founder Dmitry Muratov received the Nobel Peace Prize in 2021, has stopped covering the war amidst Muratov being declared a foreign agent.[38] Russia's Justice Ministry justified the label on the grounds that Muratov 'used foreign platforms to disseminate opinions aimed at forming a negative attitude towards the foreign and domestic policy of the Russian Federation'.[39] Notably, Muratov is among the approximately 900 individuals[40] who have been declared as foreign agents.

Other tools invoked to shape the official narrative include the Russian government introducing a new law that imposes financial penalties and jail terms of up to 15 years for spreading 'fake information' about the ongoing conflict. Reports suggest that several protestors are spending time in jail.[41]

Notably, details of Ukrainian drone attacks on Russian soil appear to be carefully calibrated. The narrative of such attacks is usually on Russia striking down the majority of the drones with the minimal damage to life and property being a collateral of a 'just' war.[42] Officials have also used the attacks to rally people around the flag.

Meanwhile, public feting of its armed forces is now a recurring phenomenon.[43] Their success and sacrifices are acknowledged and appreciated. This is likely part of the strategy to encourage more Russians to join the armed forces. Similarly, the motive of conducting a 'special military operation' against an ideologically radical and dangerous Ukrainian regime is frequently highlighted with the aim of reminding the domestic audience of the stakes involved.

Interestingly, Russia announced a new curriculum titled 'Fundamentals of Security and Defense of the Motherland' for schools with much fanfare in 2023.[44] It aims to build discipline and comradeship among the students. The youth will also be introduced to certain armed forces' way of life. These include wearing uniforms, doing parade, digging trenches and learning about weapons and ammunition. The curriculum could captivate the youth to join the services.

## Strategic Communication with Global Stakeholders

Strategic communication with select global stakeholders has also been a key part of the Russian toolkit. This is particularly relevant amidst Russia's attempts at overcoming its growing isolation. It has seen Russia reach out to the Global South where it maintains robust equities anchored to its legacy defence, energy and food grains trade diplomacy.[45] The Kremlin has also sought to leverage prevailing regional anti-West sentiments to build sympathy for Russia's actions. This includes the perceived Western double standards of maintaining its own sphere of influence while denying the same to Russia.

Similarly, the Western narrative of the war in Ukraine being a democracy versus authoritarian conflict appears to have only a few takers. Several regimes of the Global South have a different interpretation of democracy. And their models of governance appear closer to Russia's than the one propagated by the West. It helps that the US playing the 'violation of an independent country's sovereignty' card gives Russia more ammunition to highlight Washington's double standards by shining the spotlight on America's intervention in Iraq.[46]

With access to the popular media platforms of Western Big Tech being blocked, the Kremlin has sought to communicate through Russian news channels in local languages. RT's Spanish and Arabic, apart from English, channels have enabled Russia to reach out to Latin America, the Arab World, Africa and Asia. Interestingly, RT Spanish appears to have a larger audience than its CNN Spanish counterpart.[47]

Telegram too remains an effective medium of communication. Rybar, Telegram's multi-lingual flash channel that sends frequent real-time updates on the state of war, has gained popularity.

Incidentally, Russian embassies in several countries, including India, have been emailing weekly updates about the 'real status' of the conflict to the strategic community of the host nation.

Russia has also sought to cultivate right-wing groups in the Western world.[48] This move likely stems from the calculation of sowing division and dissent in the West with the objective of weakening the Western commitment to Ukraine.

Meanwhile, Russia has reached out to the post-Soviet space, particularly Central Asia, where the Russian language is still a medium of interaction. Russian television and radio channels and podcasts have sought to not only allay the fears of these countries about Moscow's perceived expansionist agenda but also cultivate an understanding of Russia's position.[49]

Russian ministers have used non-Western forums, including BRICS, SCO and bilateral meetings with counterparts of non-Western countries, to highlight Russia's interests and concerns.[50] An underlying theme has been of Russia standing up for itself with an emphasis on the virtue of global strategic balance anchored to Russia being a global pole.

In the same vein, Russia has sought to tackle discontent in the Global South, particularly in African countries that have been hit hard by the disruption to their energy and food security, by delivering aid.[51] The strategic messaging has been of Russia caring for the developing countries.

Incidentally, intimidation also appears to be a part of Russia's playbook. The dropping of leaflets[52] in eastern Ukraine that highlight dangers of a nuclear meltdown in Zaporizhzhia reflects Russia calculus of leveraging fear psychosis to garner support.

Russian leaders have also not shied away from publicly raising the bogey of nuclear escalation.[53] This could be a tactical ploy to dissuade Western countries from upping the ante through deliveries of offensive platforms such as F-16 fighter jets and Main Battle Tanks (MBTs).

## Report Card

Domestically, Russia's information strategy appears to be weathering the storm of the prolonged conflict. The ruling regime remains stable amidst the incipient dissent remaining below the threshold of undermining regime security. In fact, it seems that a significant section of the Russian population[54] has bought into the narrative of an existential war for Russia that necessitates sacrifices for the protection of their motherland.

At the global level, Russia's strategic communication has been severely undermined by tech restrictions imposed by the West. This has seen large sections of the English-speaking world demonising Russia. Nevertheless, Moscow would, inevitably, take satisfaction from the widespread understanding of its position in the Global South—reflected in multiple abstentions at the UN.[55]

## WESTERN AND UKRAINIAN STRATEGY

### Western Strategy

The West appears to be a step ahead of Russia in its information dissemination strategy which, ironically, the Kremlin had pioneered. This stems from the information blackout imposed by Western technology companies, which dominate the global information platform landscape, on official Russian media houses. As a result, Russians have been cut off from platforms such as Meta, Instagram, Facebook, LinkedIn and Twitter. Its news channels such as RT and Sputnik have been banned in Western capitals on the grounds that they promote insidious state propaganda.[56]

Big Tech, therefore, appears to be toeing the Western governments' strategy of an information boycott of Russia. Perhaps, they are also behind the throttled speed of access to official Russian websites. These dynamics have, inevitably, put Russia on the back foot.

Meanwhile, the United States Agency for Global Media (USAGM) has launched a new Ukrainian and Russian language satellite channel—Current Time TV[57]—for not just the Ukrainians but also for the audiences in Russia's neighbourhood where Kremlin has sought to cultivate support for its war. These include Belarus, Moldova and Kazakhstan. The aim of the channel is to provide 'independent coverage' of current affairs—euphemism for rendering alternative views to that of the Russian media. This includes highlighting the protests in Russia against the war and discrediting the Russian Presidential elections slated for March 2024.[58]

Notably, as the war drags onto its third year, the Western countries have sought to publicly downplay their emerging inconsistencies on the quantum of support to Ukraine. The blocking of additional funding for Kiev by the US Senate[59] as well as by the Hungarian President Viktor Orban[60] in the European Union (EU) (worth a combined US$ 100 billion) have been described as bumps in the road with allies working overtime to find a way out. This funding is needed not only for the war effort but also for Ukraine's general administration.

Similarly, issues such as the barricading of Ukrainian border crossings by Polish farmers protesting against unfair advantage to Ukrainian transporters[61] as well as the emergence of new naysayers in the form of Slovakia and Poland refusing to supply ammunition to Kiev[62] have been depicted as non-irreconcilable differences.

In fact, the EU has sought to portray the mechanism of EU minus member states not on board as a workaround[63] to keep the funds and support flowing. It has also rejected the assertion in several circles of the inefficacy of Western sanctions in forcing Russia to change course. The imposition of the 12th package of sanctions in December 2023 was aimed at 'imposing additional import and export bans on Russia, combating sanctions circumvention and closing loopholes',[64] thereby dismissing suggestions of fatigue in Western support. Similarly, President Biden[65] has sought to downplay the Senate veto as tactical vote bank politics of the Republicans.

As such, it appears that the West has sought to strengthen its portrayal of being largely united in its commitment to Ukraine. This includes frequent visits of Western leaders and officials to Kiev and reciprocal visits of the Ukrainian President to Western capitals.[66] An underlying theme of discussion has been on giving primacy to Kiev's interests on any potential peace agreement amidst speculation that Ukraine could get the raw end of the deal.

The West has also highlighted its unwavering support by referring to instances of supplying Ukraine with weapons from its own reserves. Similarly, the opening of EU's membership talks with Kiev in December 2023[67] is seen as an attempt to maintain the existing course of embracing Ukraine. Inevitably, this received widespread media coverage. The European Council President Charles Michel in a social media post called the event 'a clear signal of hope for their people and for our continent' while European Commission Chief Ursula von der Leyen labelled it 'a strategic decision and a day that will remain engraved in the history of our union'. President Zelenskyy, in a Tweet, welcomed the decision as 'a victory for Ukraine. A victory for all of Europe. A victory that motivates, inspires, and strengthens'.[68] Consequently, managing perceptions has been a key Western toolkit in the ongoing conflict.

## Ukrainian Strategy

The surprise package of this information contestation has been the phoenix-like rise of Ukraine from the war ashes to take the lead in leveraging the information space to captivate and garner international support.

President Volodmyr Zelenskyy, often dressed in combat fatigues, has led from the front in engaging global stakeholders. His outreach has seen him play the victim card at the UN and in several parliaments from the US Congress to Israeli Knesset, among others.[69] Comparison of Ukrainian peoples' suffering with the emotive events of these countries in the form of 9/11 and Holocaust have helped generate tremendous sympathy and support. He has also successfully leveraged the prevailing fear psychosis in Western capitals, especially Eastern Europe, about Russia to make the West *pièce de résistance* of Ukrainian pushback against Moscow. The Europeans, in particular, appear to have bought into the Ukrainian narrative of continental Europe's security being at stake in this war with Russia.[70]

Unsurprisingly, the West has provided resources to not only tackle the humanitarian crisis but also to withstand the Russian military pressure. And there are incipient suggestions that this support could force Russia to dilute its ambitious political goals. More importantly, the projection of 'naked Russian aggression'[71] across the information space has led to do the unthinkable—unite the West in imposing sweeping sanctions against Russia.

Meanwhile, Ukraine has also been effective in generating a wave of global sympathy among the people by highlighting human suffering and widespread destruction of property. Viral videos, including those shot on the move on GoPro, memes, photographs and podcasts have brought the war to peoples' screens. The projection of Ukrainian bravery against a numerically superior Russian foe—a David vs Goliath battle—has driven home the point of a just war to protect their motherland. In fact, President Zelenskyy's clarion call to fight a just war by equating the battle of Mariupol with the famed Russian resilience during the Second World War siege of Leningrad[72] appears to have struck an emotive chord with both the Ukrainians and the global community. His seven million plus followers on Twitter[73] ensure that his messages spread fast, far and wide.

Amidst Ukraine taking the fight right up to Russia's doorstep in the form of increasing drone attacks on Russian soil, including in Moscow,[74] the messaging that not only can Ukraine hold its own but also that the tables could be turning against the backdrop of growing scepticism in the West about Ukraine's chances has received widespread traction in Western media. Notably, there has been growing speculation of war fatigue in the West against the backdrop of Ukraine's counteroffensive in the summer of 2023 not achieving a major breakthrough.

With the conflict in West Asia hogging international limelight, thereby pushing the war in Ukraine to the back pages, President Zelenskyy also appears to be on an overdrive to rally global support. This includes a change in tactics wherein the Ukrainian President is increasingly seen making physical appearances, in a departure from his virtual addresses, in international forums, including at economic ones at Davos. An underlying theme of his speeches has been an exhortation to the global community, particularly the West, to maintain the existing course. At the World Economic Forum in January 2024, he stated:[75]

> We need you in Ukraine to build, to reconstruct, to restore our lives... Each of you can be even more successful with Ukraine ... We need peace in the world, peace in Ukraine means peace in Europe. It means peace in the world.

President Zelenskyy has also used these platforms to push the Ukrainian 10-point 'peace formula'[76] to end the human suffering. Ukrainian ministers and officials too have sought to keep the global spotlight on the war and reinvigorate global support. At the fourth meeting of national security advisors of several countries held in Davos in January 2024, the Ukrainian President's Chief of Staff Andriy Yermak sought to portray the global support for Kiev by posting photos of the meeting on social media. He also wrote, 'countries from the Global South are increasingly getting involved in our work. It shows understanding that this European conflict is in fact a challenge for all humanity'.[77] In the same vein, Ukrainian officials have publicly called upon the Western leaders to utilise the frozen Russian assets for Ukraine's reconstruction.

Also, a robust public relations exercise of Kiev appreciating the Western support seems to be in play. This seeks to counter the perception of Ukraine being 'ungrateful'[78] to the West's economic, military and diplomatic support. It has seen the Ukrainian Prime Minister Denys Shmyhal expressing 'gratitude to the Polish nation and all Polish families for the support that they have given and have provided to Ukrainian refugees'[79] amidst friction with Poland over grain export transit and Warsaw's decision to suspend weapons supplies to Kiev.

Meanwhile, President Zelenskyy has sought to publicly highlight Kiev's ongoing domestic reforms covering judiciary, minority rights and anti-corruption.[80] These are seen as key conditions for Ukraine's coveted EU membership. Notably, the reshuffling of his cabinet[81] including the firing of the high-profile defence minister was seen as an attempt to tackle systemic corruption.

It, therefore, appears that the strategic messaging of aligning Ukraine with EU's values, rules and procedures is aimed not only at the EU bureaucracy but also the EU citizens who remain circumspect of Kiev's ability to put its house in order.

Incidentally, a virtual army of cyber volunteers, estimated in excess of three lakh cyber geeks,[82] has been the proverbial force multiplier for the Ukrainian cause. With their activities being coordinated by Ukraine's Digital Minister Mykhailo Fedorov, an OSINT app—Diia[83]—has been the repository of battlefield geo-tagged pictures and videos uploaded by citizens on the ground. This has not only helped debunk several existing notions but has also provided the Ukrainian Armed Forces with actionable intelligence. In this, Elon Musk's Starlink[84] satellite internet connectivity has proven to be a game changer for information dissemination.

Notably, Ukraine's ability to withstand Russia's hybrid warfare owes its genesis to the Information Security Strategy adopted by Kiev in 2017.[85] This led Ukraine to upgrade its digital infrastructure to tackle perceived Russian disinformation campaigns. At the forefront is the Centre for Countering Disinformation (CCD)[86] under the aegis of its National Security Council.

## Psy-Warfare

Kiev has also stepped up its psy-warfare. Viral confessions[87] of captured baby-faced Russian conscripts being misled by Russian generals is aimed at undermining Russian morale. Similarly, the projected casualty figures of Russian soldiers including top-level generals, while appearing highly inflated, may undermine Russia's claims of its operation going as per plan. A radio silence from Moscow on its war casualties has only added fuel to the fire of Russia suffering severe setbacks.

In fact, comments of Ukraine being President Putin's Afghanistan have gained traction in the social media space.[88] Similarly, the mythical exploits of the Ghost of Kyiv[89]—a Ukrainian pilot—shooting down several Russian fighter jets would appear to be a part of this ongoing narrative of boosting Ukrainian morale while simultaneously undermining the Russian one.

Similarly, the disclosure of alleged personal details of more than a lakh Russian soldiers fighting in Ukraine as well as the telephonic transcripts between the Russian chain of command are a further reflection of Kiev upping its psy-warfare game.[90] Ukrainian generals have even telephonically called up the next of kin of Russian soldiers informing them of their demise. Ukraine has also used the intercepted messages to its military advantage. Incidentally, this ability to access personal information and intercept communication is a result of Ukraine tying up with Western Artificial Intelligence (AI) tech companies such as Clearview and Primer.[91]

Notably, Ukraine has been aptly supported by the US in this endeavour. The US, in a tactic similar to the Cuban Missile Crisis, has been declassifying and releasing intelligence related to the war. This includes battlefield positions of Russian Armed Forces as well information about Kremlin's order of business.[92] The visit of North Korean leader Kim Jong Un to Russia in September 2023, including minute details of his itinerary, was announced by the US[93] much before any official intimation from the Kremlin or Pyongyang. The implicit messaging from the US is that it has eyes and ears even in the core of the Russian establishment.

Similarly, the US has made several announcements that appear to undermine the existing Russian narrative. These involve Russia's plan of launching false flag events,[94] friction between Russian commanders and the political establishment[95] and human casualties[96] that far exceed official Russian figures.

Moreover, the US has frequently painted a picture of the Russian Armed Forces in terminal decline. Release of satellite imagery of seemingly Ukrainian missile attacks on Russian positions, blown-up Russian equipment and Russian soldiers fleeing their manned stations blends in with the Western narrative of the Russian Army being a shadow of its past.[97] This messaging, inevitably, also boosts the Ukrainian morale.

President Biden too has kept up the narrative of Russia in decline. At an event in Poland, he stated:

> As a result of these unprecedented sanctions, the ruble almost is immediately reduced to rubble. The Russian economy—that's true, by the way.... The economy is on track to be cut in half in the coming years. It was ranked—Russia's economy was ranked the 11th biggest economy in the world before this evasion—invasion. It will soon not even rank among the top 20 in the world.... These international sanctions are sapping Russian strength, its ability to replenish its military, and its ability—its ability to project power. And it is Putin—it is Vladimir Putin who is to blame, period.... Notwithstanding the brutality of Vladimir Putin, let there be no doubt that this war has already been a strategic failure for Russia already.[98]

Meanwhile, Ukraine has efficiently leveraged social media to alert its citizens about bombing raids, human shelters and the availability of essentials.

### Report Card

It appears that Ukraine has been far more adept than Russia in convincing its domestic and global audience about its narrative. Supported by the West in its strategic communication, Kiev has ridden the wave of sympathy to garner significant international support. Its relentless projection of Russian barbarity, Ukrainian resilience against all odds and the war being a battle for survival of democracy and rules-based order has prevented any let up in Western support to the Ukrainian cause. This is despite the growing economic pain[99] in Europe on account of European countries severing lucrative economic linkages with Russia. Ukraine also appears better equipped today to deal with Russia's perceived disinformation tactics—a far cry from the proverbial deer in the headlights scenario during Ukraine 1.0 in 2014.

## DISINFORMATION

The war in Ukraine has been emblematic of disinformation and misinformation campaigns waged by both sides. Deception and manipulation aimed at discrediting and demonising the ruling regime as well as undermining morale appear to be par for the course. In fact, it seems that each side has sought to outdo the other in spreading propaganda, half-truths and lies.[100]

This shadow-boxing has manifested in several forms. Images have been doctored, videos taken from other war theatres and the news fabricated. The deployment of bots and paid trolls in the social media space have been force multipliers in peddling false narratives. These have, inevitably, added fuel to the fire of rumour mills. Platforms such as Telegram that have limited checks and balances have emerged as a vital part of this disinformation toolkit.

Interestingly, the emergence of AI-generated deep fake software that can imitate even the minutest details of a human being's expression has added a new and dangerous dimension to hybrid warfare. Deep fake inherently undermines the long-held conviction of seeing is believing. This was particularly evident in the chaos and confusion caused by two instances of deep fake videos.[101] The first originated in the immediate aftermath of Russia's invasion. It involved President Zelenskyy imploring his soldiers to surrender. The second instance was a video of President Putin calling upon his soldiers to return home amidst perceived battlefield setbacks. Needless to say, these videos received massive traction in the online space and several social media users inadvertently became carriers of disinformation.

The following are a few examples of disinformation being propagated in the war:

(i) A large number of videos shared by Russian and Ukrainian official handles were borrowed from unrelated conflict theatres, military exercises and even video games. Blasts in Beirut and Tianjin were projected as part of the Ukrainian battlefield.[102] Similarly, news coverage of a mass grave in Ukraine blew up in the face of the audience when body bags in that site started showing movement—it was later pointed out that the backdrop was a climate protest in Vienna.[103]

a. In this, the spotlight has also been on the role of paid crisis actors as well as film shoots of war scenes, with both being part of the ongoing rhetoric.[104]

(ii) Fake websites impersonating the mother site have sprung up. This includes the prominent French newspaper 20minutes.fr.[105]

(iii) Videos of Ukrainian soldiers surrendering on Snake Island and reports of them being killed by Russian troops had gained traction, leading to much furore. This incident was confirmed by President Zelenskyy. However, the Presidential office later backtracked by stating that the soldiers were alive but had been taken as Prisoners of War (PoW).[106]

(iv) Pictures highlighting bravado of a Ukrainian farmer capturing a Russian fighter jet were later found to be part of a Croatian military parade in Zagreb.[107]

(v) Russia and Ukraine had accused each other of targeting a renowned cathedral in Odessa.[108] Similarly, both sides blamed the other for the breach in the Kakhovka dam.[109]

(vi) Russia has accused Ukraine of developing a dirty bomb while Kiev has accused Moscow of nuclear brinkmanship.[110] They have also traded barbs over culpability of the perceived Bucha massacre.

(vii) Multiple sightings (photos and videos) of the Commander of Russia's Black Sea Fleet, Russian Admiral Viktor Sokolov, have been reported after Ukraine claimed his death after a Ukrainian attack on the fleet's headquarters in Sevastopol.[111]

## TAKEAWAYS FOR INDIA

A key ponderable for India is the growing importance of information security in a country's national security. This is particularly relevant at a time when social media has made it child's play to spread information through the mere click of a button. As the Ukrainian crisis has shown, it is easy to target impressionable minds with the objective of shaping opinions. A deluge of biased information can overwhelm and impair ability to make informed decisions. In the past, India's adversaries in Pakistan and China had taken recourse to social media to spread insidious propaganda, including on Kashmir and Galwan.

Crucially, information projection also has political repercussions. Indian media houses had increasingly highlighted the Western narrative of the need to punish Russia. This could have acted as a pressure point on the government in chalking out its next course of action. Similarly, the plight of stranded Indian students in Ukraine, projected through social media platforms, moved many. It would likely have been impossible to ignore their desperate appeals even though they had gone to Ukraine on privately funded study visas without seeking the government's prior approval.

Meanwhile, the information boycott of Russia by Big Tech, which dominate the global information space, is an indication of the hold that the West has in shaping the information narrative. This is particularly relevant amidst several instances of these companies' refusal to abide by the local rules in the past. The growing weaponisation of these platforms to fulfil geo-political goals is a new reality in the face of their earlier perceived neutrality.

These dynamics, therefore, highlight the need to rely on indigenous social media platforms to project a country's narrative. Similarly, monitoring of the social media space with adequate checks and balances appears to be a compelling rationale. This includes fact checking to ensure credibility of the information being posted.

In the same vein, an updated education curriculum as well as public awareness campaigns that sensitise the audience about dangers of being agents of misinformation could be taken up. This stems from the inherent nature of social media—unconventional content is likely to increase the scope of its monetisation given its direct correlation with hits and views, yet such a theme may undermine established societal norms.

Perhaps, the most overlooked platform that may need to be monitored is the podcast. The very nature of its conversational character could lead to key objectionable words, including hate speech, escaping technology filters.

Arguably, the bottom line is the need for accountability amidst increasing propagation of misleading information in the social media space.

## NOTES

1 'As War in Ukraine Escalates with Surge of Missile, Drone Attacks, Prospects for Peace Remain 'Desperately Dim', Senior Official Tells Security Council,' *UN,* June 23, 2023, at https://press.un.org/en/2023/sc15333.doc.htm (Accessed August 1, 2023).

2 D. Trenin, 'The War in Ukraine Where is Russia Headed One Year After?,' *ORF,* 2023, at https://www.youtube.com/watch?v=g0oNvmonEG0 (Accessed June 30, 2023).

3 'Ukraine War: Is the West Out of Touch with the Global South?,' *DW*, February 25, 2023, at https://www.dw.com/en/global-eyes-one-year-since-russia-invaded-ukraine-is-the-west-out-of-touch-with-the-global-south/audio-64792319 (Accessed August 1, 2023).

4 J Shapiro and N. Weidmann, 'Is the Phone Mightier Than the Sword?,' *International Organization*, 69 (2), 2015, pp. 247–74.

5 S. Ratcliffe, *Oxford Essential Quotations*, Oxford University Press, Oxford, 2018.

6 M. Agursky, 'Soviet Disinformation and Forgeries,' *International Journal on World Peace*, 6 (1), 1989, pp. 13–30.

7 K. Pynnöniemia and M. Jokela, 'Perceptions of Hybrid War in Russia: Means, Targets and Objectives Identified in the Russian Debate,' *Cambridge Review of International Relations*, 6 (3), 2020, pp. 828–45, and T. German, 'Harnessing Protest Potential: Russian Strategic Culture and the Colored Revolutions,' *Contemporary Security Policy*, 41 (4), 2020, pp. 541–63, and M. Snegovaya, 'Putin's Information Warfare in Ukraine Soviet Origins of Russia's Hybrid Warfare,' *Institute for the Study of War,* 2015, at https://www.understandingwar.org/sites/default/files/Russian%20Report%201%20Putin's%20Information%20Warfare%20in%20Ukraine-%20Soviet%20Origins%20of%20Russias%20Hybrid%20Warfare.pdf (Accessed August 1, 2023), and J. Wilson, 'The Legacy of the Color Revolutions for Russian Politics and Foreign Policy,' *Problems of Post-Communism*, 57 (2), 2010, pp. 21–36.

8 M. Galeotti, 'The Mythical 'Gerasimov Doctrine' and the Language of Threat,' *Critical Studies of Security*, 7 (2), 2019, pp. 157–61.

9 D. Trenin, 'Russia's National Security Strategy: A Manifesto for a New Era,' *Carnegie Moscow* 2021, at https://carnegiemoscow.org/commentary/84893 (Accessed September 1, 2023).

10 'West Struggles with Russia's 'Ambiguous Warfare' Tactics,' *Reuters*, November 27, 2014, at https://www.reuters.com/article/us-russia-nato-security-idUSKCN0JB0BU20141127 (Accessed September 2, 2023).

11 'Doctrine of Information Security of the Russian Federation,' *Security Council of the Russian Federation*, December 5, 2016, at http://www.scrf.gov.ru/security/information/DIB_engl/#:~:text=683%20of%20December%2031%2C%202015,improve%20the%20information%20security%20system (Accessed September 7, 2023).

12 'Alexander Dugin Advocates a Vast New Russian Empire,' *Reuters*, August 21, 2022, at https://www.reuters.com/world/europe/who-is-alexander-dugin-russian-nationalist-whose-daughter-died-car-bomb-attack-2022-08-21/ (Accessed August 1, 2023).

13 'Defence Strategic Communications,' *Journal of the NATO Strategic Communications Centre of Excellence*, 2, 2017, pp. 61–86, at https://kclpure.kcl.ac.uk/ws/portalfiles/portal/102015136/web_fridman.pdf (Accessed September 25, 2023).

14 'Article by Vladimir Putin on the Historical Unity of Russians and Ukrainians,' *President of Russia*, July 12, 2021, at http://en.kremlin.ru/events/president/news/66181 (Accessed August 1, 2023), and 'Address by the President of the Russian Federation,' *President of Russia*, February 24, 2022, at http://en.kremlin.ru/events/president/transcripts/speeches/67843 (Accessed August 1, 2023).

15 Ibid.

16 Ibid.

17 'United Nations Not Aware of Any Biological Weapons Programmes in Ukraine, Senior Disarmament Affairs Official Tells Security Council,' *UN*, October 27, 2022, at https://press.un.org/en/2022/sc15084.doc.htm (Accessed July 16, 2023).

18 J. Watling, O. Danylyuk and N. Reynolds, 'Preliminary Lessons from Russia's Unconventional Operations During the Russo Ukrainian War, February 2022–February 2023,' *RUSI*, March 29, 2023, at https://rusi.org/explore-our-research/publications/special-resources/preliminary-lessons-russias-unconventional-operations-during-russo-ukrainian-war-february-2022 (Accessed August 1, 2023).

19 'Anti-war Protests Held in Cities across Russia, 2,000 People Arrested,' *Reuters*, February 27, 2022, at https://www.reuters.com/world/europe/police-detain-more-than-900-people-anti-war-protests-across-russia-monitoring-2022-02-27/ (Accessed August 1, 2023).

20 'Over 115 Holy Sites Damaged in Ukraine Since Start of Russian Invasion, Top UN Official Tells Security Council, Urging Respect for Religious Freedom,' *UN*, July 26, 2023, at https://press.un.org/en/2023/sc15366.doc.htm (Accessed August 1, 2023).

21 'How Sanctions Have Changed Russian Economic Policy,' *The Moscow Times*, May 14, 2023, at https://www.themoscowtimes.com/2023/05/14/how-sanctions-have-changed-russian-economic-policy-a81093 (Accessed August 1, 2023).

22 'Russia Calls up 300,000 Reservists, Says 6,000 Soldiers Killed in Ukraine,' *Reuters*, September 21, 2022, at https://www.reuters.com/world/europe/russias-partial-mobilisation-will-see-300000-drafted-defence-minister-2022-09-21/ (Accessed August 1, 2023), and 'Anger Mounts as Russian Draftees Thrown Into Battle Without Training, Equipment,' *The Moscow Times*, October 18, 2022, at https://www.themoscowtimes.com/2022/10/18/anger-mounts-as-russian-draftees-thrown-into-battle-without-training-equipment-a79120 (Accessed August 1, 2023).

23 'Where Have Russians Been Fleeing to Since Mobilisation Began?,' *Reuters*, October 6, 2022, at https://www.reuters.com/world/europe/where-have-russians-been-fleeing-since-mobilisation-began-2022-10-06/ (Accessed August 1, 2023), and 'Russia Opens First Criminal Draft-dodging Case,' *The Moscow Times*, October 5, 2022, at https://www.themoscowtimes.com/2022/10/05/russia-opens-first-criminal-draft-dodging-case-a78988 (Accessed August 1, 2023).

24 'Russia Bans Instagram and Facebook as 'Extremist',' *The Moscow Times*, March 22, 2022, at https://www.themoscowtimes.com/2022/03/21/russian-court-bans-instagram-facebook-as-extremist-a77017 (Accessed August 1, 2023).

25 'WhatsApp Drops Channels Launch in Russia Over Ban Threat,' *The Moscow Times*, September 26, 2023, at https://www.themoscowtimes.com/2023/09/26/whatsapp-drops-channels-launch-in-russia-over-ban-threat-a82564 (Accessed September 24, 2023).

26 'Russia's Authorities Are Talking About Blocking WhatsApp. What Would This Mean in Reality?,' *The Bell*, September 21, 2023, at https://en.thebell.io/russias-authorities-are-talking-about-blocking-whatsapp-what-would-this-mean-in-reality/ (Accessed September 27, 2023).

27 'Russian Social Media Flooded With Army Recruitment Ads – Report,' *The Moscow Times*, April 19, 2023, at https://www.themoscowtimes.com/2023/04/19/russian-social-media-flooded-with-army-recruitment-ads-report-a80879 (Accessed August 1, 2023).

28 'Global Community Making 'Terrible Mistake' by Ignoring Neo-Nazism—MFA,' *TASS*, September 26, 2023, at https://tass.com/politics/1680301 (Accessed September 26, 2023).

29 'Dem Party Leaders, Pfizer, Moderna Involved in US Biological Activities in Ukraine: Russian MoD,' *Sputnik*, May 11, 2022, at https://sputnikglobe.com/20220511/democratic-partys-leaders-are-ideologists-behind-us-military-biological-activities-in-ukraine-mod-

1095433497.html (Accessed August 1, 2023), and 'US Biolabs in Ukraine Created as Part of Bioweapons Programs—Kennedy Jr.,' *TASS*, August 15, 2023, at https://tass.com/defense/1660431 (Accessed August 19, 2023).

30 'Champagne Corks Popping in Moscow as US Global Influence Wanes,' *Sputnik*, January 16, 2024, at https://sputnikglobe.com/20240116/champagne-corks-popping-in-moscow-as-us-global-influence-wanes-1116186388.html (Accessed January 18, 2024).

31 'US Stops Arms Supplies to Ukraine—White House,' *TASS*, January 12, 2024, at https://tass.com/world/1731395 (Accessed January 15, 2024).

32 'Ukraine Debased to 'Pawn' on Geopolitical Chessboard Serving West,' *Sputnik*, December 14, 2023, at https://sputnikglobe.com/20231214/scott-ritter-ukraine-debased-to-pawn-on-geopolitical-chessboard-serving-west-1115586165.html (Accessed January 18, 2024).

33 'New Year Address to the Nation,' *President of Russia*, December 31, 2022, at http://en.kremlin.ru/events/president/transcripts/speeches/70315 (Accessed August 1, 2023).

34 'Kremlin Says Putin Has No Real Competitors If He Runs Again,' *Reuters*, September 11, 2023, at https://www.reuters.com/world/europe/kremlin-says-putin-has-no-real-competitors-if-he-runs-again-2023-09-11/ (Accessed September 12, 2023).

35 'Russian TV Protester Listed as Wanted Fugitive,' *Reuters*, October 4, 2022, at https://www.reuters.com/world/europe/russian-tv-protester-listed-wanted-after-escaping-house-arrest-2022-10-03/ (Accessed August 1, 2023).

36 'Undeniable Fact' That Strong Support for Putin Spans Diverse Age Groups, Kremlin Says,' *TASS*, December 29, 2023, at https://tass.com/politics/1727939 (Accessed January 18, 2024).

37 'Ekho Moskvy Radio Station Was Taken Off the Air,' *TASS*, March 2, 2022, at https://tass.com/society/1414499 (Accessed August 1, 2023), and 'VK Blocks Pages of Ekho Moskvy and TV Rain,' *Interfax*, March 2, 2022, at https://interfax.com/newsroom/top-stories/75158/ (Accessed August 1, 2023).

38 'Russia Brands Nobel Winner Dmitry Muratov a 'Foreign Agent',' *The Moscow Times*, September 1, 2023, at https://www.themoscowtimes.com/2023/09/01/russia-brands-nobel-winner-dmitry-muratov-a-foreign-agent-a82340 (Accessed September 12, 2023).

39 'Russia Labels Nobel-winning Journalist 'Foreign Agent',' *Reuters*, September 2, 2023, at https://www.reuters.com/world/europe/russia-labels-nobel-winning-journalist-foreign-agent-2023-09-02/ (Accessed September 16, 2023).

40 'Russian Authorities Maintain Secret List of People 'Affiliated' with 'Foreign Agents',' *The Moscow Times*, June 16, 2023, at https://www.themoscowtimes.com/2023/06/15/russian-authorities-maintain-secret-list-of-people-affiliated-with-foreign-agents-a81522 (Accessed August 1, 2023).

41 'Russia Issues First Criminal Conviction for Ukraine 'War Fakes',' *The Moscow Times*, June 1, 2022, at https://www.themoscowtimes.com/2022/06/01/russia-issues-first-criminal-conviction-for-ukraine-war-fakes-a77859 (Accessed August 1, 2023).
'Russian Activist Jailed for 6 Years Over Social Media Posts,' *The Moscow Times*, May 25, 2023, at https://www.themoscowtimes.com/2023/05/25/russian-activist-jailed-for-6-years-over-social-media-posts-a81288 (Accessed August 1, 2023).

42 'Ukrainian Drone Shot Down in Moscow Region, Another One Intercepted in Leningrad Region,' *TASS*, January 18, 2024, at https://tass.com/emergencies/1733731 (Accessed January 19, 2024).

43 'Military Ad Campaigns Reach Russian Schools, Metro Stations, and Kindergartens,' *Novaya Gazeta*, April 19, 2023, at https://novayagazeta.eu/articles/2023/04/19/military-ad-campaigns-reach-russian-schools-metro-stations-and-kindergartens-en (Accessed August 1, 2023).

44 'Russian Veterans of Ukraine War Will Teach Defence Course for Students,' *Al Jazeera*, September 7, 2023, at https://www.aljazeera.com/news/2023/9/7/russian-veterans-of-ukraine-war-will-teach-defence-course-to-students (Accessed September 16, 2023).

45 'Economic Partnerships, Ukraine Set to Dominate Diminished Russia-Africa Summit,' *The Moscow Times*, July 25, 2023, at https://www.themoscowtimes.com/2023/07/25/economic-partnerships-ukraine-set-to-dominate-diminished-russia-africa-summit-a81956 (Accessed August 1, 2023).

46 P. Rutland, 'Why the West is Losing the Global Information War Over Ukraine and How It Can Be Fixed,' *PONARS Eurasia,* 2022, at https://www.ponarseurasia.org/why-the-west-is-losing-the-global-information-war-over-ukraine-and-how-it-can-be-fixed/ (Accessed August 1, 2023).

47 Ibid.

48 R. Pantucci, (2023), 'Russia's Far-Right Campaign in Europe,' *Lawfare*, April 9, 2023, at https://www.lawfaremedia.org/article/russias-far-right-campaign-europe (Accessed August 1, 2023).

49 E. McGlinchey and S. Dzhuraev, 'Russia's Erosion in Central Asia,' *PONARS Eurasia* 2022, at https://www.ponarseurasia.org/russias-erosion-in-central-asia/ (Accessed August 1, 2023), and 'We Want Respect': Putin's Authority Tested in Central Asia,' *Reuters*, October 18, 2022, at https://www.reuters.com/world/we-want-respect-putins-authority-tested-central-asia-2022-10-18/ (Accessed August 1, 2023).

50 'Lavrov Calls for United Eurasian Front Amid NATO's Aggressive Posturing,' *TASS*, December 15, 2023, at https://tass.com/politics/1721879 (Accessed January 19, 2024).

51 'Russia Has Sent First Free Grain Shipments to Africa,' *The Moscow Times*, November 17, 2023, at https://www.themoscowtimes.com/2023/11/17/russia-has-sent-first-free-grain-shipments-to-africa-a83141 (Accessed January 18, 2024).

52 'Russian Forces Drop Leaflets on Ukrainian Positions in Zaporozhye Calling for Surrender,' *TASS*, March 23, 2023, at https://tass.com/politics/1593655 (Accessed August 1, 2023).

53 'Russia's Putin Issues New Nuclear Warnings to West Over Ukraine,' *Reuters*, February 22, 2023, at https://www.reuters.com/world/putin-update-russias-elite-ukraine-war-major-speech-2023-02-21/ (Accessed January 18, 2024).

54 'Why Support for Putin's War Is Rife in Russia's Worst-Hit Regions,' *The Moscow Times*, June 21, 2023, at https://www.themoscowtimes.com/2023/06/10/why-support-for-putins-war-is-rife-in-russias-worst-hit-regions-a81426 (Accessed August 1, 2023).

55 'Ukraine War Exposes Splits between Global North and South,' *France24*, February 17, 2023, at https://www.france24.com/en/europe/20230217-ukraine-war-exposes-splits-between-global-north-and-south (Accessed August 1, 2023).

56 'EU Imposes Sanctions on State-owned Outlets RT/Russia Today and Sputnik's Broadcasting in the EU,' *European Council, Council of the European Union*, March 2, 2022, at https://www.consilium.europa.eu/en/press/press-releases/2022/03/02/eu-imposes-sanctions-on-state-owned-outlets-rt-russia-today-and-sputnik-s-broadcasting-in-the-eu/ (Accessed August 1, 2023).

57 'USAGM Expands Russian-language Programming to Europe,' *U.S. Agency for Global Media*, March 9, 2023, at https://www.usagm.gov/2023/03/09/usagm-expands-russian-language-programming-to-europe/ (Accessed August 1, 2023).

58 'West Stepping Up Efforts to Discredit Russia's Presidential Election—Senate Committee,' *TASS*, January 9, 2024, at https://tass.com/politics/1730075 (Accessed January 18, 2024).

59 'Republicans Block Ukraine Aid Bill, Putting New Pressure on Border Talks,' *The Wall Street*

*Journal*, December 6, 2023, at https://www.wsj.com/politics/policy/border-fight-set-to-derail-ukraine-aid-vote-in-senate-a67e53c3 (Accessed January 1, 2024).

60 'Hungary Blocks 50 Billion Euros in EU Aid for Ukraine Following Approval of Membership Talks,' *France 24*, December 15, 2023, at https://www.france24.com/en/europe/20231215-hungary-s-orban-blocks-eu-aid-for-ukraine-following-membership-discussions (Accessed January 1, 2024).

61 'Polish Farmers Continue Ukraine Border Protest,' *Euronews*, January 4, 2024, at https://www.euronews.com/2024/01/04/polish-farmers-continue-ukraine-border-protest (Accessed January 5, 2024).

62 'Ukraine Puts on Brave Face As West Goes Wobbly,' *Politico*, October 3, 2023, at https://www.politico.eu/article/ukraine-puts-on-brave-face-as-west-goes-wobbly/ (Accessed January 10, 2024).

63 'Foreign Ministers Close Ranks to Slam Hungary's 'Deplorable' Threats to Block EU Support for Ukraine,' *Euronews*, December 11, 2023, at https://www.euronews.com/my-europe/2023/12/11/foreign-ministers-close-ranks-to-slam-hungarys-deplorable-threats-to-block-eu-support-for- (Accessed January 1, 2024).

64 'EU Adopts 12th Package of Sanctions against Russia for Its Continued Illegal War against Ukraine,' *European Commission*, December 19, 2023, at https://neighbourhood-enlargement.ec.europa.eu/news/eu-adopts-12th-package-sanctions-against-russia-its-continued-illegal-war-against-ukraine-2023-12-19_en (Accessed January 1, 2024).

65 'Remarks by President Biden and President Zelenskyy of Ukraine in Joint Press Conference,' *The White House*, December 12, 2023, at https://www.whitehouse.gov/briefing-room/speeches-remarks/2023/12/13/remarks-by-president-biden-and-president-zelenskyy-of-ukraine-in-joint-press-conference-2/ (Accessed January 2, 2024).

66 'European Officials Visit Ukraine with Pledges of More Support,' *Politico*, January 14, 2024, at https://www.politico.eu/article/europe-leaders-visit-kyiv-pledges-more-support-french-sejourne/ (Accessed January 15, 2024).

67 'Ukraine Membership Status: Candidate Country,' *European Commission*, at https://neighbourhood-enlargement.ec.europa.eu/european-neighbourhood-policy/countries-region/ukraine_en (Accessed January 15, 2024).

68 'Zelenskyy Claims 'Victory' As EU Agrees to Open Ukraine Membership Talks', *AlJazeera*, December 14, 2023, at https://www.aljazeera.com/news/2023/12/14/zelenskyy-hails-victory-as-eu-agrees-to-open-membership-talks-for-ukraine (Accessed January 15, 2024).

69 'Speech by President of Ukraine Volodymyr Zelenskyy in the Knesset,' *President of Ukraine*, March 20, 2022, at https://www.president.gov.ua/en/news/promova-prezidenta-ukrayini-volodimira-zelenskogo-v-kneseti-73701#:~:text=Dear%20members%20of%20the%20Government,both %20joy%20and%20pain%20together (Accessed August 1, 2023), and 'Full Transcript of Zelensky's Speech Before Congress,' *The New York Times*, December 21, 2022, at https://www.nytimes.com/2022/12/21/us/politics/zelensky-speech-transcript.html#:~:text=We%20 have%20no%20fear%2C%20nor,protect%20freedom%20and%20international%20law (Accessed August 1, 2023).

70 'Statement by President Charles Michel at the UN Security Council Debate on Ukraine,' *European Council, Council of the European Union*, September 20, 2023, at https://www.consilium.europa.eu/en/press/press-releases/2023/09/20/statement-by-president-charles-michel-at-the-un-security-council-debate-on-ukraine/ (Accessed September 21, 2023).

71 'Remarks by President Biden on Russia's Unprovoked and Unjustified Attack on Ukraine,' *The White House*, February 24, 2022, at https://www.whitehouse.gov/briefing-room/speeches-

remarks/2022/02/24/remarks-by-president-biden-on-russias-unprovoked-and-unjustified-attack-on-ukraine/ (Accessed August 1, 2023).

72 'Zelenskiy Compares Mariupol to Leningrad Siege As Russia Launches Fresh Strikes on Kyiv,' *The Guardian*, March 17, 2022, at https://www.theguardian.com/world/2022/mar/17/ukraines-zelenskiy-compares-mariupol-to-leningrad-siege-as-russia-launches-fresh-strikes-on-kyiv (Accessed August 1, 2023).

73 'Volodymyr Zelenskyy / Âîëîäèìèð Çåëåíñüêèé,' *Twitter Handle* - @ZelenskyyUa, at https://twitter.com/ZelenskyyUa?ref_src=twsrc%5Egoogle%7Ctwcamp%5Eserp%7Ctwgr%5Eauthor (Accessed August 1, 2023).

74 'Russia Says It Downed Dozens of Moscow-bound Ukrainian Drones After It Struck Kyiv,' *NPR*, November 26, 2023, at https://www.npr.org/2023/11/26/1215233625/russia-says-it-downed-dozens-of-moscow-bound-ukrainian-drones-after-it-struck-ky (Accessed January 16, 2024).

75 'Zelensky Calls for Peace, Not More Weapons, in Davos,' *The New York Times*, January 16, 2024, at https://www.nytimes.com/2024/01/16/world/europe/ukraine-zelensky-davos-switzerland-peace.html (Accessed January 18, 2024).

76 'Ukraine Peace Talks End Without Agreement As Kyiv Insists China Must Be Involved,' *Independent*, January 16, 2024, at https://www.independent.co.uk/news/world/europe/ukraine-peace-plan-davos-world-economic-forum-b2478607.html (Accessed January 18, 2024).

77 'More Countries Join Talks on Ukraine Peace Formula, But China Is Missing,' *Euronews*, January 15, 2024, at https://www.euronews.com/2024/01/15/more-countries-join-talks-on-ukraine-peace-formula-but-china-is-missing#:~:text=Zelenskyy%20has%20presented%20a%2010,roughly%201%2C500%2Dkilometre%20front%20line (Accessed January 16, 2023).

78 'Diplomatic Spat After Poland Calls Ukraine 'Ungrateful',' *Euronews*, October 10, 2023, at https://www.euronews.com/2023/08/03/diplomatic-spat-after-poland-calls-ukraine-ungrateful (Accessed January 16, 2024).

79 *Politico*, no. 62.

80 'Ukraine's EU Accession Process Faces Bureaucratic and Political Hurdles,' *Atlantic Council*, December 19, 2023, at https://www.atlanticcouncil.org/blogs/ukrainealert/ukraines-eu-accession-process-faces-bureaucratic-and-political-hurdles/ (Accessed January 16, 2024).

81 'Ukraine Fires 6 Deputy Defense Ministers As Heavy Fighting Continues in the East,' *AP*, September 18, 2023, at https://apnews.com/article/ukraine-russia-deputy-defense-ministers-fired-ab8f88ff31f26ae29b35bd14406e62f3 (Accessed August 16, 2023).

82 'The IT Army of Ukraine,' *Center for Strategic and International Studies*, August 15, 2023, at https://www.csis.org/blogs/strategic-technologies-blog/it-army-ukraine (Accessed August 16, 2023).

83 'Ukraine's Diia Platform Sets the Global Gold Standard for E-government,' *Atlantic Council*, May 30, 2023, at https://www.atlanticcouncil.org/blogs/ukrainealert/ukraines-diia-platform-sets-the-global-gold-standard-for-e-government/ (Accessed August 1, 2023).

84 'Elon Musk's Unmatched Power in the Stars,' *The New York Times*, July 28, 2023, at https://www.nytimes.com/interactive/2023/07/28/business/starlink.html (Accessed August 1, 2023).

85 'Decree of the President of Ukraine: On the Decision of the National Security and Defense Council of Ukraine Dated December 29, 2016 "On the Information Security Doctrine of Ukraine",' *National Security and Defense Council of Ukraine,* February 25, 2017, at https://www.rnbo.gov.ua/ua/Ukazy/439.html (Accessed August 1, 2023).

86 'About Center for Countering Disinformation,' *Center for Countering Disinformation,* at https://cpd.gov.ua/en/category/docs/ (Accessed August 1, 2023).

87 'Captured Russian Soldier Cries Whilst Being Allowed to Speak to His Mother,' *The Telegraph*, March 3, 2022, at https://www.youtube.com/watch?v=7Y3YqgWtPq4 (Accessed August 1, 2023).

88 'Putin's Afghanistan: Ukraine and the Lessons of the Soviets' Afghan War,' *Foreign Affairs*, March 24, 2022, at https://www.foreignaffairs.com/articles/afghanistan/2022-03-24/putins-afghanistan (Accessed August 1, 2023).

89 'Fact Check: The 'Ghost of Kyiv' Fighter Pilot,' *DW*, April 5, 2022, at https://www.dw.com/en/fact-check-ukraines-ghost-of-kyiv-fighter-pilot/a-60951825 (Accessed August 1, 2023).

90 'Ukrainian Intercepts Show Russian Soldiers' Anger at Losses, Disarray,' *Reuters*, September 5, 2023, at https://www.reuters.com/investigates/special-report/ukraine-crisis-intercepts/ (Accessed September 10, 2023).

91 'Exclusive: Ukraine Has Started Using Clearview AI's Facial Recognition during War,' *Reuters*, March 15, 2022, at https://www.reuters.com/technology/exclusive-ukraine-has-started-using-clearview-ais-facial-recognition-during-war-2022-03-13/ (Accessed August 1, 2023).

92 'How the U.S. Adopted a New Intelligence Playbook to Expose Russia's War Plans,' *The New York* Times, February 23, 2023, at *https://www.nytimes.com/2023/02/23/us/politics/intelligence-russia-us-ukraine-china.html (*Accessed August 1, 2023).

93 'State Department Holds Briefing Amid Reports Putin Will Meet North Korea's Kim Jong Un,' *PBS News Hour*, September 5, 2023, at https://www.youtube.com/watch?v=dB_Hqc1l0bQ (Accessed September 6, 2023).

94 'U.S. Says Russia Is Laying the Groundwork to Attack Civilian Ships and Blame Ukraine,' *NP*R, July 20, 2023, at https://www.npr.org/2023/07/20/1189040872/russia-ukraine-black-sea-grain-ships (Accessed August 1, 2023).

95 *Reuters*, no. 90, and 'Vladimir Putin Feels His Military Leaders Misled Him about Ukraine, Declassified Intelligence Shows,' *CNBC*, March 30, 2022, at https://www.cnbc.com/2022/03/30/russias-vladimir-putin-feels-military-leaders-misled-him-about-ukraine.html (Accessed August 1, 2023).

96 'The 'Stunning' Scale of Russian Deaths in Ukraine Signals Trouble Ahead for Putin,' *NBC News*, May 2, 2023, at https://www.nbcnews.com/news/world/russia-casualties-soldiers-killed-ukraine-counteroffensive-putin-war-rcna82380 (Accessed August 1, 2023).

97 'US General Says Russian Army in Disarray,' *Al Jazeera*, June 15, 2023, at https://www.aljazeera.com/news/liveblog/2023/6/15/ukraine-russia-war-live-kyiv-says-three-missiles-hit-kryvyi-rih#:~:text=Top%20US%20general%20Mark%20Milley,re%20sitting%20in%20defensive %20positions%E2%80%9D (Accessed August 1, 2023).

98 'Remarks by President Biden on the United Efforts of the Free World to Support the People of Ukraine,' *The White House*, March 26, 2022, at https://www.whitehouse.gov/briefing-room/speeches-remarks/2022/03/26/remarks-by-president-biden-on-the-united-efforts-of-the-free-world-to-support-the-people-of-ukraine/ (Accessed August 1, 2023).

99 'The Euro-zone Economy is Set for a Painful Reckoning,' *Bloomberg,* August 7, 2023, at https://www.bloomberg.com/news/articles/2023-08-07/ecb-rate-hikes-return-to-spending-restraint-raise-euro-zone-recession-risk#xj4y7vzkg (Accessed August 16, 2023).

100 'Ukraine: One Year of Misinformation and How It Has Shaped the War Narrative,' *France24*, February 24, 2023, at https://www.france24.com/en/tv-shows/truth-or-fake/20230224-ukraine-war-fake-news (Accessed August 1, 2023).

101 'Fact Check: Deepfakes and Disinformation in the Ukraine War,' *DW*, July 18, 2023, at https://www.dw.com/en/fact-check-how-deepfakes-spread-disinformation-in-russias-war-against-ukraine/video-66278320 (Accessed August 1, 2023).

102 'Ukraine War: Five of the Most Viral Misinformation Posts and False Claims Since the Conflict Began,' *Euroenews*, August 24, 2022, at https://www.euronews.com/my-europe/2022/08/24/ukraine-war-five-of-the-most-viral-misinformation-posts-and-false-claims-since-the-conflic (Accessed August 29, 2023).

103 'Fact Check - Video Shows Climate Demonstration, Not Staged Body Bags in Ukraine War,' *Reuters*, March 3, 2022, at https://www.reuters.com/article/factcheck-ukraine-body-bags-idUSL2N2V6241 (Accessed August 1, 2023).

104 'Fact Check - Footage Shows TV Production, Not 'Crisis Actors' in Ukraine Conflict,' *Reuters*, March 3, 2022, at https://www.reuters.com/article/factcheck-tvfootage-notcrisisactors-idUSL2N2V61K1 (Accessed August 1, 2023).

105 'Ukraine: Disinformation on the Battleground of a Hybrid War,' *Polytechnique Insights*, November 2, 2022, at https://www.polytechnique-insights.com/en/columns/geopolitics/ukraine-and-the-russian-disinformation/ (Accessed August 1, 2023).

106 'AI and Disinformation in the Russia-Ukraine War,' *TechTarget*, March 14, 2022, at https://www.techtarget.com/searchenterpriseai/feature/AI-and-disinformation-in-the-Russia-Ukraine-war (Accessed August 1, 2023).

107 'Ukraine: One Year of Misinformation and How It Has Shaped the War Narrative,' *France24*, February 24, 2023, at https://www.france24.com/en/tv-shows/truth-or-fake/20230224-ukraine-war-fake-news (Accessed August 1, 2023).

108 'Russians and Ukrainians Blame Each Other for Bombing in the Heart of Donetsk,' *Le Monde*, August 5, 2022, at https://www.lemonde.fr/en/international/article/2022/08/05/russians-and-ukrainians-blame-each-other-for-a-bombing-in-the-heart-of-donetsk_5992612_4.html (Accessed August 7, 2023).

109 'Explainer: What the Kakhovka Dam Catastrophe Means For the Ukraine-Russia War,' *The Moscow Times*, June 7, 2023, at https://www.themoscowtimes.com/2023/06/06/explainer-what-the-kakhovka-dam-catastrophe-means-for-the-ukraine-russia-war-a81415 (Accessed August 1, 2023).

110 'Russia, Without Evidence, Says Ukraine Making Nuclear "Dirty Bomb",' *Reuters*, March 6, 2022, at https://www.reuters.com/world/europe/russia-without-evidence-says-ukraine-making-nuclear-dirty-bomb-2022-03-06/ (Accessed August 1, 2023).

111 'Russian Black Sea Fleet Commander Appears at Defense Ministry Meeting After Ukraine Reports His Death,' *Meduza*, September 26, 2023, at https://meduza.io/en/news/2023/09/26/russian-black-sea-fleet-commander-appears-at-defense-ministry-meeting-after-ukraine-reports-his-death?utm_source=email&utm_medium=briefly&utm_campaign=2023-09-27 (Accessed September 27, 2023).

# SECTION IV

# Strategic Dimensions of the Conflict

# 14

# Impact of Russia's Military Transformation on the Ukraine Conflict: Lessons for India

*Vivek Chadha*

The immediate focus of attention for any discussion on military transformation, more often than not, shifts toward the Western world. In particular, the United States and the United Kingdom. Both countries have gone through a long-standing debate followed by several iterations of implementing structural and doctrinal changes. More importantly, the deliberations surrounding the process are available in the public domain for reference.

The Ukraine War has brought the focus of strategic analysts back on Russia. Its military modernisation efforts had taken a backseat, especially after the end of the Cold War, constraints on economic resources and the disintegration of the Soviet Union. Russia's operations short of war and eventually the war in Ukraine have forced a reassessment of Russia's capabilities, which amongst other factors has been influenced by the ongoing transformation of its armed forces—a process that began in 2008.[1] Possibly, the immediate trigger for the restructuring initiative was the inadequacy of the Russian military machine, which was found to be constrained by legacy issues of an industrial-age war-fighting machine.[2] However, as more recent events suggest, the challenges to a successful transformation were not limited to structures alone. They were related to the operational culture within the Russian defence establishment, which included the armed forces.

A number of factors including leadership, military capability and platform effectiveness have been assessed and questioned in an attempt to better understand the performance of Russia's war in Ukraine. This chapter focuses primarily on the circumstances that led to Russia's military transformation and resultantly, its effectiveness during the Ukraine War. Consequently, it will help derive useful lessons for India's ongoing structural changes.

## BRIEF ASSESSMENT OF RUSSIA'S MILITARY TRANSFORMATION

Prior to describing the fundamental aspects of Russia's military modernisation, it would be useful to understand the context in which the exercise was undertaken. This is best provided by someone responsible for initiating the process—former Defence Minister of Russia, Anatoly Serdyukov. In a rare interview, Serdyukov provided a forthright perspective and an intimate understanding of the circumstances under which the Russian Armed Forces were forced to change. This underlined in no uncertain terms, the accompanying criticality for the transformation of the military.

Interestingly, Serdyukov was handed over the responsibility for the transformation not as much because of his deep understanding of the military, but due to his background in economics and finance. The implication was clear. There was a need for better rationalisation of resources being allocated to the armed forces in terms of the capability that this created.

After an extensive tour of the military stations and an understanding of weapons and equipment the broad parameters of the envisaged change became clear. Instead of focusing merely on restructuring, Serdyukov attempted to address morale and motivation as well. He identified two major challenges: first, 'monetary allowance and housing for the military personnel, as well as schools and kindergartens in military camps, employment of wives,' and second, 'how to change the attitude of military personnel to service.'[3] In other words, he was keen to bring about a change in the approach to soldiering, in addition to military structures.

The funding for these improvements came from the privatisation of a large number of state enterprises and releasing officers in charge of such establishments for active duties. Facilities were created to provide social support for the armed forces, salaries were increased to make the job more attractive and procedures that improved efficiency and encouraged corruption were put in place.[4]

Serdyukov cut down on wasteful expenditure on maintaining 22,800 military camps, bringing these down to 700 by the time he left in 2012. He also found units with commanders but with practically no manpower they could command. These were disbanded.[5]

One of the most important areas of reform was related to the training of the officer cadre. Serdyukov found that a unit had sub-unit commanders (platoon and company commanders) but with little experience in the command of men. 'There are 100–150 soldiers in the military unit. And ten times as many officers. The officer is listed as a company commander, two years later as a battalion commander. And he has neither a company nor a battalion. He grows up to be the commander of the army and he doesn't know how to command anyone.'[6]

Serdyukov found a disproportionate number of officers being trained for the size of the Russian Armed Forces. In comparison to the US Navy training 1,200 officers, including 300 from foreign navies, Russia was training 1,665 officers annually. 'Because in the first three years, half of us quit.'[7]

It was therefore not surprising to find that Russian military planners witnessed a serious setback during the Georgian War in 2008. Based on wartime experience the Chief of General Staff made his displeasure evident.

> Commanders who, commanding regiments and divisions that existed only on paper, were simply not able to solve issues that arose during a real war. When they were given people and equipment, they were confused, and some even refused to perform tasks.[8]

Serdyukov's description of the officer cadre suggests a disturbing trend that could only have a negative impact on leadership in war. 'When my son took oath, I was amazed to see on the parade ground young officers with bellies who no longer fit into the uniform sewn on the occasion of graduation. I thought: how will they fight?'[9]

The former defence minister's interview is revealing in terms of the challenges that were faced by the Russian Armed Forces in 2007–08. Correspondingly, it reflected the magnitude of the changes that were desirable if the armed forces had to develop the capability of a modern fighting force.

Serdyukov indicates some of the corrective measures he oversaw during his tenure. However, it became evident that there were differences within the armed forces over the changes he was implementing. Further, the existing beneficiaries of the system were unlikely to take kindly to the proposed changes.[10]

The challenges before the Russian military hierarchy and political leadership were immense. It becomes evident from Serdyukov's interview that bringing changes to the military leadership and operational ethos that had evolved over the years could prove to be more difficult to change than the structure of industrial-age armed forces. This included a shift from conscription to an all-volunteer army, severing vested interests in maintaining a top-heavy force and imbibing an all-arms military culture beyond the newly created integrated structures.

Despite the resistance and differences that existed, it goes to the credit of the Russian leadership that they were able to push reforms. Major changes were undertaken based on the direction provided by the 2010 doctrine and thereafter a refreshed doctrine in 2014.[11] These documents provided an understanding of Russian priorities and visualisation of perceived challenges. The reforms that took place simultaneously reflected the capability the Russian state was desirous of creating by 2020.[12]

This capability development was anchored in Russia's threat assessment. Two of the primacy challenges envisaged included a move of 'military infrastructure of North Atlantic Treaty Organisation (NATO) member countries closer to the borders of the Russian Federation, including by expanding the bloc.' And second, a bid to destabilise 'the situation in individual states and regions and to undermine strategic stability.'[13] In essence, Russia saw the use of force and the show of force in states contiguous to its territory as a violation of international treaties and law and a threat in the making to the Russian state itself.

Russia had been observing the changing contours of warfare closely. Most recent advances in the employment of modern weapons and experimentation with force structures had been undertaken by the United States (US) forces. It is therefore not a surprise that Russia had taken note of such shifts and these became an important source for its own assessment of military transformation.[14] Some of the important areas identified by the Russian military included the 'integrated utilization of military force'; the employment of conventional weapon systems that could be 'comparable to nuclear weapons in terms of effectiveness'; 'broadening' the employment of troops and resources in 'airspace and outer space'; 'intensification of the role of information warfare'; reduction in preparation time for operations and an improved command and control system that facilitated faster decision making.[15]

The impact of this vision started becoming evident by the time the Russian forces were employed in combat in 2014 during the Crimean campaign, in contrast with their involvement in Georgia in 2008.

This military transformation was undertaken with the complete support of the government, more specifically President Putin. This was not only reinforced by Serdyukov but also became evident with the substantial increase in the defence budget. In 2012, it went up by 16 per cent and the modernisation budget from 2011 to 2020 saw an allocation of USD 730 billion.[16]

Some of the major changes proposed included the following:[17]

- Create a volunteer army; reliance on conscripts initially to be reduced from 50 per cent to 20 per cent, with an eventual reliance on an all-volunteer force in a permanent state of readiness.
- Increase the strength of the military from 700,000 to a million.
- Abolish intermediate divisional headquarters with increased reliance on brigade-sized formations. This is needed to create a highly mobile, adaptable and flexible force.
- Create regional commands around four military districts with a joint structure. The Eastern District to include four armies, while the Western and Southern districts to include two each. The Central District was given a supporting responsibility. The Army should have 38 combat brigades and 41 combat support brigades, with a plan to raise an additional '26 to 40 brigades' by 2020, 'including 14 new army aviation brigades.'
- Divide the Air Force into two staffs including the 'strategic Long Range Aviation Command and the Military Transport Aviation Command.' There should be four territorial air force and air defence commands.
- Organise the Navy to operate through six fleets including the 'Northern Fleet, the Pacific Fleet, the Black Sea Fleet, and the Baltic Fleet and a flotilla (Caspian Sea).'
- Create four independent organisations under the Russian Armed Forces, including the Strategic Rocket Forces with land-based nuclear ICBMs; Airborne Troops to be divided into four air assault divisions and four air assault brigades along with an airborne reconnaissance regiment; 10 special forces units and an Aerospace Defense Force.[18]

## FIRST TEST AND ITS IMPLICATIONS

After the initial reforms had been implemented by 2012, the Russian Armed Forces faced their first test in 2014 in Ukraine with the annexation of Crimea. Arguably, the limited operation, though against negligible military resistance, achieved the desired political and strategic objectives. Russia displayed decisive use of force and effective unity of effort. There was appreciable cohesion between political aims and military means.[19]

It became evident even during the 2014 operations that the Russian Armed Forces, including their special forces, were effective when dealing with a limited objective against a weak opposition. The employment of a covert force, the availability of forces in close proximity and small areas of operations facilitated the employment of special forces, which led to the achievement of a larger strategic prize.

However, success was not as easy to come by in the Donbas region, which put up greater resistance. The sub-conventional approach that had been successful in Crimea, created at best a limited opening for the Russians in Donbas.[20]

These actions could be seen as a successful demonstration of Russia's improving military capability as part of the ongoing transformation. However, there were limitations that continued to adversely impact a more conventional approach to warfare against a well-entrenched adversary. These limitations were a result of legacy challenges faced by the Russian military and its inability to undertake transformation merely through the creation of integrated structures alone. The scope of limited operations of the kind witnessed in Crimea allowed Russia to work around these weaknesses. However, large-scale operations spread over a wider geographical area and for a longer duration raised questions regarding similar military effectiveness.

More importantly, while the creation of organisational structures could be completed over such a short period, it was a bigger challenge to re-orient the military culture of the armed forces, especially the Army, which was no longer trained and ready for a major war. Middle and senior-rung military officers who had moved up the leadership hierarchy without adequate combat and functional experience could come under the kind of combat stress that can only be developed over time and through live exposure in combat.

A previous study of the Indian experience with military change management by the author revealed five key factors that influence the implementation of a successful transformation. These factors will be used as a framework to evaluate the Russian endeavour prior to assessing its impact during the Ukraine War of 2022–23. The five critical factors that drive successful military change are long-term strategic assessment; political support; visionary and committed military leadership; strong institutional structures; and follow-up action to progress changes to their logical conclusion.[21]

An evaluation of these factors provides indications regarding the potential for success or failure of military transformation in Russia.

## PARAMETERS FOR DEFENCE REFORMS IN RUSSIA

The task of military transformation must pursue an objective long-term strategic assessment. In Russia, this was attempted through a rigorous process of guidance basis successive doctrines and strategies to provide clarity for all stakeholders. The relative success achieved in Crimea in 2014 provides a contrast to the challenges faced more recently in 2022 during the Ukraine War. This suggests that either the process of capability development did not take into account future military employment or worse that the Russian military failed to build the requisite professionalism for a task that was considered well within its ability. Either way, there is evidence of a gap between military capability development and the long-term strategic assessment that would dictate military employment. The Russian military was possibly better equipped and trained to handle limited operations against a weak opposition instead of major wars against a determined adversary. The war experience of Russian Armed Forces remained focused upon limited and special operations of the kind that leveraged unstable political and social conditions to employ special forces for an impact beyond their numbers. This was seen in Crimea and parts of Donbas. However, this experience while useful and valuable under certain specific conditions, did not replace the needs and demands of a large-scale conventional war.

Over time, the Russian leadership and in particular President Putin were convinced about the need for military reforms. They were also aware of over-reliance on numbers and the industrial-era approach to warfare that the military had excelled at in the past. The leadership was also cognisant of the bloating up of the senior military ranks and the vested interests that had come to influence decision-making instead of professional factors alone. This made defence reforms imperative for Russia, especially if they were to contend with the rapid modernisation of their potential adversary—the US—with the hope of protecting their strategic interests against the expanding influence of NATO. The acknowledgment of the need for reforms led to the necessary political patronage of tough decisions, including cutting down numbers of the armed forces, reducing military establishments, initiating action against corrupt practices and placing the development of operational capability ahead of individual service-specific interests. Military modernisation is almost never an exercise in cost-cutting. This was evident from Russia's experience as well, which saw a sharp increase in the allocation of the defence budget during the initial years of military modernisation. It is also evident from the budgetary support provided by the Russian leadership that even as this total amount reduced in the more recent past, it remained a substantial percentage of the total government expenditure and a percentage of the GDP. This indicates the desire of the Russian leadership to continue with its effort towards transforming its armed forces through the provision of necessary budgetary outlay.

Military transformation is best progressed when the reform process is supported by the political leadership and benefits from the professional guidance and implementation of the senior military hierarchy. While there is adequate evidence of political support for the reforms, as seen above, the ability of the senior military leadership to navigate the process has raised serious questions after the Ukraine War of 2022–23. The foremost failure of the leadership emerges from its attempt at shielding and hiding the true nature of Russian military weaknesses for fear of reprimand. The relative success of the Crimean Operation and the challenges faced in the Donbas region should have indicated these concerns within the Russian military. The limited exposure to combined arms manoeuvres became evident from the very commencement of operations in 2022. This was either a result of inadequate planning or capacity. At worst, it could have been an outcome of both. This implies that force structures that were created as a result of military modernisation were not tested during wargames and exercises that were meant to validate their effectiveness. In addition, the military leadership failed to guide the creation of requisite capability for the intended strategic objectives, which had been stated in no uncertain terms in the Russian doctrine.

These aspects stemmed from the critical weaknesses of Russia's transformation process. While some of these had been overcome over a decade of reforms, other limitations remained. The Russian military planners failed to convert the conscript model of recruitment to an all-volunteer one as had been planned. The size of the army was clearly inadequate to undertake the kind of offensive that was launched to invade Kyiv, especially in light of the sub-optimal implementation of a technologically driven force that could create the enabling conditions for the numerically smaller land forces to overcome a substantially weakened opposing force.

The ability to undertake a follow-up action remains critical for the success of any military reforms. The Russian reforms began in 2008. The military planners were afforded the opportunity in 2014 to reassess the direction and scope of these changes. However, the Ukraine War suggests that the requisite follow-up that was needed was not undertaken until 2022. On the contrary, it was the Ukrainians, duly supported by NATO, who learned from their failures of 2014 and developed capabilities that were tailored to stand up to the Russian forces. In fact, they also identified Russian military weaknesses with the ability to exploit them at critical junctures. These specific aspects will be discussed in other chapters of this volume dealing with specific arms and niche areas of military employment.

Despite making initial mistakes, the Russian Armed Forces have displayed an ability to adapt on the battlefield during the course of a long-drawn conflict. While most of these instances relate to the tactical battlefield, these are positive signs of flexibility and the ability to make amends despite the reverses.[22] An assessment of the Second World War also indicates that the Russians have the ability to bounce back after losing ground initially. This includes reinventing themselves and taking losses as part of the learning process. Russia has been successful in blunting Ukrainian offensives successfully. At the time of writing this paper, there is inadequate evidence to relate these successes to structural changes. The experience gained could likely provide the impetus for successful reforms. However, these will need follow-up over time to ensure that reforms are institutionalised if the intended objective of a modern fighting force has to be achieved.

## ACHIEVING BATTLEFIELD EFFECTIVENESS WITH DEFENCE REFORMS

In an interesting book, *The Dictator's Army: Battlefield Effectiveness in Authoritarian Regimes*, Caitlin Talmadge proposes a framework for assessing military effectiveness.[23] While making the assessment, Talmadge considers a dual ability. It includes tactical-level skills as well as the ability to execute complex operational manoeuvres.[24] These factors can create multiple possibilities for the effectiveness of armed forces as a combination of these two aspects. As an illustration, a tactically brilliant army could suffer serious losses as a result of poor offensive or defensive planning. And the reverse could be equally true, where an excellent plan can be let down by inept tactical execution. The worst-case scenario could result from ineffectiveness at both levels. In effect, a recipe for military disaster.

Talmadge goes on to identify four aspects of military behaviour that can impact the performance of a military.[25] This includes promotion patterns that reflect on the quality of leadership, training regimens that impact military skills, command arrangements that impact the quality of decision-making and finally, information management for coordination of the warfighting effort.

When these aspects are seen in relation to battlefield effectiveness in the context of military transformation undertaken by Russia, its influence on the Ukraine

War becomes evident. The creation of military structures and the introduction of technology-centric reforms are important elements on the modern battlefield. However, this by itself is not a guarantee for success unless these are accompanied by tactical acumen and professional leadership.

Serdyokov's observation of the state of the Russian Army provides a useful perspective on both these aspects. The rise of military leaders without necessarily having been tested for the employment of forces under their command points towards a flawed assessment and promotion system. Despite the reforms, this anomaly was not corrected. Resultantly, senior military leaders clearly did not have the requisite experience to lead their troops under battlefield conditions. In light of the challenges faced by the Russian military, it can also be concluded that exercises were conducted on the basis of unrealistic parameters that did not reflect the reality of challenges in Ukraine. Simultaneously, Russia did successfully create islands of military excellence within its armed forces, including special operations units with combat experience. Their ability to achieve results emerged as a silver lining in 2014 and more recently in Ukraine. This, however, was not a reflection of the training standards of the armed forces in general. Unlike previous military engagements when Russia wanted to retain a degree of deniability of their involvement, the employment of the Wagner Group under testing battlefield conditions such as those prevalent in Bakhmut, further reinforces the limitations of regular military organisations, which should have logically been better suited for conventional warfighting responsibilities. Forces such as the Wagner Group should ideally augment conventional military forces, not replace them in battle!

The inability to imbibe professionalism at the tactical level was unfortunately aggravated by the failure to make soldiering at the grassroots level attractive enough for fresh recruits. The decision to convert a conscript army to an all-volunteer force could not be implemented. Further, the employment of conscripts in war and the high desertion rate were all indicative of weaknesses that persisted despite the reform process.[26]

The war in Ukraine witnessed an uncharacteristically high rate of deaths among senior military officers.[27] This has been attributed to the lack of initiative at the tactical level and the failure to imbibe decentralised command and control. Evidently, it led senior officers to move forward to the frontline to force the pace of operations.[28] Such actions indicate the absence of a directive style of command that allows subordinate commanders to operate with flexibility based on a clear directive from their commanders. Further, the sacking of senior military leaders further reinforced the challenges faced by the Russian leadership in achieving their national objectives effectively on the battlefield.[29] In other words, senior leaders failed to ensure the time-bound achievement of the war plan as had been envisaged, leading to their attempt to force the pace from vulnerable positions on the battlefield instead of their subordinates achieving it themselves.

One of the most important contributors to a successful decentralised campaign is the command and control network, which allows the seamless flow of information, facilitating a faster decision cycle. Referred to as the OODA loop (Observe, Orient, Decide and Act), evidently the pace of completing this cycle can make a critical difference in the ability to achieve success between two opposing sides. The concept of an informationalised or network-centric battlefield aims to achieve an advantage in this domain against an adversary. Russia's reorientation towards a technology-driven, modern army was meant to replicate this attribute. The results of the first year of the war seem to suggest either an incomplete transformation to create a seamless information structure or an inadequacy to exploit its full potential.

Amongst the changes that were initially considered a positive initiative was the creation of Battalion Tactical Groups (BTGs), which are combined arms units capable of swift manoeuvres. The employment of these battalions prior to the Ukraine conflict was largely seen as successful. Russia also chose to re-create divisions along its western and southern borders in a bid to improve command, control and the speed of deployment.[30] Conceptually these battalions were a good option from the perspective of having integrated structures at the most fundamental level of warfighting. However, their employment under conditions that demand battles in built-up areas, infantry-heavy roles and hybrid battlefield conditions led to serious challenges. This was specially related to the need for an infantry-heavy deployment, which could not be achieved by an equipment-biased structure such as the BTG.

It is evident from the budgetary outlay Russia made over the years that it was a substantial part of the national expenditure, as also in terms of percentage of the GDP. However, when the same budget is seen in absolute terms and co-related to the ambitions of the Russian state, limitations become evident. This is all the more relevant when compared with the US and Chinese budgets instead of India's. Therefore, even as Russia did well to enhance its outlay for building a technologically oriented defence force, the transformation is difficult to achieve when co-related with the envisaged role and the size of the force.

## LESSONS FOR INDIA

At the outset, prior to drawing lessons from Russia's experience with its military transformation it would be pertinent to underline differences with the Indian context. The Indian and Russian military represents fundamentally different models in terms of their organisational structures, the role played by the military within the government, combat experience and most importantly, military culture. These differences stem from the experiences, circumstances and evolution of the two organisations over the years. This makes drawing relevant lessons that much more challenging, raising obvious concerns regarding the relevance of such an exercise. Keeping this reality in perspective, the focus of this analysis remains on military aspects alone despite the inherent influence of aforementioned differences on the defence forces of any country.

India's decision to undertake military reforms was an attempt at enhancing operational effectiveness through the integration of its armed forces. In addition to this requirement, Russia's challenges also related to issues of morale, motivation and a seemingly incongruent officer–men ratio. In contrast, a disproportionately low number of officers are available in battalions, given the deficiencies at lower officer ranks in the Indian Army for over three decades now. India did not face issues such as officers being promoted without being adequately tested in either combat or simulated combat-like conditions. Similarly, officers are not considered for career progression without the command of their sub-units and units. Challenges associated with conscription are a non-issue for the reform process in India. On the contrary, more often than not recruitment processes in India face the challenge of managing crowds seeking to join the armed forces.[31]

There were also certain similarities in the reform process undertaken by Russia and India. The senior leadership in both countries acknowledged the need for military reforms and eventually gave a directive for its implementation despite reservations within some sections of the uniformed community. This ensured support for reforms at the highest level and facilitated the process of transformation.

Both countries made integration of their armed forces a key outcome of the reform process. In this regard, the single-service approach to military matters was a common limitation that existed within the two setups. This was accompanied by the desire to reduce redundancies and improve the efficiency of delivery systems.

Arguably, both countries did assess advanced military modernisation models that had undergone similar transformative changes. In this regard, the US experience was an important reference point, without necessarily the need to replicate it. This was especially relevant since the US had experience with successive iterative changes to its military structures. This became all the more valuable with its operational validation in Iraq and Afghanistan, leading to valuable insights that included both successes and failures of the model.

Before assessing the limitations of the Russian experience it is important to reinforce the strength of their endeavour. Russia acknowledged the challenges it faced in 2008 and undertook reforms in due earnest thereafter. This was an important starting point for subsequent changes—some more transformative than others. Second, Russia undertook a deliberate process of doctrinal guidance in 2010 and 2014 to enable coherence of thought and action to its military transformation. There was complete clarity in the assessment of the country's challenges. Third, arguably, Russia succeeded in creating niche capabilities through specialists in an attempt to build capabilities. This included special forces, militia and information warfare expertise, to name a few. Fourth, until the Ukraine War, Russia also demonstrated the ability to balance its military capability with its strategic objectives during the period of military transformation. In other words, it did not suffer from the debilitating challenge of military overreach.

Having seen some of the strengths of the Russian model, the focus needs to shift towards the limitations of the Russian military reforms that India or for that matter any other country attempting military transformation must draw lessons from.

Resistance within certain quarters against any change is expected and predictable in all bureaucracies. It is all the more relevant for military bureaucracies. This was evident in Russia, before that in the US, and more recently in India as well.[32] The perception of diluting influence, numbers and how things should be done is always difficult to accept. If the decision-making hierarchy is blind-sighted or taken in by this resistance, it raises the potential for either half-baked reforms or the possibility of failure when the new organisation is tested in combat. Russia has witnessed a series of sackings of its senior military leaders.[33] This has been accompanied by the unfortunate reality of a disproportionate number of star-ranked officers being killed in combat. These incidents are in part a reflection of an inadequate or dysfunctional reform process. An integrated organisation will yield far better results on the battlefield when compared with a disaggregated single-service organisation. However, as difficult as it is to lead forces in war, it becomes more complex in an integrated environment. Military leaders who may have delivered the bare minimum in an industrial-age battlefield environment will almost certainly fail to do so in a more complex joint theatre battle. The resistance to change that attempts to preserve service-specific domains and positions of senior officers at the cost of efficiency in peace, resulting in paying a heavy price in war. The inability of some senior officers to deliver in Ukraine as well as their casualties is a sharp reflection of this weakness.

In the face of such opposition–often very vocal and passionate—an unbiased assessment of key military transformation outcomes becomes important. This must come not merely from the armed forces, who could well be a part of the vocal opposition to those very outcomes, but from the highest levels of the government. The objectives must be laid down clearly and in as much detail as needed to thereafter allow professionals to implement the directives. Ideally, this process must be accompanied by a public debate that allows different views to be aired and debated.

One of the most important lessons from Russia's military reforms relates to what is possible in a short period and what is not. It is far easier to create new military structures. After all, their efficacy or in the worst-case scenario their failure will only be seen in a combat situation. In contrast, it is far more difficult to change the military culture of an institution. And irrespective of the excellence of structures, their integration and efficiency, failure is guaranteed if an organisation is adversely influenced by a negative culture, especially when related to professionalism.[34] The weaknesses in Russian military culture that seem to have crept into their system, as outlined by the former defence minister, are bound to adversely affect military effectiveness. It, therefore, becomes imperative for Indian planners to ensure that the existing strengths of the services create a multiplier effect in a future integrated environment.

The Russian experience also suggests that capabilities cannot be created overnight. This became evident in raising additional manpower for the war effort and niche military capabilities in the face of opposition.[35] This directly affects the allocation of budgets and, more importantly, a long-term plan for capability development that remains closely aligned with intended objectives and evolving threats.

The Russian military decision-making remains centralised within their military hierarchy.[36] This has adversely influenced the decentralised execution of plans. Further, it seems to have curbed the initiative of local commanders in combat. The Indian reforms process must therefore allow space for debate and deliberation on major decisions at the planning stage without centralising decision-making. Simultaneously, the integrated structures must allow decentralised command wherein commanders can take initiative within the broad parameters of the assigned responsibility.

The Russian experiment with a mix of a standing army and conscripts has clearly not worked as was desirable. Seeking to get the best of both—a ready and fast mobilised army along with a percentage that can be brought in when needed—led to neither working to expected levels of effectiveness. It led to sub-optimal operational performance and poor cohesiveness in operations. In addition, the numbers that were desirable for an operation of this scale could never be mobilised over time, leading to a severe crunch, especially of foot infantry for critical manpower-intensive operations.[37]

The constraints of Russia's budgetary outlay despite an increase in percentage terms suggest that the creation of technologically advanced defence forces of the size that India possesses will demand a substantially higher defence outlay. In the absence of such funding, it would be prudent to undertake the endeavour in phases based on priorities or reduced ambitions.

Russia's experience yet again reinforces the importance of realism in training, wargaming and testing the strengths and weaknesses of the armed forces under conditions short of war. This requires fielding the forces under conditions that not only test their plans but also what they are not prepared for.

Russia experimented successfully with cutting down on static establishments, which raised the costs of maintenance and contributed little to the efficiency of the armed forces. India too has attempted to cut legacy establishments to improve the tooth-to-tail ratio. This must be progressed both within military and civil support organisations.

Advanced militaries such as the US defence forces have spent a fortune and decades of effort to create the kind of networked forces that exist today. Yet these are not infallible. Russia's experience with forces that are possibly still in the process of achieving optimisation as a joint organisation is therefore understandable. India too must tread this path with the realisation and acceptance that a networked army or defence forces will not be created in the near future. Instead, this endeavour will see a progressive and incremental culmination instead.

## NOTES

1 Jonas Gratz, 'Russia's Military Reform: Progress and Hurdles,' *CSS Analyses in Security Policy*, 152, April 2014, at https://css.ethz.ch/content/dam/ethz/special-interest/gess/cis/center-for-securities-studies/pdfs/CSSAnalyse152-EN.pdf (Accessed June 22, 2023).

2 Michael Kofman, 'Russian Performance in the Russo–Georgian War Revisited,' *War on the*

*Rocks*, September 4, 2018, at https://warontherocks.com/2018/09/russian-performance-in-the-russo-georgian-war-revisited/ (Accessed May 16, 2023).

3 Anatoly Serdyukov, former Defence Minister of Russia in an interview, *Ogonyok*, May 28, 2018, at https://www.kommersant.ru/doc/3635559 (Accessed April 19, 2023). This is a translation into English from the original article in Russian.

4 Serdyukov gives the example of bringing in a single electronic register for housing to break the influence and corruption of the chairmen of commissions at each military station.

5 Anatoly Serdyukov, *Ogonyok*, May 28, 2018, Note 3.

6 Ibid.

7 Ibid.

8 Quoted in *Ogonyok*, May 28, 2018, at https://www.kommersant.ru/doc/3635559 (Accessed April 19, 2023). This is a translation into English from the original article in Russian.

9 Anatoly Serdyukov, *Ogonyok*, May 28, 2018, Note 3.

10 Ibid.

11 See *The Military Doctrine of the Russian Federation*, February 05, 2010 and 2014, at https://carnegieendowment.org/files/2010russia_military_doctrine.pdf (Accessed April 20, 2023) and at https://web.archive.org/web/20150721195150/http://www.rusemb.org.uk/press/2029 (Accessed June 22, 2023).

12 See Mandip Singh, 'Learning from Russia: Comparing Russian and Chinese Military Reforms,' *Journal of Defence Studies*, October–December 2020, 14(4), at https://idsa.in/jds/14-4-2020-learning-from-russia (Accessed June 20, 2023).

13 Para 8(a) and 8(b), *The Military Doctrine of the Russian Federation*, February 05, 2010, at https://carnegieendowment.org/files/2010russia_military_doctrine.pdf (Accessed April 20, 2023).

14 See Jonas Gratz, 'Russia's Military Reform: Progress and Hurdles,' Note 1.

15 Para 12, *The Military Doctrine of the Russian Federation*, February 05, 2010, Note 13.

16 Jonas Gratz, 'Russia's Military Reform: Progress and Hurdles,' Note 1.

17 Ibid.

18 Ibid.

19 See Michael Kofman, Katya Migacheva, Brian Nichiporuk, Andrew Radin, Olesya Tkacheva and Jenny Oberholtzer, 'Lessons from Russia's Operations in Crimea and Eastern Ukraine,' *Rand*, at https://www.rand.org/pubs/research_reports/RR1498.html (Accessed April 24, 2023).

20 Ibid, p. xiii.

21 Vivek Chadha, *Even if Ain't Broke Yet, Do Fix It: Enhancing Effectiveness Through Military Change*, Pentagon Press, New Delhi, 2016, p. 70.

22 Mick Ryan, 'The Russians Keep Evolving,' *Futura Doctrina*, April 17, 2023, at https://mickryan.substack.com/p/the-russians-keep-evolving (Accessed June 27, 2023).

23 Caitlin Talmadge, *The Dictator's Army: Battlefield Effectiveness in Authoritarian Regimes*, Cornell University Press, Ithaca, 2015.

24 Ibid, pp. 7–8.

25 Ibid, p. 13.

26 Zoe Strozewski, 'Russian Force Sees 'Mass Desertion' Amid Putin's Recruitment Push: Report,' *Newsweek*, September 8, 2022, at https://www.newsweek.com/russian-force-sees-mass-desertion-amid-putins-recruitment-push-report-1741284 (Accessed June 22, 2023).

27 Alia Shoaib, 'How the Russian Officer Elite was Decimated in Ukraine – 29 Generals and Commanders Who Were Killed in Action,' *Business Insider India*, December 31, 2022, at https://www.businessinsider.in/international/news/how-the-russian-officer-elite-is-being-

decimated-in-ukraine-9-generals-and-commanders-who-were-killed-in-combat/articleshow/90175870.cms (Accessed June 22, 2023).

28 Meredith Deliso, 'Why Russia has Suffered the Loss of an 'Extraordinary' Number of Generals,' *abc News*, May 8, 2022, at https://abcnews.go.com/International/russia-suffered-loss-extraordinary-number-generals/story?id=84545931 (Accessed June 22, 2023).

29 Peter Beaumont and Pjotr Sauer, "Russia Replaces General In Charge of Ukraine War in Latest Military Shake-up,' *The Guardian*, January 11, 2023, at https://www.theguardian.com/world/2023/jan/11/russia-replaces-general-in-charge-of-ukraine-war-in-latest-military-shake-up (Accessed June 27, 2023).

30 Keir Giles, 'Reassessing Russia's Reorganized and Rearmed Military,' *Carnegie Endowment for International Peace*, May 03, 2017, at https://carnegieendowment.org/2017/05/03/assessing-russia-s-reorganized-and-rearmed-military-pub-69853 (Accessed June 20, 2023).

31 S Raju, 'Exercising Running: Craze for Army Recruitment Beats Covid – 19 Fears in West UP Villages,' *Hindustan Times*, April 11, 2020, at https://www.hindustantimes.com/india-news/exercising-running-craze-for-army-recruitment-beats-covid-19-fears-in-west-up-villages/story-ujUOzvvZirseX8zyXbP2iJ.html (Accessed June 22, 2023).

32 Rajat Pandit, 'Gen Rawat Challenged Status Quo, Pushed Reforms Even If It Ruffled Feathers,' *The Times of India*, December 09, 2021, at https://timesofindia.indiatimes.com/india/challenged-status-quo-pushed-reforms-even-if-it-ruffled-feathers/articleshow/88173830.cms (Accessed June 22, 2023).

33 Matthew Loh, '"Highly Likely" That Russia Has Lost or Fired 16 of Its Top Generals Since the Start of the War in Ukraine: UK Intelligence,' *Business Insider India*, August 08, 2022, at https://www.businessinsider.in/international/news/highly-likely-that-russia-has-lost-or-fired-16-of-its-top-generals-since-the-start-of-the-war-in-ukraine-uk-intelligence/articleshow/93426931.cms (Accessed June 16, 2023).

34 Max Boot, 'Russia Keeps Losing Wars Because Its Dysfunctional Military Culture,' *The Washington Post*, April 12, 2022, at https://www.washingtonpost.com/opinions/2022/04/12/ukraine-military-culture-advantage-over-russia/ (Accessed June 16, 2023).

35 See Michael G. Anderson, 'A People Problem: Learning From Russia's Failing Efforts to Reconstitute Its Depleted Units in Ukraine,' *Modern War Institute West Point*, January 26, 2023, at https://mwi.usma.edu/a-people-problem-learning-from-russias-failing-efforts-to-reconstitute-its-depleted-units-in-ukraine/ (Accessed June 16, 2023).

36 Maxim Shipenkov, 'Ukraine War: Russia's Problems on the Battlefield Stem from Failures from the Top,' *The Conversation*, September 14, 2022, at https://theconversation.com/ukraine-war-russias-problems-on-the-battlefield-stem-from-failures-at-the-top-189916 (Accessed June 16, 2023).

37 Michael G. Anderson, 'A People Problem: Learning from Russia's Failing Efforts to Reconstitute Its Depleted Units in Ukraine,' Note 33.

# 15

# Arming Ukraine: The Dynamics of External Military Support

*S Samuel C Rajiv*

## INTRODUCTION

Ukraine has been the recipient of significant amounts of military aid since the start of the Russian special military operation in February 2022. Ukraine was the third largest arms importer in the world in 2022, after Qatar and India. Over $60 bn worth arms and ammunition have been provided to Ukraine by its allies, with the majority of aid coming from the United States (US). This support has significantly aided Ukraine's military in standing up to the Russian military onslaught.

Given these supplies, Ukraine occupied the 14th position in the Top 40 largest arms importers in the world during the period 2018–22, accounting for 2 per cent of the total global arms imports.[1] This is significant given that Ukraine was not even listed in the Top 40 arms importers list during 2017–21, by the Stockholm International Peace Research Institute (SIPRI).

To be sure, Ukraine has one of the most robust defence industries in the world. During 2018–22, Ukraine was the 17th biggest arms exporter in the world, as per SIPRI data, accounting for 0.5 per cent of the world's total. Ukraine's share of global arms exports during 2017-21 were slightly higher at 0.7 per cent, making it the 14th biggest arms exporter during that period.[2] Despite having such a robust domestic industrial base, the Russian onslaught has forced it to expend domestic reserves such as those of ammunition and depend on foreign sources to replenish its stocks. Further, some of the niche equipment provided by its allies has also enabled it to more effectively counter the Russian invasion.

The US and European countries, among others who have helped Ukraine militarily, have also had to make changes in their domestic defence industry, arms procurement policies and their own stockpiles, in light of their massive support to Ukraine. Debates about these countries' military industrial complexes profiting from the war in Ukraine have also been raised.

Russia continued to be the second biggest arms exporter in the world during 2018–22, but its share in the global arms trade declined to 16 per cent from 22 per cent during 2013–17. Analysts also noted that Russia's invasion of Ukraine will further lead to a reduction in the volume of its own arms exports, as it will have to prioritise arms production for its own forces rather than for exports.

The chapter examines issues relating to the global efforts to arm Ukraine. It begins with placing in perspective the nature of the military support that Ukraine has received. Three key implications of such massive support are then highlighted: the impact of the Western military support on Ukraine's warfighting capabilities; the debate around the possible escalation concerns associated with certain equipment and platforms such as fighter aircraft or longer-range ammunition; and the impact on the domestic arms industry and stockpiles of the Western countries providing critical equipment such as ammunition.

## ARMS AND EQUIPMENT

Since January 2022 till July 2023, out of the $77 bn of humanitarian and military aid that the US has sent to Ukraine, more than 60 per cent is related to military aid, including weapons and equipment as well as security assistance (which includes training and logistics support).[3] US security assistance and military aid have ranged from Stinger anti-aircraft systems to 155 mm howitzers, 125 mm tank ammunition, High Mobility Rocket Systems (HIMARS) and ammunition, mortar rounds, anti-tank missiles, HAWK air defence systems, anti-aircraft guns and munitions, precision aerial weapons, main battle tanks, infantry fighting vehicles, armoured personnel carriers, mine resistant vehicles, unmanned aerial systems, unmanned coastal defence vessels, riverine patrol boats, anti-tank mines, satellite communication antennas, Chemical, Biological, Radiological and Nuclear (CBRN) protective equipment, electronic jamming equipment as well as support for training, maintenance and sustainment activities.[4]

The total value of this equipment and security assistance exceeded $44 bn since February 2022 (and more than $47 bn in the aftermath of Russia's 2014 invasion of Ukraine).[5] The value of US military assistance since February 2022 therefore was more than 10 times Ukraine's defence budget for 2022, which stood at $3.5 bn.[6] Nearly $24 bn of the US assistance since August 2021 was in the form of Presidential Drawdown Authority (PDA), which authorises the transfer of equipment from US weapons stockpiles due to 'unforeseen emergency'.[7] The US has also transferred Excess Defense Articles from its inventories to Ukraine, including Coast Guard cutters and helicopters.[8] It is pertinent to note that US Direct Commercial Sales (DCS) to Ukraine during the five-year period from 2015–2020 were only $274 m.[9] As of December 2023, active government-to-government foreign military sales (FMS) to Ukraine stood at around $600 m.[10]

Apart from the US, other countries that have provided significant amounts of military aid include the United Kingdom (UK), Poland, Germany, Canada, the Netherlands, Italy, France and Norway. The UK has provided long-range conventional precision strike missiles such as Storm Shadow, Harpoon cruise missiles, anti-tank missiles such as Javelin and Brimstone, Challenger 2 main battle tanks, artillery ammunition, extreme weather clothing, counter drone capabilities and Sea King helicopters, among others. The value of UK military aid to Ukraine in 2022 was nearly $3 bn (GBP 2.3 bn) and the UK has pledged a similar amount of military help in 2023 as well.[11]

**Table 1: Military Aid to Ukraine (Top 20 Countries) (Euros Billion)**

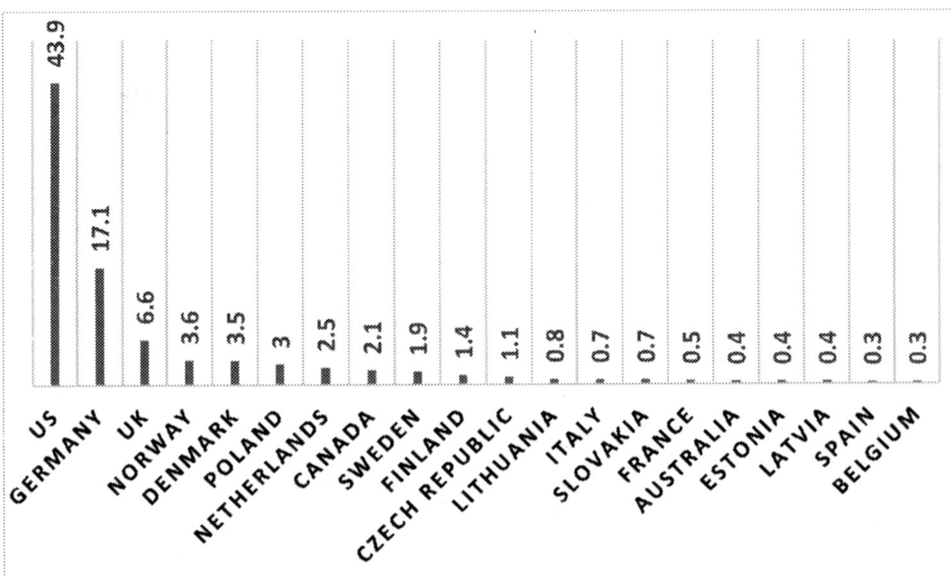


*Source:* Ukraine Support Tracker, Kiel institute for the World Economy (Accessed December 7, 2023).

The European Peace Facility (EPF) has played a pivotal role in providing European military equipment to Ukraine. By mid-2022 itself, the Euros 5.7 bn EPF budget for 2021–27 was spent on Ukraine, half of its total budget of Euros 12 bn.[12] The EPF was established in 2021 as an off-budget mechanism to fund EU military and security assistance measures. The US has also approved 'third-party transfers' of US-origin weapons and equipment from NATO allies' inventories to Ukraine. Such weapons include anti-air missiles, night visions devices and anti-armour systems, among others.[13]

As for individual European countries, Germany provided funding of Euros 2 bn for Ukraine's security and capacity building in 2022 while Euros 5.4 bn have been pledged to be spent in 2023. Additional authorisations amounting to more than Euros 10 bn have been pledged in the coming years to support Ukraine's security and capacity building activities. Among the equipment that Germany has provided includes armoured fighting vehicles, air defence radars and missiles such as Patriot, man portable air defence systems such as Stinger and Strela, precision guided artillery ammunition, self-propelled howitzers, bridge laying tanks and mine clearing tanks, reconnaissance drones and anti-drone sensors, tank transporters and all-terrain vehicles. As of December 2023, more than 100 Leopard main battle tanks (in a project jointly financed by Denmark), air surveillance radars, ammunition, howitzers, drone detection systems, among others were in the process of being distributed to Ukraine.[14]

France has supplied shoulder-launched anti-aircraft missiles and short-range anti-air missiles and in June 2023 it also pledged to supply long-range cruise missiles, SCALP (similar to UK's Storm Shadow), which are usually launched from fighter aircraft in France's inventory such as the Eurofighter or the Rafale. The missiles being supplied to Ukraine are expected to be integrated into the country's Russian-made fighter jets.[15] A French parliamentary report in November 2023 estimated the value of the country's military assistance to Ukraine at more than Euros 3 bn.[16] France has also been involved in training of Ukrainian soldiers as part of the EU Military Assistance Mission. In 2023, it trained over 7,000 Ukrainian soldiers.[17] Other countries such as Belgium, Canada, the Netherlands, Poland (Ukraine's neighbour), Greece, Finland, Estonia and Sweden, among others, delivered self-propelled howitzers, main battle tanks, assault rifles, military transport aircraft, grenade launchers, bullet proof vests, de-mining equipment and armoured personnel carriers.

Reports in February 2023 meanwhile noted that a Polish company had signed a Memorandum of Understanding with a Pakistani company associated with the Pakistan Ordnance Factories for the supply of arms and ammunition to Ukraine.[18] Other reports also flagged the supply of rockets for use in multi-barrel rocket launchers through German ports and the supply/refurbishment of T-80 main battle tanks.[19] While the Pakistani Foreign Office insisted that the country maintained a 'policy of non-interference in military conflicts', analysts have highlighted the irony of Pakistan militarily supporting Ukraine while its all-weather friend China is supporting Russia.[20]

## KEY IMPLICATIONS

### Ukraine's Warfighting Capabilities

There is no doubt that the massive equipment and training support that Ukraine has received from its benefactors has helped it to stand up to the Russian onslaught. Russia launched the invasion with more than 200,000 troops in February 2022. This was eight years after seizing the Crimean Peninsula from Ukraine in 2014 in another military operation. Since 2014, more than 40,000 Russian troops have been stationed in the Crimea, Donetsk and Luhansk regions, occupying more than 7 per cent of Ukraine's territory.[21]

Ukraine's military, therefore, has already been engaged in a conventional and hybrid warfare since 2014, when it had to further counter the massive Russian invasion in 2022. In 2014, Ukraine had 200,000 troops (including around 80,000 paramilitary forces), apart from around a million in reserves. In 2022, the active personnel strength reached nearly 300,000 while by 2023, the number of active troops swelled to nearly a million (inclusive of 250,000 paramilitary) and 400,000 in reserves.[22]

Equipment such as loitering and direct attack munitions and high mobility artillery rocket systems, which Ukraine did not have in its inventory as of February 2022 and have been since supplied by Ukraine's benefactors, have had a decisive impact on the course of the war. This is given the fact that while Russia made significant territorial gains in the initial stages of the war, by October 2022, Ukraine was able to beat back the Russian offensive in many sectors in the east and the north. This was assisted no doubt by equipment such as High Mobility Artillery Rocket System (HIMARS) and scores of cutting-edge equipment and ammunition, as listed in the earlier sections.

Since their usage in the war from June 2022, the 70 km range US-supplied HIMARS rockets and GPS-guided rocket launched glide bombs have enabled

Ukrainian forces to target and destroy Russian ammunition depots and weapons storage facilities. Ukraine's civilian as well as military infrastructure–which took a pounding in the initial stages of the war–have been protected by air defence systems ranging from the Patriot to medium-range systems such as NASAMS to short-range systems such as the vehicle-mounted Avengers.[23]

By February 2023, a year into the conflict, the US had supplied Ukraine with more than a million 155 mm artillery shells, while the European Union (EU) provided 350,000 155 mm artillery shells.[24] EU foreign policy chief Josep Borrell pointed out in February 2023 that the Russians fired more than 50,000 artillery shells per day, compared to around 7,000 by Ukraine.[25] Kiev, therefore, needed additional supplies to at least stand up to the Russian artillery barrage, even after accounting for the massive Western support. It is pertinent to note that prior to the start of the Russian offensive, Ukraine did not have self-propelled 155 mm howitzers. As per the US Department of Defense, more than 800 artillery systems have been pledged or delivered by March 2023, along with more than 2 million rounds of ammunition.[26]

Apart from equipment and training support (over 20,000 Ukrainian soldiers completed training in the US and NATO countries in 2022),[27] intelligence support of Ukraine's allies has been critical. One of the most decisive acts in the early stages of the war was the sinking of the Russian missile cruiser Moskva, the flagship vessel of Russia's Black Sea Fleet. While the warship was sunk on April 14, 2022, by Ukrainian Neptune anti-ship missiles, reports noted that the intelligence about the ship's location was provided by the Americans. The White House later insisted that the US did not provide specific targeting information nor was it involved in the decision to strike the warship.[28] Officials though admitted that the US confirmed the ship's identity and its location, which helped Ukrainian forces to target the ship.

The fact of the positive impact on Ukraine's war fighting capabilities as a result of the Western military support though does not discount deficiencies and inadequacies in the Russian war effort that prevented them from reinforcing the territorial gains secured in the initial stages of the war. The Russians also deliberately did not use the full force of their air power assets. Their personnel policies have also been under the scanner, especially so as regards the significant role of the Wagner militias in executing their war plans as well as in recruiting Russian citizens to buttress the war effort.

## Weapons Systems and Escalation Concerns

As per International Institute for Strategic Studies (IISS) Military Balance 2023, prior to the start of the Russian invasion, Ukraine had about 80 combat capable aircraft made up entirely of Russian-origin equipment such as Su-27 and MiG-29 aircraft.[29] Reports noted that in the first few weeks of the war, Ukraine lost as many as 30 of these aircraft.[30] Ukraine's repeated requests for fighter aircraft has been one of the significant issues of contention vis-à-vis the military equipment and training support that has been provided by its Western allies. This was even as Russia warned that providing fighter jets to Ukraine will be a 'colossal risk'.[31]

President Biden in February 2023 stated that US military assessment showed that Ukraine did not need US F-16s at that period in time, after saying emphatically in January 2023 that the US will not provide fighter jets to Ukraine. President Zelensky toured European capitals (Rome, Berlin, Paris and London) in May 2023 to put in place what he termed a 'coalition of fighter jets' and received a more positive reaction from these countries.[32] As against the US position in the first half of 2023, European countries such as France, Poland and the UK were more open about the proposal to provide Ukraine with fighter jets. This was after Ukraine succeeded in its efforts to secure equipment such as main battle tanks in early 2023.

French President Emmanuel Macron in January 2023, when asked by reporters whether Ukraine will be provided with fighter jets, insisted that 'nothing is excluded' when it came to providing military assistance to Ukraine. Macron, however, flagged the need to avoid escalation and insisted that the jets should not 'touch Russian soil'.[33] British Prime Minister Rishi Sunak, told President Zelensky in early February 2023–during his first visit to the UK after the Russian invasion– that the UK will provide training to Ukrainian fighter pilots to be able to fly NATO-standard fighter jets as and when Ukraine receives such jets.[34] In March 2023, Poland became the first NATO member country to announce that it will supply around 12 Mig-29 fighter jets to Ukraine, followed by Slovakia, which pledged to provide at least 13 similar jets. Poland also was the first country to provide main battle tanks to Ukraine.

Analysts noted that Ukraine's requests for Western fighter jets was to bridge capability gaps relating to Suppression of Enemy Air Defences (SEAD), Intelligence, Surveillance and Reconnaissance (ISR) and ground attack. These are capabilities that Ukraine's inventory made up of older generations of Russian-origin aircraft was not effectively carrying out. Western fighter aircraft such as the

F-16s, on the other hand, could be useful for SEAD operations as well as to target Russian artillery positions.

Analysts have also pointed to possible issues relating to the training of Ukrainian pilots and maintenance of Western fighter aircraft, among others, apart from escalation concerns, that have prevented a more positive response to the Ukrainian requests from the US.[35] It has also been pointed out that the limited number of Western-sourced fighter jets such as F-16s may not lead to a significant change in conflict dynamics, especially in the face of the dense and multi-layered Russian air defence systems. These range from the long-range systems such as the S-400 to medium-range SAMs such as SA-15 (Tor) and SA-17 (Buk).[36] In order to evade Russian missile defences, analysts noted that Ukraine's Western-sourced fighter jets would have to fly at very low altitudes, effectively reducing their lethality and strike options.[37]

At the meeting of the G7 leaders in Japan in May 2023, President Biden finally stated that the US will indeed support partners and allies to train Ukrainian fighter pilots, not on US soil but at European bases. The Pentagon insisted that the training on F-16 fighter aircraft was to support Ukraine's mid- and long-term defence needs and not necessarily for use in a counteroffensive against Russian forces.[38] It was noted that Ukraine was strictly told that the fighter planes will not fly over Russian territory.

NATO Secretary General Jens Stoltenberg in June 2023 revealed that the training of Ukrainian fighter pilots had indeed begun. At the sidelines of the NATO Summit in Lithuania in July 2023, it was reported that a coalition of nations (Belgium, Canada, Denmark, Luxembourg, Norway, Poland, Portugal, Sweden and the UK) will start training Ukrainian pilots at bases in Denmark and Romania. By August, however, it was still not clear which countries will provide the F-16 fighter jets and there was still uncertainty whether US fighter pilots will be involved in the training regimen. The training itself was expected to take at least four to five months.

Apart from the escalation concerns associated with fighter aircraft, equipment such as the 300 km range surface-to-surface missile, MGM-140 Army Tactical Missile System (ATACMS) has also not been provided to Ukraine by the Biden administration on account of escalation fears. Reports noted that even the widely used HIMARS rocket systems were modified by the US prior to delivery to Ukraine in order to prevent them from being fired too deeply into Russian territory, to obviate escalation concerns.[39] The HIMARS can fire the less than 100 km range

Guided Multiple Launch Rocket Systems (GMLRS)—at least six of them—or a single 300 km range ATACMS.

It is pertinent to note that the UK and France have provided cruise missiles such as Storm Shadow and the SCALP to Ukraine, which have a slightly lesser range than the US ATACMS (at less than 250 km). Even as the Biden administration debates whether to supply Ukraine with the ATACMS, it has decided to provide Ukraine with cluster ammunitions, despite widespread criticism.[40] Ukraine's Foreign Minister Dmytro Kuleba meanwhile specifically called up US Secretary of State Anthony Blinken on August 7, 2023, to plead for the ATACMS system to be supplied to 'enhance Ukraine's long-range capabilities'.[41]

The US Vice Chief of Army Staff, in his confirmation hearings in July 2023 before an US Congressional Committee to become the Chief, admitted that the ATACMS will indeed provide Ukraine the ability to attack 'deeper targets'.[42] Analysts specifically noted that ammunition such as the ATACMS will help Ukraine strike at key logistical nodes such as the Kerch bridge, which is the only land bridge connecting the Russian mainland to Crimea.[43] Ukraine though attacked the Kerch Bridge in mid-July without ammunition such as the ATACMS in an attack that apparently used naval drones.[44] President Zelensky confirmed in October 2023 that Ukraine used the US-supplied ATACMS for the first time, without giving details of where they were used. He was responding to reports of destruction of Russian helicopters in Berdyansk and Luhansk and noted that the 'ATACMS have proven themselves'.[45]

## Stockpiles and Domestic Defence Industry

The US debate about whether to provide the ATACMS to Ukraine also related to the number of such missiles in its own inventory and the possibility of sparing such missiles for Ukraine.[46] Lockheed Martin revealed that only about 4,000 ATACMS have been manufactured since the missile was developed in the 80s and US officials have been cited as stating that the missile was essential for US war plans in conflict zones such as the Korean peninsula.[47]

As for 155 mm ammunition that the US has supplied to Ukraine in large numbers, reports noted that the production rate of such ammunition by the US domestic arms industry was around 30,000 rounds per year.[48] Ukraine, however, expended similar amounts in about two weeks. As noted in the previous section, the US has supplied close to two million rounds of 155 mm artillery ammunition to Ukraine till March 2023.

Even then, Ukraine's Defence Minister Oleksii Reznikov wrote to the EU member countries in March 2023, requesting them to provide a quarter of a million artillery shells every month to tide over the critical shortages facing the country in its war effort. As per Reznikov, Ukraine was firing more than a 100,000 155 mm calibre shells a month, which was still at least 4–5 times less than the ammunition being expended by Russia.[49]

President Putin also asserted that the Western countries cannot sustain the weapons supply to Ukraine for ever, and that Russia has far greater industrial capacity to produce tanks and other types of ammunition than that of Western countries. Western analysts, however, rubbished such claims and noted that the Western economies were many times larger than that of Russia and insisted that Russian military industrial capabilities were 'hopelessly unmatched'.[50]

Despite the touted large economic strength and GDPs of Western countries, given the large numbers of equipment and ammunition that was supplied to Ukraine and in a relatively short period of time, issues relating to weapons stockpiles, the ability of the domestic arms industry to cater to the needs of Ukraine as well as their own armed forces and the possibility of deficiencies in military readiness levels, among other aspects, were challenges that were flagged.

President Biden, while touring a Javelin anti-tank guided missile plant in May 2022, reiterated that his administration will do everything in its power to quickly replenish stocks that have been sent to Ukraine. As with the 155 mm ammunition, reports noted that the US sent to Ukraine more than 8,000 Javelins, while the normal production rate of the missile was around 800 per year. Ukraine was therefore sent inventory worth a decade of production.[51]

A September 2022 study by the Center for Science and International Security (CSIS) noted that out of the15 types of equipment that the US sent to Ukraine, the US stockpiles in around half of them were 'limited' while they were deemed to be 'adequate' in around five categories of weapons systems. The adequate quantities related to Harpoon missiles, 105 mm ammunition and howitzers and small arms ammunition while the limited numbers spanned 155 mm ammunition, Stinger missiles, M-777 howitzers, Javelin missiles and HIMARS launchers, among others.[52]

As with US weapons stockpiles and inventories, the issue was also seen as acute vis-à-vis the weapons and equipment that were supplied by NATO member countries to Ukraine. NATO Secretary General, ahead of a meeting of NATO defence ministers in February 2023, admitted that the Ukrainian Armed Forces were consuming ammunition at a faster rate than that could be produced in the West. Jens Stoltenberg noted that it could take more than two years for ammunition orders placed then to be realised, given extant Western production capacities.[53] German Defence Minister Boris Pistorius urged the German defence industry to 'to ramp up all capacities to the maximum as quickly as possible'.[54] As pointed out in earlier sections, Ukraine has secured ammunition supplies from a wide range of countries, including South Korea and Pakistan, to meet its ammunition requirements.

The EU, in early March 2023, meanwhile agreed to not only transfer individual country national stocks of ammunition to Ukraine (Track 1) but also engage in joint procurement of one million rounds of 155 mm ammunition (Track 2), in response to Ukraine's requirements. This ammunition will be procured from the EU defence industry and Norway before September 2023 and individual members will be eligible for reimbursement from funds of the European Peace Facility (EPF) provided they are procured as part of any existing European Defence Agency (EDA) project or through complimentary joint acquisition projects. The Euros 1 bn EPF facility for enabling joint procurement and reimbursement was activated in May 2023.[55] Twenty-four EU member States along with Norway signed the EDA Project arrangement for the joint procurement of ammunition.

Further, as part of the Track 3 of the above approach to address Ukraine's ammunition shortages, it was also decided to ramp up the domestic production capacities of the European defence industry. To enable this effort, the Act in Support of Ammunition Production (ASAP) was adopted in July 2023, as part of which Euros 500 mn was budgeted till June 2025. The ASAP provisions seek to identify bottlenecks in the defence industry supply chains, if any, and tackle these bottlenecks to increase production capacities.

The key objectives of the Act include securing the availability and supply of critical raw materials and components and facilitating access to public finance as well as private funding for European defence companies to help them more effectively respond to Ukraine's defence requirements pertaining to ammunition and missiles.[56] The Act, however, specifically excludes the production of lethal autonomous weapons systems.

The Act also provides for a Ramp-Up Fund to the tune of at least Euros 50 mn to provide support to companies facing difficulties in accessing finance or help accelerate investments to manufacture relevant defence products 'while increasing the security of supply for the whole Union defence industry value chain'.[57] While the financial envelope of Euros 500 mn has been provided till June 2025, the Act will be evaluated in June 2024 for possible extension of its applicability and additional funding if required, depending upon the prevailing security situation and consultations with member states and key stakeholders.

## IN CLOSING

Russia's special military operation in Ukraine is a full-scale, high-intensity, inter-state land war being fought on European borders. As Josep Borrell, the High Representative of the European Union for Foreign Affairs and Security Policy stated in May 2023, Europe has not seen a war of such high intensity in decades. The consequences of the war and the challenges being encountered in assisting Ukraine face up to the Russian aggression have forced European countries to re-examine their defence and security strategies and policies.

This has been most pertinent as regards the impact the war has had on their defence industrial capabilities, given the massive amounts of military aid these countries are supplying to Ukraine. Borrell has flagged the need for the EU to more effectively pool resources to tackle defence industrial challenges going forward in a cooperative manner rather than by just increasing national defence expenditures to a certain percentage of respective GDPs.[58]

As for the US, it has been cautious in providing ammunition or platforms given the possibility that the extant production rates of these equipment may not help plug the resultant gaps in US readiness and stockpiles adequately enough, apart from reasons associated with possibility of escalation of the war with US weapons and equipment. This is indeed a significant barometer of the unpredictability infused into the contingency planning and associated military readiness levels of the US and its allies as a result of a large-scale conventional war. The need to maintain and sustain large-scale stockpiles therefore is being flagged as an essential requirement, given the high equipment losses that can be expected in high-intensity conventional wars.

US Secretary of State Anthony Blinken, while announcing additional military assistance to Ukraine on November 3, 2023 asserted that the US and its coalition partners will continue to stand with Ukraine until Russia withdrew its forces from the country.[59] Blinken, however, on December 6, 2023, while announcing another package of military assistance worth $175 mn including air defence and artillery munitions, anti-armour missiles, among others, noted that this could be one of the last assistance packages to Ukraine unless the US Congress passed the

President's national security supplemental funding request of more than $100 bn.[60] The request included more than $30 bn of funds for Ukraine, $14 bn for Israel and $13 bn for border security.

President Biden, speaking on December 6, urged the Congress to approve of his funding request and stated that any disruption in US ability to support Ukraine "strengthens Putin's position".[61] The 49 Republicans in the US Senate though voted against the request demanding additional funds for border security while independent Senator Bernie Sanders expressed concern about Israel's "inhumane military strategy" vis-à-vis the Palestinians and voted against the request.[62]

The vote was an indication of US domestic politics as well as other security concerns relating to the Mexican border – apart from concerns over replenishment of US military stockpiles, increasingly impacting US security assistance policies towards Ukraine. Given the above, in order to bolster Ukraine's domestic ability to produce critical military equipment and spare parts, the launch of the US-Ukraine Defense Industrial Base Partnership on December 6, 2023, assumes significance.

Ukraine has not only stood up to the Russian aggression for nearly two years on the back of military support and security assistance of more than 50 countries but has also taken back nearly half of the territory captured by Russia, at huge human and material cost. It remains to be seen when and how Ukraine will be able to completely beat back the decade-long Russian territorial aggression.

The Ukraine War has highlighted the challenges related to defence industrial complexes, as a result of protracted conflicts. Despite massive support from the West, Ukraine has been facing the challenge of replenishment of its arsenal. Ammunition shortages and dependence on imports for critical equipment such as engines, among others, have also been highlighted in the Indian context.

Reports of the Comptroller and Auditor General (CAG) in 2015 and 2017, for instance, highlighted that only stocks of 20 per cent of armoury were found to be satisfactory.[63] The government has subsequently taken steps to address these issues, including setting up a working group to review availability of critical items, defining a roadmap to build up adequate stocks through imports wherever required, as well as advancing five-year orders with ordnance factories.[64]

In the aftermath of the 2016 Uri terrorist attacks, the army has placed orders worth over Rs 30,000 crores to fill critical firepower shortages.[65] The government has also taken steps such as delegation of financial powers for revenue procurement to bridge ammunition shortages. Former Army Chief MM Naravane asserted in

January 2020 that procurement has been fast-tracked and issues with shortages have been resolved.[66]

Given that India's partner nations and sources of arms and equipment are unlikely to raise their production capacity in a buyer-seller relationship, as against ideological and strategic support that has been given to Ukraine in the past nearly two years, the steps that the Ministry of Defence and the government have taken to effectively address shortages of critical equipment such as ammunition are indeed welcome.

Further, the series of steps taken in recent years relating to defence indigenisation and domestic procurement, be it positive indigenisation lists or a significant portion of the capital procurement budget being allotted to the domestic defence industry, are expected to further reduce dependence on imports for critical equipment.

## NOTES

1 Pieter D. Wezeman, Justine Gadon and Siemon T. Wezeman, 'Trends In International Arms Transfers, 2022', March 2023, p. 6, at https://www.sipri.org/publications/2023/sipri-fact-sheets/trends-international-arms-transfers-2022 (Accessed December 5, 2023).

2 Pieter D. Wezeman, Alexandra Kuimova and Siemon T. Wezeman, 'Trends In International Arms Transfers, 2021', March 2022, p. 2, at https://www.sipri.org/publications/2022/sipri-fact-sheets/trends-international-arms-transfers-2021 (Accessed December 5, 2023).

3 Jonathan Masters and Will Merrow, 'How Much Aid Has the US Sent Ukraine? Here Are Six Charts,' *Council on Foreign Relations*, July 10, 2023, at https://www.cfr.org/article/how-much-aid-has-us-sent-ukraine-here-are-six-charts#:~:text=Since%20the%20war%20began%2C%20 the,Economy% 2C%20a%20German%20research%20institute (Accessed December 6, 2023).

4 'Fact Sheet on US Security Assistance to Ukraine', US Department of Defense, December 6, 2023, at https://www.defense.gov/News/Releases/Release/Article/3426389/biden-administration-announces-additional-security-assistance-for-ukraine/ (Accessed December 6, 2023).

5 Ibid.

6 The International Institute for Strategic Studies, *The Military Balance* 2023, Routledge, 2023, p. 201.

7 'Fact Sheet on US Security Assistance to Ukraine', no. 4.

8 Defense Security Cooperation Agency, Excess Defense Articles at https://www.dsca.mil/programs/excess-defense-articles-eda#_blank (Accessed August 5, 2023).

9 'Fact Sheet on US Security Assistance to Ukraine', no. 4.

10 Ibid.

11 Alex Candlin, 'UK Pledges Further £2.3 bn to Support Ukraine in 2023,' *Forces News*, December 29, 2022, at https://www.forces.net/news/uk-pledges-further-ps23bn-support-ukraine-2023 (Accessed August 10, 2023); See also "Defence Secretary Oral Statement," UK Ministry of Defence, May 11, 2023, at https://www.gov.uk/government/speeches/defence-secretary-oral-statement-on-war-in-ukraine--3 (Accessed August 10, 2023).

12 Max Bergmann and Naz Gocek, 'Europe Needs Its Own Ukraine Assistance Act,' *Center for Strategic and International Studies*, June 22, 2022, at https://www.csis.org/analysis/europe-needs-its-own-ukraine-assistance-act (Accessed August 10, 2023). See also European Commission, 'European Peace Facility', at https://fpi.ec.europa.eu/what-we-do/european-peace-facility_en (Accessed August 10, 2023).

13 'Fact Sheet on US Security Assistance to Ukraine', no. 4.

14 'Military Support for Ukraine,' *The Federal Government*, December 1, 2023, at https://www.bundesregierung.de/breg-en/news/military-support-ukraine-2054992 (Accessed December 5, 2023).

15 'What Are France's SCALP Missiles, and How Can They Help Ukraine?,' *Al Jazeera*, July 11, 2023, at https://www.aljazeera.com/news/2023/7/11/what-are-frances-scalp-missiles-and-how-can-they-help-ukraine (Accessed August 10, 2023).

16 The estimation does not represent the price of the equipment sent to Ukraine but the budgetary cost of replacing the equipment in French arsenals. This estimation will place France as the sixth largest provider of security and military assistance to Ukraine, after the US, Germany, UK, Norway and Denmark. The Ukraine Support Tracker at Kiel University (Table 1) though places France at the 15th position amongst largest providers of military aid, at Euros 500 mn. See Cédric Pietralunga, 'French military aid to Ukraine estimated at € 3.2 billion', November 9, 2023, at https://www.lemonde.fr/en/international/article/2023/11/09/french-military-aid-to-ukraine-estimated-at-3-2-billion_6241996_4.html (Accessed December 7, 2023).

17 'Thousands of Ukrainian soldiers undergo French military training before being sent to the front', *Euronews*, November 13, 2023, at https://www.euronews.com/2023/11/13/thousands-of-ukrainian-soldiers-undergo-french-military-training-before-being-sent-to-the- (Accessed December 7, 2023).

18 Dipanjan Roy Chowdhury, 'Pakistan, Polish Entities Ink MoU for Supply of Defence Equipment to Ukraine,' *The Economic Times*, February 17, 2023, at https://economic times.indiatimes.com/news/defence/pakistan-polish-entities-ink-mou-for-supply-of-defence-equipment-to-ukraine/articleshow/97996207.cms?from=mdr (Accessed August 6, 2023).

19 Dipanjan Roy Chowdhury, 'Pakistan to Supply Rockets to Ukraine via Germany Ports Now,' *The Economic Times*, February 11, 2023, at https://economictimes.indiatimes.com/news/defence/pakistan-to-supply-arms-to-ukraine-via-german-port-now/articleshow/97808726.cms?utm_source=contentofinterest&utm_medium=text&utm_campaign=cppst (Accessed August 6, 2023).

20 Kamran Yousaf, 'Pakistan Rubbishes Claims of Arms Supply to Ukraine,' *The Tribune*, February 16, 2023, at https://tribune.com.pk/story/2401542/pakistan-rubbishes-claims-of-arms-supply-to-ukraine (Accessed August 6, 2023).

21 '10 Facts You Should Know About Russian Military Aggression against Ukraine,' Ministry of Foreign Affairs of Ukraine, December 19, 2019, at https://mfa.gov.ua/en/countering-russias-agression/10-facts-you-should-know-about-russian-military-aggression-against-ukraine (Accessed August 4, 2023).

22 The International Institute for Strategic Studies, *The Military Balance 2014*, Routledge, 2014, p. 194; See also The International Institute for Strategic Studies, no. 6.

23 Gerry Doyle, Anurag Rao and Vijdan Mohammad Kawoosa, 'Shaping the Battlefield: How Weapons from Western Allies Are Strengthening Ukraine's Defence,' *Reuters*, March 10, 2023, at https://www.reuters.com/graphics/UKRAINE-CRISIS/ARMS/lgvdkoygnpo/ (Accessed August 4, 2023).

24 Jacopo Barigazzi, 'EU Nears Deal to Restock Ukraine's Diminishing Ammo Supplies,' *Politico*, March 15, 2023, at https://www.politico.eu/article/ukraine-war-european-union-ammunition-supplies-deal/ (Accessed August 4, 2023).

25 Sanya Mansoor, 'Why the West Is Getting Nervous About Ammunition Shortages for Ukraine,' *Time*, March 16, 2023, at https://time.com/6263802/ukraine-west-ammunition-shortages/ (Accessed August 4, 2023).

26 Jim Garamone, "US Sends Ukraine $400 Million in Military Equipment", US Department of Defense, March 3, 2023, at https://www.defense.gov/News/News-Stories/Article/Article/3318508/us-sends-ukraine-400-million-in-military-equipment/#:~:text=They've%20delivered%20 or%20pledged,advanced%20Multiple%20Rocket%20Launch%20Systems (Accessed August 6, 2023).

27 Phillips Payson O'Brien, 'Time Is on Ukraine's Side, Not Russia's,' *The Atlantic*, January 14, 2023, at https://www.theatlantic.com/ideas/archive/2023/01/russia-ukraine-weapon-production-nato-supply/672719/ (Accessed August 4, 2023).

28 Ken Dilanian, Courtney Kube and Carol E. Lee, 'US Intel Helped Ukraine Sink Russian Flagship Moskva,' *NBC News*, May 6, 2022, at https://www.nbcnews.com/politics/national-security/us-intel-helped-ukraine-sink-russian-flagship-moskva-officials-say-rcna27559 (Accessed August 4, 2023).

29 The International Institute for Strategic Studies, no. 6, p. 203.

30 'List of Aircraft Losses during the Russian Invasion of Ukraine,' *Oryx*, March 20, 2022, at https://www.oryxspioenkop.com/2022/03/list-of-aircraft-losses-during-2022.html (Accessed August 4, 2023).

31 'Russia: Giving F-16 Fighter Jets to Ukraine a "Colossal Risk",' *Al Jazeera*, May 20, 2023, at https://www.aljazeera.com/news/2023/5/20/russia-giving-f-16-fighter-jets-to-ukraine-a-colossal-risk (Accessed August 4, 2023).

32 'President of Ukraine: We Are Working to Create a Coalition of Fighter Jets,' President of Ukraine, May 14, 2023, at https://www.president.gov.ua/en/news/mi-pracyuyemo-nad-stvorennyam-koaliciyi-vinishuvachiv-prezid-82885 (Accessed August 4, 2023).

33 'Western Allies Differ Over Fighter Jets for Ukraine as Russia Claims Gains,' *Reuters*, January 31, 2023, at https://www.nbcnews.com/news/world/western-allies-differ-fighter-jets-ukraine-russia-claims-gains-rcna68322 (Accessed August 4, 2023).

34 'PM Extends Ukraine Military Training to Pilots and Marines as President Zelensky Makes First Visit to the UK Since Russian Invasion,' Gov.UK, February 8, 2023, at https://www.gov.uk/government/news/pm-extends-ukraine-military-training-to-pilots-and-marines-as-president-zelenskyy-makes-first-visit-to-the-uk-since-russian-invasion#:~:text=The%20UK%20will%20continue%20to,main%20battle%20tanks%20to%20Ukraine. (Accessed August 4, 2023).

35 John Hoehn and William Courtney, "Why Does Ukraine Want Western Jets?," RAND, May 3, 2023, at 'Why Does Ukraine Want Western Jets?'. (Accessed August 4, 2023); See also, "Transferring Fighter Aircraft to Ukraine: Issues and Options for Congress," Congressional Research Service, March 17, 2023, at https://crsreports.congress.gov/product/pdf/R/R47476 (Accessed August 4, 2023).

36 Justin Bronk, 'Why the West Is Reluctant to Give Ukraine F-16s,' *The Spectator*, February 5, 2023, at https://www.spectator.co.uk/article/why-the-west-is-reluctant-to-give-ukraine-f-16s/ (Accessed August 4, 2023).

37 Holly Ellyatt, '"We Will Get F-16s": Ukraine Aims for NATO's Fighter Jets after Winning Battle for Western Tanks,' *CNBC*, January 26, 2023, at https://www.cnbc.com/2023/01/26/

ukraine-aims-for-f-16-fighter-jets-after-winning-battle-for-tanks.html (Accessed August 4, 2023).

38 C. Todd Lopez, 'F-16 Training, Aircraft, to Fill Ukraine's Mid-Term, Long-Term Defense Needs,' *DoD News*, May 23, 2023, at https://www.defense.gov/News/News-Stories/Article/Article/3405085/f-16-training-aircraft-to-fill-ukraines-mid-term-long-term-defense-needs/ (Accessed August 4, 2023).

39 Michael R Gordon and Gordon Lubold, 'US Altered Himars Rocket Launchers to Keep Ukraine from Firing Missiles Into Russia,' *The Wall Street Journal*, December 5, 2022, at https://www.wsj.com/articles/u-s-altered-himars-rocket-launchers-to-keep-ukraine-from-firing-missiles-into-russia-11670214338 (Accessed August 8, 2023).

40 For an analysis see Abhay Kumar Singh, 'US Cluster Munitions for Ukraine: Military Context and Legal Considerations,' MPIDSA Issue Brief, July 14, 2023, at https://www.idsa.in/issuebrief/us-cluster-munitions-for-ukraine-aksingh-140723 (Accessed August 8, 2023).

41 'Ukraine's Foreign Minister Asks US for ATACMS Long-Range Missiles,' *Reuters*, August 7, 2023, at https://www.reuters.com/world/europe/ukraines-foreign-minister-asks-us-atacms-long-range-missiles-2023-08-07/#:~:text=Ukraine's%20foreign%20minister%20asks%20U.S.%20for%20 ATACMS%20long%2Drange%20missiles,-By%20Reuters&text=KYIV%2C%20Aug%207%20 (Reuters),requested %20ATACMS%20long%2Drange%20missiles (Accessed August 8, 2023).

42 'Ukraine Would Benefit from ATACM Missiles, US Army General Says,' *Reuters*, July 12, 2023, at https://www.reuters.com/world/us/ukraine-would-benefit-atacm-missiles-us-army-general-2023-07-12/ (Accessed August 4, 2023).

43 John Hardie, "Biden Is Wrong: Ukraine Needs ATACMS," Foundation for Defense of Democracies, July 14, 2023, at https://www.fdd.org/analysis/2023/07/14/biden-is-wrong-ukraine-needs-atacms/ (Accessed August 4, 2023).

44 Josh Pennington, Alex Stambaugh, Brad Lendon and Christian Edwards, 'Ukraine Claims Responsibility for New Attack on Key Crimea Bridge,' *CNN*, July 17, 2023, at https://edition.cnn.com/2023/07/16/europe/russia-crimea-bridge-intl-hnk/index.html (Accessed August 4, 2023).

45 Robert Greenall and Chris Partridge, 'Ukraine uses US-supplied ATACMS for the first time, says Zelensky', *BBC News,* October 17, 2023, at https://www.bbc.com/news/world-europe-67135163 (Accessed December 7, 2023).

46 'US in No Hurry to Provide Ukraine With Long-Range Missiles,' *The Washington Post*, July 23, 2023, at https://www.washingtonpost.com/national-security/2023/07/22/ukraine-us-long-range-missiles/ (Accessed August 8, 2023).

47 Lara Jakes, 'Biden Administration Is Quietly Debating Whether to Send Ukraine ATACMS Missiles,' *The New York Times*, July 11, 2023, at https://www.nytimes.com/2023/07/11/world/europe/atacms-missiles-ukraine-us.html#:~:text=But%20for%20now%20at%20least,other%20munitions%20in%20its%20counteroffensive (Accessed August 8, 2023).

48 Natasha Turak, 'The US and Europe Are Running Out of Weapons to Send to Ukraine,' *CNBC*, September 28, 2022, at https://www.cnbc.com/2022/09/28/the-us-and-europe-are-running-out-of-weapons-to-send-to-ukraine.html (Accessed August 8, 2023).

49 'FT: Ukraine Appeals to EU to Provide 250,000 Artillery Shells Per Month,' *The Kyiv Independent News Desk*, March 4, 2023, at https://kyivindependent.com/ft-ukraine-appeals-to-eu-for-250-000-artillery-shells-per-month/ (Accessed August 8, 2023).

50 Joshua Askew, 'West Cannot Sustain Arms Supplies to Ukraine, Claims Putin,' *Euro News*, March 26, 2023, at https://www.euronews.com/2023/03/26/west-cannot-sustain-arms-

supplies-to-ukraine-claims-putin (Accessed August 10, 2023).

51 Mark F Cancian, "Is the United States Running Out of Weapons to Send to Ukraine?," Center for Science and International Security, September 15, 2022, at https://www.csis.org/analysis/united-states-running-out-weapons-send-ukraine (Accessed August 10, 2023).

52 Ibid.

53 Stephanie Höppner and Ralf Bosen, 'Ukraine War: Is the Army Running Out of Ammunition?,' *DW*, February 15, 2023, at https://www.dw.com/en/ukraine-war-is-the-army-running-out-of-ammunition/a-64710592 (Accessed August 10, 2023).

54 Ibid.

55 'EU Joint Procurement of Ammunition and Missiles for Ukraine: Council Agrees €1 Billion Support Under the European Peace Facility,' European Council, May 5, 2023, at https://www.consilium.europa.eu/en/press/press-releases/2023/05/05/eu-joint-procurement-of-ammunition-and-missiles-for-ukraine-council-agrees-1-billion-support-under-the-european-peace-facility/ (Accessed August 10, 2023).

56 See "Regulation (EU) 2023/1525 of The European Parliament and of The Council of 20 July 2023 on Supporting Ammunition Production (ASAP)," European Commission, July 24, 2023, at https://defence-industry-space.ec.europa.eu/eu-defence-industry/asap-boosting-defence-production_en (Accessed August 10, 2023).

57 Ibid.

58 Josep Borrell, 'Lessons from the War in Ukraine for the Future of EU Defence,' European Union External Action, May 29, 2023, at https://www.eeas.europa.eu/eeas/lessons-war-ukraine-future-eu-defence_en (Accessed August 10, 2023).

59 'Additional U.S. Military Assistance for Ukraine', US Embassy in Ukraine, November 3, 2023, at https://ua.usembassy.gov/additional-u-s-military-assistance-for-ukraine-6/ (Accessed December 7, 2023).

60 'Biden Administration Announces Additional U.S. Security Assistance for Ukraine', US Department of State, December 6, 2023, at https://www.state.gov/biden-administration-announces-additional-u-s-security-assistance-for-ukraine/ (Accessed December 7, 2023).

61 'Remarks by President Biden Urging Congress to Pass His National Security Supplemental Request, Including Funding to Support Ukraine', The White House, December 6, 2023, at https://www.whitehouse.gov/briefing-room/speeches-remarks/2023/12/06/remarks-by-president-biden-urging-congress-to-pass-his-national-security-supplemental-request-including-funding-to-support-ukraine/ (Accessed December 7, 2023).

62 Patricia Zengerle, 'US Senate Republicans block Ukraine, Israel aid bill over border dispute', *Reuters*, December 7, 2023, at https://www.reuters.com/world/us/us-senate-sets-test-vote-ukraine-aid-despite-republican-opposition-2023-12-06/#:~:text=WASHINGTON%2C%20Dec%206%20(Reuters),the%20U.S.%20border%20with%20Mexico (Accessed December 8, 2023).

63 Rajat Pandit, 'India Faces Severe Ammunition Shortage, Can Fight War for Only 20 Days: CAG,' *The Times of India*, May 9, 2015, at https://timesofindia.indiatimes.com/india/india-faces-severe-ammunition-shortage-can-fight-war-for-only-20-days-cag/articleshow/47209011.cms (Accessed August 12, 2023); See also Sudhi Ranjan Sen, 'Indian Army's Ammunition Stock Will Exhaust after 10 Days of War: CAG Report,' *India Today*, July 21, 2017, at https://www.indiatoday.in/india/story/indian-army-ammunition-war-supply-shortfall-cag-report-1025676-2017-07-21 (Accessed August 12, 2023).

64 'Shortage of Ammunition for Armed Forces,' *Press Information Bureau*, February 5, 2018, at https://pib.gov.in/Pressreleaseshare.aspx?PRID=1519144 (Accessed August 12, 2023).

65 Amrita Nayak Dutta, 'Army Buys Ammo Worth Rs 30,000 Crore to Fill Shortage Exposed after 2016 Uri Attack,' *The Print*, February 3, 2020, at https://theprint.in/defence/army-buys-ammo-worth-rs-30000-crore-to-fill-shortage-exposed-after-2016-uri-attack/357816/ (Accessed August 12, 2023).

66 'Ammo Reserves Full, Stocks High: Army Chief Says Preparedness Not Dependent on Budget Allocations,' *India Today*, January 28, 2020, at https://www.indiatoday.in/business/budget-2020/story/ammo-reserves-full-stocks-high-army-chief-says-preparedness-not-dependent-on-budget-allocations-1641027-2020-01-28. (Accessed August 12, 2023).

# 16

# The Road to War Termination: Navigating Strategies and War Termination Efforts in Russia–Ukraine War

*Rajneesh Singh*

## INTRODUCTION

Russia launched a 'special military operation' in Ukraine on February 24, 2022 in the hope of a quick victory but finds itself embroiled in a protracted war with no end in sight. The Russia–Ukrainian war has left a trail of devastation and suffering, prompting urgent calls for negotiations and conflict resolution to bring an end to the hostilities. This chapter delves into the efforts being made to bring an end to the war.

The chapter begins by shedding light on why predicting the outcome of war is difficult and negotiations even more difficult. It thereafter analyses the political and military objectives of the stakeholders and critical moments and turning points in the war that have played a decisive role in shaping its outcome. Subsequently, the chapter deliberates on the various attempts at negotiations and diplomatic engagement that have taken place throughout this war and the challenges involved in war termination because of the deeply entrenched positions and demands of the two principals—Russia and Ukraine. Lastly, the chapter attempts to prognosticate the possible war termination scenarios, including political settlement. In doing so the chapter attempts to highlight the intricacies of navigating a lasting resolution to one of the defining wars of the recent times.

## VICTORY, NEGOTIATIONS AND WAR TERMINATION

Defence analysts have suggested there are three possible ways the Russia–Ukraine war could eventually end: absolute victory, armistice and political settlement.[1] This is notwithstanding the fact that predicting outcomes of war is risky because it involves anticipating events in the future and choices that are yet to be made.[2] During the course of war there are possibilities of the warring sides undertaking operational pauses and conditional ceasefires, but that would be temporary in nature and not dictate the eventual form of the war termination, hence, is not being considered.

Victory is often equated with decisive battles that vanquish the enemy. Military historian John Keegan has described such battles as two armies fighting to the point of moral and physical disintegration of one of them, such that the remaining soldiers are dissuaded from wanting to fight any more.[3] There are, however, others who find the idea of victory ambiguous and problematic because there are no absolute criteria to define victory. The assessment parameters of victory are contestable and the political objectives of war, an important determinant, are in most cases opaque and subject to change. J Boone Bartholomees in his essay, *Theory of Victory*, has asserted that victory in war is an assessment of the situation and not a fact or condition.

> Victory in war is at the most basic level an assessment, not a fact or condition. It is someone's opinion or an amalgamation of opinions. Victory in war may or may not have anything to do with objective criteria such as casualties or territory taken or lost. In winning a war, those things matter—at least at some level and always in terms of their effect on perception—but what matters most is the ultimate perception of the situation, not the facts. Different people, depending on their perspective, can legitimately differ in their assessment.[4]

Since victory and defeat are a matter of perception everyone can have an opinion based on one's understanding of the war. Moreover, as the concept of victory and defeat is a matter of perception political leadership can create narratives that do not reflect reality and if the narrative is successfully advanced by the political leadership, it becomes a form of reality.[5]

Victory and conflict termination are two distinct and sometimes mutually antagonistic concepts. It is not necessary that victory always leads to a preferred outcome. It is quite possible and sometimes desirable to terminate conflicts without producing a winner. Conversely, it is also possible to continue a war in the hope of achieving victory or avoiding defeat. Winning a war, however, almost certainly implies that a state of peace exists even if the existence of peace does not necessarily imply victory.[6]

There are two categories of negotiated ends to war—armistice and political settlement. In an armistice agreement the two sides commit to stop fighting and often create mechanisms, such as demilitarised zones, to prevent the resumption of violence.[7] Despite a comprehensive armistice agreement it is possible that it does not address the political drivers of the conflict, in which case antagonistic relations can endure and the diplomatic and economic relations between the parties often remain at a minimal level.[8] On the other hand, a political settlement or peace treaty would involve both a durable ceasefire and a resolution of at least some of the disputes that sparked the war or emerged during it. A political settlement might be more difficult to reach than an armistice agreement since the latter would be narrowly focused on maintaining a ceasefire, not resolving the increasingly deep and broad set of issues disputed between the warring sides.

War termination through negotiations is a choice that all parties to the conflict make to cease military operations and adopt some form of a settlement model through concessions and conciliation. The choice may be made when the parties to the conflict realise that military operations have become ineffective and costly and are unlikely to achieve the desired end state. The victor may then take a call to terminate the war, which may involve setting terms of surrender, in case of absolute victory, or through negotiations by the warring sides by making some sort of compromise, in case of stalemate. The decision to terminate a war, however, becomes problematic when there is a credibility issue among the adversaries. The adversaries may continue with military operations if one or both do not trust the other to honour any peace deal that may be reached. In addition, domestic politics of the country and the form of government too has a role in deciding when it is the right time to terminate a war.[9]

## REASONS FOR WAR

The 2015 Minsk Agreement,[10] brokered by France and Germany, sought to halt the conflict between the Russian-backed separatists and Ukrainian forces following the seizure of large swaths of territory in Donetsk and Lugansk by the separatists in 2014. The deal was, however, interpreted differently by Russia and Ukraine and has never been implemented fully. The main point of contention is Russian insistence that it is not a party to the conflict and therefore is not bound by its terms, while Ukraine sees the agreement as an instrument to re-establish control over the rebel territories.[11] Just before the launch of 'special military operations' Moscow recognised the two Donbass republics and told Kiev to vacate the parts of Donetsk and Lugansk then under Ukrainian control. Kiev refused, and the hostilities began. On 24 February 2023, Russia launched a military operation in Ukraine and the official reason forwarded for the operation was the defence of the two newly recognised republics, which had asked for military assistance.[12] In his address President Putin announced that operations were aimed at '*demilitarising and denazifying*' the country.[13]

While the trigger for the 'special military operations' may have been the non-implementation of the Minsk Agreement, the crisis has been in the making for a long time. Russia has been extremely concerned about the eastward advance of NATO and has been asking for a list of security guarantees from the US that have included: Ukraine's formal neutrality between Russia and NATO ('*no Ukraine in NATO*');[14] and no deployment of US and other NATO weapons and military bases in Ukraine, as well as a ban on military exercises on Ukrainian territory ('*no NATO in Ukraine*').[15] The US and NATO have openly and publicly rejected the Russian proposals.

There have been contra arguments to absolve the US and the West of the culpability by suggesting that NATO membership was never a realistic prospect for Ukraine,[16] or suggesting that President Putin believes that Ukraine is not a legitimate country with a right to exist separate from Russia.[17] It has even been suggested that the war is a result of an initial miscalculation by the Russian President that he could overrun Ukraine in a matter of days.[18]

## POLITICAL AND MILITARY OBJECTIVES AND CHANGES WITH THE PROGRESS OF WAR

The Russia–Ukraine war has multiple players with differing national interests that translate to diverse war objectives. The West rather than being an integrated and a cohesive player guided by singular war objective is a disparate group of countries guided by their respective and differing national interests. The varying war objectives and a desire for different outcomes has resulted in an incoherent approach that has, at times, acted on cross purpose to that of Ukraine's. The Russian war objectives have also evolved as the war has progressed, perhaps not anticipated by the Kremlin. An analysis of the war objectives will provide an understanding of the course in which countries' war efforts are being directed.

Russia initiated a 'special military operation' to deter Ukraine from joining NATO and to protect the interests of ethnic Russians in two eastern provinces of Ukraine—Donetsk and Lugansk. President Putin also spoke of the need for Ukraine's 'demilitarisation and denazification', which implied regime change.[19] The second time the Russian war termination objective was revealed was in late March 2022 during the peace talks between the two countries in Istanbul. Russia demanded that Ukraine recognise the sovereignty of the two Donbass republics within their constitutional borders, as well as Russia's own sovereignty over Crimea, plus accept a neutral and demilitarised status for territory controlled by Kiev.[20]

Overtime Russia's attitude towards Ukraine has hardened and President Putin has added the '*de-Communization*' of Ukraine to his war objectives. One of the assessed implications of President Putin's 'de-communization' effort is to severe from Ukraine the Russian-populated or Russian-speaking territories that had been awarded to the Soviet Ukrainian republic of the USSR by the Communist leaders in Moscow, Vladimir Lenin, Joseph Stalin and Nikita Khrushchev. These territories include, besides Donbass, the entire southeast of Ukraine, from Kharkov to Odessa.[21]

By September 2022 it was apparent that the Russian operation was making limited progress, but Russia upped the stakes by announcing the annexation of Kherson, Zaporizhzhia, Donetsk and Lugansk, along with the already-seized Crimea. Russia was unable to completely capture any of these provinces, other than Crimea, and since then the announcement has lost ground in Kherson significantly and to a limited degree in Lugansk.

The Russian military objectives, which flow from the Russian political objectives, include a decisive victory over Ukrainian Armed Forces to assist in regime change and capture Russian-speaking areas in the east and south of Ukraine. On 24 February 2022, the Russian Army and airborne forces attempted a lightning assault on Kyiv, and simultaneously launched offensives against Kharkiv, Sumy, Chernihiv, Kherson, Melitopol, Mariupol and on the line of contact in the Donbas region. Russia failed to take these cities, except for Kherson and Melitopol, and suffered heavy casualties. On 25 March 2022, the Russian Ministry of Defence announced that the 'first phase' of the invasion of Ukraine was over.[22] The announcement was interpreted as an admission of Russian incapability to affect a regime change and an attempt to have a more modest military objective of capturing territory and destroying Ukrainian forces in the Donbas.[23] The Russian announcement was pragmatic considering it stood a reasonable chance of achieving military successes in Donbas and also to moderate the expectations of the Russian population fed on propaganda of 'demilitarisation and denazification' of Ukraine.

In the early days of the war Ukraine held a relatively more conciliatory approach to war termination. In March 2023, a peace deal was being negotiated between the two countries and reportedly Ukraine was amenable to abandon ambitions of NATO membership in return for Russian withdrawal from occupied territories. President Zelensky even considered the idea of changing the country's constitution and abandoning aspirations of NATO membership in return for a guaranteed EU membership and legally binding security guarantees.[24] The Austrian and Swedish model of neutrality was discussed during the peace negotiations, however, it was unacceptable to Ukraine since it was now in a state of direct war with Russia and the model had to suit the changed situation and Ukraine was insistent on legally verified security guarantees by the West. No other model or option was acceptable to Ukraine.[25]

Fom May 2022 onwards the Russia–Ukraine war saw the reversal in fortune with Ukrainian Armed Forces making advances against Russian troops in the east and south, recapturing the city of Kherson and pushing Russian forces back in the northeastern region of Kharkiv. Ukraine also planned a much-publicised offensive to drive Russia from the areas it occupied in the country's south as well as the eastern Donbas region.[26] It was under these changed circumstances that President Zelensky called on the G20 leaders to adopt a 10-point peace formula and end the war,[27] which reflects changed circumstances and the hardening of Ukrainian stand following the battlefield success. The formula included: cessation of hostilities, Russian troops withdrawing and restoring Ukraine's territorial integrity and Russia reaffirming it according to the U.N. Charter.[28]

The Ukrainian war effort and its economy is surviving on the aid being provided by the West led by the US. It is, therefore, only natural that the interests and the concerns of the disparate community of the 'West' will have a significant impact in the manner the conflict resolution efforts are directed.

Since the beginning of the war the Western response has been clear, even though the objective—the endgame of this war—has been nebulous. The US has been pursuing the 'Win and Weaken' strategy articulated by the U.S. Secretary of Defense Lloyd Austin at a conference with allies at the Ramstein Air Base in Germany in late April 2022. Russia is the primary adversary of the US, not very far behind China. This war provides an opportunity for the US to erode and degrade Russia's conventional defence capability[29] with little risk to US lives and minimal expenditure.[30] From the US' perspective it is an incredibly cost-effective investment to spend 5.6 per cent of the defence budget to destroy nearly half of Russia's conventional military capability. The US, however, is unsure how Ukraine will achieve victory or even define victory. In an op-ed published in the *New York Times*, US President Joe Biden attempted to define the US war objectives. The aim of American support for Kyiv, he wrote, isn't to confront or attempt a regime change in Russia, but rather to create conditions for a diplomatic solution that puts a democratic and sovereign Ukraine in 'the strongest position at the negotiating table.'[31] He did not elaborate what, precisely and realistically, is that 'strongest position'? In June 2022, National Security Advisor (NSA) of the United States Jake Sullivan stated, 'We have in fact refrained from laying out what we see as an endgame.... We have been focused on what we can do today, tomorrow, next week to strengthen the Ukrainians' hand to the maximum extent possible, first on the battlefield and then ultimately at the negotiating table.'[32] In February 2023, the US Secretary of State Antony Blinken, announced that the war must end in what he called a durable peace. He said, 'that means making sure that Ukraine has the capacity to deter aggression and, if necessary, to effectively defend against it.'[33]

## UKRAINE'S SUCCESSFUL COUNTEROFFENSIVE AND DECISION DILEMMAS

Wars follow an unpredictable trajectory, making assessment about the outcome extremely challenging, if not impossible. The imponderables and uncertainties of the Russia–Ukraine war have a direct bearing on conflict resolution efforts and its outcome. The successful Ukrainian counteroffensive in Donbas in August 2022 led to the withdrawal of Russian forces from swaths of occupied territory, including Kherson and Kharkiv. This created a paradoxical situation from the Western perspective that the better Ukrainian forces perform on the battlefield, the more difficult it is to discuss a negotiated settlement, even though it is to Ukraine's advantage to negotiate from a position of strength. Ukrainian interests are not necessarily identical to those of its Western partners. Kyiv has little to lose in risking escalation or continuing the war, whereas for the Western alliance, which is bearing substantial economic costs from the war, any risk of escalation or nuclear exchange poses a direct threat to the West itself. This has led some to argue that the US and its partners should provide future aid with an eye on putting Ukraine in the best negotiating position, not simply continuing the war.[34]

Despite the battlefield successes of the Ukrainian Armed Forces the US

Department of Defence (DoD) was not very optimistic about the war termination being in favour of Ukraine. General Mark Milley, Chairman of the Joint Chiefs of Staff, shared his assessment that neither Ukraine nor Russia can win militarily. The general sense of DoD was that Ukraine will be challenged to expel Russian forces from all occupied areas, which is Kyiv's stated end objective. The US DoD was at pains to explain its stand that Ukraine should not capitulate and cede any part of its sovereign territory to Russia, yet seize any available window of opportunity for a negotiated settlement.[35] The US did attempt to tone down the Ukrainian military objective when NSA Jake Sullivan recommended that it should start thinking about realistic demands and priorities for negotiations, including a reconsideration of its stated aim of Ukraine regaining Crimea, which was annexed in 2014.[36] The US stand is also amplified by the kinds of weapons and platforms it is willing to provide to Ukraine. President Zelensky has been ratcheting up campaigns for the West to send F-16 jets and long-range missiles. President Biden has so far declined to agree to the request, which exposes the dilemma that defines the US war strategy: How far to go to help Kyiv win while avoiding a direct clash between the West and Russia.[37]

On the first anniversary of the war, two contradictory trends played out: there was renewed fighting in Donbas with Russians making a desperate attempt to capture Bakhmut and there were renewed calls for a negotiated settlement. It was around this time that there was an expectation that Ukraine would launch its much-anticipated spring/summer counteroffensive, which was finally launched in June 2023. Amidst all this and despite public assurances by the West to back Ukraine 'as long as it takes,' US officials noted that aid packages from Congress and America's allies represent Kyiv's best chance to decisively change the course of the war, raising doubts about West's long-term appetite for funding the war effort.[38]

In February 2022, when Russia launched its special military operation it was expected that Ukraine will not be able to withstand the attack. Not only did Ukraine halt the Russian advance but also reversed some of the gains by recapturing territories under Russian occupation. Overtime the Russian Armed Forces have learnt from their multiple failures and adapted to the changing situations. They executed some complex operations and have deployed multiple layers of defences to thwart the Ukrainian summer 2023 counteroffensive. It was for over a month that Ukraine's counteroffensive was on and during this time there was a dramatic challenge to President Putin's authority when Yevgeny Prigozhin launched his short-lived 'mutiny'. The Wagner 'mutiny' did weaken, to some extent, President's position, yet a dramatic reversal in Ukrainian fortunes is not appreciated at the moment. This assessment is in sync with the US assessment revealed through the 'Discord Leaks'. Wherein dozens of highly classified US documents leaked online reveal profound concerns about the war's trajectory and Kyiv's capacity to wage a successful offensive against Russian forces.[39]

## CONFLICT RESOLUTION EFFORTS

The US had made attempts to dissuade Russia from launching a 'special military operation'. After the war commenced on 24 February 2022, several countries have attempted to bring the two warring sides to the negotiating table. Many world leaders have articulated peace plans, some of which have been outrightly rejected and others have been debated and taken forward.

Ever since 2021, the Biden administration has made efforts to avert the war.[40] Later, when the war started, one of the first backchannel efforts to de-escalate the situation was initiated by the former Israeli prime minister Naftali Bennett, who visited Moscow on 5 March 2022.[41] Recep Tayyip Erdogan, President of Turkey, also made an attempt to terminate the war when he spoke with Ukraine's President Volodymyr Zelensky, and his top officials intensified their efforts to help broker a peace deal between Kyiv and Moscow.[42] By mid-March 2022 a 15-point draft proposal was in an advanced stage of consideration.[43] This draft required Kyiv to renounce its ambitions to join NATO[44] and not to host foreign military bases or weaponry in exchange for protection from allies such as the US, UK and Turkey.[45] It has also been reported that talks between Russia and Ukraine became 'more constructive' and that Russia had softened its stand by no longer airing its demands that Ukraine surrender before the two sides hardened their stand and the talks broke down.[46] Recently, in June 2023, during a meeting with leaders of African Union, Russian President Vladimir Putin, referring to the Istanbul peace talks, accused Ukraine of signing a peace treaty with Moscow to end the ongoing war and later discarding it as soon as Russia obliged the request and withdrew troops from Kyiv.[47] President Putin informed that it was called 'Treaty of permanent neutrality and security guarantees of Ukraine' and the document included 18 articles and appendixes, including clauses on neutrality and guarantees of security. The issues, which were contentious and possibly led to the breakdown in talks, include the nature of security guarantees to Ukraine and the status of territories seized by Russia and its proxy forces since 2014—Crimea and the self-proclaimed republics of Lugansk and Donetsk.

After the breakdown in peace talks between Russian and Ukraine in March

2022, others including France, Germany, G7 countries, China, Indonesia and the African Union have articulated their version of a peace plan.

The Ukrainian Armed Forces launched their much-anticipated spring/summer counteroffensive in early June 2023 andhave performed creditably and beyond expectation by limiting the Russian advance and forcing them to withdraw from large swaths of territory in eastern Ukraine. Despite the successes of 2022 there are doubts that Ukraine will be able to recapture all Ukrainian territory including Crimea. Some of the European countries see stronger ties between NATO and Ukraine as a way to encourage Kyiv to start peace talks with Russia later this year.[48] French President Emmanuel Macron and European Commission Chief Ursula von der Leyen have even visited China to call on Beijing to help convince Moscow to end its year-long invasion of Ukraine.[49] President Macron has kept his channels of communications with the Russian President open and has consistently maintained that the Russians should not be humiliated.[50] He favours a non-confrontational approach with Russia and yet ensuring the security of Ukraine.

In October 2022, the G7 leaders announced their version of a just peace plan. The leaders declared that it should include the following elements: respecting the UN Charter's Article on protection of territorial integrity and sovereignty; safeguarding Ukraine's ability to defend itself in the future; ensuring Ukraine's recovery and reconstruction, including exploring avenues to do so with funds from Russia; and pursuing accountability for Russian crimes committed during the war.[51]

President Zelensky too announced his peace formula on 15 November 2022 during the summit of the Group of 20 (G20) major economies in Bali, Indonesia.[52] Since then, the Ukrainian President has been vigorously promoting his 10-point peace plan, discussing it with US President Joe Biden among others, and urging world leaders to hold a Global Peace Summit based on it. Moscow has rejected the peace formula and has announced that it will not give up any territory it has taken by force. Other countries have been cautious with G7 leaders saying that they were committed to bringing peace to Ukraine and President Biden announcing that he and Zelensky 'share the exact same vision' for peace and that the US is committed to ensure that Ukraine can defend itself.[53]

On 17 February 2023, China released a 12-point peace proposal that called the two countries to respect the sovereignty of all countries, cease hostilities, keep nuclear power plants safe and promote post-conflict reconstruction, among other points. The proposal was rejected by the US and EU since the plan called for a ceasefire, which would freeze Russian troops in place on Ukrainian territory, and for an immediate end to all sanctions not endorsed by the UN Security Council, where Russia holds veto power.[54] President Putin has favoured the Chinese proposal, saying, China's peace plan for Ukraine could be used as a basis to end the war.[55]

On 03 June 2023, Indonesian Defence Minister Prabowo Subianto proposed a peace plan to end the conflict in Ukraine, calling for a demilitarised zone and a UN referendum in disputed territories, during the Shangri-La Dialogue. Reportedly, the proposed plan involves withdrawal of troops by 15 km from each side's forward position, and monitoring of the demilitarised zone by UN Peacekeeping Forces. In response, Kyiv's Foreign Ministry spokesperson Oleg Nikolenko dismissed the plan, reiterating his country's position that Russia should withdraw its troops, and instead urged Jakarta to support the 10-point peace plan forwarded by President Zelensky.[56]

In June 2023, an African delegation, made up of representatives from South Africa, Egypt, Senegal, Congo-Brazzaville, Comoros, Zambia and Uganda visited Moscow to impress upon the warring sides to end the war. Members of the delegation were from different parts of Africa with differing stands on the war. South Africa and Uganda are seen as leaning towards Russia, while Zambia and Comoros are closer to the West. Egypt, Senegal and Congo-Brazzaville have remained largely neutral. The delegation asked the two leaders to end the war, however, no concrete outcome was expected from the visited.[57]

There are some Western officials who believe that Ukraine's successful summer offensive and a 'nudge' by the Chinese President to President Putin may pave the way for negotiations between Russia and Ukraine. This understanding is based on the belief that neither side has the ability to continue fighting indefinitely. Even though the Western stand is to continue supporting Ukraine as long as it takes to defeat Russia, there is evidence to suggest that President Zelensky has been advised, both in public and in private, to commence negotiations following the anticipated gains of the summer counteroffensive. The counteroffensive allows Ukraine a chance to recapture some important territory it has lost in the east and south and claim victory, while Russia retains control over some of the territory it has occupied since the start of the special military operation.

Even though there is a general understanding that Russia and Ukraine should commence negotiations, there are differences as to when and under what conditions

Ukraine should commence them.. There is a concern among the Western alliance that aid to Ukraine will be hard to match in the future if the war grinds into a stalemate. The contours of the negotiated settlement for the moment remain unclear, even though some Western officials favour having China as one of the guarantors.[58] The US has also considered the possibility of enlisting the support of President Xi Jinping and Prime Minister Narendra Modi, two world leaders who are believed to have significant sway over President Putin.[59]

## CHALLENGES TO PEACE NEGOTIATIONS

Peace negotiation efforts to end the war are facing significant challenges due to a number of factors. Deep-rooted mistrust accumulated over years of conflict has created an environment of suspicion, hindering the establishment of trust necessary for successful negotiations. Furthermore, divergent interests and positions have created significant hurdles as each party is holding firm to its demands and non-negotiable positions. The complex power dynamics inherent in war have further complicated the initiation of the negotiation process and asymmetrical bargaining positions have made compromise elusive. Moreover, the involvement of outside stakeholders and external influences, along with the need to balance humanitarian and security concerns, has further complicated the path to resolution. Addressing these challenges requires skilled diplomacy, patience and a genuine commitment from all parties involved to overcome mistrust, bridge gaps and find mutually acceptable solutions. Only then there can be hope for a negotiated end to the war, which can pave the way for sustainable peace and stability.

Ukraine has announced its territorial integrity, including the return of Crimea, as the precondition for any talks. Russia has repeatedly rejected the call for withdrawal from Ukrainian territory. The US President has even offered to speak to the Russian President if Russian troops fully withdraw from Ukraine.[60] In May 2023, the Chinese envoy visited Ukraine in a bid to end the war. During the meeting with Li Hui, China's Special Representative for Eurasian Affairs, Ukrainian Foreign Minister Dmytro Kuleba emphasized that Ukraine does not accept any proposals that would involve the loss of its territories or the freezing of the conflict.[61] Another related issue that has the potential to cause an impasse during negotiations will be to reconcile Ukrainian sovereignty with Russian security concerns. For Kyiv, sovereignty is about reversing the Russian occupation of eastern Ukraine and Crimea and seeking long-term security guarantees from third parties. For Moscow, security is about limiting the sovereignty of Ukraine and its neighbours to the west. Preventing the presence of other powers on its periphery is at the heart of Russian security concerns. Aligning these two mutually conflicting requirements will challenge the diplomatic skills of all involved.[62]

Ukraine is seeking NATO membership to guarantee security from Russian invasion. On 11 July 2023, NATO leaders gathered for a summit in Vilnius, Lithuania, seeking to overcome divisions on Ukraine's membership bid. During the summit NATO members agreed that Kyiv cannot join NATO during the war, they have, however, disagreed over how quickly it could happen afterwards and under what conditions. NATO members in Eastern Europe have backed Kyiv's stance, arguing that bringing Ukraine under NATO's collective security umbrella is the best way to deter Russia from attacking again, while the US and Germany have been more cautious, wary of any move that they fear could draw NATO into a direct conflict with Russia, and potentially spark a global war.[63]

After the NATO failed to issue an invitation, the G7 announced a long-term security framework for Ukraine. The framework seeks to bolster Ukrainian ability to defend itself and deter Russian aggression in the future by providing modern military equipment across land, air and sea, training for Ukrainian forces and intelligence sharing.[64] G7's announcement has been criticised by Russia, which considers the move as dangerous and escalatory.

## LIKELY WAR TERMINATION SCENARIO AND POSSIBLE OUTCOME

As discussed elsewhere is the chapter, predicting outcomes of war is risky because it involves anticipating events in the future and choices that have yet to be made. Despite the uncertainties associated with wars and battles, the Russia–Ukraine war in all likelihood may possibly end in one of the three possible ways: absolute victory, armistice or political settlement.

The victory for Ukraine, as distilled from President Zelensky's 10-point peace plan, has to fulfil three basic conditions, besides others—regaining every inch of occupied territory, reparations and war-crimes tribunals. This would entail defeat of Russian Armed Forces and possibly a regime change, an unlikely outcome as the situation stands now. Russia on the other hand had initiated the special military operation with plans to install a new regime in Kyiv and demilitarise the country. Over time Russia's declared objectives have changed since the operation has progressed unfavourably. For the moment the Russian primary objective seems to be holding onto territory in the east and south of Ukraine that Russia now claims as its own. But even if Russia took control of those regions, that would hardly be an absolute victory as it would be unable to effect a fundamental change in

Ukraine's political system and would always with under military threat from Ukraine, supported by its Western partners.

From the foregoing it appears that neither Russia nor Ukraine has the capability to achieve absolute victory. The war will most likely end with some sort of negotiated outcome. Two of the possible negotiated settlement in this case could be: lasting ceasefire, armistice agreement or a political settlement between the belligerents. In practice an armistice agreement and political settlement are not easily differentiated but the two types do have nuanced differences between them. A negotiated end to the war in Ukraine is likely to fall somewhere between these two ideal types. A negotiated settlement is likely to result in a durable ceasefire and resolve some of the disputes that led to the war.[65]

A negotiated end to the war in Ukraine could freeze the front-line with the Russian side agreeing to cease capture of additional territory, missile attacks on civilian and military targets while Ukraine would agree to halt the counteroffensive. During the negotiation stage the Russian side may seek to ensure Ukraine's non-alignment and prevention of eastward expansion of NATO, an essential and pre-condition to dispute resolution. Ukraine, on the other hand, is likely to seek security guarantees from Western partners that would be legally binding and agreeable to Russia. In addition, the negotiations are likely to address multiple issues such as a reconstruction fund, bilateral trade, cultural matters and freedom of movement and conditions for relief of Western sanctions on Russia. A negotiated end to war is likely to endeavour normalisation of ties between the two adversaries, even though all issues may not be resolved between them, including the status of certain territory.

## NOTES

1 Samuel Charap and Miranda Priebe, 'Avoiding a Long War U.S. Policy and the Trajectory of the Russia–Ukraine Conflict,' *RAND Corporation Perspective*, January 2023, pp. 11–3.

2 Lawrence Freedman, "Is Russia Losing? And If It Is, When Will It Concede?," Blog Post, November 23, 2022, at https://samf.substack.com/p/is-russia-losing?sd=pf (Accessed June 26, 2022).

3 Brad Roberts, 'On Theories of Victory, Red and Blue,' *Livermore Papers on Global Security No. 7*, June 2020, at https://cgsr.llnl.gov/content/assets/docs/CGSR-LivermorePaper7.pdf, pp. 33–4 (Accessed June 22, 2021).

4 J. Boone Bartholomees, 'Theory of Victory,' *U.S. Army War College*, 2008, at https://apps.dtic.mil/sti/pdfs/ADA490503.pdf, pp. 26 (Accessed April 2, 2023).

5 Dr Cris Tuck, "Losing as Winning:' Putin's Developing Narrative of Victory,' *Defence-in-Depth*, February 1, 2023, at https://defenceindepth.co/2023/02/15/losing-as-winning-putins-developing-narrative-of-victory/ (Accessed February 16, 2023).

6 J. Boone Bartholomees, no. 4, pp. 29.

7 Virginia Page Fortna, 'Scraps of Paper? Agreements and the Durability of Peace,' *International Organization*, 57 (2), 2003.

8 Samuel Charap and Miranda Priebe, no. 1.

9 For the impact of internal pressures on the government of a modern nation-state on war termination see, Keith Gessen, 'How the War in Ukraine Might End,' *The New Yorker*, September 29, 2022, at https://www.newyorker.com/culture/annals-of-inquiry/how-the-war-in-ukraine-might-end (Accessed September 30, 2022).

10 For details of Minsk II Agreement see, 'Minsk Agreement: Full text in English,' *UNIAN*, February 12, 2015, at https://www.unian.info/politics/1043394-minsk-agreement-full-text-in-english.html (Accessed July 5, 2023).

11 'Ukraine–Russia Crisis: What is the Minsk Agreement?,' *Aljazeera*, February 9, 2022, at https://www.aljazeera.com/news/2022/2/9/what-is-the-minsk-agreement-and-why-is-it-relevant-now (Accessed July 5, 2023).

12 Dmitri Trenin, 'Six Months into the Conflict, What Exactly Does Russia Hope to Achieve in Ukraine?,' *RIAC*, September 8, 2022, at https://russiancouncil.ru/en/analytics-and-comments/comments/six-months-into-the-conflict-what-exactly-does-russia-hope-to-achieve-in-ukraine/?sphrase_id=99688667 (Accessed May 30, 2023).

13 Ilya Tsukanov, 'Putin Puts Russian Nuclear Deterrence Forces on High Alert Over Aggressive Statements by NATO,' *Sputnik International*, February 27, 2022, at https://sputniknews.com/20220227/putin-slams-western-permissiveness-of-aggressive-speeches-in-russias-direction-by-nato-officials-1093422175.html (Accessed February 27, 2022).

14 On November 10, 2021, the U.S. and Ukraine signed a Charter on Strategic Partnership, which asserted America's support for Kyiv's right to pursue membership in the NATO. See Tunku Varadarajan, 'The Two Blunders That Caused the Ukraine War,' *West Street Journal*, March 4, 2022, at https://www.wsj.com/articles/cause-ukraine-war-robert-service-moscow-putin-lenin-stalin-history-communism-invasion-kgb-fsb-11646413200?st=hxwqtokpk05awud&reflink=desktopwebshare_twitter (Accessed March 5, 2022).

15 Ibid.

16 Ian Bremmer has noted that Ukrainian aspirations, NATO membership was never a realistic prospect for Ukraine. While it's true that at the Bucharest NATO Summit in 2008, NATO promised Ukraine and Georgia accession at some indeterminate time in the future, it didn't offer a roadmap for it. Indeed, when Ukraine applied for a NATO Membership Action Plan, NATO members rejected the application. See, Ian Bremmer, 'No, the US Didn't "Provoke" the War in Ukraine,' *Gzero Media*, May 31, 2023, at https://www.gzeromedia.com/no-the-us-didnt-provoke-the-war-in-ukraine (Accessed June 2, 2023).

17 Ibid.

18 Keith Gessen, no. 9.

19 Russian President Vladimir Putin on Thursday announced a special military operation in Ukraine's eastern Donbas region, in a move he said was aimed at protecting civilians and countering the encroaching threat of the North Atlantic Treaty Organization. In a televised address, Mr. Putin said the decision was made following appeals for help from leaders of two Russian-controlled breakaway regions that he recognised as independent this week. "Circumstances require us to take decisive and immediate action," Mr. Putin said. The goal, he said, "is to protect people who have been subjected to abuse, genocide by the Kyiv regime for eight years, and for this we will strive to demilitarize" and rid Ukraine of what he described as Nazis, "as well as bring to justice those who committed numerous bloody crimes against peaceful residents, including citizens of the Russian Federation," Mr. Putin said. See, Ann M.

Simmons, 'Putin Announces Special Military Operation in Eastern Ukraine,' The *Wall Street Journal*, March 23, 2022, at https://www.wsj.com/livecoverage/russia-ukraine-latest-news/card/putin-announces-special-military-operation-in-eastern-ukraine-BBbiFSHMKssPMTur01Vh (Accessed March 11, 2022).

20 Dmitri Trenin, no. 12.

21 Ibid.

22 Justin Bronk, 'Russia Has Effectively Admitted Defeat In Ukraine,' *Aljazeera*, March 30, 2022, at https://www.aljazeera.com/opinions/2022/3/30/russia-has-effectively-admitted-defeat-in-ukraine/ (Accessed March 31, 2022).

23 In January 2023, President Putin offered a 'serious dialogue' with Ukraine, provided Kyiv acknowledges the regions of Donetsk, Lugansk, Zaporizhzhia and Kherson as Russian territory. See, 'Putin Signals Readiness for Peace Talks if Kyiv Cedes Occupied Regions,' *The Moscow Times*, 5 January 5, 2023, at https://www.themoscowtimes.com/2023/01/05/putin-signals-readiness-for-peace-talks-if-kyiv-cedes-occupied-regions-a79877, ( Accessed July 10, 2023).

24 Isobel Koshiw and Daniel Boffey, 'Russia and Ukraine 'Close to Agreeing' on Neutral Status, Says Sergei Lavrov,' *The Guardian*, March 16, 2022, at https://www.theguardian.com/world/2022/mar/16/russia-and-ukraine-close-to-agreeing-on-neutral-status-says-sergei-lavrov (Accessed March 17, 2022).

25 Ibid.

26 'Zelenskiy Urges G20 to Adopt Ukraine's Plan to Restore Peace,' *Reuters*, November 15, 2022, at https://www.reuters.com/world/we-will-have-fight-longer-liberate-ukrainian-land-says-zelenskiy-2022-11-15/ (Accessed June 20, 2023).

27 Ibid.

28 'What is Zelenskiy's 10-point Peace Plan?,' *Reuters*, December 28, 2022, at https://www.reuters.com/world/europe/what-is-zelenskiys-10-point-peace-plan-2022-12-28/ (Accessed June 20, 2023) and "Ukraine Has Always Been a Leader in Peacemaking Efforts; If Russia Wants to End This War, Let It Prove It With Actions," speech by the President of Ukraine at the G20 Summit, November 15, 2022, at https://www.president.gov.ua/en/news/ukrayina-zavzhdi-bula-liderom-mirotvorchih-zusil-yaksho-rosi-79141 (Accessed May 18, 2023).

29 By the end of 2022 the Ukrainian forces had wounded upwards of 100,000 Russian troops, half its original fighting force; there have been almost 8,000 confirmed losses of armoured vehicles including thousands of tanks, thousands of APCs, artillery pieces, hundreds of fixed and rotary wing aircraft and numerous naval vessels. See, Timothy Ash, 'It's Costing Peanuts for the US to Defeat Russia,' *CEPA*, November 18, 2022, at https://cepa.org/article/its-costing-peanuts-for-the-us-to-defeat-russia/ (Accessed June 16, 2023).

30 The Biden administration received Congressional approval for $40bn in aid for Ukraine for 2022 and has requested an additional $37.7bn for 2022. More than half of this aid has been earmarked for defence./ These sums pale into insignificance when set against a total US defence budget of $715bn for 2022. The assistance represents 5.6 per cent of total US defence spending. Ibid.

31 Joseph R. Biden Jr., 'What America Will and Will Not Do in Ukraine,' *The New York Times*, May 31, 2022, at https://www.nytimes.com/2022/05/31/opinion/biden-ukraine-strategy.html (Accessed July 11, 2023).

32 Samuel Charap, 'An Unwinnable War Washington Needs an Endgame in Ukraine,' *Foreign Affairs*, June 5, 2023, at https://www.foreignaffairs.com/ukraine/unwinnable-war-washington-endgame?utm_source=twitter_posts&utm_campaign=tw_daily_soc&utm_medium=social (Accessed June 9, 2023).

33 Bojan Pancevski and Laurence Norman, 'NATO's Biggest European Members Float Defense

Pact With Ukraine,' *The Wall Street Journal*, February 24, 2023, at https://www.wsj.com/articles/natos-biggest-european-members-float-defense-pact-with-ukraine-38966950 (Accessed February 26, 2023).

34 Emma Ashford, 'The Ukraine War Will End With Negotiations,' *Foreign Policy*, October 31, 2022, at https://www.foreignaffairs.com/ukraine/ukraine-war-will-end-negotiations (Accessed November 1, 2022).

35 Alexander Ward, Lara Seligman and Erin Banco, 'U.S. Scrambles to Reassure Ukraine After Milley Comments on Negotiations,' *Politico*, November 14, 2022, at https://www.politico.com/news/2022/11/14/u-s-ukraine-milley-negotiations-00066777 (Accessed November 15, 2022).

36 Washington has signalled to Ukraine that at a minimum Kyiv needs to appear open to a negotiated solution. Mr. Biden's National Security Adviser, Jake Sullivan, conveyed that message to President Volodymyr Zelensky and his lieutenants in Kyiv on November 4, suggesting that Kyiv would gain leverage by showing openness to negotiations, see, Gordon Lubold, Nancy A. Youssef, Laurence Norman and Drew Hinshaw, 'As Ukraine Retakes Kherson, U.S. Looks to Diplomacy Before Winter Slows Momentum,' *The Wall Street Journal*, November 13, 2022, at https://www.wsj.com/articles/as-ukraine-retakes-kherson-u-s-looks-to-diplomacy-before-winter-slows-momentum-11668345883 (Accessed November 15, 2022).

37 Stephen Collinson, 'Biden's Trip to Kyiv Delivers the Starkest Rebuke Possible to Putin,' *CNN*, February 20, 2023, at https://edition.cnn.com/2023/02/20/politics/joe-biden-kyiv-visit/index.html (Accessed June 23, 2023).

38 Yasmeen Abutaleb and John Hudson, 'U.S. Warns Ukraine It Faces a Pivotal Moment in War,' *The Washington Post*, February 13, 2023, at https://www.washingtonpost.com/politics/2023/02/13/us-ukraine-war-critical-moment/ (Accessed February 15, 2023).

39 Shane Harris and Samuel Oakford, 'Leaker of U.S. Secret Documents Worked on Military Base, Friend Says,' *The Washington Post*, April 12, 2023, at https://www.washingtonpost.com/national-security/2023/04/12/discord-leaked-documents/ (Accessed April 13, 2023).

40 CIA Director William Burns was sent to Moscow in early November 2021 to warn Mr. Putin against an invasion. Mr. Biden spoke twice with Mr. Putin in December 2021 and again in February 2022 to try to avert a Russian attack while U.S. diplomats engaged with their Russian counterparts. See, Vivian Salama and Michael R. Gordon, 'Senior White House Official Involved in Undisclosed Talks With Top Putin Aides,' *The Wall Street Journal*, November 7, 2022, at https://www.wsj.com/articles/senior-white-house-official-involved-in-undisclosed-talks-with-top-putin-aides-11667768988?mod=article_inline (Accessed November 11, 2022).

41 According to Bennett, during his mediation efforts Zelenskiy agreed to give up the idea that Ukraine would join NATO, and Putin dropped a vow to seek Ukraine's disarmament in order to end the war. "Everything I did was coordinated with the US, Germany and France," he said. See, Hu Wei, 'Putin Promised Me He Would Not Kill Zelenskiy, Says Former Israeli PM,' *The Guardian*, February 5, 2023, at https://www.theguardian.com/world/2023/feb/05/putin-promised-me-he-would-not-kill-zelenskiy-says-former-israeli-pm-naftali-bennett (Accessed February 6, 2023).

42 Turkey's facilitation of the meeting between Ukrainian Foreign Minister Dmytro Kuleba and Russian Foreign Minister Sergei Lavrov, on the margins of the Antalya Diplomacy Forum on March 10, was an important first step to ensure that sides engage with each other at a high level and pave the way for settling the conflict. See, Tacan Ildem, Defne Arslan, John Herbst, Dimitar Bechev and Ariel Cohen, 'After Russia–Ukraine Talks in Istanbul, Is an End to War Imminent?,' *Atlantic Council*, April 1, 2022, at https://www.atlanticcouncil.org/blogs/turkeysource/experts-react-after-russia-ukraine-talks-in-istanbul-is-an-end-to-war-imminent/ (Accessed November 6, 2022).

43 Sergei Lavrov, Russia's foreign minister, said that "absolutely specific wordings" were "close to being agreed" in the negotiations. See, Max Seddon, Roman Olearchyk, Arash Massoudi and Neri Zilber, 'Ukraine and Russia Explore Neutrality Plan in Peace Talks,' *Financial Times*, March 17, 2022, at https://www.ft.com/content/7b341e46-d375-4817-be67-802b7fa77ef1 (Accessed November 6, 2022).

44 It was reported that Ukraine was willing to forego membership of NATO, which is enshrined in its constitution, in exchange for guaranteed membership of EU. See, Isobel Koshiw and Daniel Boffey, no. 24.

45 "We propose a 'Ukrainian model of security guarantees', which implies the immediate and legally verified participation of a number of guarantor countries in the conflict on the side of Ukraine, if someone again encroaches on its territorial integrity," - Mykhailo Podolyak, a senior adviser to President Zelensky. See, Max Seddon, Roman Olearchyk, Arash Massoudi and Neri Zilber, no. 43. Ukraine also sought agreement with the West that they would come to Ukraine's aid in the event of any future conflict with Russia and that there would be no hesitation in imposing a "no-fly zone" in such a war. See, Isobel Koshiw and Daniel Boffey, no. 24.

46 Isobel Koshiw, Jon Henley and Julian Borger, 'Zelenskiy Says Russia's Position in Negotiations Is Becoming 'More Realistic' As Fears Deepen For Mariupol,' *The Guardian*, March 16, 2022, at https://www.theguardian.com/world/2022/mar/16/zelenskiy-says-russias-position-in-negotiations-is-becoming-more-realistic-as-fears-deepen-for-mariupol (Accessed March 17, 2022).

47 "It was called Treaty of permanent neutrality and security guarantees of Ukraine," Vladimir Putin showing the supposed draft of the treaty. "We never agreed with the Ukrainian side that the text will be confidential but we never showed it before nor commented on it. This draft of the treaty was initialled by the leader of the negotiation group from Kyiv. He put his signature. There it exists," he added. See, Mallika Soni, 'Russia–Ukraine Signed Peace Treaty, Vladimir Putin Says. Then, Shows Document,' *Hindustan Times*, June 18, 2023, at https://www.hindustantimes.com/world-news/russiaukraine-signed-peace-treaty-vladimir-putin-says-then-shows-document-101687079021115-amp.html (Accessed June 20, 2023).

48 Bojan Pancevski and Laurence Norman, no. 33.

49 'Macron and Ursula von der Leyen Will Visit China to Urge Peace in Ukraine,' *Le Monde*, March 24, 2023, at https://www.lemonde.fr/en/international/article/2023/03/24/macron-and-ursula-von-der-leyen-will-visit-china-to-urge-peace-in-ukraine_6020563_4.html (Accessed March 27, 2023).

50 'Macron Favors Maintaining Ability for Dialogue With Russia,' *TASS*, January 19, 2023, at https://tass.com/world/1564551 (Accessed January 23, 2023).

51 'G7 Statement on Ukraine,' The White House, October 11, 2022, at https://www.whitehouse.gov/briefing-room/statements-releases/2022/10/11/g7-statement-on-ukraine-11-october-2022/ (Accessed November 6, 2022).

52 Volodymyr Zelenskyy, 'Ukraine has always been a leader in peacemaking efforts; if Russia wants to end this war, let it prove it with actions,' - speech by the President of Ukraine at the G20 Summit, November 15, 2022, at https://www.president.gov.ua/en/news/ukrayina-zavzhdi-bula-liderom-mirotvorchih-zusil-yaksho-rosi-79141?fbclid=IwAR0r3lTXwo4wl38e8G1KS4rlv_7luNKoRIM-qPpk5GYBkz37VW8ZSmzhG0s (Accessed July 17, 2023).

53 *Reuters*, no. 28.

54 Robert Delaney, Orange Wang and Khushboo Razdan, 'US Joins EU in Rejecting Beijing's Peace Proposal, Sanctions More Chinese Firms,' *SCMP*, February 25, 2023, at https://www.scmp.com/news/china/diplomacy/article/3211510/us-joins-eu-rejecting-beijings-peace-

proposal-sanctions-more-chinese-firms (Accessed July 17, 2023).

55 In a joint news conference after talks with Mr Xi during his visit to Moscow in March 2023, Mr Putin said: "Many provisions of the Chinese peace plan can be taken as the basis for settling of the conflict in Ukraine, whenever the West and Kyiv are ready for it." See, James Gregory, 'Putin: China Plan Could End War, But Ukraine And West Not Ready For Peace,' *BBC News*, March 22, 2023, at https://www.bbc.com/news/world-asia-65030929?xtor=AL-72-%5Bpartner%5D-%5Bbbc.news.twitter%5D-%5Bheadline%5D-%5Bnews%5D-%5Bbizdev%5D-%5Bisapi%5D&at_link_origin=BBCNews&at_campaign_type=owned&at_medium= social&at_ ptr_name= twitter&at_link_ id=5B79B20A-C80C-11ED-9093-8FB94744363C&at_format=link&at_link_type=web_link&at_bbc_team=editorial&at_campaign=Social_Flow (Accessed March 22, 2023).

56 Kanupriya Kapoor, 'Indonesia Proposes Demilitarised Zone, UN Referendum For Ukraine Peace Plan,' *Reuters*, June 3, 2023, at https://www.reuters.com/world/indonesia-proposes-demilitarised-zone-un-referendum-ukraine-peace-plan-2023-06-03/ (Accessed July 17, 2023).

57 Antoinette Radford, 'Ukraine War Must End, South African President Ramaphosa Tells Putin,' *BBC News*, June 18, 2023, [Online: web] URL: https://www.bbc.com/news/world-europe-65940655?xtor=AL-72-%5Bpartner%5D-%5Bbbc.news.twitter%5D-%5Bheadline%5D-%5Bnews%5D-%5Bbizdev%5D-%5Bisapi%5D&at_link_id=606A4ECA-0D3D-11EE-8BE6-9290D772BE90&at_link_type=web_link&at_campaign_type=owned&at_format=link&at_ campaign= Social_ Flow &at_ptr _name=twitter&at_ medium=social&at _link _origin=B BCWorld&at_bbc_team=editorial (Accessed June 18, 2023).

58 Bojan Pancevski, Laurence Norman and Vivian Salama, 'U.S. and Allies Look at Potential China Role in Ending Ukraine War,' *The Wall Street Journal*, May 7, 2023, at https://www.wsj.com/articles/u-s-and-allies-look-at-potential-china-role-in-ending-ukraine-war-2d6cbb4d?st=8ovk0vjht9921uj (Accessed May 7, 2023).

59 Bryan Bender, 'Calls Grow For China and India to Talk Sense Into Putin,' *Politico*, September 28, 2022, at https://www.politico.com/news/2022/09/28/china-and-india-on-putin-in-ukraine-00059382 (Accessed October 3, 2022).

60 'Kremlin Turns Down Biden's Conditions for Putin Talks,' *The Moscow Times*, December 2, 2022, at https://www.themoscowtimes.com/2022/12/02/kremlin-turns-down-bidens-conditions-for-putin-talks-a79573 (Accessed January 20, 2023).

61 James Marson, 'Ukraine, China Meeting Shows No Breakthrough to End Russian Invasion,' *The Wall Street Journal*, May 18, 2023, at https://www.wsj.com/articles/ukraine-china-meeting-shows-no-breakthrough-to-end-russian-invasion-f71a871d (Accessed May 18, 2023).

62 C. Raja Mohan, 'Xi, Modi and Peace in Ukraine,' *The Indian Express*, February 22, 2023, at https://indianexpress.com/article/opinion/columns/c-raja-mohan-xi-jinping-narendra-modi-ukraine-peace-8458767/ (Accessed July 17, 2023).

63 Andrew Gray, John Irish and Sabine Siebold, 'NATO Summit Seeks Agreement on Ukraine Bid After Turkey Deal on Sweden,' *Reuters*, July 11, 2023, at https://www.reuters.com/world/nato-summit-seeks-agreement-ukraine-bid-after-turkey-deal-sweden-2023-07-10/ (Accessed July 11, 2023).

64 Ruxandra Iordache and Sam Meredith, 'G7 Countries Sign Declaration Outlining Long-Term Security Guarantees for Ukraine,' *CNBC*, July 12, 2023, at https://www.cnbc.com/2023/07/12/g7-announces-long-term-security-guarantees-for-ukraine.html (Accessed July 17, 2023).

65 Samuel Charap, Miranda Priebe, no. 1.

# Conclusion

*Abhay Singh and Vivek Chadha*

The Ukraine War, like any other war in the past, will remain the focus of attention of the strategic community not only for its geopolitical impact but also for the military lessons that will emerge from it. This volume has focussed on the latter. The observations made are more from the perspective of objective bystanders rather than an involved side in the conflict. It was not the intention of the contributors to argue the case of either side. The diplomatic corps of the warring nations do that best. Instead, the focus has remained on doctrines, strategic choices, use of weapon systems, their employment philosophy, the impact of supply chains on military operations, the influence of technologically advanced weapon systems, analyses of attempts at military restructuring and the employment of arms as part of an integrated national war effort.

The lessons drawn by contributors have an India focus, even though these have wider applicability, given the broad-based relevance of military issues. It is also relevant to point out that individual authors have written their chapters based on their perspective of a designated theme. Consequently, there are conforming and competing views that are simultaneously held with similar convictions. It becomes important to underline this aspect given the ongoing and often contentious debate around military assessment during a war. The case of Ukraine is no exception. On several issues, the jury is still out; this volume will contribute to the issues under discussion.

Over the years, there was consensus amongst the strategic community that the frequency and possibility of long-drawn major wars had receded. Consequently, the focus of militaries across the world shifted to fighting short, swift and limited wars. While individual wars and conflicts cannot prove or disprove the logic of multi-decadal data indicators, the Russia–Ukraine war has forced a cautionary pause in the wisdom of this thought process. The duration of wars is relevant from the perspective of its strategic bearing on geopolitics. It also has a direct impact on the ability of countries to sustain long-drawn wars. The challenges of supply chains, availability of critical munitions and weapons and impact of mounting casualties have seen an adverse fallout on the ability of both Russia and Ukraine to maintain a sustained intensity of war effort. If this indeed be the potential reality of protracted wars, then a country should fight a war based on its inherent capacity to sustain it over the probable duration. The support of allies and partners cannot be taken for granted over time, especially in the long run. India's experience has shown that support notwithstanding, the onus of fighting wars will remain primarily on the country itself. This must therefore continue as the basis of planning for conflicts and if need be, the decision to go to war.

India has always given the highest priority to strategic autonomy in the implementation of international relations. Therefore, the post-independence period witnessed strategic partnerships, preferred relationships and issue-based support. This allowed India to make decisions based on national interest. It is not necessarily the easiest path to ensuring security. The policy of strategic independence raises the cost of safeguarding national security. It does not guarantee military or even diplomatic support in times of need. Despite this reality, India's diplomatic experience and the policy of strategic autonomy have led to capacities that can address potential challenges. In that sense, as welcome as the support of partners will remain and as important as it is to cultivate those partnerships, this cannot become the basis for planning national capacities.

The ongoing war has demonstrated to both Russia and, more recently, Ukraine that taking control of territory and keeping it in the face of fierce opposition is a difficult task, especially when the opposing country has external support. Russia failed in its initial attempt to capture Kyiv. Similarly, Ukraine's much-anticipated offensive did not yield favourable results. This has lessons for countries that may seek territorial annexation or integration in the face of not only the adversary but also a strong support structure. This can be related to a possible attempt by China to forcefully take over Taiwan, especially in the face of direct United States (US) military intervention, and enforce unification.

Since the onset of the Russia–Ukraine war, there has been growing concern about the risk of escalation in the Taiwan Strait. Ukraine's ability to continue its war efforts relies heavily on the military support it receives from the US and its allies. However, some voices in the US are now arguing that continuing to support Ukraine is distracting from the more significant threat of a Chinese invasion of

Taiwan. They claim that providing this aid is using up valuable resources that could be used to prevent a takeover and defeat China in case of a war.[1] On the other hand, it is also being argued that steadfast support to Ukraine against Russian aggression by the US and its allies signals their resolve to counter potential Chinese aggression in the Taiwan Strait.

In recent years, China has been aggressively pursuing the goal of resolving Taiwan's ambiguous status in its favour. Beijing had initially attempted to bring the island under its control by using economic incentives and political pressure. However, many Taiwanese policymakers are now of the opinion that, as the Chinese Communist Party recognises the futility of these measures, and with its armed forces modernising rapidly, Xi Jinping might consider military action to achieve his objectives.[2]

Probably, Beijing is closely observing how deeply involved US becomes in the Ukraine conflict, given that the US provides the majority of direct military aid, including essential weapons and munitions that are currently in short supply. Ukraine is currently using up the entire US yearly production of 9,000 HIMARS missiles every two months. Critics of ongoing aid to Ukraine argue that the US should prioritise military assistance to Taiwan to deter a potential Chinese invasion and defeat it if it occurs. They suggest that even if this comes at the expense of supporting Ukraine, it is necessary to protect Taiwan.

While the Russian invasion of Ukraine has focused attention on the potential threat to Taiwan, there is one big difference between the two situations: a Chinese war on Taiwan could be a war with the US given Washington's commitment under the Taiwan Relation Act. While China's strategic intention towards Taiwan remains unclear, the growing anxiety about a potential Chinese invasion is reshaping the way Washington and Taipei think about defending the country.

The Russia–Ukraine war is an interesting example in terms of the importance and relevance of supply chains to sustain the war effort. In the case of Ukraine, the events suggest that the West has failed to maintain a desired level of supply of critical military hardware and ammunition. This has adversely influenced Ukraine's ability to sustain its war effort. In contrast to traditional military allies, it is South Korea that has been able to supply Ukraine with critical military supplies such as ammunition. Conversely, in the case of Russia, while its inherent ability to sustain logistics is far stronger than in Ukraine, the role of suppliers such as North Korea has proved to be invaluable. This reinforces the importance of a domestic military–industrial complex, which is being attempted through the Atmanirbhar policy of the Government of India. Further, it also suggests that supply chains for critical spares, equipment, replenishments and weapons when reliant on external sources cannot be taken for granted. Beyond the intention of a partner nation, supplies are also likely to be influenced by competition demands.

After two years of a full-scale invasion of Ukraine, the North Atlantic Treaty Organization (NATO) has managed to maintain its unity against Moscow. The alliance has expanded with the accession of Finland and Sweden is expected to join soon. Russia's invasion of Ukraine has significantly complicated its strategic geography. The ascension of two Nordic nations to NATO, who had previously adopted a neutral stance, has brought the alliance virtually to Russia's doorstep. This development was inconceivable before February 2022. There is a consensus across Western capitals that a Russian victory in Ukraine could shift the international geopolitical order and harm the West's strategic interests. Additionally, NATO has initiated the process for Ukraine's accession. In July 2023, NATO leaders declared that 'Ukraine's future is in NATO', adding that Kyiv's Euro–Atlantic integration had moved beyond the need for a Membership Action Plan.

Notwithstanding repeated assertions of the Western government to support Ukraine 'as long as it takes', it's unclear how far NATO can go. There are limits to the amount of material and money Western countries can send to Ukraine. In addition, the war in Ukraine has also exposed NATO's fault lines, particularly on its southern front. Furthermore, the conflict in Ukraine has revealed the weaknesses of NATO, especially on the southern front. Due to sentimental attachment, past hostilities and reliance on Russian energy supplies, Hungary, Bulgaria, Turkey and even Romania have reacted to Russia's incursion with increased circumspection, if not ambivalence.

Doubts were raised about the US' commitment to European security due to its pivot to Asia, but the invasion of Ukraine brought NATO together around its core purpose of collective defence. The conflict also revealed NATO's vulnerability and Europe's disproportionate reliance on US security. There are urgent and unanswered questions about the sustainability of this commitment and long-term US military support to Ukraine. While Russia has a thriving war economy, NATO countries are still searching for a business model that aligns with their new military requirements. Given the European Union and NATO's deep strategic commitment to the European theatre, their broad strategic vision of seeking greater involvement in the Indo–Pacific will likely take a backseat.

Technology often tends to emerge as the most visible factor in any war. The images from the 1991 US–Iraq war became a long-term advertisement for precision-guided munition. Similarly, the Ukraine War has reinforced the relevance of drones and unmanned aerial vehicles as a battle-winning factor. Another example of this is the immediate obituary of tanks written by analysts after the initial setbacks that Russian armour faced. In contrast to the technologically advanced battlefield in Ukraine and the innovations that were being adapted to battlefield conditions, the conflict in Gaza suggests that a side that has a clear technological disadvantage could still breach one of the most advanced surveillance systems in the world. None of these observations are intended to suggest the irrelevance of technology. Technology was and will remain one of the primary drivers of military success. However, technology alone is not a panacea for all battlefield challenges. If anything, recent experiences suggest that technology by itself is not a solution to military contests. The manner of its employment, the ability to adapt and innovate in quick time and the desire to continually evolve will possibly do more for success than technology alone.

The Russian nuclear threats have cast a shadow on the fighting in Ukraine. By threatening to use nuclear weapons either explicitly or implicitly, Russia has used nuclear signals to sway Western decision-makers and prevent direct Western engagement and support for Ukraine. Moscow has frequently brought up Russia's nuclear doctrine and has made overt threats, such as threatening to cross a 'red line' in September 2022 if the US provides Ukraine with longer-range missiles. In an effort to manipulate risks and erode Western support for Ukraine, Russia has also deployed disinformation campaigns, drills and fresh nuclear force deployments to Belarus. The idea that nuclear weapons prevent conflict and competition has been called into question by the war between Russia and Ukraine. Russia's nuclear signalling has been evolving since the beginning of the war both in words and actions. Moscow significantly calibrated its nuclear messaging, ramping up its threats in the face of setbacks on the battlefield while at times showing a receptiveness to external pressures.

Initially, when the Kremlin believed that it could seize Kyiv in a matter of days, Russian officials used the threat of nuclear use in an attempt to deter direct NATO intervention in the war. As it became clear that the war would drag on, the Kremlin attempted to use nuclear signalling to deter a wider range of activities. Russian nuclear sabre-rattling was at its shrillest in September 2022 when it conducted a referendum in the occupied territory of Ukraine. Subsequently, nuclear risks began to be downplayed by Moscow, despite deep Ukrainian strikes inside

Russia and the supply of new types of weapons by NATO. While Western officials took Russian warnings seriously, they perceived a decreased risk of nuclear escalation. Since nuclear coercion was not working, Russia soon began manipulating risk by other means. The Kremlin suspended participation in the final strategic arms control treaty between Russia and the US and announced plans to station nuclear weapons in Belarus.

Russia's nuclear messaging has consistently pointed to Russia's nuclear arsenal as the ultimate security guarantor, and it has used nuclear signals—whether explicit rhetoric and messaging or posturing—as part of a wider strategy. This nuclear calibration is an important trait of Russia's war in Ukraine and will likely continue to shape its actions going forward.

The Russia–Ukraine war poses a significant challenge for policymakers as they consider the conflict's long-term effects on the future role of nuclear weapons in international conflicts and competition. The use of nuclear weapons by Russia to hold on to captured territory, while using conventional forces to seize it, has been a significant concern for analysts since the post-Cold War era. In addition to the short-term challenge of supporting Ukraine's war efforts while avoiding nuclear escalation, the outcome of the current conflict will likely influence how leaders of nuclear-armed countries view the usefulness of nuclear weapons for territorial expansion in the long term.

A key takeaway of the Ukraine War is not only about being cognizant of the adversary's red lines but also about being accurate in one's impact assessment of crossing them. For instance, while Russia's red line in the run-up to its 'special military operation' had been known to be NATO's expansion and the Western arming of Ukraine, Moscow's military offensive seemingly took the European stakeholders by surprise. This is despite the Kremlin having repeatedly highlighted its concerns about the Western embrace of countries in its neighbourhood since March 1999 when the first lot of Eastern European countries were included as NATO members. Perhaps Russia's feeble protests and inaction during the subsequent co-option of new members led NATO to ignore Russia's growing insecurity and warnings. Ukraine's membership, however, was apparently the straw that broke the camel's back given the geostrategic and geo-economic relevance of Kiev for Moscow. Therefore, it is imperative to give due credence to an adversary's red line irrespective of its justification, or lack thereof.

The Russia–Ukraine war has been a test of military leadership and strategic guidance. There are as many examples of successes as there are of failures in this regard. Both sides have attempted several innovations in a bid to seek advantage. This was seen in the use of militia, information warfare techniques and weapon systems such as drones not only taking the aerial route but also making a significant impact over the seas. However, as the war has progressed, the mental and psychological resilience of combatants and citizens of the two countries facing the brunt of the war is being put to the test. There have been claims and counter claims of soldiers breaking down under the stress of battlefield environments. The conditions under which troops are fighting are taxing their resolve and resilience. Military leaders under pressure to produce results have often been found wanting by their political leadership. Neither country is a stranger to similar long-drawn wars, even though these were fought several decades ago. Nor are they unfamiliar with large-scale casualties. Yet, the ability to sustain a prolonged attrition in men and material will test the will of competing sides and may well be the most important factor in the eventual outcome of the war.

## NOTES

1 Michael Poznansky, 'The Ukraine-Taiwan Tradeoff,' *Foreign Affairs*, January 5, 2024, at https://www.foreignaffairs.com/china/ukraine-taiwan-tradeoff (Accessed January 12, 2024).

2 Demetri Sevastopulo and Kathrin Hille, 'Taiwan: Preparing for a Potential Chinese Invasion,' June 7, 2022, at https://www.ft.com/content/0850eb67-1700-47c0-9dbf-3395b4e905fd (Accessed November 23, 2023).

# Index